Beyon

Beyond Jihad

The Pacifist Tradition in West African Islam

LAMIN SANNEH

OXFORD
UNIVERSITY PRESS

Oxford University Press is a department of the University of Oxford. It furthers the University's objective of excellence in research, scholarship, and education by publishing worldwide. Oxford is a registered trade mark of Oxford University Press in the UK and certain other countries.

Published in the United States of America by Oxford University Press
198 Madison Avenue, New York, NY 10016, United States of America.

CIP data is on file at the Library of Congress
ISBN 978–0–19–935161–9

1 3 5 7 9 8 6 4 2
Printed by Sheridan Books, Inc., United States of America

In tribute to the Jakhanke clerics who follow the pathways of tolerance and commitment with learning and humor

CONTENTS

AUTHOR'S NOTE

Studies of Islam and of Africa form a divided picture. Studies of Islam tend to view the religion as an intellectual, Arab civilization remote from Africa—a view that oversimplifies the complex, layered nature of Arab religion. Studies of Africa cast Islam as foreign and marginal, relegating it to its local function (or dysfunction) on the grounds that Islam's intellectual heritage has no place in Africa's unwritten past. A distinction, however, between Islamic Africa and Black Africa is nowhere found in Islamic teaching, and there are some notable exceptions to the prevalent dichotomous approach, such as Jamil Abun Nasr's *Muslim Communities of Grace*. Yet an academic gulf has been created between the history of Islam and the history of Africa.

This book presents Islam as part of the history of Africa as well as a religious heritage in its own right. I use the framework of religious discourse and teachings to explore the historical impact of Islam on society in terms of its orthodox creed as well as its local appropriation.

Despite the dominant focus on jihad, and the syncretism condemned by that focus, many scholars have observed Islam's peaceful development in societies throughout Africa. In answer to the current climate of political tension and cultural stereotypes, this book offers an explicit examination of Islam's pacifist achievement in Africa in the larger framework of Islam's centuries-long intellectual tradition. Where they might be illuminating, I have introduced historical and thematic comparisons with the Western tradition.

As everywhere else, Islam was introduced in Africa with demarcations that properly distinguished it from other religions, but that still left a significant margin of overlap and parallels with local religions. Indeed, the history of Islam is at heart the process of negotiation and adjustment with other traditions and cultures, including the modern West. Islam was not insulated from that historical process, however particular and distinct the African phase was.

This is another reason why it is important not to treat Islam in Africa or anywhere else as an exotic exception.

The use of the term "pagan" has been maintained in this book largely for reasons of historical consistency but also for religious considerations. Islamic and Western historical sources use the term widely, and in Islamic sources it is used in several senses to describe unbelievers, idolaters, polytheists, and so on. Academic religious writing employs other terms, such as animist, fetichist, traditional religion, primal religion, and, in an earlier era, heathen. Because of the Islamic context of this book, I have adopted the word "pagan" without the theological stigma of Muslim or Western authors. I apply the term to indicate the religious tradition that Islam encountered in Africa, one it recognized as worthy of challenge and often as a necessary critical phase of Islam's local appropriation. Even when Muslims and others use the term pejoratively, I try to draw attention to the strength and influence it is able to exercise on society and persons, including the serious attention and respect it receives from antagonists. This is quite different, though, from setting out to defend or to criticize the tradition associated with the term, for that is not the role of the historian. Religion and religious encounter matter in the history of human societies; with the tools of critical investigation it is the task of the historian to make that as plausible as is consistent with the evidence.

The term "non-Muslim" sometimes used for this pagan tradition gives it a negative marker, saying what it is not in relation to Muslims. It does not seem to indicate any more neutral a view of pagans to see them as non-Muslims whose religion is shown to fall short of Islam, its notional destination. I have used the term here in a limited way rather than as a general classification. The historian need not be tied to one prescriptive position to the neglect of context, detail, and circumstances, but should be guided by events on the ground and by rules of evidence. As long as scholars are not contenders in issues between and among religions, a justification exists for using terms that contribute to historical understanding.

The work of the Muslim groups of this study has long been overshadowed by militant efforts to spread the religion. When we consider the steadying effects of clerical work in running Qur'an schools, managing the pilgrimage, maintaining mosques, providing services for disciples and clients seeking professional religious service, and generally overseeing observances of the religious calendar, we can see the vital part these groups have played in promoting a quietist, tolerant form of Islam. Rather than a splinter group, pacifist clerics are revealed to be the flying buttress of the structure of sustained Muslim self-expansion. Without the drama of battle, religious practices offer assurance and solidarity, giving solid expression to belonging and identity. Pacifist teaching about the equality of believers in the eyes of God takes a concrete form in religious settlements. Pacifist religious teaching helped Muslim society to rise and flourish despite historical setbacks. There is much about the pacifist heritage to justify claiming it as an important but long-neglected aspect of Islam's religious heritage.

On a return visit to one of these centers in Kombo-Brufut in the Gambia in 2013, I was able to update information on clerical succession in places as far apart as Marssasoum in Casamance and Macca-Kolibantang in Senegal Orientale. I circulated that information to other clerical centers in Senegal and Gambia and received additional details that brought the story to 2015.

In response to the challenge of community representatives at field sessions at several centers, I committed to give as faithful an account of the subject as is consistent with the rules of impartial inquiry—to general approbation, I am relieved to report. An incident at a field session at Bakadaji illustrates how field inquiry can change the scholarly perspective. Noticing my unspoken reluctance to record information the audience was giving about the clerics' involvement in acquiring slaves for their settlements, witnesses asked how scholarship can be reliable when scholars omit writing about objectionable matters. How tenable is the idea of impartial scholarship when my personal scruples about slavery decide what to include and what to exclude? How is a scholar to be believed and his work respected in that case? Is that how the university trains students to prosecute scholarship? How can inquiry expand the frontiers of knowledge when it coyly conceals and evades the truth?

That embarrassing episode concluded with my apology and promise to report as accurately as possible local views about slavery. I report the incident here to keep faith with the field informants. This does not exonerate from taking personal responsibility for evaluating and interpreting the significance of the evidence. Where appropriate, I have tried to respect the distinction between clerical self-understanding and outsiders' view of Muslim religious life. The clerics were not always aware of the range of historical and religious scholarship available on particular subjects, such as developments in scholarship on *hisbah*, understood as commanding right and forbidding wrong; *maslahah* with respect to the common good; and discussions on *takhayyur* (legal hybridization), which is pertinent to issues of pluralism and accommodation. It would be useful to place the clerics' understanding of religious separation from politics in the light that more general Islamic thought sheds on the subject.

One external point of reference is the tradition of the separation of church and state, so long established in the United States and elsewhere. Separation is unfamiliar to the clerics in that specific form, but its significance for them could not be greater. The common view that religion and politics are inseparable where Islam is concerned does not give due recognition to pacifist teaching. Muslim pacifist teaching is not an exception; it is a recurring theme in religious and historical sources, even if local community expression of it falls short of an established tradition. I try to identify in the sources the peaceful understanding of Islam and where cross-cultural parallels and similarities may broaden our grasp of the subject.

In a culture of moderation, Islam's religious profile often casts its shadow over prevailing customs without sharp dichotomies. A pacifist tradition may develop from this moderation or may be attracted to it. In the cases examined in this study, pacifism became confident enough of its mandate vis-à-vis advocates of jihad to strike out on a mission of its own to instill values of moderation and tolerance in the society.

Pacifist groups spread in many parts of West Africa where their reputation won them disciples and supporters. These groups stayed within the Muslim community, rather than becoming sectarian splinter groups. They added to the experience of diversity, not only of cultural practices but also of the spiritual values that guide behavior and conduct. Islam's spiritual unity is compatible with its growing cultural diversity. It is important not to split the religion's spiritual unity from its diverse cultural expressions in the pursuit of an elusive, abstract ideal. As a religious tradition with a historical heritage, Islam endures through time and place by affecting and being affected by diverse encounters and experiences. It is not always possible to resist the temptation, but as a matter of historical credibility we must not lose sight of the immense complexity that rides on Islam's unifying code. In any case, I ask the reader's indulgence where I have failed in that and other ways.

ACKNOWLEDGMENTS

Many people have contributed to this book, and I gladly acknowledge my indebtedness to them for helping me think through the issues set out here. My thanks to Sandra, who as companion for most of my life has been a witness and sounding board for the ideas and views contained in these pages. I am grateful to Humphrey J. Fisher for his role in the initial phase of the development of the subject and for his care and friendship in subsequent years and to the late John Ralph Willis for initiating me into the field. John B. Taylor laid the foundation of my studies in classical Arabic and Islam, and I owe him a huge debt of gratitude for his expert knowledge that he placed unstintingly at my disposal. The late Johann Bauman of the University of Marburg introduced me to the sources of classical Islamic theology when he was on the faculty of the American University of Beirut (AUB), and I owe him profound gratitude for the scrupulous standards of scholarship to which he held his students. I also mention the late J. Spencer Trimingham, at the time also at the AUB, whose encyclopedic knowledge of Islam and Islam in Africa he shed on his students in tutorials, in the course of which we became friends. I am grateful for his guidance and generosity.

The late Thomas Hodgkin, whom I consulted at Balliol College, Oxford, and corresponded with subsequently, was extremely encouraging as I embarked on the research that led eventually to this book. Hodgkin's willingness to advise and guide students was legendary, and few scholars were more open with their knowledge, contacts, and research materials, all of which left his beneficiaries with a sense of nobility of spirit. I count myself fortunate in the ranks of scholars he inspired and challenged. The late Nehemia Levtzion of the Hebrew University of Jerusalem was a friend and colleague who placed at my disposal his commanding knowledge of the field. Over the years I benefited greatly from his penetrating comments and observations on the subject of this book. I wish to acknowledge the assistance of friend and colleague, Boubacar

Barry, of Cheikh Anta Diop University, Dakar, and the late Ousman Njie of Taru Photo Studio, Banjul, for his kind help with field photographs.

As a senior colleague, the late Wilfred Cantwell Smith of Harvard was generous and unstinting with his advice and encouragement, and I owe him much gratitude. With interest and care he followed my career after Harvard, combining it with personal solicitude about family members. I learned much from him about the imperative of scholarship to be engaged in the cause of our common humanity. No one was more distinguished in that effort than Kenneth Cragg, now deceased, whose long and distinguished life was dedicated to that high purpose. I am thankful to have been the beneficiary of his friendship and companionship in many events over several decades. I am grateful to Jane I. Smith at Harvard who as a colleague and a life-long friend has stood steadfast as a generous scholar and humane teacher. My admiration for her has only grown with the years. With his wife, Nancy, and children, Kathy and Stephanie, George Rupp as dean of the Harvard Divinity School was a source of much encouragement and help when I served on the faculty there and in subsequent years.

I am grateful to many generations of my undergraduate students, first in West Africa and then at Yale, who took my course on West African Islam where the material of this book was presented. I am grateful for their keen observations and for the stimulating questions they brought to the course. All of that helped me to grapple with issues of evidence and interpretation and encouraged me to move forward with my investigation.

I am grateful to Ian Shapiro, who as director of the Macmillan Center at Yale has supported my work in this and other fields. The Yale Divinity School has backed the research and travel connected with the writing of this book, and I gladly acknowledge the assistance of Harry Attridge, the former dean, and Greg Sterling, the current dean, for their help. I benefited from the criticism and comments of the anonymous reviewers of an earlier draft of the manuscript. For any remaining inadequacies and shortcomings, I take full responsibility.

Thanks to the kindness of James Billington, the Librarian of Congress, with the congenial collegiality of Prosser Gifford, then director of Scholarly Programs, and Carolyn Brown, his successor, I spent a year at the Library of Congress as the recipient of the Kluge Award for Countries and Cultures of the South. It was a stimulating and productive time for thinking over the issues of this book and embarking on the research and scholarship for this study. I wrote drafts of the manuscript there, and although I did not realize it at the time, I benefited greatly from scholars who were working in cognate fields but who had yet to publish the results of their research. By the time I returned to the subject some years later those results were available in published form and proved to be critical to the subject of this book. In hindsight, the delay in finishing my book proved to be an advantage. It also increases my gratitude and indebtedness to the generosity of the Library of Congress.

My thanks are due to Chee Seng Yip for technical assistance with the maps and table of clerical succession. I acknowledge the support of the Lundman Family Trust and the friendship of Phil and the late Nancy Lundman in the research and writing of this book. However small, I hope Phil and his family will accept the book as a token of my thanks and appreciation. My grateful thanks go to Theo Calderara, the Editor-in-Chief at Oxford University Press, for his interest and guidance.

I owe an incalculable debt to the clerical leaders among whom I spent much productive time over years of research and investigation. Despite my not being a member of their community, these leaders opened their homes and hearts to me without hesitation or reservation. The confidence of the clerics was a boon for field investigation, particularly with respect to rounding up subjects to be interviewed. The relay system the clerics used to convey messages and material across the clerical diaspora was extremely beneficial in providing a structure for site visits and for collection of evidence. Relationships play an important role in the life and work of clerical centers, the significance of which I was able to observe on site visits.

I am grateful to Sanna Jawneh and Mbemba Sanneh for that follow-up and for the documents written by the clerics they acquired for me. Family relationships help maintain the educational careers of clerics, with pastoral visitations renewing and expanding the network of contacts. All this provided a stimulating setting for my investigations and for historical reflection on the pressures and opportunities of the pacifist vocation. I appreciate the trust the clerics placed in me to try to represent the tradition as fairly as possible but, I insisted, without compromise to the rules of critical reconstruction in which I was engaged. Yet such defensiveness on my part was unnecessary as I found out nearly five years after the fact as this book was going through production that at the inaugural meeting of the Association Internationale Karamokhoba pour l'Education la Culture et la Solidarité Islamique en Afrique at Dakar in June, 2011, I was elected an honorary member. It is a great honor, one impossible to foresee when I set out on this inquiry. The Association is an official public forum dedicated to promoting the pacifist vocation and to commending its importance for contemporary Muslim Africans. I hope this study of that legacy will contribute to the renewed efforts at expanding knowledge of the Islamic pacifist cause the Association seeks to promote.

Beyond Jihad

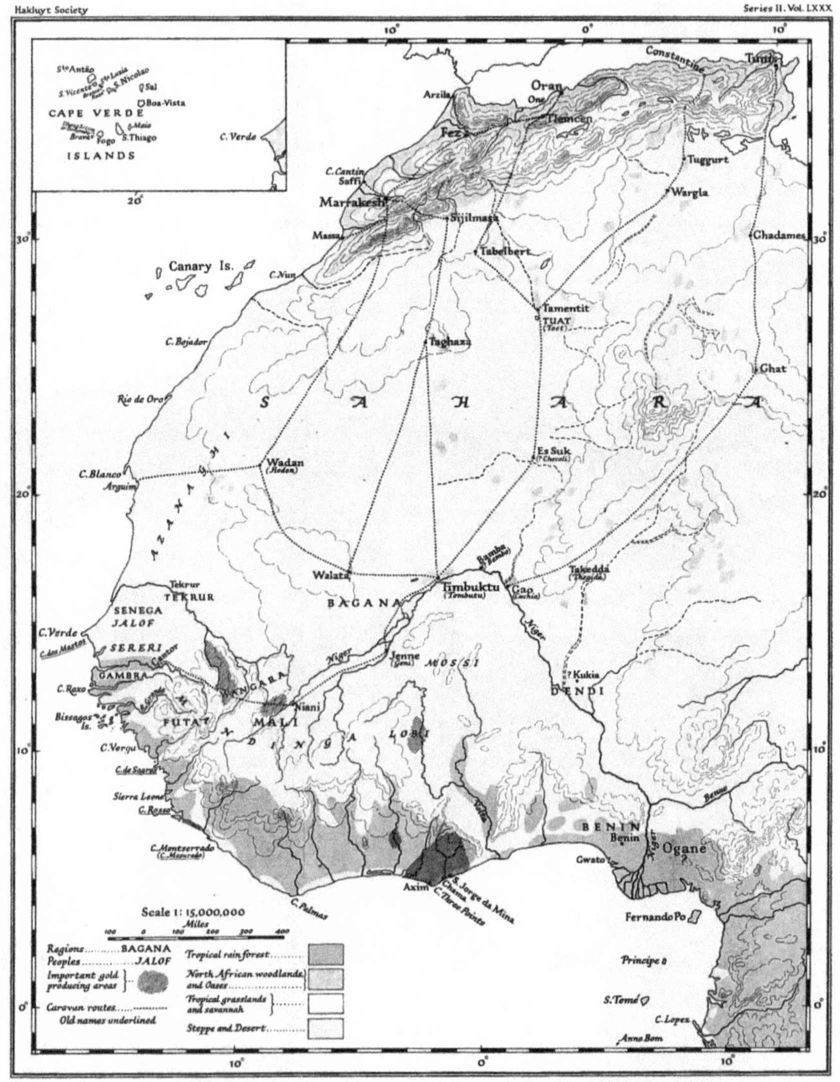

NORTH-WESTERN AFRICA IN THE FIFTEENTH CENTURY

Figure 1 Northwestern Africa in the Fifteenth Century. Courtesy Hakluyt Society.

Introduction

Issues and Directions

> History compels us to fasten on abiding issues, and rescues us from the temporary and transient. . . . Ours is a domain that reaches farther than affairs of state, and is not subject to the jurisdiction of governments. It is our function to keep in view and to command the movement of ideas, which are not the effect but the cause of public events. . . . If the Past has been an obstacle and a burden, knowledge of the Past is the safest and the surest emancipation. . . . The law of stability was overcome by the power of ideas [. . .], ideas that take wing and traverse seas and frontiers, making it futile to pursue the consecutive order of events in the seclusion of a separate nationality. They compel us to share the existence of societies wider than our own [. . .], to live in the company of heroes, and saints [. . .] that no single country could produce.
>
> —Lord Acton, *Essays in the Study and Writing of History*, 505–506, 508, 509–510

This book is about pacifist practice, primarily in Muslim West Africa. It explores Islam's seventh-century beginnings and expansion in North Africa and subsequent transmission by trans-Saharan trade routes to West Africa, showing how the religion spread and took hold—without jihad—and what that peaceful assimilation process means for ongoing religious and social change in Muslim West Africa and other places. Essential to the study of the Muslim pacifist practice is the clerical vocation promoted by religious masters, who set themselves apart from the warrior class and the political class. The clerics formed a distinct religious community by specializing in educational, religious, and legal scholarship. With the support of the wider religious network of clerical settlements, this scholarship enabled them to appropriate and promote Islam's heritage of peaceful persuasion—work that came to define the clerical identity. In time, the clerics emerged as a recognized source of stability and transmission of religion in the midst of political changes and cultural shifts.

They opposed the spread of radicalism, choosing the "greater jihad" of moral and spiritual discipline over the "lesser jihad" of armed combat.

Pathways of Transmission

The term *transmission* is generally understood by historians to mean the spread of Islam through informal and incidental channels of trade, travel, pilgrimage, and general exchange: activities not expressly dedicated to the propagation of the religion and not directly concerned with local reception or acceptance of it. Many historical studies of religious conversion focus heavily on transmission in this external sense, reducing conversion to a mechanical process that overlooks the role of clerics in adapting Islam in their own societies. A process initiated and dominated outside of local communities, transmission credits foreign agents and external logistics with the spread of Islam: camels and caravans brought the religion to commercial transfer points; the transfer points developed into towns and cities, which then became embryonic states; increased learning led to the formation of a scholarly class that inculcated sentiments of jihad; undertaking raids and sorties increased the demand for weapons and tools; the arms buildup stiffened the fledgling jihad impulse; ports of entry in the Sahel and on the coastline provided channels for trade, pilgrimage, and the other cosmopolitan advantages of a world religion. These forms of transmission chronologically and geographically coincided with the earliest outbreaks of jihad. External influence has, therefore, been regarded by scholars as a safeguard against local syncretism.

This emphasis on transmission has been a guiding principle of historical scholarship on the expansion of Islam and cannot be ignored, but it is inconsistent and requires revision. Islam's manner of introduction is crucial to the religion's missionary character of embracing converts regardless of race, gender, culture, rank, or nationality. This missionary mandate can be traced to the Qur'an, but to understand the introduction of Islam fully, one must study not only the message of Scripture but the realities of local reception and adaptation. With this shift in focus, there is no clear-cut religious distinction between core and periphery, between Arab heartland blueprints and frontier adoption in Africa.

Rather than a remote outpost feeding off orthodox norms at long range, Africa has been an integral part of the missionary process that has characterized the history of Islam's expansion. This missionary process is evident in many other parts of the Muslim world, as we shall see. Local accommodation of Islam means a process of give and take: expansion means reappropriation, not simply repetition. The progress of Islam is by local engagement, not by franchise extension. Local Islam emerges through favorable disposition and flexible social mediation and is not necessarily a case of an interminable recovery process that requires jihad for a sound and reliable outcome.

Though a universal religion, Islam has a local, concrete impact on the lives of Muslims. The religion is involved in both the historical process in general and exposure to the African environment in particular.[1] Islam has shaped and also been shaped by events and movements, and the African setting has left its mark on the religion while undergoing transformation. As carriers of Islam, rulers have drawn on it to support court rituals and ceremonies. It has been argued that the tendency to speak of "folk" or "corrupt" Islam encourages essentialization of the religion and the disparagement of local beliefs that might otherwise have provided readily for the introduction of Islam.[2] To essentialize Islam in that way is to do away with peaceful gradual alternatives for introduction of the religion—in other words, it is to insert jihad into the calculus of reform.

Trans-Saharan transmission and the commercial and political development of African towns have converged to promote conversion as a quietist, pacifist phenomenon, sustained by a benign, preexisting religious environment. Walking makes the road, and the pacifist way found in accommodation a formula for securing religious commitment. Trans-Saharan societies afforded opportunities for trade and for propagating Islam, as did many sedentary societies and organized institutions, which upheld the tradition of peaceful coexistence and facilitated the movement of goods/people and the accoutrements of religion. Sedentary societies offered beneficiary links to Saharan centers and pastoralists of the Sahel—Arabic for "coast," the Sahel is the "shoreline" fringing the "sea" of the desert on its southern border with the African Savannah. This fostered a process of exchange between the Islam of towns and cities and the footloose demands of desert life. In this accommodationist milieu, Islam transcended its reputation as a foreign creed and took hold among Africans, in most cases without force or outside interference (see Figure 1.1).

In many parts of West Africa, centers of Muslim life emerged in the course of time as "self-reliant, productive, independent and dominant, supporting, without countenance or patronage of the parent country, Arabia." Muslim communities began to "erect their mosques, keep up their religious services, conduct their schools, and contribute to the support of missionaries from Arabia, Morocco, or Futah [Futa Jallon] when they visit them."[3] Jihad was not necessary to implant the religion or to reform and renew it.[4] The pacifist tradition that developed by local initiative illustrates the autonomous character of religious change. Far from taking the acceptance and efficacy of pacifist teaching for granted, the clerics mounted a moral defense of it. As will be discussed in this book, the clerics prevented the rulers of Mali from entering their centers except as pilgrims during Islamic festival observances. The clerics based their position on giving fidelity to religious teaching over cooption by rulers.

Long-range transmission of Islamic influence converged with the conscientious appropriation of local Muslim professionals to give the religion a secure stronghold in African communities.

As a bridge for trade and cultural exchange between the societies of North Africa and West Africa, the Sahara is critical to understanding how populations came to embrace Islam peacefully and in gradual steps. In the jihad perspective, the Sahara was the channel for the spread of the aggressive proselytization that culminated in the purported eleventh-century Almoravid invasion of Ghana. The invasion coincided with increasing commercial and cultural exchange, bringing about the kingdom's conversion. This is the basis for the questionable theory that the Berbers imposed Islam forcibly on the people of Ghana and maintained it through trade and pilgrimage. This theory perceived caravan routes as an ideal transmission belt for jihad, as well as a barrier against local syncretism.

The Almoravid Invasion of Ghana: Fact and Myth

As will be discussed here and in chapter 2, despite the longstanding nature of the Almoravid claim, there is little support for it in Arabic sources contemporary with the invasion. Islam's ascendancy in Ghana was a protracted, gradual process with a mixed outcome, in large part because prior religious customs and practices continued to be observed even after Islam entered the kingdom. People cultivated a mixed, tolerant form of Islam throughout the history of its trans-Saharan phase, suggesting that Ghana had not been targeted because of its non-Islamic reputation and that the Berbers did not force a choice upon the people. On the contrary, Arab writers indicate that the Berbers were subject to Ghana's jurisdiction and were accommodated into the prevailing pluralist ethos. The fact that Islam was part of the cultural landscape for at least a century before the Almoravid invasion proves that it was not the Almoravids who introduced the religion in the region. Writing in 950–951, Ibn Hawqal says that life in Sijilmasa as a transit town linking Saharan routes and Ghana compares favorably with conditions elsewhere in the wider Muslim world. "I came to Sijilmasa in the year 40 [340 of the Hijrah] [950–951 AD] and I saw there, more than anywhere else in the Maghrib, *shaykhs* of blameless conduct and devotion to scholars and scholarship combined with lofty broadmindedness and elevated and pure ambition."[5] Ibn Hawqal reported seeing at Awdaghast a check with a statement of a debt owed to someone in Sijilmasa by a merchant of Awdaghast, who was himself from Sijilmasa, in the sum of 42,000 dinars. "I have never seen or heard anything comparable to this story in the East. When I told it to the people of 'Iráq, Fárs [Persia], and Khurásán it was consideredremarkable."[6] AprogressiveIslamizationprocesshadbeenunderway, promoted not at state directive but as an active social process of ongoing contact and exchange, with local initiative guiding the course of religious change.

The evidence at our disposal indicates that, rather than the Almoravid Berbers conquering Ghana with Islam as their weapon, the kingdom of Ghana dominated the Berbers. This jihad hypothesis subverted the facts: the claim that the Almoravids conquered Ghana emerged centuries after the supposed event, with Ibn Khaldun (d. 1405–1406) reporting it as fact and the fiction solidified into accepted consensus with the passage of time. Scholars did not challenge the theory; few writers gave any credence to the idea of local initiative as an alternative quietist force for the penetration of Islam. This will be examined in chapter 2.

As we shall see, contemporary sources blend with local perspective to offer a convincing account of the conversion of Ghana, supporting the tie between trans-Saharan traffic and Islam's gradual, quietist entry. This is consistent with written accounts. It explains the nonthreatening role of minority Muslims as autonomous enclaves in predominantly non-Islamic societies and accounts for the gradual, staged introduction of Islam without the upheaval of war; it also accounts for the two-religion policy of Ghana and successor states to foster Islam alongside traditional religions. Finally, it explains the considerable religious overlap between Ghana and the succeeding Mali Empire. In both kingdoms, Muslims filled roles in traditional social and political structures that were congruent with existing practices. Indeed, the conversion of the king of Mali took place not on the battlefield but on the prayer mat, in supplication for rain. Although Mali embraced Islam by royal initiative, it nevertheless allowed a generous margin of coexistence with traditional religious practices.

By way of intervening trans-Saharan crossing points, the kingdom of Mali was fully engaged with centers of law, religion, and politics in Egypt, North Africa, and beyond—and without jihad. By the fourteenth century, it was clear that peaceful clerical communities led by local Muslims had grown and were flourishing in society, a picture that can be drawn from fifteenth-century Portuguese sources, discussed in chapter 5, as well as from traditions recounted in Arabic sources. The evidence is consistent with the enduring pacific impulse of Islam's expansion in West Africa; local initiative did not need jihad to inscribe the religion into the hearts and minds of Africans. Islam expanded in gradual stages without duress or interruption.

Religious Accommodation

By the time of the Almoravids, religious exchange and trade across the Sahara had developed patterns that were becoming more clearly distinct from the power of rulers, fostering a centuries-long tradition of piety and enterprise as civil activities. Muslim traders and visitors operated independently within West African societies, though they had recourse to officials of the state in Mali in cases of fraudulent or unjust treatment. Islam had its center in civil society from where it exerted its impact with securing the conversion of the court. The emergence of communities of scholars as imams, jurists, clerics, muezzins, and spiritual leaders strengthened the role of civil society in religious affairs. The term *elite* has been used to describe this class of scholars, which is not to suggest that they held political positions: the cleric was not a chief or a warrior in waiting. Communities emerged in Egypt and North Africa where political power came to devolve on the invading Arabs, while religious affairs and scholarship fell into the hands of Berber scholars. As will be discussed in the following chapter, Khárijite ideas show Berber influence on the formation of Islam's religious and ethical canon as the foundation of civil society. The religious clericalism that is the subject of this book was based and fostered in civil society, the point of similarity with Kharijite theology.

Even at its zenith, Islam in Mali retained the marks of cultural accommodation, best illustrated by the famous fourteenth-century pilgrimage to Mecca of Mansa Musa. With raised eyebrows at the mixed religious practices of Mansa Musa's court, the Cairene scholars still praised their royal guest's commitment and knowledge of Islam. As P. F. de Moraes Farias observed, Mansa Musa's attitude of accommodation toward his non-Muslim subjects, which was acknowledged by scholars of Cairo, fell remarkably short of the treatment prescribed by jihad doctrine.[7] On Mansa Musa's return journey, his pilgrimage caravan was stocked with scholarly books on law and religion and with cultural artifacts, inaugurating in Mali an era of lively interchange with the wider Muslim world.

Apart from operations and measures to tackle internal unrest, there is little evidence that Mansa Musa imposed Islam on his subjects. His attitude is best explained by his making the resolve while on pilgrimage that when he returned he would reform social custom concerning the treatment of women as a matter of personal repentance, not at the point of the sword, an example he bequeathed to his successors. The prerogative of royal power, Mansa Musa acknowledged, must be subordinate to the norms of religious observance and ethical conduct. This acknowledgment is not a late concession by a lukewarm Muslim ruler but an expression of a fundamental conviction that earthly power is not a duplicate of the higher law and that religious obedience falls under the sovereignty of the religious code. In an environment influenced by the intermixture of diverse social groups observing different customs and speaking different languages, local clerics developed their distinctive brand of "soft" Islam as a social paradigm. This Islam did not ignore or seek to eradicate jihad; it merely characterized it as a harmful exception.

Islam's religious calendar and daily rituals organize the institution and implementation of religious prescriptions. This organization often involved accommodation: in West African societies, this meant the coopting of preexisting institutions and customs. Even when it had the status of the religion of visitors to the court, Islam was exposed to royal customs that involved mixing and compromise. It suited the merchants to remain unattached to the religious life of the court, because whether temporary or permanent residents, merchants have always been outside the religion of the state, usually indicated by residential separation.[8] Buckor Sano, a local merchant, shared with Richard Jobson, the English traveler, his unflattering view of rulers as self-indulgent layabouts, saying as fellow traders he and Jobson had more in common than either of them with the king. "I seek abroad as you doe; and therefore am nearer unto you," said Sano.[9] As such "traders were very sensitive to the attitude of the local authorities, and would defy a governor by deserting his town, as did the merchants and the *'ulamá* of Jenne in 1637."[10] Accordingly, the court, home, tribal council, shop, school, mosque, market, and courthouse have functioned in relevant cases as facilitators or as promoters of the spread of Islam. This will be explained in more detail in due course.

Clerics as religious specialists pursued their work independent of the court and trading centers. Oral traditions confirm this separation by supplying local titles for this class of religious specialists, who are normally identified by the all-purpose term of *'ulamá* (scholars of religion). The local titles of diviners, soothsayers, shrine attendants, oracles, rain-makers, dream-interpreters, and healers reveal very specific understandings about the provision of a wide range of religious services, with roots going back to Ghana. It is from the Serakhulle, the dominant ethnic group of Ghana, that the clerical class among the Jakhanke people emerged as an intentional community under a charismatic itinerant scholar and became major carriers of Islam. "Quietist" is how Western scholars describe Islam in its unresolved, syncretist phase; the pacifist designation is one the local clerics themselves make for their style of peaceful Islam. In pursuing this pacifist vocation, the clerics set out with deliberate purpose to steer their history in a vocational direction. The pacifist narrative is made up of community observance and social boundaries. Observance of community rituals in common with other Muslims is combined with the sense of being set apart rather than set against the *ummah*, the Islamic faith community.

Clerics and Politics

Most Western societies draw a distinction between the public sphere and the private. This distinction is absent in much of Muslim society in Africa. The relationship between the public and the private in Islam is generally fluid, governed by rules of obligation and prohibition, of what is commendable and what is condemned. *Halál* and *harám* (lawful and forbidden) apply equally to the sacred and the secular; both are religious categories. Something can be *halál* by reason of its being designated mundane and therefore removed from stigma; such is the case with *halál* meat. *Harám* does not mean simply forbidden but, depending on the context, also hallowed, which is how it is used with respect to the holy precinct of the Ka'ba. *Halál* and *harám* illustrate how the religious code spreads to all spheres of life. Morally indifferent acts are part of Shari'ah classification that comprises the obligatory, commendable, reprehensible, and forbidden. Moral neutrality is such by virtue of the religious rule that gives it that status; despite being considered indifferent, an act is not without standing in religion. The adaptable Islam of the clerics came about in part through this fluid, incorporative understanding of religion.

Societies throughout Muslim West Africa are divided into spheres of responsibility based on different occupational groups; religious specialists are one such group. The fourteenth-century Moroccan explorer Ibn Battuta describes the existence of such groups in Mali, testifying that there were prominent communities of religious specialists with deep local roots. These specialists were quite distinct from the Muslim communities who lived in separate quarters of the town. As will be discussed in chapter 2, al-Bakrí describes residential separation between Muslims and non-Muslims in Mali. At his own request, Ibn Battuta took lodging in the Muslim quarter. The picture of Mali painted by Ibn Battuta is one in which Muslims and non-Muslims occupied their respective places in society, without being subjected to meddling by the king.

How did pacifist teaching survive the challenge of jihad and political meddling? A study of the founding clerical centers provides possible answers. Muslim religious leaders created these centers in areas with easy access to towns and trading routes but without the religious leaders turning into traders; the centers were similarly separated from the larger Muslim community. The clerics formed a pact with political leaders: rulers would not enter the centers except on a prearranged schedule and for the purpose of undertaking religious exercises. The clerics abjured political office for themselves and required rulers to recognize this clerical neutrality. Without a homeland to claim or to defend, pacific clerics adopted pastoral itinerancy as a way of life: the dispersion trail provided a defense against danger and an instrument of expansion. Spread out over a wide arc, the pacifist trail embraced towns, villages, and hamlets. As a result, clusters of settlement emerged as a network of teaching centers and contacts. They maintained educational *isnáds* (chains of transmission) on which religious chronicles used in this study are based. In addition to their explicit withdrawal from political life, this network strengthened the clerical community's autonomy and afforded it a further safeguard against political meddling.

The satellite clerical centers, located close to trading routes and markets, became recognized for their work in the transmission and establishment of Islam. While they were sometimes pressed to forgo their pacifist commitment and merge with wider society and dealt with dissidents within their ranks, the centers survived, either by being granted political immunity or by relocating. In the clerical view, one is obligated to seek the peaceable kingdom by acts of peacemaking, rejecting the use of political offices for the propagation of Islam. For the clerical profession, political subservience undermined fidelity to pacifist teaching. The clerics offered political compliance in the sense that they would not accept political office as chiefs and they would not take sides in political disputes. But their compliance would not be at the expense of their religious conscience. Religion was the high moral wall erected to protect the clerics from, as well as to impede, the excess of politics. This clerical view is in striking contrast to the jihad view of religion as a matter of military and political enforcement.

Local family chronicles document the sense of community solidarity and kinship of religion distinguished by learning and devotion. The chronicles are evidence of the unified purpose of the dispersed religious settlements. They describe the intellectual achievements of leading clerics who founded the settlements and promoted their development and provide details about teachers, scholars, clerics, and students. Together with early Arabic sources and the accounts of travelers, explorers, and scholars who journeyed or lived in West Africa, the chronicles help to fill gaps in knowledge about what took place in the clerical centers. Field investigation is indispensable for a true grasp of the spirit and outlook of these centers.

The leaders of these clerical centers distanced themselves from political families, with the clerics deriving their legitimacy from pursuing religion as a calling rather than from political attachment. The autonomous religious office furnishes the basis for an independent clerical vocation; in clerical hands Islam transfuses society, communal rituals, and kinship observances with norms of behavior and conduct. The clerics of this study belong to a community of trained religious officials. Like those officials, the clerics lead their communities in prayer, teach the young the rudiments of faith, preside over the community in Ramadan and the pilgrimage festival, officiate at the naming ceremony of the newly born, perform marriages, and direct burial customs and interment. Unlike other religious officials, however, the clerics created an unbroken historical tradition of performing these functions. Religious centers emerged to support clerics specializing in the routine, peaceful, nonpolitical cultivation of Islam, including provisions for learning. The distinctive design of Muslim society in West Africa was largely the consequence of the work of such religious clerics with the backing of the general Muslim community.

Clerical Biography and Muslim Identity

Clerical biographies offer important insight into the nature and function of clerical settlements, as illustrated by the story of Karamokhoba and his Sufi counterparts (discussed later). In the clerical vocation, ethnicity is subsumed into religion. Among the Manding/Malinke, a West African ethnic group descended from the Mali Empire, the term for cleric is *karamokho*. *Karamokho* is usually adopted as a *jamu*, a name used in salutation, and it becomes a professional designation: his ethnic origin notwithstanding, a *karamokho* is a member of the circle of learned clerics and becomes the people's chaplain.

The cleric's education draws on the network of centers, which are connected to allow the distribution of religious and intellectual resources through travel and exchange. A scholar rarely finishes his education without having undertaken a rigorous, extensive travel regime that brings him into personal contact with important clerical centers and with their *barakah* (blessing). The "tanning of travel" accomplished these objectives at once, which explains the prevalence of the travel motif in the chronicles. (See chapter 6 for a description of travel as an element of *barakah*.)

The evolution of Muslim religious identity in West African societies reflects a high degree of accommodation with little inclination to judge a person's faith and conduct. It is enough to claim the name of Muslim: time and practice will lead to faith. There is no notion of Islam *manqué;* in most circumstances, the spirit of accommodation will absorb nominal believers without designating them second-class Muslims. This conforms to the general Muslim attitude: unlike a lapsed Christian in the West, a nominal or a lapsed Muslim may still claim the prerogatives of the name. For these adherents of the faith, submitting to the voice of religious authority is enough to secure their allegiance; they are "not given to speculation or else [are] content to regard fulfillment of ritual as an end in itself."[11] Islam does not share the modern Western intellectual view that religion is a free speech issue and thus a matter of individual rights. In the Western view, religion is a matter of individual will and personal choice. This understanding of religion comes of the Western classical heritage, of which Islam is relatively free.[12] Islam regards religion as revealed truth; in Africa, that sits well in light of the notion of sacred oracle. In Islam, accommodation is congruent with the elastic nature of custom, without the radical dichotomy of church and state, of sacred and secular, conservative and liberal. The conflict-personalities of Christianized populations in Africa, who are prickly about their close identification with European culture, are not typical of Islamized groups in Africa, leading a French scholar-administrator to observe that Qur'an schools "do not create any *déclassés*."[13]

As advocates of "soft" Islam, pacifist clerics are not separatists, in contrast with the Western tradition of pacifism. They do not reject the *ummah*, the constituted faith community of Sunni Islam. Social pluralism mitigated the tendency toward political and communal separatism, and the absence of centralized government power removed political coercion in conversion and religious affiliation. The authority of the universal Arabic Qur'an, buttressed by commentaries anchored in language and tradition, averted or diminished the tendency for an individualistic interpretation of Scripture and, equally, for political control of religion, leaving religion's place in civil society. This authority allowed the clerics to affirm the *ummah* (the faith community) as the repository of Scripture and *sunnah* and to place their moral example before and within the *ummah* in public teaching and witness. The clerics experienced their share of trials and tribulations, but they adhered to peace and moderation as defining qualities of their profession. The clerics claimed no political entitlement or reward for the peaceful propagation of religion. They felt the obligation of faith would be fulfilled better by forbearance and accommodation than by waging jihad. Accommodation led the clerics to accept a fluid boundary with traditional religions in the process of conversion to Islam. The idea is well enunciated by Gregory III, namely, "whoever wishes to climb to a mountain top climbs gradually step by step, and not in one leap."[14] The question relates to how people should move from following local religion to faith in a Scripture-based religion. The clerics of this study would concur.

Divergent Forms of Islam

We are familiar in the puritan tradition with austere, earnest religious souls, who, "full of pious worry and tense watchfulness," work themselves up to such a pitch of piety that they adopt a secluded lifestyle to separate themselves from the rest of the world in order to "walk warily with the Lord."[15] Islam has had its own brand of the fervent, self-isolating *záhid* (ascetic); a relatively tame version of the type has appeared in West Africa, where he follows the religion with a solicitous, social disposition and sets out on the path of prayer with Qur'an and rosary in hand and with little more than bare necessities and the expectation of ample reward in wives, compounds, and material blessings. Whatever his flair for mystical seclusion, the Sufi in West African Islam is a charismatic figure with social appeal. Sufism is a social phenomenon, making *barakah* (grace) beneficial as material blessing. Votive prayer flourished by the abundance of the social benefits it received. The religious space that enabled Sufis to flourish was appealing environment, too, for the professional clerics in their own right. The clerics provide numerous religious services to their followers, including prayer, holy water collected from washing wooden slates containing Qur'anic verses, amulets for protection from the evil eye, and dream interpretation (Figure 9.1). The Sufi connection was an important point of religious convergence with pacifist clerics.

Regional political interests, such as the leaders in Futa Jallon, Guinea, sometimes coveted the presence of scholars of religion, including Sufi scholars, in their societies. That was one way in which the Qádiriyah *ṭaríqah* and its offshoots like the Shádhiliyah spread in West Africa. By the time the clerics of this study arrived in Futa Jallon, the political system had been weakened to the point of becoming dysfunctional, thanks to the inconclusive jihad waged in the eighteenth century by Karamokho Alfa and his Fulbe compatriots. The ensuing political inertia carried the risk of political instability, in part because the violent jihad compromised Islam's appeal to local communities and in part because Fulbe secularists had not come to an understanding with the advocates of jihad. The split between Fulbe religious elements and their secular cousins persuaded both sides that compromise was preferable to a contest for partisan superiority. The Muslim religious party recognized that not all Fulbe were united behind Islam, despite the considerable gains Islam had made. With both secular and religious Fulbe willing and eager to grant concessions to pacifist teaching, the clerical prescription seemed destined to prevail; the clerics reforged weapons of jihad into plowshares and pruning hooks.

The coming of the Jakhanke, a people originating in ancient Ghana, was followed by the French colonial administration, whose comprehensive view of religion dispensed with the finer shades of local adaptation. Global Islam, or what the French called "Islam *arabe*," was the enemy of imperial power and must be checked and disarmed at every turn. "Islam *noir*," its African counterpart, also required monitoring for its mischievous influence on gullible populations easily roused to fanaticism. With their moral authority, clerical centers posed a double threat as magnets of Islam *arabe* and as hatching grounds of a nefarious Islam *noir*. The French colonial classifications of Islam were motivated by a demand for collaboration as the logical corollary of capitulation, a policy that threatened the very raison d'être of pacifist religious independence.

The jihad hypothesis has dominated scholarship with the idea that Islam matters only as an issue of political choice and economic inducement.[16] Spencer Trimingham, a pioneer scholar of African Islam, presents a similar view by noting, somewhat casually, that it was when Islam entered West Africa that a religion of historical revelation and monotheism first arrived to challenge the timeless recurring mythology of local beliefs and rituals and forced a disruption of the old ways. Like many other places, West Africa never underwent an Arabization process as a complement to Islamization. Islamization and Arabization seldom converged outside the Arab heartlands. The indigenous religious outlook subsisted through the Islamic phase; evidence of this can be seen in the return to divinatory practices in areas where jihad once prevailed.[17] Still, the Islam embraced by Muslim Africans comprised of the Five Pillars of the faith is no different from what Muslims elsewhere embraced. And the same is true of the supple and nuanced ways in which Muslim Africans have approached the religious code.

This book will identify several ways in which the structure of Islamic institutions, from quotidian rituals to annual rites, impresses itself batik-like on the fabric of West African life and fashions a distinct Muslim culture. This structure is described in biographies, which are invested with *barakah*, the divine gift of blessings and grace, as well as in personal stories and anecdotes, which are offered as instructive parables. The cleric is above all a religious emissary, not the heroic bearer of tribal or ethnic valor. Hero worship is little cultivated in the clerical community; in Muslim thought, faith is based not on blood relationship, nationality, territorial affinity, or personal heroism but on *dín* (religion). Islam's religious frame is original and consistent with its message, not a side issue of ethnic or racial preeminence. The religious focus of clerical biographies resonates with Islam's transethnic and transnational appeal, as demonstrated by examples in and beyond Muslim Africa.

Local and Global Islam

Islam's caliphal heritage long ceased to define the worldwide Muslim community. In the course of their history Jakhanke clerics occupied the space normally filled by traditional religions, adding to it the advantage Islam offered of the network assets of a world religion. The tendency of scholars, including Trimingham, to speak of folk in opposition to orthodox Islam overlooks the advantages, direct and indirect, that came with Islam. Despite the different peoples and contexts it embraced, the Muslim world was of one mind by virtue of the single revealed Arabic Qur'an and the canonical code of the Five Pillars of faith. That fundamental structure, while undergoing countless internal modifications, did not change much in outline. It was a framework of unified aspiration and practice that continued to define Muslim identity for a long time. Distinctive religious institutions and structures continued to emerge and to overlap with politics, but the Islamic spirit was expressed through Scripture, worship, morality, law, scholarship, architecture, and art.

As numerous studies have shown, there is no monolithic Islam—even at its origination, caliphal authority was tentative and nebulous where it existed at all. Yet the religious canon remained in force. Many user-friendly versions of legal works circulated widely and freely. Children carrying slates of Qur'anic passages, or seated on the ground chanting their lessons under the attentive eye of a genial schoolmaster, were familiar sights across the Muslim world, as were pilgrims returning to their communities from Mecca, wearing the headband. The pilgrim, teacher, imam, and legal expert remained emblematic figures, illustrative of the religion's impact on individuals and society. The cleric was another such figure.

In light of widespread adaptation of the religious code, historical perspective is necessary to correct the prevalent picture of an unchanging, monochromatic Islam. According to the fourteenth-century Tunisian historian Ibn Khaldun, scholars seeking to describe and interpret are inclined to judge by comparison and analogy, and to that extent are liable to error, particularly when they are inattentive or rushed. [18] Any treatment of the past must reckon with the truth that great changes and even revolutions have occurred in human conditions and institutions. To do that, writers must not draw analogies between the events of the past and those that take place around them, judging the past by what they know of the present. Difference is intrinsic to the nature of history because change is what defines time, Ibn Khaldun argues, and the failure to understand this principle is what accounts for historians accepting and transmitting "stories about events which are intrinsically impossible."[19] But difference does not mean fragmentation, and change is not incoherence.

The Muslim pacifist tradition is one example of how, involved in a complex and dynamic spiritual exchange with its African ideas of accommodation and coexistence, Islam became appropriated in ways that helped to unify it with the Islam of Arabia. This accommodation was not syncretism, since the idea that Islam is prescribed by the Qur'an was not overlooked or rejected despite extensive borrowing from African customs. Rather, both unity and difference were maintained in a pattern of accommodation and change, of absorption and differentiation. The Qur'an was introduced into this process as an oracle of power. Converts saw it as a source of spirit power and a protection against ill will and misfortune. The potency of the Qur'an assured success while also providing protection against the evil eye. The battlefield was no longer the secret groves and nocturnal rituals of local, pre-Islamic religions but the public, material form of sacred Qur'anic scripture, with daily practice to reinforce it. Even in societies affected by jihad, where reformers attempted to eradicate practices deemed repugnant to the religious code, the pattern of accommodation and peaceful change emerged. West Africa offers ample ground for revising Islam's message, such that it harmonized with specifically African conversion and construction of identity. Being Muslim and being African were compatible.

The French Colonial Challenge

The clerical community proved problematic for French colonial officials. There were competing interests at issue. The argument made in this book, that benign forms of Muslim clericalism were key to the gains of Islam in Africa, was conceded by the French—but with a very different perception of those gains. Clericalism's pervasive nature, the French argued, enabled subterfuge for conspiracy, and its humble profile was craftily designed to disguise evil intent. In the colonial discourse, pacifist clerics were the Trojan horse of religious radicalism and had to be confined at every opportunity. It is this view of Islam as a conspiracy that framed the official colonial outlook, and even when scholars contested the premise, the discussion was still constrained by it. To the extent that the colonial power believed in an Islamic conspiracy and acted on that belief, Muslims became sitting targets of colonial action. The stereotypes and caricatures of Islam and of Muslims as dangerous and unreliable and therefore requiring *apprivoisement* (breaking in) justified a policy of targeting Muslims with the goal of making them submit as colonial collaborators and clients. In the colonial perception, Islam attracted to itself irrational and unstable elements of primal Africa and, as such, constituted an unacceptable challenge to France's *mission civilisatrice.* A colonial administrative campaign was orchestrated and launched against the marabouts perceived as masterminds of a Muslim jihad that existed only in the imagination of an insecure colonial power.

This situation presented pacifist clerics with an unenviable challenge: the loyalty and cooperation of the clerics that had been sufficient to safeguard their reputation now must serve the comprehensive demands of an ascendant colonial power. Committed to the pacifist vocation, the clerics found in submission and clientage, with religious leaders coming under the authority of local officials, the space they needed to regroup and to retrieve the heritage. Though it was too little too late, the clerics were assisted in this retrieval work after the return of their leaders from imprisonment and exile by a penitent colonial administration and by allies in the Muslim community. The clerics' quiet sincerity and dogged persistence won the respect and sympathy of administrators and helped to lift the stigma of suspicion from them.

The Muslim world was fundamentally altered by colonial rule. Nowhere was this more evident than in the establishment of the nation-state as the unit of the international order and as the foundation of individual rights and citizenship. This led to the proliferation of independent national jurisdictions where citizenship as a function of national origin was set above religious adherence, with the expectation that religion would shrink proportionately as progressive national forces expanded. Shared citizenship with non-Muslims, the theory continues, would overtake truculent religious attitudes and render the *ummah* (the Islamic religious community) obsolete. As in the modern West, the resulting nation-state would have no religious communities within it capable of challenging its unified national identity. In addition, the advent of modern means of travel and communication—and of the Internet revolution—would accelerate the pace of change, pull the Muslim world further into the secular orbit, and expose it to the individualism of market forces. The end result was that emerging economic structures overtook Islam's legal and political institutions and ushered in a world largely free of religion in terms of state jurisdiction.

Yet, despite the changes, upheavals, and disruptions following colonial rule and the challenging impact of transnational pressures, the continuing vitality of Muslim society proved that the modern encounter did not sap Islam's energy or weaken its hold on communities. Although their roles changed, sometimes radically, clerics as a religious class did not lose their social importance, thanks to their resourcefulness in taking charge of opportunities of localization and mediation of new influences. The continuing social influence of religion vindicated the idea of freedom *of* religion while making freedom *from* religion a speculative, remote idea.

Jihad and the State

The traditional Western understanding of the relationship between Islam and society presumes unity of religion and politics, of church and state. That understanding, seen in colonial attitudes toward Islam and Muslims, casts Islam as political in nature and Muslims as predisposed to exploit that political potential. The jihad view of religious change affirms a political role for religion and thus a rationale for Islam as an anticolonial force. *Beyond Jihad* challenges this standard view of Islam despite the fact that Muslims established caliphates to project the religion as the object and justification of power, as well as being active in anticolonial struggles. The short-lived nature of the caliphates, along with their mixed record and heritage, shows the cost of trying to force religion and government into a single enterprise. The history of caliphates might incline us to believe that Muslim backed the integration of religion and state power, yet caliphates never succeeded completely in taking over the religious and legal jurisdictions of Islam. No evidence, including Scripture, supported the idea of the state as a prerequisite and substitute of religion. That would amount to *shirk* (idolatry).

The political and military engagement involved in jihad sometimes worked against it. The haphazard and opportunistic ways Muslim warlords embarked on military operations to promote their cause divided the Muslim community and undercut the promotion of jihads and other such operations. That Muslim warlords allied with non-Muslim leaders in operations in which Muslims suffered deepened divisions gave jihad a controversial reputation. The open challenge of leading clerics to the jihads happening around them denied jihad critical, uncontested acceptance. Jihad was compromised because it was so often attempted in an environment marked by ambition and opportunism. The inconclusive outcomes of religious wars challenged the notions of universal support or of divine mandate, and that hard lesson was used by the clerics to bolster the case for pacifist teaching. If, as Hobbes maintains, force and fraud are the two cardinal virtues in war, it is not difficult to make the case that jihad is not moral enough to spare religion or society.

Clerical practice created a strikingly distinctive religious tradition; it should challenge us to examine afresh the case for separation of religion and politics in the Islamic canon, as well as in the daily lives of Muslims. Muslim scholars generally insisted that Muhammad's heritage could not be abandoned into the hands of the rulers of this world and that the religious office was such not by state fiat. Dismay and disenchantment with a much-maligned caliphate could account for this distrust but not for all of it. The idea of revealed law in Islam is predicated on God as the lawgiver and as ruler of the universe. Human affairs belong in the realm of the created order while religion has its foundation in the transcendent will of God. Muslim authorities use the term *mukhálafah* for the distinction between the Creator and what he created.[20] This radical contingency of the created order (radical in the sense that the created order is mutable and in flux while the Creator is not) has implications for treating religion and politics not as one and the same thing, at least not in pacifist clerical discourse. A clue about the distinction can be found in the way political disenchantment or defection normally has not been accompanied by religious disenchantment or defection, and political disarray does not implicate religious adherence. Muslims do not abandon their faith because they have lost faith in politics. The distinction gives new meaning to clerical views of religion and will shed light on the special character of the West African setting and historical parallels elsewhere in the Muslim world.

PART ONE

HISTORICAL GENESIS

1

Beyond North Africa

Synthesis and Transmission

In human progress unity and complexity are the two great correlatives forming together the great paradox. Life is manifold, but it is also one. So it is seldom possible, and still more seldom advisable, to divide a civilization into departments; life nowhere can be cut into two with a hatchet. And this is emphatically true of Islam. Its intellectual unity . . . is its outstanding quality . . . its life and thought are a unity.

—Duncan B. Macdonald, *Development of Muslim Theology, Jurisprudence and Constitutional Theory*, 3

Geography and Cultural Diffusion

To amend archaeologist Merrick Posnansky, the key to the religious and cultural history of Africa lies in its position and shape.[1] The solid mass of the continent at the northeastern corner, the oldest and the second-largest area, is connected to the Sinai by a 70-mile-wide isthmus. For millennia, the isthmus has acted as a conveyor of linguistic, religious, and cultural influences ranging in origin from beyond the Horn of Africa to southwest Asia. At its northwestern projection Africa is separated from the nearest landmass, Europe, by 9 miles of Mediterranean Sea at the Strait of Gilbratar. On the eastern flank of the continent, the most prominent geographical feature linking Africa to Asia is the Great Rift Valley, whose 4,000-mile course runs from the Dead Sea in the Jordan Valley at 1,300 feet below sea level to Malawi in Central Africa. The continent's 4,500-mile width across its shoulder in the northern half nearly matches the 5,000-mile length of its spine from north to south, with the relative population density of the Rift Valley hardly making up for the sparse settlements of the arid wastes. The process of populating the other continents with migrations out of Africa resulted in growth levels that Africa never saw, with Asia and Europe showing the largest population growth.

The contrast of sparse population density with the vast land mass of Africa is quite striking. With a total area of over 11.7 million square miles, Africa is 3.23 times the size of continental United States and contains 22 percent of the earth's land surface. Africa could contain within its coastline the United States, Europe, India, Argentina, and China, with room to spare. The only continent dissected by the tropics of Cancer and Capricorn, the African land mass consists of two contrasting rectangles. The horizontal northern rectangle is made up of low ground mostly below 3,000 feet, and the vertical southern rectangle is formed by a plateau above 3,000 feet. The climate and seasons north of the equator mirror those to the south of it. The position and shape of Africa caused the southern half to remain relatively isolated from outside influences compared to the northern half.

West Africa lies at the center of a geological formation consisting of a large, stable mass of rock, called a craton. This West African craton set the continental contours of the continent as early as 3,600 million years ago, making it the earliest land formation and Africa the oldest continent. The craton extends from the coastlines of present-day Sierra Leone, Liberia, Ivory Coast, and Ghana north to Mauritania. Narrowly defined, the belt extends from 5° to 20° north and 15° west to 15° east, which is the area roughly from the Atlantic coast to the Lake Chad region. Two other cratons, the Congo and the Kaapvaal, completed the formation of the continent when Africa emerged as a single stable mass some 550 million years ago. The rest of the earth's terrestrial mass, still short of its critical cooling threshold, subsisted in a state of flux.[2] The defining geological structure of the African continent, once at the requisite degree of thermal equilibrium, remained relatively stable despite surface changes of climate, massive lava flows, relentless soil and rock erosion, and sedimentation. Exceptions to this stability were the formations of Atlas Mountains to the north, the Hoggar and Tibesti massifs at the center, and the Cape Fold Mountains at the southern tip, which show evidence of more recent flux in the earth's crust. With striking linear dunes hugging the entire coastline in southern Africa, the Namib Desert, an estimated 43 million years old, is reckoned to be the world's oldest desert and, by some, the finest.

The West Africa region covered by this study is contiguous with the northern horizontal rectangle, an area of religious and cultural life with which it has had long-standing contact. The geometrical arrangement of the continent's land mass explains the history of culture contact between North Africa and southwest Asia, as is evident from the course of trans-Saharan traffic and, in subsequent centuries, the rise of Islam in Arabia and its spread within a generation to Egypt and North Africa.

This is the physical backdrop to Africa's recorded history. In the dim, distant centuries before the rise of Islam and its spread to North Africa, the continent was exposed to traffic and influences stemming from Egypt and beyond, with the winds and sands of the desert bearing more than simply the random drift of their rotation. The Sahara, the world's largest desert at some 4 million square miles, constituted a communication barrier between North Africa and regions to the south, but scattered settlements facilitated travel and trade prior to the advanced desertification of later periods. In the majority of cases, pools and waterholes resulting from surface drainage were subjected to wind, drift, and evaporation and so made little difference to the significant movement of people. Still, this topographical variation allows natural vegetation to occur in the form of scattered clumps of desert scrub and clumps of bunch grass on the margins. The mountainous territory at the western end of the desert, which carries coniferous and evergreen scrub and forest from the southern frontiers of Morocco across some 1,400 miles to the Gulf of Gabes, shows markedly different climate conditions.

The broad topographical variety of the desert, induced by surface processes of drainage, wind currents, and erosion, defies categorical generalization.[3] Some 12,000 years ago, much of the area was a lush savannah. Even today, far from being an area of dead life, conditions in the desert can be quite dynamic. One report describes a torrential downpour of rain in the central Sahara:

> On the 15th of January 1922 at 8 p.m. a hurricane followed by torrential rain struck the area. The roofs of the houses (of dried mud) nearly all collapsed and the native population took refuge in the fort and bordj. The water swept away houses and gardens along the edge of the wadi. On the 16th the rain continued and the wadi, which had burst its banks, was flowing as fast as a horse at gallop. At 5 o'clock the outer wall of the fort collapsed, burying 22 people; . . . On the 17th the rain began to let up, the level in the wadi fell and the weather began to clear; snow could be seen on the summit of the hills.[4]

Yet in the same area there might not be a single drop of rain for years. One oasis reported that there was no rain for twelve years. In Cairo, there was no rain to speak of between 1916 and 1919 and then in 1919 43 millimeters of rain fell in a single storm.[5] Some forms of vegetable life have adapted to this extreme environment. In the form of seeds, the so-called *asheb* flora of the western desert, for instance, is said to be capable of surviving ten years between rainfalls. Other resilient plants include dwarf scrub, with long, sturdy roots that can retain their moisture for long periods.

Even though the duration varies considerably, the pattern of intermittent rainfall supports extensive areas of vegetation at the northern and southern margins of the desert. In these areas, irrigated by natural springs or underground water sources called aquifers, oases exist in the form of small fertile areas where crops and livestock, including big game, can subsist. A. J. Arkell, an English authority on the archeology of the Sahara, reports how in the Gebel Marra area a young elephant went foraging in the succulent pasture that grows at the head of narrow ravines and gullies, some with very narrow cleft-like passages. In weeks of foraging in the thriving pasture, the young elephant gained so much weight that it could not fit in the narrow opening through which it came and was stranded for several months before local hunters found it and killed it.[6] A story in the *National Geographic News* reported that in 2008 a visitor to the Western Sahara was told of significant rainfall in the area.

> "The nomads there told me there was never as much rainfall as in the past few years," Kröpelin said. "They have never seen so much grazing land. Before, there was not a single scorpion, not a single blade of grass . . . Now you have people grazing their camels in areas which may not have been used for hundreds or even thousands of years. You see birds, ostriches, gazelles coming back, even sorts of amphibians coming back."[7]

Commanding the trans-Saharan trade routes and offering halting stations where traders and merchants could replenish food and water supplies, these oases made it possible to undertake long, arduous journeys across the desert. This was the vital role played by the towns of Sijilmasa and Taghaza, situated 25° north, not to be confused with towns of the same name in the region of Taodeni on 23° north and Taghaza al-Gharbi, to the west. From very early times, the oases emerged as important strategic settlements that controlled major trade routes and thus formed an important bridge in the desert. Satellite pictures have shown underground dry water beds and lakes that once supported traffic and settlement.

The Rise of Islam

Tradition dates the founding of Islam to the year 622 AD, with the *hijrah* (journey) to Mecca. The Prophet died in 632 AD, and under his successors, called caliphs, the new faith spread quickly into new acquired territories (*futuh al-buldan*). The Muslim forces had scarcely finished taking control of Syria in 636 AD before they moved into Africa to chase what remained of Byzantine hegemony there. Most of the resistance came from the Berbers, though for some fifty years isolated pockets of Byzantine resistance remained entrenched behind the natural barrier of the Tunisian Dorsal and in the fortified town of Carthage.

On the heels of the conquest of Egypt in 642 AD, the caliph 'Uthman ordered the expansion to Ifriqiya under the command of 'Abd Allah b Sa'd, who in 656 concluded a treaty with the Byzantine authority in return for a heavy tribute. Shortly after coming to power in Syria, Mu'áwiya dispatched the commander Uqba ibn Náfi to undertake the conquest of North Africa. In the course of that campaign, Uqba ibn Náfi founded Qayrawan, eventually the capital of the Muslim West, in Tunisia. In 666–667, 'Uqba penetrated the Fezzan region and eventually led his forces to Morocco. He was killed in clashes with the Berber chief, Kusayla, in 682–683. His death brought to an abrupt halt the effort to incorporate North Africa into the Arab empire, and Morocco was evacuated and abandoned. A second offensive was launched between 701 and 708 to resume the conquest; it was led by Hassan b. al-Nu'mán, who found his path to victory blocked by an old Berber woman known as al-Káhina, "the Soothsayer," described by Ibn Khaldun as being of the Jewish faith. Her resistance by way of military campaigns resulted in al-Nu'mán's confinement to the borders of Tunisia. After the fall of Carthage in 698 and the triumph of al-Káhina, the Berber resistance mysteriously crumbled. The Muslim forces, led by Musa b. Nusayr, pressed forward with lightning speed to establish a stronghold in remote Morocco and then use that as a position from which to launch the assault on Spain in 710. The perimeter of Europe was breached for the first time.

The process of absorbing surviving Christian populations of the towns of North Africa into the Islamic sphere was slow and gradual; the sword is too blunt an instrument with which to turn recalcitrant hearts into believing souls. That work of conversion relied on the prestige of Islam as the new religion of the rulers as well as on debilitating splits and divisions among the Christians. Christian life crumbled with the collapse of structures of religious life, and the stimulating effect of a vigorous Islam swept away the drifting Christian remnants. The fate of a community of Christian captives in Qayrawan who were converted to Islam hints at a social pattern of captives and slaves as carriers of Islam. Traders of Sardinia established a colony of Christian captives in the city, who in time adopted the language and religion of their Muslim masters.[8]

The victorious Arabs used military recruitment into their armies to secure the allegiance of the Berber populations to Islam and subdue the Maghrib (the northwest region of the African continent along the Mediterranean), establishing it as a beachhead. From there, the tide of conquest carried the Muslim forces into Spain, which surrendered without too much struggle. Under Islam, Spain was realigned with the momentum of Islamic ascendancy in the Maghrib and beyond, with a Muslim-dominated Mediterranean world offering a channel of contact to the wider Islamic civilization. Islam created a *cordon sanitaire* insulating Spain from its European cultural hinterland. Ibn Juzayy, the editor of Ibn Battuta's *Rihlah* ("Journey") speaks of Gibraltar as "the citadel of Islam" planted "as an obstruction stuck in the throats of the idolaters."[9] The note of defiance struck here reflects confidence in Islam's rising power.

The strategy of military conscription as a means of overcoming Berber opposition and reconciling them to Arab ascendancy broke down under the strain of Berber nationalist agitation and factionalism. The western Maghrib remained outside the orbit of Arab power, which called it "The Far West" (*al-maghrib al-aqsá'*). In that form, the "West" carried the connotation of unfamiliar wilderness. Other areas of the Maghrib, the middle and eastern, were far from being pacified as Khárijite unrest gripped the country. As Berbers who were embroiled in the succession dispute of the caliphate between 'Ali and Mu'áwaiyah, governor of Syria, the Khárijites got their name as "those who went out in opposition" to the arbitration that was called to decide rightful succession in Islam.

Khárijites adopted the extreme view that faith can be voided by sin, which fueled their fierce nationalist anti-Arab opposition, adding an incendiary element to the rash of dissident outbreaks that beset the fledgling Islamic empire. Khárijite extremists were as uncompromising as their opponents. The conflict came to a head with the anathema against the Caliph 'Uthman for abandoning the ideals of religion, particularly the dogma of a race-blind, egalitarian Islam.[10] In 656, 'Uthman was pursued to Medina where, in his caliphal chambers, with the Qur'an open on his lap, he received the death blows. This opened the *fitnah* (civil strife) that ended the unity of Islam; the Sunni-Shi'ite split became institutionalized. The austere terrain of North Africa provided ideal incubation for Khárijite nationalism and for the accompanying Shi'ite manifestation. Together they ensured that in the Maghrib the establishment Islam of Arab inspiration was exploited to stoke the energy and direction of Berber independency. New states under Arab leadership rose and fell in quick succession as the Berbers continued to resist Arab highhandedness. This instability may have accounted for the defeat of the Arabs at the hands of Frankish ruler Charles Martel in 732.

The Arab-Berber racial problem was resolved by a theological distinction made by the Berbers: by "rejecting their *islám*, their submission to the Arabs, in the name of their Islam, their submission to God."[11] Thus the Berbers embraced Islam with their egalitarian view that all believers are on an equal moral footing, despite Shi'ism's introduction of the variant teaching of hierarchy based on veneration of the descendants of the Prophet. Notions of sharifian title indicating that the Prophet's descendants had the right to rule thus found fertile ground in the Maghrib. In that way, Shi'ism became the catalyst of Arab settlement and leadership in Berber society. In the late eighth century, Idris b. 'Abd Allah, claiming descent from the family of the prophet, fled political oppression in Baghdad. He came to settle in the Maghrib, where he became chief of a Berber tribe and founded the city of Fez. He died of poisoning at the hands of agents of the Abbasid caliph. His tomb became a national shrine and pilgrimage center, a passageway from politics to religion. Built by Idriss II, the Idrisid house flourished at Fez, where Tunisian and Andalusian settlers arrived to help transform the city into Morocco's intellectual and spiritual center.[12] The ruling house became one of the most renowned Muslim dynasties of North Africa, though division and decline followed the death of Idriss II; his twelve sons presided over a disintegrating power structure. Despite its extremism, Berber Kharijism laid convincing claim to Islam's egalitarian spirit of the brotherhood of believers and went on to deepen knowledge of the religion by advancing orthodox teaching, especially at Qayrawan. Kharijism gave North African Islam the rigor and puritan temper that mark it even today.[13] It relieved religion of the burden of hierarchy and interminable theological debates.

Shi'ism spread in North Africa through the activities of a Shi'ite *dá'í* (missionary), called Abú 'Abd Alláh al-Shí'í, who was active in 893. His teachings found fertile soil in the milieu of Berber conversion and rising Arab power. In its wake, the Fatimid rule of the *mahdí* 'Ubayd Alláh was established in 910 over a wide area of the Maghrib, with the Shi'ite wave carrying the Fatimids to power in Egypt in 969. It was under the Fatimids in 972 that Jawhar al-Siqilli, "the Sicillian," a Christian of Byzantine background brought as a slave to Qayrawan, founded Al-Azhar, which was turned soon afterward into an academy by the caliph al-'Aziz.

Religious Realignment Around the Mediterranean

Over the centuries, Islam's formative structures and institutions developed and took hold to create a cultural frame aligning Egyptian and North African society as no other religion had done before. David Wasserstein of Vanderbilt University noted this integrative force of Islam with respect to the scattered Jewish and other *dhimmí* (non-Muslim protected people) communities of the seventh century. Buffeted by pressures from within and without, Judaism was in crisis. The rise of Islam brought it relief and new life. Islam united the Mediterranean world and offered a chance for threatened diaspora communities to obtain religious respectability, as well as economic and social freedoms "that made possible a major renaissance of Judaism and the Jews." [14]

The pattern of the spread of Islam helping marginal groups to acquire cohesion was repeated in several other places.

> Merchants from the Caliphate were found in places as far apart as Senegal and Canton ... The negro lands south of the Sahara were drawn into the stream of world commerce. ... Cities expanded, fortunes were made, a wealthy middle-class of traders, shippers, bankers, manufacturers and professional men came into being, and a rich and sophisticated society gave increasing employment and patronage to scholars, artists, teachers, physicians and craftsmen.[15]

The rich alluvial flood of the diverse cultures of the world started to irrigate the arid Bedouin soil of Islam's origin. As Joseph Stamer put it, "the foundation of a fraternal community, based on a simple but inspiring message" swept the newly acquired territories and populations into "Islam's political order governed by a revealed text."[16] This description applies well to the kingdom of Mali, as will become apparent in this book.

The earlier unification of the Mediterranean world and its subsequent disintegration allowed the victorious Arabs to plant the seeds of a potent Islam, however difficult the path of progress and however mixed the outcome. Egyptian society had resisted being drawn into mainstream Latin Christianity and was therefore susceptible to the systematic, long-term cultural assimilation Islam fostered. Barriers were leveled and frontiers abolished as Islam expanded into new territories. It provided cover for Coptic Christianity as the exception that proved the rule of Islam's unrivaled ascendancy; by a successful mixture of choice and necessity, the Copts separated from the rest of the Christian world only to find themselves borne on the Islamic tide as an isolated faith community. Muslim rule spared their religion once the Byzantine threat was removed. In due time the new Muslim rulers substituted sequestration for separation and made it a necessity of survival for the Copts.

According to tradition, the Byzantine emperor Heraclius received a conciliatory letter from the Prophet Muhammad inviting him to repent and embrace Islam. The letter appeared to confirm an old prophecy of the emperor's astrologers that the Byzantine Empire would be abrogated by a circumcised people. This was a veiled reference to Muslims, who practiced circumcision; however, it threw the emperor into a fit of sanguinary vengeance against the Jews, who also practiced circumcision. The foreboding mood brought on by these events was an indicator of the growing political crisis, and, with the rise of Islam, Byzantine power felt threatened. It took nearly three centuries for theologians of a fragmented Christianity to acknowledge the challenge of

Islam, by which time Islam's imperial power had engulfed Eastern Christians as *dhimmís*.

The reaction to the Crusades in the east that brought Saladin to power in Egypt shares an ideological affinity with the movements in the west that vaulted the Almoravids to power in North Africa and Spain in the eleventh century, followed by the Almohads in the twelfth century. The Almohads (Ar. al-*muwahhidún*, "Unitarians," advocates of the unity of the Godhead against syncretist anthropomorphic associations) were disaffected Berbers who, under the iconoclastic Ibn Tumart (d. 1130), rose against the Almoravids, denounced by Ibn Tumart as anthromorphists "who divided up the godhead into little pieces."[17] Yúsuf ibn Tashfín, the Almoravid leader, and Saladin both set out to institute Islam as taught in the law books and as prescribed in canonical practice. Islam spread by the twin channels of political power and religion, but eventually religious authority, as exemplified by legal scholars and Sufi masters, crystallized as a sphere distinct from the political. Islamization of the Berbers was achieved by the class of religious scholars and lawyers while Arabization brought about Arab dominance in politics and government. Along with the legal schools, the Sufi confraternities played a formative role in the development of a Muslim society still subject to the ebb and flow of political events. The combined, stabilizing influence of religion and law offered a critical counterbalance to volatile political events.

The orthodoxy of the legal schools had a calming influence on the storm whipped up by Berber-Arab racial and tribal conflict. The explosive Khárijite and Fatimid Ismá'ílí tension was considerably mitigated by the unifying power of religion; Fatimid rule used the veneration of the Prophet's family as a political counterweight to anti-Arab sentiment. The course of Islam's progress was a checkered one, made more so by the invasion of marauding Arab nomads in the twelfth century. The invasion overshadowed the Khárijite agitation by causing widespread devastation in the region. With the hindsight of developments in eleventh- and twelfth-century North Africa, Ibn Khaldun says that the Berbers apostatized twelve times before Islam gained a firm hold over them. Similarly, the earlier Christian influence, selective in its impact by being largely confined to the urban elite, was a residue of Roman and Byzantine hegemony. Its imperial association and restricted appeal presented but token obstacles to the Arabs. Nubia bought time by submitting in 651 to the *baqt* treaty, under which Nubia supplied slaves to the Muslim rulers. Centuries later, the Nile valley capitulated with the fall of Dongola in 1317 and Alwa on the lower escarpment of the Ethiopian plateau in 1505. Ethiopia was saved by the intervention of Portugal against an Ottoman-led attack in 1543, but Portuguese high-handedness resulted in their expulsion, leaving behind a heritage of deep resentment. Ethiopia henceforth jealously guarded its Christian tradition against Western interference.

Law and Society

In due course, Islam's great legal structures were created and promoted by scholars without state backing, with the kind of intellectual autonomy political authorities often feared and opposed.[18] As will be made clear in subsequent chapters, in a technical sense Sharí'ah cannot be state law because that would "be inconsistent with its nature."[19] Accordingly, the consolidation of Málikí law in Egypt in the ninth century was independent of the establishment of the Tulunid dynasty there, while in North Africa (*Ifríqiya*) the influential legal school of Qayrawan maintained its independence from the Aghlabid dynasty. The legal schools fostered by Qayrawan emerged as centers of orthodox teaching that the Khárijite movement indirectly inspired, a result of the ambivalence and mutual distrust between scholars and political leaders. Writing of the influence of legal scholars in eleventh-century North Africa, historian Michael Brett calls attention to this issue: "Jurists of the required eminence formed a small and distinguished elite, all the more influential because of their pious reluctance to become involved in any way in the sinful business of government." Al-Qábisí (935–1012 AD), a Málikí jurist of Tunisia, would not offer his services to the state until demonstrators "broke into his house to insist that a jurist of his eminence had a duty to do so."[20] The tradition persisted with Jalál al-Dín al-Suyútí (1445–1505), the eminent Egyptian Hanafí scholar-jurist who criticized scholars for having too close an association with men of power.[21]

Given its central importance to this study, it may be helpful at this point to pause and reflect on the relation of religious law and society. Sir Hamilton Gibb has noted that, in the hands of jurists, the religious code rather than the state was the force of cultural synthesis, setting out how the code evolved in a changing social milieu to reflect the exigencies of lived experience, which the legal framework helped to shape. Between the real content of Muslim thought and its legal expression, Gibb contends, there is not so much a contradiction as a gap similar to the dynamic nexus between creed and action. If we look only to the legal expression, we would not be able to infer how Muslims live in real time. The great diversity of the life Muslims live defies a rigid formulation, for lived reality exerts a constant pressure "whose influence is to be seen in the unobtrusive reshaping of theory which, beneath an outward inflexibility, characterizes all branches of speculative activity in Islam, where Islam has remained a living organism."[22] David de Santillana considers the particular way law and society are related in the Muslim canon. Society, he says, is a necessary fact in Islam; "it is not a confused rabble, but an aggregation held together by a common end and by mutual help; hence the social and moral conception of the state."[23] The long-held view in Islam is that law exists to enable government to lead human beings to prosperity in this world and to salvation in the next. This prescriptive view of society shapes the structure of law, and the legitimacy of law depends on it. The importance to Muslims of obeying God and the Prophet is lived out in the everyday needs of social life. "Muslim jurists supposed that God desired the best for man, and therefore social utility could most reliably be attained through obedience to the divine will."[24] The legal code exists to guide those living in the real world. Lofty rules must still have solid ground beneath them. This effort to bridge the gap between injunction and practice shows that aspiring to be a faithful believer is as much a matter of explicit religious teaching as it is a process of social mediation.

That is why, as Carl Becker pointed out, a legal injunction is not a binding rule to be followed blindly in all circumstances but one that has attached to it a reasonable margin of discretion. It is how jurisprudence (*fiqh*), particularly the principle of consensus (*'ijma*), developed to channel and mediate the divine law (*Sharí'ah*). It provided Islam with freedom of movement, with the capacity for adaptation, and "a corrective against the tyranny of the dead letter."[25] In time, *Sharí'ah* and *fiqh* became functionally interchangeable in the sense that *fiqh* provided understanding of *Sharí'ah,* framing it for interpretation and implementation. The river of God's law, though elevated, is still not removed from the banks of human interpretation. Muslims know *Sharí'ah* because *fiqh* conveys it to them.[26] They can take confidence in the knowledge that the authorities of law had never intended "to embitter the life of the Muslim by imprisoning him in a stockade of legal restraints," relying for that purpose on the words of the Qur'an as well as on the sayings of *hadith* (the writings and speeches of the Prophet).[27] Abú Hanífa famously defines *fiqh* as "the self's knowledge of what is to its advantage and disadvantage," hinting at the enormous scope for law as a vehicle of social change and personal improvement. Al-Ghazali echoes that ethical view of law when he lays stress "on the *value for us* of a doctrine or a piece of knowledge."[28] The Sanhaja Berber scholar-jurist, Shiháb al-Dín b. Idris al-Qaráfí (d. 1285), taught that laws must change in reponse to changing circumstances.[29]

To return to the progress of Islam: the new Islamic cultural assimilation in North Africa can also be seen in what happened to the remains of Roman civilization in the new Islamic world. About three hundred columns from nearby Roman and Byzantine buildings were used in the construction of the Great Mosque of Qayrawan, which emerged as a revered seat of Islamic legal scholarship. The only evidence of the long Roman occupation in Ghadames (in what is now northwestern Libya) was a few Doric and Corinthian columns incorporated into the two principal mosques there. In time, these brittle mementos of the area's distinguished past were swept away by the destructive storm of the invading Banu Hilal and Banu Sulaym tribes. By the time the affected areas recovered, Islam was ready to resume its forward momentum with the leavening of society. Some historians have argued that the French colonization of Africa was a belated attempt to recover the Mediterranean world's pre-Islamic standing and to avenge the Christian basilicas looted for the construction of the Great Mosque.[30] This claim helped create the myth of colonialism as a Western crusade.

Breaching the Desert Barrier

In the Roman period, the Sahara was an impenetrable barrier. This changed momentously with the introduction of the camel, "the ship of the desert." It is uncertain when the camel was first introduced in the desert, with historians inclined to the view that it was sometime during the second century AD. By the end of the Byzantine period, the camel had become a well-established presence in the Sahara. Travel by camel was as revolutionary for desert travel and trade as the discovery of the compass was for maritime navigation. The camel afforded an immense range of mobility for Berber activity and allowed the caravan trade to develop and commercial towns to flourish in the Sahel. The introduction of the camel brought West Africa for the first time into permanent contact with the Muslim Mediterranean world, and thus Islam spread and took root in sub-Saharan Africa (see Figure 3.1). The first wave of the Islamization of West Africa was the work of Muslim Berbers as traders, pilgrims, holy figures, travelers, entrepreneurs, fortune-seekers, and missionaries.

The nomadic Sanhája of the western Sahara began to spread from Mauritania to Ahaggar. Their descendants are the present-day Moors of the west and the Tuareg of the central Sahara. By the ninth century, the Tuareg were a confederation of three main branches: the Lemtuna, the Masúfa, and the Gudála. Their strength derived from their dominance of the trans-Saharan trade between Zenata in the north and the state of Ghana in the south. The Lemtuna moved from the Mauritanian Adrar in the second half of the eighth century to Awdaghast in eastern Tagant, a center of the caravan trade.

The gradual penetration of nomadic groups such as the Lemtuna into areas where the populations were cultivators began a process of intercultural and social exchange. For their livelihood, the nomads depended on control of the caravan trade and on the tribute they exacted from the cultivators. Nomadic pressure forced the cultivators to move further south toward the Senegal River in the African Savannah. In his report on the struggle between the Lemtuna nomads and the African cultivators, Ibn Khaldun, drawing on al-Bakrí and others, casts the encounter in terms of jihad, saying after the Lemtuna subdued the desert regions they waged jihad against the Africans to force them to adopt Islam or else pay the *jizya*, the poll tax.

> Later the authority of the people of Ghana waned and their prestige declined as that of the veiled people [*mulaththimún*, Arabic for Almoravids], their neighbours on the north next to the land of the Berbers, grew. . . . These extended their dominion over the Súdán, and pillaged, imposed tribute (*itáwát*) and poll tax (*jizya*), and converted many of them to Islam.[31]

But this account leaves too many gaps in the conquest theory of Ghana to be conclusive.

The degree of successful resistance to conversion noted by Ibn Khaldun is evidence that the alleged invasion fell well short of jihad. The fact that local populations could decline Islam suggests a complex relationship with the invaders, if they could be characterized as such. This is confirmed by contemporary sources, which indicate that if jihad was waged, it must have been in a desultory fashion with uneven results. One historical source, the *Rawd al-Qirtás* of Ibn Abí Zar', says that the Lemtuna Tuareg, who commanded an impressive cavalry of camels, were able to impose their will on the Berbers and the blacks of Mauritania but could not extend their power to Ghana in the south. This would seem to rule out jihad.

According to Ibn Abí Zar', the Lemtuna dynasty collapsed by the beginning of the tenth century from internal weakness but also from an exhausting external conflict with Ghana. This left Ghana the dominant power in the region. Taking advantage in 990 AD of internal dissension, the ruler of Ghana captured Awdaghast to end the dominance of the Sanhája. Awdaghast was an important commercial entrêpot and a nerve center of trans-Saharan trade with Ghana, the land of gold. Stripped of power, the Sanhája sought compensatory solace in religion, embracing a nominal form of Islam while biding their time for an opportune attack on Ghana. The advantages of peace and security during this time made it difficult to justify persisting with the idea of waging war. (For their part, the Tuareg of the central Sahara eventually founded the town of Agades in about 1413, though Takedda to the west, visited by Ibn Battuta in 1353, was older and more important politically.)

Given this evidence, it is clear that the idea of imposing Islam on Africans at the hands of foreigners or by means of jihad was widely contested where it is reported and produced complex results even among the Lemtuna themselves.

Neither military pressure nor the machinery of jihad seemed to have made much difference to the diffusion of Islam in the region. The first strong evidence we have of Islam making a noteworthy impression on the Sanhája is a description of their strongman, Tarsina, as a Muslim ruler in power in 1020 AD. It is reasonable to conclude that neither jihad nor economic leverage was the chief cause of the people converting to Islam or at least of staying with it after the initial contact.

Almoravid Movement

For all his religious zeal, Tarsina came and passed like a comet. In the course of his pilgrimage to Mecca, he developed the idea of waging jihad against the state of Ghana. His reasons for wanting to do so are neither clear nor consistent, save that Ghana's trade was something the Sanhája long coveted. Tarsina scarcely began the campaign before losing his life in the effort in 1023. According to custom that allowed power to alternate between the branches of the Sanhája, the succession passed to Tarsina's son-in-law, Yahyá ibn Ibráhim, of the Gudála. In the company of the other Sanhája chiefs, inspired by Tarsina's pious example, Yahyá set off in earnest on the pilgrimage in 1035 and on the way back halted at Qayrawán, where he asked a prominent jurist, Abú Imrán Músá b. 'Isá, for help finding someone to instruct his ignorant countrymen in the true doctrine of Islam. Unable to persuade any of his trustworthy acolytes to assume missionary responsibility for the conversion of the Sanhája, the jurist directed Yahyá to Waggág ibn Zalwí with an accompanying letter. This was in 1039. Waggág was the head of a religious educational institution, called *dár al-murábitín*, in the town of Nafís, which, according to Ibn Khaldun, was in the region of Sijilmása (in what is now Morocco), founded in 758.[32] Impressed with Yahyá's sincerity, Waggág persuaded 'Abd Alláh ibn Yásín to undertake the mission. The historical account describes 'Abd Alláh ibn Yásín, among other things, as "an outstandingly able student, keen and alert, well versed in law (*fiqh*), literature (*adab*), and diplomacy, knowing something of all sciences."[33] Like many generous student recommendations, this endorsement seems a little overly enthusiastic, especially in light of ibn Yásín's reception among the Gudála.

The name ibn Yásín assumed on his conversion indicates an overly pious estimate of himself as a proud Berber setting out as God's avenging angel by adopting the path of judgment on the world. His name tells a message: 'Abd Alláh, servant or slave of God; ibn Yásín, son of Yá Sín; that is, one begotten of, and beholden to, the revealed book, the Arabic letters *Yá Sín* being the mysterious title of chapter 36 of the Qur'an.[34] The opening words of the chapter are in the form of a commissioning of one who is sent as an envoy with a warning to a stiff-necked people whose forebears were heedless of admonition. "Surely We have put on their necks fetters up to the chin, so their heads are raised" in stubborn defiance (Qur'an 36:1–8). Yá Sín is also one of the sixteen canonical subdivisions (*hizb*) of scripture, a ritual stage in learning and memorization of the Qur'an. That Scriptural message was what Ibn Yásín took to be his ultimatum (*intidhár*), with the notion of being given a public mandate just as tradition claims Muhammad was vested with a similar inaugural public ultimatum in surah 74.

Ibn Yásín underestimated the resistance he would face among the Gudála, whose lax morals seemed to mock his learning. He was shocked to find men who married six, seven, or ten wives, men who did whatever took their fancy, and he chided them that their behavior was a violation of religious teaching. Their easygoing lifestyle under attack, two of the Sanhája scholars challenged his credentials, including his poor grasp of law. The Sanhája at once moved to strip him of his authority, to destroy and loot his property, shunning him as a foe. In the long tradition of resistance to conversion, the people turned against Ibn Yásín, resenting his effort to change their customs and break their will. By this time, Ibn Yásín had heard reports of Islam spreading among African populations to the south, and he wanted to go where his labors stood a better chance of producing fruit, but Yahyá ibn Ibráhim would not hear of it and barred his way. Said he, "I shall not let you go away for I brought you here only that your learning might profit my person, my religion, and those of my people, for whom I am responsible." Yahyá ibn Ibráhim made him a counter-offer of retreat to "an island in the sea" where the tidal flow ebbed enough to allow convenient access by foot. Such cloistered sojourn would facilitate undistracted devotion and study, set an example of the pious life, and build momentum for reform.

'Abd Alláh ibn Yásín relented, and, with his missionary mandate reaffirmed, regrouped and resolved to experiment with a ritually prescribed form of religious propagation. Accompanied by seven companions, among them Lemtuna leaders Yahyá ibn 'Umar and his brother, Abú Bakr, Ibn Yásín, set off for the "island in the sea" to the southeast. There, in the *rábita* or *ribát,* he and the others entered the consecrated state of *khalwah* (ritual seclusion) to hatch their strategy of orthodox reform. Though often associated with jihad, the idea of *khalwah* need not be jihad-bound to be valid. *Khalwah* occurs widely in personal and collective spiritual ritual where, undertaken by clerics and detached from jihad, it is spoken of as *luzúm al-khalwah,* "adjourning in solitude."[35]

Contemporary sources disagree on the precise location of this "island in the sea," and confusion mounted as scholars attempted to reconcile widely different accounts. This confusion places in doubt even the idea that the Almoravids are so-called because they originated in a jihad-based ribát (Ar. *al-murábitún;*

people of the *rábita, ribát*). According to the reports of al-Ya'qubi and Ibn Hawqal, who wrote in the ninth and tenth centuries, respectively, ribáts were constructed along the coast of Ifriqiya as military posts for defense against attacks on Islam by the Byzantine fleet. Ibn Marzuq says that for the Sufis a ribát means "the place in which a man shuts himself up for the purpose of worship."[36] Ribáts appear to have evolved from fortified bastions with a military purpose to become centers of militant proselytization (*ribát fí sabíl li-lláhi*) and, later, centers of Sufi teaching. As centers of retreat, ribáts were a form of hijrah, a preparatory stage of renewal for the devotees. Writing in the fourteenth century, al-'Umari refers to this religious purpose of ribát when he speaks of "the pious men who are called *murábits*," whence the French *marabout*. Once Muslims gained control of the Mediterranean, ribáts lost their military purpose and were adopted as centers of religious devotion and the means of waging the "greater jihad" of spreading the faith by the word, rather than the "lesser jihad" by the sword.[37] As we shall see, this distinction between the two kinds of jihad was carried forward into West Africa where the clerical profession promoted Islam as a pacifist cause.

It would distract us here to attempt to follow the historical trail of the ribát in question, or even to attempt to verify the related Almoravid references, important though that may be in other respects.[38] Of critical note in al-Bakrí's account is the way 'Abd Alláh ibn Yásín conceived the ribát as an incubation phase of religious conversion—what the sources refer to as *hijrah*. In the reform canon originating with Muhammad's move to Medina, *hijrah* means withdrawal in symbolic rejection of a corrupt, oppressive world; it is a crossing of the Rubicon vis-à-vis the status quo. In a ribát for ritual seclusion, the initiates are plunged into the observances and obligations of the religious code and offered an imagined idealization of the soon-to-be coming dispensation, which is modeled on the pattern of the Prophet's life in Medina, the place of the first *hijrah* that set the stage for the ultimate triumph of the cause.

In his ribát, 'Abd Alláh ibn Yásín had his disciples spend three months in sequestration following a stringent regime of worship, devotion, and study in order "to win them over to what is good, to plant in them a desire for the divine reward, and to warn them against His painful punishment until love for him was firm in their hearts."[39] Adopting a phased program of religious change, Ibn Yásín confronted his people with an ultimatum that gave them little excuse for their customary prevarication. The call to action was preceded by seven days of public warning and an invitation to repent. When he judged that the number of his disciples had reached critical mass, Ibn Yásín moved to sound the call to conversion. He summoned his disciples, now called the Almoravids, and charged them to sally forth, declaring,

> Go with God's blessing, said he. Warn your people. Make them fearful of God's punishment. Tell them of His [binding] proofs (*hujja*). If they repent, return to the truth, and abandon their ways, let them be. But if they refuse, continue in their error, and persist in their wrongheadedness, then we shall ask for God's help against them and wage holy war on them till God shall judge between us.[40]

Taking note of the endemic nature of interclan rivalries, Ibn Yásín decided to exploit it by picking off the Sanhája piece by piece, to split the weak stem of intertribal unity rather than challenge united opposition. First he waged war on the Gudála, cutting them down and imposing Islam on the survivors. He made sure of their submission before next turning on the Lemtuna, whom he vanquished, extracting from them a pledge of allegiance. He dealt similarly with the Masúfa, who were made to promise to follow the teachings of Scripture and the Law, including paying the *zakát* (alms) and the customary tithe (*'ushr*). A hundred lashes of the cane were applied to each penitent as punishment for their acknowledged recalcitrance and as a warning to likely delinquents. To provide a systematic way of regulating affairs, Ibn Yásín established a public treasury (*bayt mál*) and put in place a structure for the application and collection of levies and taxes. There is a suggestion here that financial administrative reform may have played a more pivotal role in the Almoravids' work than a jihad hatched in a ribát, however defined.[41]

Nomadic Impetus

With his cohorts, 'Abd Alláh ibn Yásín resolved the sticking point of religion with respect to the nomadic tribes, calling for radical obedience in answer to prevailing recalcitrance. His engagement with the nomads revealed that, despite their seeming incompatibility with Islam, they had the capacity for a singular understanding of it. This idea is well expressed by T. E. Lawrence (Lawrence of Arabia). The nomads Lawrence encountered in his famous desert campaign (1916–1918) saw the world, he said, with no half-tones in their register of vision. A people of primary colors, they viewed the world in contour; dogma dispensed with doubt, which is "our modern crown of thorns." They discriminated between truth and falsehood, between belief and unbelief, "without our hesitating retinue of finer shades."[42] They invented no complex mythologies of teasing curiosity and abstract speculation, no intricately wrought syllogistic webs to impress and bamboozle, and while surrounded on the fringes of their deserts with evidence of broken faiths, their thoughts were essentially at ease in extremes. They lived simply; though considered their only substance, camels still "are the occasion of all their contending."[43] The nomads did not clutter themselves with the pleasures of acquisition and accumulation; they suffered no fettering of allegiance, which, in a sense, made them ready disciples.

The Almoravids did not forget their desert roots, and so after appointing his cousin, Yusuf b. Tashfin, his deputy in Morocco, Abu Bakr b. 'Umar, military leader of the Lemtuna since the death of his brother Yahya ibn 'Umar in 1056–1057, returned to the desert he regarded as a more hospitable environment for his brand of religion than the grandeur of power. The desert was the ideal religious habitat. Describing his own experience of joining the caravan trails of the desert, Ibn Battuta testifies: "This wilderness is luminous and bright (*muníra mushriqa*). The spirit is gladdened and the soul rejoices."[44] "I cannot live out of the desert," Abu Bakr told Ibn Tashfin. It happened to suit the calculating Ibn Tashfin to have Abu Bakr thus confined to the desert. In that spirit, the same Sanhája who as the *murábitún* possessed ascetic scruples rallied under Ibn Tashfin to help suppress rebellion of the Zanata who had risen in revolt against Abu Bakr's authority. The campaign to put down the rebellion in Morocco, which occurred between 1061 and 1071, pinned down between a half and a third of Abu Bakr's forces. Ibn Yásín in time elevated his *nazirate* into an *emirate*, "his jurisdiction into a state. For this conquest was necessary; the community became an army, and its neighbours the object of attack and subjugation."[45] The offense of opponents was tantamount to *'adáwa* (enmity to the religious code by those who had been outsiders). It called for decisive religious alignment.

It took time for the alignment to occur. The impulse of conversion proved to be precocious, and when the novelty of the new creed began to wear off, the brief memory of attachment faded rapidly, though not irretrievably. Whatever the creed, nomadic energy prevailed as well by tenacity as by rejection. The nomads inhabited religion much as they inhabited the desert, by defiance or abnegation, not by inducement and concession and certainly not by building and defending monuments. Ibn Tumart (d. 1130), who would become the Messianic mastermind of the Almohad revolt of 1121–1122 AD against the Almoravids, grasped this point when he stipulated not material incentives but moral surrender as a rule of coming under Almohad authority. The first thing to which to summon would-be converts is "worship of God" and the duties God has laid on them.[46] This suggests that Ibn Tumart's movement was more interested in purifying Berber Muslim practice than in the overthrow of the Almoravids.[47] Power over the desert was not about gaining control of fixed structures and amassing assets but about overcoming fatalism to force a choice. By its nature, the desert itself is unconquerable, yet the spirit of the desert can be claimed by the creed irreducible to calculations of pecuniary gain and the comforts of settled life. In the North African desert, Islam entered upon its second birth with the elemental energy of its first conception, without the thrills of intellectual sport.[48]

The Almoravids learned that taming souls required sacrifice and energy, not wooing with entreaties and incentives. As ibn Yásín understood, unbelief is not so much an intellectual disposition as it is a matter of decisive authority, the kind of authority needed to take mastery of people and launch jihad. Al-Bakrí describes it as something that was distinctive of the Almoravids' chosen style of religious propagation. Disenchantment with the Almoravids grew as their zeal faded and their ideals became corrupted—or so their opponents claimed. Economic discontent fueled the downfall of the Almoravids, and the unpopular taxes they imposed spread disenchantment, taxes that covered a random list of items such as locusts, soap, and skewers.[49] As *al-muwahhidún* (Almohads), their opponents ratcheted up the stakes by declaring the Almoravid vision for Muslim society bankrupt and promising a better dispensation.

The Almohads took up the challenge and once more called on the faith and sacrifice of their followers, setting out on the path of reclaiming the true faith, or what they took to be the true faith. The Almoravids were denounced for their easy-going lifestyle, including wine drinking, taking up musical instruments, indulging in luxury, and allowing free movement of unveiled women even though the men were veiled.[50] No other religion had made so arid a desert environment so conducive to its creed and mission and so compatible with the opposite instinct of civilization—after all, under Islam the worldly Ibn Tashfin and the ascetically minded Abu Bakr had collaborated to advance a common faith in very different environments, one steppe and nomadic, the other town and settled. The versatility of Islam seemed designed to endure even if it was too dependent on desert stamina to be safe from anarchic unrest.

Great Disruption

The energy and momentum of the nomadic restlessness, with no landmarks for boundaries or targets for direction, would eventually engulf the whole region and set back the progress Islam made under the Almoravids. The event with the most far-reaching of repercussions in the history of Muslim North Africa had its roots in an intra-Shi'ite political dispute. When in 1045 the governor of Ifriqiya, al-Mu'izz ibn Bádís, renounced Shi'ism and declared himself independent, the Fátimid caliph of Egypt al-Mustansir resolved to restore his authority in Ifriqiya. Al-Mustansir goaded the Banú Hilál, who, like the Banu Sulaym, were sectarian dissidents and who had emigrated from Syria. Their leader, Hamdán Qarmat, "the esoteric teacher" of Nabatean peasant stock, set up a religious enclave, *dár al-hijrah*, in Kufa in 890 where he prescribed a radical social program of common ownership of property and possessions, including women, with revenues and earnings handed over to collective control. It was the doctrine that "dominion is founded in grace."[51] Qarmat was hailed by his followers as "the emissary," and "the proof" and addressed with obscure titles of Scripture as "the she-camel" of the Prophet Salih who, according to Qur'an 7:74–80, was hamstrung by the unbelievers, and as "the beast" mentioned in Qur'an 27:83. It provided a heady brew of Mahdist excitement whose political manifestation after the death of Qarmat would create widespread agitation and unrest in North Syria where the community sought refuge. By the time the Qarmatians emerged in Fatimid Egypt, they had created a political creed. The followers declared: "Truth has appeared, the Mahdí has risen, the rule of the 'Abbásids, the jurists, the readers of the Koran and the teachers of tradition is at an end. There is nothing more to wait for; we have not come to set up a government, but to abolish a law."[52] In Upper Egypt, where they eventually settled, they became a grave military nuisance. Minded to be rid of them, the hard-pressed Fatimid caliphate of Cairo, faced with increasing territorial losses of Jerusalem in 1071 and Damascus in 1076, saw the defeats as the writing on the wall and, in a desperate gambit to buy time, decided to deploy the Banu Hilal on the mission of exacting vengeance on the renegade governor of North Africa as reprisal for his irredentist subversion. "I make you a gift of the Maghrib," he wrote, "and [of that of] the rule of al-Mu'izz ibn Bádís, the Sanhájí, the runaway slave. No longer will you be in want."[53] The caliph had no idea he was unleashing on the region a hurricane with centuries-long effects, cultivating a time when "mere anarchy is loosed upon the world." Ibn Khaldún sums up the effects of the Hilalian invasion thus:

> In North Africa and the Maghrib, which were invaded by the Banu Hilal and Banu Sulaym at the beginning of the fifth century of the Muslim era [eleventh of the Christian era] and ravaged by them during three hundred and fifty years, ruin and devastation still prevail. Yet before that time all the country lying between the Sudan and the Mediterranean was the centre of a flourishing civilization, as witnessed by the remains of buildings and statues and the ruins of towns and villages.[54]

Sadly, Qayrawan, the renowned center of Málikí legal scholarship, was sacked by the Hilalian invasion and never regained its former glory completely. Teaching and scholarship are intellectual crafts, and crafts, says Ibn Khaldún, "do not exist in nomadic societies." The Hilalian nomads were true to their name. They had little in common with the Arabs of the first invasion who settled in towns and became political elites. The identity of the first Arabs was bound up with their role as colonizers, with the instincts of settler communities maintaining themselves as a privileged minority. "The Arabs," Ibn Khaldún observes, "did not establish themselves in these parts as tent-dwellers nor as nomadic tribes because the need to maintain their authority did not allow them to occupy the open country but restricted them to towns and cantonments."[55]

It was only in the middle of the eleventh century that the Arabs established themselves in colonies among the Berbers. All that changed with the Almohads, who expanded from Morocco to Tunisia. Almohad rule produced the golden age of Maghribi civilization. Two contrasting cultural streams developed: on one side the Bedouin Arabs imposed their pastoral economy on a region where civilization once flourished; on the other side the Berber nomads were poised to become carriers of Andalusian civilization. Islam united them. "When the Arab East broke up after the death of Saladin, the Almohad West was ready to pick up and to carry the torch."[56] Almohad power in turn crumbled within two generations. But by this time an Arabo-Islamic Maghribi society had emerged to produce the civilization by which the region remains defined to this day.

The great historical movements that transformed Europe after the Middle Ages—monasticism, the Renaissance, the Protestant Reformation—largely bypassed Muslim Spain. Much of Spanish art in the age of the Renaissance was essentially Italian art. Only in the age of Columbus were Spain and Portugal able to break out of their Islamic confinement by launching the maritime expeditions from Italy and looking for bases beyond zones of Muslim control.[57] Some of these expeditions, aiming to discover the New World, sailed via the west coast of Africa where at the mouth of the Senegal River the emissaries of Prince Henry of Portugal, moved by the prospects of taking control of unoccupied territory and gaining unhindered range, carved there Henry's arms and motto, *Talent de bien faire* (To do good is my desire). In 1482 the Portuguese built a massive fortress, São Jorge da Mina, or Elmina, on the West African coast in what is now Ghana. Of such feats, the chronicler, Zurara (1410–1473/1474), declared, "Of a surety, I doubt if since the great power of Alexander and of Caesar, there hath been any prince in the world that ever had the marks of his conquest set up so far from his own land."[58] Once out of the Muslim chokehold, the Iberian Peninsula tried to make up for lost time by turning its attention to the transatlantic slave trade, the "Black Gold" on which was founded the Iberian sea-borne empires.

2

Beyond the Veil

The Almoravids and Ghana

Among the tribes our creed could only be like the desert grass—a beautiful swift seeming of spring; which, after a day's heat, fell dusty. Aims and ideas must be translated into tangibility by material expression. The desert men were too detached to express the one; too poor in goods, too remote from complexity, to carry the other. If we would prolong our life, we must win into the ornamented lands; to the villages where roofs or fields held men's eyes downward and near.
—T. E. Lawrence, *Seven Pillars of Wisdom*, 336

Al-Bakrí on Religion in Ghana

The many scattered references to the Almoravids and Ghana pieced together are crucial for understanding how Islam penetrated into *bilád al-Súdán* (land of the blacks), as the sources refer to West Africa. These references have been marshaled and contextualized by Abú ʿUbayd ʿAbd Alláh b. ʿAbd al-ʿAzíz al-Bakrí (d. 1094). Born to a princely family in Spain, al-Bakrí lived for most of his life in Cordoba and Almeria and was recognized as a botanist, a theologian, a philologist, and, significantly for our purposes, a geographer with keen historical research instincts. The relative scope and accuracy of his information are remarkable considering the fact that he never left Spain. His curious and organized habits of mind allowed al-Bakrí to consult many sources in order to produce his work, *Kitáb al-Masálik wa al-Mamálik* ("The Book of Routes and Kingdoms"), with a section in the work called *Kitáb al-Mughrib fí dhikr bilád Ifríqiya wa al-Maghrib* ("The Account of the History of North Africa and the Maghrib"), which deals specifically with the Maghrib and the Sudan. Much of his information, particularly the reports on Ghana and West Africa, he culled from sources oral and written, from people with firsthand knowledge of the events and the regions described.

An important source for al-Bakrí was the geographical work of Muhammad b. Yúsuf al-Warráq, who was born in Guadalajara in 904. Al-Warráq lived for many years in Qayrawan before returning to Cordobá, where he died in 973. Al-Bakrí borrowed the title of al-Warráq's work, *Kitáb al-Masálik wa al-Mamálik*, for his own, written in 1067. The detailed and accurate nature of the information he supplied on Ghana and its peoples suggests that al-Bakrí was in touch with people in Spain who had traveled to West Africa and knew well the places, people, and the events described. Al-Bakrí's account shows Spain as part of the extended Islamic corridor that stretched as far as sub-Saharan Africa, which al-Bakrí terms "the farthest limits of the domains of Islam." Such a description raises a crucial question about what not to include in "the domains of Islam." The doctrine of the universal validity of Islam dismisses distinctions of geography, society, race, and culture.

Accordingly, al-Bakrí's account of the spread of Islam in sub-Saharan Africa focuses not on race and culture but on "routes" and "kingdoms"—that is, on channels of transmission and organized structures of state and society. It is an important way to understand the nature of Islamic expansion. People, goods, and materials flowed through channels of transmission and with them came religious ideas, values, and cultural aspirations. The organized structures of state and society gave shape and impetus to the transmission process, reinforcing the appeal of Islam, especially its religious and civil code. Islamic law on finance, commerce, trade, duties, levies, debts, property, and inheritance shaped and bolstered the transmission process. In ordinary circumstances, warfare can only disrupt this process, not aid and abet it.

Al-Bakrí offers critical evidence of the progress of Islamization in West Africa. Following his conversion to Islam, the ruler of Takrúr, Wár Jábí introduced it to his people along with Muslim law, requiring adherence by the people. By the time of Wár Jábí's death in 1040–1041, Islam had taken root among the people, including those of Silá, a neighboring state of Ghana. Al-Bakrí claims that the people of Ghana also were Muslims. In light of the rest of his evidence about the strength of traditional religion in Ghana, it is not clear if this claim reflects confusion in the sources he used or whether it is based on the formula of the ruler's religion defining the religion of the country (*cuius regio eius religio*).[1] Such a rule, however, is not strictly Islamic.[2] As we shall see, however, even before he settled into his stride, telling of the triumph of Islam, al-Bakrí yielded to evidence of the force of ancient custom in Ghana, where Islam's hold seemed rather precarious. At any rate, by the time al-Bakrí arrived in Ghana, he had effectively joined the early phases of the Islamization process in West Africa at the point where local custom, though no longer pristine, was still predominant. The description of Ghana in other sources bears many resemblances to al-Bakrí's portrait of Muslim life in the shadow of customary practices. The effective religious boundaries are those set for Muslims, not by them.

The Ghana of al-Bakrí's description has twelve mosques, in one of which the Friday congregational prayer is observed. Religious officials—imams, muezzins, jurists, and scholars—are maintained at state expense. The king is said to reside some 6 miles away in the royal town of Al-Ghába (Arabic for "forest"). The king maintains a circle of officials that includes interpreters, the royal treasurer, and a number of ministers, all of whom are Muslims. The king and his heir apparent, normally the son of the king's sister, are required to wear "sewn clothes," possibly a reference to the traditional garment made of long strips of woven cotton cloth that is still worn today. Depending on their means, the other Ghanaians wear robes of cotton, silk, or brocade, indicating an active trans-Saharan trade in these materials. The houses of the inhabitants are constructed of stone and acacia wood, and the royal palace is composed of domed dwellings with an enclosure like a city wall. Adjacent to the court of justice is a mosque for Muslim visitors to the town. In a designated quarter of the town is the dwelling place of practitioners of traditional religion. Their sacred groves are out of bounds, making them suitable for the king for use as his maximum security prison.

The report that describes the king dressing in the custom of pre-Islamic traditional attire is strengthened by al-Bakrí's account that the king's ceremonial royal dress makes him look like a woman: he adorns himself with necklaces and bracelets for his forearms and puts on a high cap decorated with gold and wrapped in a turban of fine cotton.[3] He holds court in a domed pavilion to receive visitors or to hear grievances against officials, with the pavilion surrounded by ten horses decorated with gold-embroidered materials. Behind the king stand ten pages holding shields and swords decorated with gold; on his right he is flanked by sons of the vassal kings of the country wearing splendid garments with their hair plaited with gold.

The entrance to the royal pavilion is guarded by dogs "of excellent pedigree." They are fitted with collars of gold and silver. A drum is sounded to announce the arrival of visitors to court. The people observe the traditional style of royal greeting by falling on their knees and sprinkling dust on their heads as a sign of respect. Exempt from this traditional custom, Muslims greet the king by clapping their hands, thus sparing them having to compromise the required prostration (*sujúd*) of Muslim worship. Much of this court life Mali inherited in its turn but, bowing to Islamic custom, replaced the dogs with two rams as protection against the evil eye.

In spite of the presence of Muslims and the existence of numerous mosques, the kingdom of Ghana maintained a robust practice of traditional religion centered in the royal cult. The use of the groves as a place of incarceration, however, would appear to suggest that religion, used as punitive sanction, may have played a role as a social deterrent as well. The account of court ceremony and ritual shows the central role religion played in court life, as does the description of the royal attire and its transvestite overtones. The accounts depict a society with an air of confident pomp and wealth, thanks to an abundance of gold, which would explain why Muslim traders were attracted to Ghana, the odious whiff of heathen rituals notwithstanding.

The mortuary rites observed on the occasion of the death of the king indicate the existence of a vigorous imperial cult, maintained as an elaborate system of ceremony and ritual and assiduously patronized on state occasions. The tomb is a dome made of wood, either teak or acacia. It is covered with carpets and cushions, and beside the body are laid various of the deceased king's ornaments, weapons, and vessels that he used for drink and food. The king is buried with the men who served him food. The door to the dome is covered with mats and furnishings and is closed. The people heap earth upon it to form a raised mound, with a ditch dug around that is made impassable except at one point. This is the cult of the dead, fortified with offerings of fermented drinks - the old pre-Islamic tradition in regal panoply.

Al-Bakrí looks askance at the structural institutions of a kingdom sunken in pagan religious observance, where on state occasions the royal court observes traditional ritual while giving a polite nod to Muslim scruples. By accommodating his Muslim subjects such that they may pay him allegiance without denying their faith, the king affirms his stake in the old and the new at the same time. He recognizes that society is still too attached to its traditional roots for him to break cleanly and make what would be a suicidal bid to institute Islamic reform. At the same time, Muslims in his kingdom are as yet too small a minority to warrant the king casting his lot in with them irrevocably, even though he cannot turn his back on them and on their rising political importance. The prospects of growing Muslim influence in the kingdom necessitate that the royal court act the part of broker with the people. In that respect, the king serves both as guardian of custom and as patron of Muslims. The mixed religious practice over which he presides offers recognition and encouragement to Muslims while keeping faith with traditional custom. If the day arrives when Islam has acquired too large a following to be ignored, the king will have had his finger on the religion's pulse sufficiently long to avert the peril of being outflanked. The channels and institutions that facilitate the introduction of Islam also serve as a valve for regulating the timing and degree of religious change, with the king as broker-in-chief. An astute ruler knows how to predict events that have long cast their shadows on the royal court. The practice of extending royal patronage to Muslims was an investment in a favorable outcome.

In spite of the relatively high mortality rate of foreign visitors to the kingdom, Ghana remained a magnet for Muslim traders because of the abundance of gold in the realm, a subject of equally great interest to al-Bakrí and presumably to his informants. Gold was the standard currency in Ghana, and the king took measures to prevent an oversupply of the precious metal to guard against inflation and a collapse of commodity prices. The king imposed duty on goods entering and leaving the kingdom: one gold dinar for a donkey-load of salt coming in and two when it went out. The king also had a controlling interest in the gold mines: he had first rights to mined nuggets, while his people had access only to the gold dust. The nuggets ranged in weight from an ounce to a pound.

With this wealth, the king could afford to raise a large army of men, though the figures given—200,000 troops, including 40,000 archers—seem exaggerated. There were horses in Ghana, though they were of small stature, and the king maintained a cavalry. Al-Bakrí makes a curious reference to a group of people called the Hunayhín, claiming that they are descendants of the troops sent to Ghana by the Umayyad caliphate in the first flush of Islam. It is a curious story, but we do not have much more information on them.[4] Al-Bakrí says the Hunayhín had by the time of his writing lapsed from Islam and adopted the traditional customs of Ghana, though they did not marry local women or give their daughters in marriage to the men. The Hunayhín lived in Ghana as a stranger community, adopting measures to preserve their racial identity without feeling the need to preserve the fading Islam of their forbears. It would not be unlikely that they were involved in the gold trade as middlemen or even as the caravan guides of Ibn Battuta's description.[5]

In connection with the purported Umayyad origin of the Hunayhín, we should note that there are other references to Umayyad links with Saharan history. In excavations more recently conducted at Awdaghast, pottery and iron tools were discovered along with imported glassware, enameled ceramic objects, and oil lamps that were in wide currency in the Muslim world until the thirteenth century. The relics of buildings discovered were of Mediterranean style. Also, copper ornaments unearthed in Tegadaoust are similar to those found at Koumbi-Saleh, the capital of Ghana.[6] The economic links between Awdaghast and Ghana were quite strong, though Ghana triumphed in conflict, as described earlier.

Accommodation and Adaptation

As can be seen in al-Bakrí's accounts, the driving engine of Islam in Ghana was not jihad or economic leverage but the policy of tolerance and accommodation of the court. In this early phase of coexistence and quietism, Islam subsisted as a religion of informal contact, with local awareness not rising much above simple inquiry or plain curiosity. The king and his senior officials offered an open hand to Muslims in their midst, welcoming mosques and ancillary institutions that upheld Muslim religious life. The arrangement did not nullify any Muslim obligations. The rules of religion and the affairs of society allowed citizens and foreigners to share amicably in the public life of the kingdom. Customary law in situ had the home advantage of closeness to its accommodating indigenous sources, and the routine and conduct they prescribed. Meanwhile, enjoying the prestige of a written Scripture, literacy, and a universal faith, the Islamic code had the benefit of prescribing the opportunities and demands of trans-Saharan traffic and a growing cosmopolitan society of Africans, Berbers, and Arabs.

Before the opening of the Atlantic sea lanes with sub-Saharan Africa, the trans-Saharan overland route was the only corridor of contact with the outside world.[7] Islam commanded that corridor; its presence in Ghana and elsewhere is proof of that. The inclusion of West Africa for the first time in the sphere of the civilization of the Mediterranean world and beyond "was achieved by the spread of Islam to the south of the desert." Islam was absorbed into local customary law, which is how matrilineal succession edged out Islamic law to remain the lynchpin of the political system, providing the organizational structure of society in which Muslims learned the art of accommodation. The spirit of such accommodation is a recurring theme of Islam's historical course in West African societies.[8]

Some of the geographical clues al-Bakrí gives of place names in Ghana suggest that he possessed remarkably accurate information. His directions for the region around the Niger bend between Ra's al-Má' and Gao, for example, are too precise not to have been obtained from informants with firsthand knowledge. The meticulous details al-Bakrí gives of "routes" shows how well-trodden the pathways of travel and communication were. That information was well disseminated at the hands of others, but al-Bakrí folded knowledge of these well-beaten trails into his historical overview of Islam, routes, and kingdoms. His rule of "follow the religion" opens vistas onto the expanding horizons of human enterprise. The allure of gold could have mesmerized him into fabricating an imaginary Eldorado, shrouded in remote native regions waiting to be possessed for profit and fame. In that case, he would have overlooked much valuable religious and historical information about the land and the people themselves and written only about what stirred his imagination, not about what interested the subjects of his account. Instead, his attention to detail and instinct for historical clarity led al-Bakrí to observe closely people in an area of the world rather remote from the Muslim heartlands. This area was not entirely removed from Muslim religious interest, however: Islamic jurisdiction is not determined by geography but by the teachings and impetus of a universal religion.

Through the Arabic language medium and its cultural diffusion, al-Bakrí and his contemporaries helped to reveal people and places that would otherwise be excluded from the cultural map of the world. For the jurists, in particular, West Africa was not so much an issue of geographical remoteness as an issue of Islamic legal jurisdiction: Can it be said of non-Muslim societies that their status of unbelief (*kufr*) and enmity (*'adáwa*) de facto voids Islamic law, or are Muslim traders and travelers entitled to the provisions of the legal code, whatever the religion and custom of the countries affected? Islamic legal opinion determined that contracts made under Islamic law in Islamic countries are valid even if the traders involved lived in "the lands of the blacks." The significance of this legal principle for West Africa is that, so long as Muslims continued to travel and live there, the validity of Islam for them and for African states could not be denied, which gave tacit recognition to non-Muslim jurisdiction. Law was a structural force for expanding the influence of Islam[9]. The application of the universal rules of the legal code "allowed the Muslim merchant to enter the particular society of West Africa with its multiplicity of customs and laws."[10] In time, the growing merchant community was absorbed into the web of the multiplicity of customs and laws that characterized society in West Africa.

Almoravid Legacy: Ghana and Mali

Citing Ibn Hawqal from the tenth century and al-Bakrí from the eleventh century, Yáqút (d. 1229), a freed slave of Greek origin, reported that the king of "Záfún" (Jafunu) traveled to the Maghrib on his way to the pilgrimage in Mecca. The king of Jafanu paid a courtesy call on the Almoravid Lemtúna sultan of the Maghrib. Yáqút describes the king of Jafunu as "stronger and more versed in the art of kingship" than the Lemtúna sultan, who bears the title *amír al-muslimín* (Commander of the Muslims). Acknowledging the superior power of his royal guest, the Lemtúna leader deferred to the Jafunu ruler when he met him "on foot, whereas the King of Záfún did not dismount for him." An eyewitness described the king as "tall, of deep black complexion and veiled."[11] Jafunu is described as a place adjoining "the land of the veiled people (*mulaththamún*)," where rainfall is intermittent and where there was a growing mixed population of Berbers and Africans.

In many accounts, the history of Ghana is intertwines at important points with that of the Almoravids, and when Yáqút describes the adoption of the veil (*lithám*) by the people of "Záfún," he invokes the connection by describing a cultural habit—whether imposed in a jihad or borrowed through peaceful contact, he does not say. It seems to be confirmation of the suggestion that as a constituent part of the Ghana empire, Jafunu was on the frontline of the Almoravid encounter, though this is far from saying that an Almoravid jihad had once vanquished Ghana. Relying on the highly manipulated account of Ibn Abí Zar' (d. 1315), Ibn Khaldun writes of Ghana's imperial power extending over areas where the footprint of the Almoravids was also visible. But it is a different matter to infer from this that jihad was how Ghana and the Almoravids came into sustained contact or that evidence of the adoption of the *lithám* in Jafunu can be construed as evidence of religious change by jihad. That would be a highly unsatisfactory way to make historical judgment, as it relies on the questionable hypothesis of an Almoravid jihad.

In his critical translation of Ibn Battuta's *Rihlah* ("Journey"), Sir Hamilton Gibb offers a chronology of Ghana and Mali along the following lines. Ghana was founded in the fourth century by white (Berber) immigrants, but in the ninth century the Soninke people of Koumbi-Saleh won control and ruled it until its destruction by the Almoravids of Morocco in 1076. A number of small states splintered off and were reconstituted on the ruins of Ghana. Then the Soninke dynasty, with its capital at "Sosso," situated to the west of the town of Sansanding, recaptured Ghana in 1203 and restored the non-Muslim Soninke empire. Walata was founded at this time as a refuge for the Muslim inhabitants fleeing Ghana. Sumanguru, the conqueror of Ghana, was in turn killed by Sunjata, the Mandinka (Malinke) ruler in 1235, who subsequently converted to Islam. He created a new capital for the empire and died in 1255. Mansa Músá, who established the preeminence of Mali, was the grandson of a sister of Sunjata. Mansa Músá's grandfather, Sáraq Játa, was converted to Islam by the grandfather of Mudrik ibn Faqqús, on whom Mansa Músá lavished much wealth and welcome attention. After a brief decline in Mali's political fortunes, Mansa Sulayman, a brother of Mansa Músá, restored the empire's power and prestige. A long decline ensued that ended with the fall of Mali and the rise of the Songhay empire (see Figure 2.1).

There are, however, many baffling problems with this timeline, among which is that it makes the Almoravid invasion the narrative that explains how Islam came to that part of West Africa. In the first place, the Mali empire, according to Gibb, did not disappear finally until 1670, a timeline that makes it difficult to explain how Mali's western tributary state of Kaabu emerged in the sixteenth century as an independent entity.[12] Second, Gibb's chronology makes it difficult to distinguish between Sumanguru, the Susu leader, conquering Ghana in 1203 and the Susu again taking the kingdom in 1215, with the confusing implication that Islam suffered a setback with the rise of the non-Muslim Susu.

In his study of the issue, historian Marvyn Hiskett acknowledges the difficulty by modifying the jihad hypothesis to the effect that the cultural practice of the Almoravids as *muththalimún* (the veiled ones) was adopted by the people of Jafunu because Ghana "enjoyed cordial relations with the Almoravid court in Marrákush."[13] This amendment still leaves fragments of the jihad hypothesis cluttering the field, and Hiskett attempts to tidy up by switching the terrain to the non-Muslim Susu, fellow tribesmen of Ghana's founder, Sumanguru Konte, as the real targets of the Almoravid jihad, not the "Soninkes" of Ghana. This clarification does not disprove the jihad claim; it merely compounds it. It assumes an Almoravid jihad, but allows that the Soninke of Ghana escaped it by virtue of the fact that they had been Muslim in a pre-Almoravid era, though their Susu neighbors were not. Written and oral sources contradict this, indicating that Ghana continued to exist as a non-Muslim kingdom.

Writing in 1067, a decade or so before the purported Almoravid conquest, al-Bakrí provides evidence for Islamic contact in Ghana in a pre-Almoravid era. Muslims formed only a small proportion of the people, and, along with the stranger Muslim community who settled in the *zango* or stranger quarter, they were residentially separated from the general population. In effect, the king remained the guardian of traditional religion and maintained it in court ritual and funeral observances. Writing in the mid-twelfth century, al-Zuhrí reduces the Almoravid jihad theme to the vague statement that, after Ghana converted, around the time of the coming of Masufa leader Yahyá b. Abí Bakr, the Ghanaians "sought the help of the Almoravids," presumably to defend Ghana against attacks by neighboring peoples. A seasoned scholar and a contemporary of al-Zuhrí, al-Idrísí similarly makes no claims for the Almoravid conquest despite the fact that he reports on Islam being present in Ghana. Hiskett's promotion of the Susu taking the hit for Ghana does not shift the premise of the Almoravid conquest of Ghana; it merely reassigns it without disputing that the conquest took place; only that it bypassed Ghana. It is a revisionism that preserves a claim only dubiously supported by contemporary evidence but one that looms ever larger in the short end of the telescope. The farther away Arab writers were from the supposed Almoravid conquest of Ghana, the more credulity they invested in it, and the more modern historians, in turn, echoed the conquest theory.[14] Unable to escape the old-school view, Hiskett moves inconclusively between growing confidence in the idea of the conquest and the receding ground of any supporting contemporary evidence. The Almoravid conquest seems to cast a spell all its own.

Hiskett's treatment of the issue does not offer a satisfactory solution. Not unlike Gibb, Hiskett seeks to resolve the problem by diverting focus to the

Susu and away from Ghana, whose pagan reputation can now be blamed on the pernicious influence of the unconverted Susu. This allows Hiskett to argue that the Soninke of Ghana adopted Islam by peaceful means to become allies of the Almoravids.[15] By this stage, the solutions had become far more vexing than the Almoravid hypothesis they were designed to salvage. In a brief spell of logical consistency, Hiskett concedes the point and abandons the Almoravid hypothesis, admitting that the evidence does not support the claim that Ghana was conquered by the Almoravids or anyone else. On the contrary, the sources "speak of Ghana as if it continued to be a sovereign state of the Soninke long after the 5/11 century. Thus the whole story of the conquest becomes rather doubtful."[16] Soon after that statement, though, Hiskett reasserts the conquest theory he just repudiated.[17] It is hard to know what to make of this, for even Ibn Khaldun's generous concession of inattentiveness as a forgivable occupational hazard cannot entirely explain why the fragile Almoravid hypothesis has been so resistant to evidence even in skilled hands. [18]

Quite apart from their common roots in traditional religion, the so-called Soninke and the Susu share broadly what Tocqueville might have called "habits of the heart," understood here as the inherited customs and observances that infuse and render experientially credible and politically viable the structures and institutions of society.[19] Hiskett's main argument is based on the offsetting hypothesis that the Soninke were Muslim before the Almoravids, but if that is so, why would an Almoravid jihad be necessary for the Susu?

On available evidence, it is not credible to argue that the pagan Susu caused Muslim Ghana to lapse or to contend that an Almoravid-directed jihad accomplished the kingdom's now-improbable conversion as a concomitant of its still more doubtful political subjugation. The Almoravid *amír al-muslimín* described by Yáqút tellingly does not give credence to that theory, nor does the account of al-Maqrízí, for all its derivative way of giving different explanations.[20] It sounds as if al-Maqrízí is cutting and pasting over the gap between Ghana and Mali with a speculative Susu middle link. Sunjata, also called Mari Jata (Our Lord the Lion), succeeded Sumanguru after defeating him at the battle of Kirina (Krina in some sources) in 1235 and went on to build Mali into the empire it became; both he and Sumanguru were non-Muslim rulers, and their memory is hallowed as such in the traditions still handed down.[21] Sunjata was succeeded in 1255 by his son, Mansa Wulé (Ulí) (d. 1270), who performed the pilgrimage during the reign of Záhir Baybars, the Mamluk sultan of Cairo (ruled 1260–1277). Somewhat implausibly, though, Trimingham asserts the Almoravid conquest of Ghana only to cloud the issue by noting that in 1090, before the dust settled, Ghana regained its independence,[22] which is tantamount to saying that the conquest did not happen. The chronology in either case rules out the idea of the Almoravid conquest and conversion of Ghana in its integral imperial phase in 1076. It does not, however, rule out the existence of Islamized parts of the scattered provinces that had once formed the exposed northwestern flank of the Ghanaian empire.

Why did the flimsy, speculative theory of the Almoravid conquest of Ghana, appearing in full only after some three hundred years, loom so large in the works of later writers when the contemporary sources were silent on it? Fisher's explanation is that a certain bias intervened, altering the record by framing Ghana as fit to be plucked. There is a tendency, he argues,

> to assume that it is in the nature of things for conversion to Islam to be a dramatic about-face, for Muslims to be superior to pagans, whites to blacks, nomads to sedentary people—cowboys to farmers, a perennial problem from Cain and Abel down to the musical "Oklahoma." Had white, Muslim nomads conquered black pagan sedentaries, there would have been no reason at all for later Arab writers to hush up such events: but if the Almoravid *amír* walking before the mounted black king of Záfún is, in some sense, symbolic of the whole real relationship, then perhaps a certain reticence in the Arab sources is more easily understood. It is bad enough to have the farmer and the cowboy friends: for the farmer to ride while the cowboy has to walk oversteps the limits.[23]

We need not probe motives to appreciate how an idea can snowball if conditions are favorable. Scholars do not work in a vacuum, and receptivity to scholarship has its share of influence on the craft of scholarship. The Almoravid hypothesis resonated in a favorable environment that gave it range and durability. That is how, in a different part of West Africa, writers came to believe that it was the Almoravid conquest that enabled the Masufa Berbers of the Sahel to establish a power base of the Kel Tadmekkat and the Kel Tingeregif, who acted as overlords of Timbuktu. Yet

> there exists no coherent support for the theory advanced by the early French writers to the effect that the militant Islamic Almoravid movement which arose in the Western Sahara during the late eleventh century gave rise to a vast but short-lived empire in the Sahelo-Sudan. . . . Locally, the Masúfa seem to have been a junior partner (if anything) in an alliance which was headed by the kingdom of Ghana.[24]

There is, indeed, nothing even in this cautious summary of the evidence to contradict the idea of the Masúfa as vassals of Ghana, much as has been suggested for the Lemtuna of Awdhagast.

The view prevailing among Muslim African scholars has rarely been taken into account. Assessing the conquest thesis for communities of his time, 'Uthman dan Fodio (d. 1817), the nineteenth-century founder of the Sokoto caliphate (discussed in chapter 12), concluded that in the hands of the most reliable scholars the thesis is roundly rejected.

> If you ask whether the Muslims among the people of the Sudan accepted Islam through being conquered or whether they professed it voluntarily, I would say that the answer to this is as stated by Shaykh Ahmad Baba in his *Kashf* when he said: "They accepted Islam without being conquered by anybody." In another place he said, "It appears from what Ibn Khaldun and others said that those who became Muslims from among the Sudanese did so voluntarily without being conquered by anybody."[25]

Ahmad Baba said he was aware of a speculative tradition articulated by an unknown *qadi* (judge) that purports to support the conquest theory but found no record of it or backing for it. He asked on whose authority the claim was based. It is very likely, Baba concluded, that the qadi's "account is untrue, for if you inquire nowadays you will not find anybody who can confirm the truth of what he said. So what is based on his report cannot be taken into consideration and it appears most likely that it is unauthentic."[26] The cloud of witnesses attesting to the Almoravid conquest of Ghana loomed large enough in retrospect to seem incontestable. Yet the claim lacks substance.

Local Tradition in Mali

It is worth noting that oral traditions maintained by the guild of poet-raconteurs called *jeli* (*griots* in French sources), who are a part of the Manding people in Senegambia, the two Guineas, and Mali, are preoccupied with the Sumanguru-Sunjata saga about which the Arabic sources are relatively tight-lipped.[27] Tradition maintains that in Mali every prince was assigned his own *jeli* from whose mouth the prince would hear the deeds of his ancestors and the art of governing Mali in line with "the principles which our ancestors have bequeathed to us . . . never forget that Niani is your capital and Mali the cradle of your ancestors."[28] In referring to Niani as Mali's capital, the jeli are employing a rhetorical device for emphasis. The intense local interest in Sunjata as the epic founder of Mali accounts for why his story

> appears to have greater historical foundation, in spite of the remoteness of the event, than anything else in Máli tradition, whilst Mansa

> Musa, who figures prominently in both native and external Arabic writings in consequence of his [. . .] pilgrimage, is almost unknown to native tradition except as a magician who imported idols from Mecca.[29]

It is instructive that, despite his proven historical significance, Mansa Músá has no musical tradition identified with him and that the otherwise legend-hungry griots have steadfastly ignored him. Sunjata is the epic champion of custom and tradition whereas Mansa Músá is the exemplar of Islam. A divided heritage developed in which the art of recounting the stories of the Muslim rulers of Mali and undertaking embassies for them was reserved to a specialized traditional caste of *jeli,* called the *fina* or *fina-ké,* who became generally court clients under the ruler's patronage.[30]

The Sunjata epic style was transferred and developed in the Mandinka kingdom of Kaabou (Gabou) (c. 1560–1867) that survived the breakup of Mali. Under the Sanneh *nyancho* nobility, Kaabou renounced Islam and became patrons of the numerous caste groups that maintained continuity with Mali's pre-Islamic heritage.[31] The term Kaabou *nyancho* distinguishes the Sanneh from two other *nyancho* groups, among them the Manneh and the Sanyang families who acquired their princely status by becoming masters of territories beyond Kaabou. Along with the ruling class, the griots converted to Islam without dropping their attachment to the pre-Islamic patrons of Manding history and without embracing Muslim champions like Mansa Músá. The Kaabou kingdom was overthrown in a jihad launched from Futa Jallon by the Fulbe. Alfa Yahya, the Fula king of Labé, married a *nynacho* princess to seal the defeat of the kingdom. Although the griots were Muslims, their music, furnished now with an expanded Kaabou repertoire, was excluded from the mosque and from general Islamic ritual observances. It is a revealing ambivalence: the griots are Muslims when they pray; they are champions of the Manding secular heritage when they play. As happened in old Mali, Islam is both the griots' safety net and their alibi at the same time. Their inclusion in the Muslim tradition protects them from social stigma, while their music thrives outside the strictures of religion.[32] It is an outstanding example of inclusion with restriction but without cultural forfeiture.

3

Beyond Desert Trails

Religion and Social Change

Even in dreams good works are not wasted.
—Pedro Calderón de la Barca (d. 1681)

Climate and Agriculture in the Desert

Historians generally agree that while climatic changes account for much of the desertification process, including social and migratory patterns, human activity is largely responsible for causing the Sahara and the Sahel to converge how and where they did. The area that lies well west of the Niger River, once inhabited by nomadic Moors, is characterized by thorny scrub, low pasture grass, and scattered acacia trees. But evidence of villages in former times suggests that the region had once been more densely populated and that human activity was responsible for accelerating the encroachment of the desert along with the southward movement of the people. It shows that the Sahara was a connecting frontier that, far from impeding the movement of nomadic Berbers, facilitated it and, by extension, trade and cultural exchange with black populations to the south (see Figure 3.1). These changes are in line with what the sources tell us of the range and effects of the Almoravid movement and its encounter with Ghana in "the land of the blacks," and it supports the view that there was a close connection between events in North Africa and social and climatic changes in West Africa.

The southward population drift eventually subjected the freewheeling nomads to the culture of political organization found in sedentary societies. Ibn Khaldun writes of wandering desert nomads who founded an empire in Morocco and Spain and became consumed by the regular demands of running a state. The culture of material success they acquired eventually sapped their strength and enfeebled them. Those who remained in the desert survived in fragmented, disorganized bands and were reduced to tutelage by the "king of Sudan," to whom they paid tribute and into whose army they were conscripted.

Nomadic communities that had been weaned on raids and sorties, as befitted the unregulated rhythm of life in the windswept sandy wastes, were transformed by the adoption of structures of political organization. The sedentary life was a congenial setting for promoting structures of organized political life, which in turn facilitated the spread of Islam into communities beyond the oases. The Berbers who immigrated into those communities received a boost to their religious profession as they gave up their nomadic habits.

Al-Bakrí confirms the existence of a flourishing sedentary life in the area, describing wells with sweet, potable water used to irrigate vegetable gardens. Even today, wells can be dug to a relatively shallow depth of ten feet under the surface sand before striking water. This suggests that the populations there were dislocated by raids and external threats and pushed down south before the sand covered the wells. Dwindling pasture and its surviving cultivation was destroyed by nomads, resulting in creeping desertification. Climatic changes alone would have taken much longer and produced a far more arid environment than is consistent with the shallow water table. We must conclude that human activity accounted for a good deal of the climatic change.[1]

The significance of this human impact for the kingdoms of Ghana and of Mali cannot be exaggerated, and the evidence aligns rather well with the accounts of al-Bakrí and other contemporary Arab writers concerning the evolving interface between desert and sown land. It forms the backdrop to the developing drama of conversion to Islam in the context of unrelenting environmental stress in the borderlands. There the challenges of agriculture made urgent the need for religious intervention, offering Muslim missionaries a welcome chance to promote Islam.

Religion, State, and Society in Mali

Conversion

When al-Bakrí turns his attention to the kingdom of Mali, the successor of Ghana, he writes of Islam being established through peaceful channels: the religious revolution he describes is of a gradual kind. He proceeds to give details. (Tellingly, he makes no reference to the conquest theory of the Almoravids.) Al-Bakrí's account of religion in Mali is noteworthy in several important ways. He begins by referring to the king as a "Muslim" (*al-musulmání*), explaining the manner and circumstances under which the king came to embrace Islam. It was all because of prayer for rain (*salát al-istisqá*). Mali faced a severe drought "one year after another," which threatened the very survival of the kingdom. In vain the people prayed for rain and sacrificed their invaluable livestock. At this critical point, the king remembered that he had as a court guest a Muslim cleric, whose custom it was to read the Qur'an and to study the *sunnah* of the Prophet. The king thought that the cleric might have access to spiritual powers beyond those of his own shrine priests and that, if such powers could avert the crisis, their foreignness would be of little consequence: the benefits of their intervention would offset any local backlash. The people, increasingly disenchanted with the failed oracles invoked at shrines and in divination rituals, offered little resistance. The king took his predicament to the cleric.

> "O King," the cleric responded, "if you would believe in God (who is exalted) and bear witness that there is none other than God and that Muhammad (may God bless him and grant him peace) is the messenger of God, and if you accept all the religious teachings of Islam, I would pray for deliverance from your predicament and that God's mercy would envelop all the people of your country and that your enemies and adversaries might envy you on that account."

The promise of relief coupled with the persistence of the cleric paid off. According to al-Bakrí, the king made a sincere profession of faith.

The cleric then took the king under his wing and instructed him in the tenets of Islam, teaching him to memorize simple passages from the Arabic Qur'an and to carry out the obligatory injunctions and practices incumbent on all Muslims. After that rudimentary initiation into the ritual demands of the faith, the cleric prepared the king for *salát al-istisqá*, the rogation ritual that was the king's real interest. According to the rules of the ritual, it must be performed as an all-night vigil on a Thursday, leading to the break of day the following Friday. Accompanied by the cleric, the king donned a cotton garment and, for personal purification, performed the ritual ablution (*wudú*), then adjourned to a mound where the cleric stood praying, "while the king, standing at his right side, imitated him." Thus they prayed together, cleric and acolyte, until dawn broke and ushered in the answer to their prayers: the clouds gathered and thickened, heavy with rain. The ensuing downpour brought on a transformation not only of the physical landscape but also of the religious.

The events that followed occurred in a seemingly inexorable pattern. His hand strengthened with a public demonstration of the benefits of the new religion, the king ordered the confiscation of the sacred images (*dakákir*) and the expulsion of their custodial priests. The new order faced no resistance from the traditional priestly establishment to delay driving out the old, or so it seemed. Al-Bakrí is too faithful to the evidence to permit the impression that royal patronage was enough to sweep away ancient custom and launch Islam on a triumphant course in Mali. It did not happen that way. Al-Bakrí commends the faith of the king and his designation of *al-musulmání* and, by implication, the devotedness also of his visiting confessor, without ignoring the continuing sway of the old religion over the general populace.

We are left with a mixed picture. In al-Bakrí's account, there are four major factors in the conversion of Mali. The first is that, situated in the Sahel, the country of Mali was drought-prone enough to make the farming cycle unpredictable, and the stress of that reflected in standard attempts at religious intervention. Geological environment and religion remained symbiotic, thrusting the visiting cleric into the habitual role of purveyor of rain. The second is the role of organized states as a channel and outlet of new influences, an important thesis of al-Bakrí. The third is the dualism or parallelism we noted earlier: Islam coexisted with traditional religions without friction and, over time, demonstrated its superior efficacy in the public setting of royal acceptance, eclipsing the now-defunct cult of the court. The fourth factor, and a critical one, is the process by which the ruler acted first as host of Muslim strangers as traders and visitors and then became their guardian and local patron until, finally, he submitted to Islam as a believer and a witness for Islam. Without resort to jihad or to political penalties, the conversion of king and court was accomplished through a gradual, peaceful process. Religious change in this situation is about "cognitive adjustment to change in the conditions of social life,"[2] quite distinct from jihad that involves tension, conflict, and violence.

All of these factors are legitimate ways of understanding Islamic conversion and its effects on people, structures, and institutions. It is also possible that economic motives—wishing to attract traders, for example—played a role in swaying the king to Islam. Though al-Bakrí is noticeably demure on this point, it is not an unreasonable assumption; other evidence shows that economic motivation is a common element of the conversion process. The ruler of Jenne, for instance, asked his leading scholars to pray for commerce so that the town might prosper and the citizens become wealthy.[3] Still, it would not do to overlook the agency role of the visiting cleric, who, under royal patronage, presides over fundamental religious change through the instruments of Scripture, public prayer, and devotion. In the bottom-up pattern of the transmission of Islam, the cleric assumes the role of royal chaplain, presiding over religious change by demonstrating Islam's effectiveness to end the drought.

Islam's success in Mali results not so much from its exclusive superiority as a religion as its readiness to fill in gaps in traditional religion—the gap in this case between the onset of a drought and the time leading to a representative Muslim figure intervening with effect. Islam did not invent a new eschatology of supernatural intervention; it simply affirmed and validated the local practice of it. Prayer for rain seems to be the litmus test of efficacious religion, as well as of a viable imperial cult, and Islam had to pass muster by meeting that challenge, which it reputedly did with resounding success.

This is not to say that fundamental change did not occur but that it can be effected in unlikely ways, such as by sleight of hand. The art of rainmaking predates the coming of Islam but is not incongruous with it. Islam's written Scripture, obligatory practices and ritual, and sartorial habit are harmoniously inclusive of the work of the old priests, oracles, and spirits. Religious conversion in Mali occurred because Islam aligned with the structure of traditional ideas, without confrontation and conflict. The ruler embraced Islam because it fulfilled the ancient expectation that religion must be useful to be valid. Islam may be blamed for causing droughts, the explanation being that droughts were rare before its introduction. The criticism makes Islam look like one of the traditional religions, to be refracted through "changes in the conditions of social life."

For a while the Accra township of Medina in Ghana was a settlement of Muslim Hausa from Nigeria who arrived there during the colonial era. In just over a generation Islam was in retreat there before the advancing tide of new Christian charismatic groups. The Muslim response was to embark on open-air preaching with the use of loudspeakers, billboards, and mobile youth groups. The strengthened Muslim presence in Accra testified to the success of the religion in adapting to changed situations.

Islam's cultural imprint similarly was not readily discarded. Society was indelibly marked by Islamic education, law, Arabic terms and concepts and loan words dealing with ethical obligations, metaphysics, the calendar, patterns of trade, dress styles, the mosque, and pilgrimage customs. The idea of jihad, the summary imposition of Islam's penal code, is too restrictive to account for localization as a religious process.

The Cleric

The trader, the ruler, and the warrior are all recognized carriers of Islam. It is important to acknowledge the equally distinctive role of the cleric, loosely defined, as an agent of religious expansion and diffusion. The visiting cleric of al-Bakrí's account makes his presence felt as a professional in his own right. His relationship with the ruler is by virtue of the religious service he renders as "seller of rain" (*bayyá' al-maṭar*), with religious demands on the king in return for the favor.[4] While the cleric might be engaged with social, political, or economic problems, he did so as a professional practicing his religious métier. He might offer prayer services for commerce or for war without the community considering him a surrogate trader or jihadist.[5] Prayer for commerce is often linked to prayer for the prevention or cessation of war. In the trans-Saharan setting and in accounts, for example, by Mungo Park and Jobson, it was often the case that religion and trade traveled together, the trader and cleric were both Muslims, merchandise included religious items or items allowed under religious law, trading advantage might also be religious advantage, and factors conducive to trade might also be conducive to the spread of religion. This is often a matter of coincidence. Trade might attract Islam and Islam trade, without indicating long-term consequences for religious change. Despite long periods of residence and close proximity to Africans, Arab and Berber traders played little direct role in religious change. Committed to the religious life, local agents used the opportunities and channels of contact traders created to raise greater awareness of Islam. As will be described later this was the spirit that guided the conduct of a largely Muslim Mali with respect to a gold-rich, largely non-Muslim Ghana. However much it might be a hospitable environment for it, the trade did not create the religious vocation because, in spite of being coveted, merchandise is not religion. Another step and other resources were necessary for religious conversion. In response to an inquiry about the commercial motivation, the pacifist clerics explained in field interviews that clerical pedigree alone was not sufficient for the vocation. Choice was necessary.

Trade and Politics

Because of the way Ghana and Mali are linked in contemporary sources, we cannot assume an abrupt, clear-cut break between the two kingdoms. Long after the Egyptian ruler Ahmad ibn Túlún (868–884) placed a security ban on traders conducting business along the treacherous route from al-Wahát to Ghana, al-'Umarí, writing in the fourteenth century, describes an active caravan route from Upper Egypt through the desert to Ghana and Mali.[6] Furthermore, as if aiming to correct a widespread misconception, al-'Umarí notes that some writers' description of the ruler of Ghana as a king is inaccurate: that title in reality belongs to the king of Mali, and "the ruler of Ghana is like a deputy to him even though he be a king." Al-'Umarí offers an elegant solution, saying that Mali granted autonomy to Ghana in return for an annual "heavy tribute" of gold—an economic calculation.

> If the sultan [of Mali] wished he could extend his authority over them but the kings of this kingdom have learnt by experience that as soon as one of them conquers one of the gold towns and Islam spreads and the muezzin calls to prayer there the gold there begins to decrease and then disappears, while it increases in the neighboring heathen countries. When they had learnt the truth of this by experience they left the gold countries under the control of the

> heathen people and were content with their vassalage and the tribute imposed on them.[7]

In this transparent calculation, the imposition of Islam was not worth a potential disruption of the valuable gold-trade of Ghana.[8] That was the reason, al-'Umarí contended, why Mali granted relative political autonomy to Ghana. The overlap between the two kingdoms may explain the confusion in the sources about the precise nature of their religious makeup.[9]

It suited neighboring states that Ghana kept the source of gold (the lucrative goldfields of Bambouk and Bure) a secret from foreign traders. Arabic and Portuguese accounts describe the elaborate measures taken to prevent foreign traders from coming anywhere near the gold-mining region. Merchants who pressed for information risked exclusion from the whole trade. Trade in the precious metal was conducted with a bartering process that required minimal contact between the two sides. Al-'Umarí reported that a witness, Abú 'Abd Alláh b. al-Sá'igh, told him that gold from the land of the blacks was traded for salt brought there by merchants. The commodities were swapped in heaps: each heap of salt for its like in gold. The Africans were very secretive about the source of the gold and so did not enter into direct communication with the traders. "When the salt merchants come they put the salt down and then withdraw. Then the Súdán [blacks] put down the gold." Only after the merchants retrieved the gold and departed did the Africans emerge to take the salt. In his *Mu'jam al-buldán* (*The Dictionary of Countries*), Yáqút describes an identical custom of dumb barter in Ghana. The foreign merchants beat drums to announce their arrival. Upon confirming that they had been heard, they laid out their merchandise and retreated a day's journey away. Emerging from their "underground hiding places and burrows," the Africans then approached and set down a pile of gold for each kind of merchandise and in turn withdrew to the sound of drums. The merchants returned and retrieved the gold, beating their drums to signify they had accepted the terms of trade and were leaving the area. Thus concluded the transaction.[10]

Farias's review of the evidence on dumb barter or, as he calls it, "silent trade," indicates that the accounts of it were colorfully exaggerated.[11] Still, there seems to have been a widespread attitude among the people—or else a widespread impression among observers—that gold was trafficked in deepest secrecy and that, whatever their personal convictions as Muslims, rulers took great care not to jeopardize the gold trade (and a number of other economic endeavors) by requiring that traders adhere to Islam. Ghana was allowed to forgo Islam for practical economic reasons. Such economic motivations interrupted the spread of Islam but did not halt it.

Since the famous pilgrimage of Mansa Músá to Mecca via Cairo in the fourteenth century, outsiders had been mesmerized by African gold, though they were largely unsuccessful in the pursuit of it. Eager to penetrate to the source of the fabulous gold on the Gold Coast, the Portuguese in the sixteenth century fretted at the Africans' secrecy as well as the obstacles of climate and disease that ensured that all routes to the interior were blocked. João de Barros, a Portuguese trader who as a young man served many years at Mina, expressed the frustration of his European compatriots when he noted that in spite of the fact that the trade of Guinea "yields a more regular annual revenue, with no tenant alleging drought or loss" than any revenue source in Portugal, it remained little prospected. The country, he pleaded,

> is so peaceful, meek, and obedient an estate, that, without our having one hand holding a lighted lunt on the touch-hole of a gun and the other hand holding a lance, it gives us gold, ivory, wax, hides, sugar, pepper, malaguetta; and it would give us more things if we would only penetrate into the hinterland. . . . But it seems that for our sins, or for some inscrutable judgment of God, in all the entrances of this great Ethiopia that we navigate along, He has placed a striking angel with a flaming sword of deadly fevers, who prevents us from penetrating into the interior to the springs of this garden, whence proceed these rivers of gold that flow to the sea in so many parts of our conquest.[12]

The desire to acquire gold was a major reason for Portuguese exploration of Africa, and this report describes that desire and how the path was blocked by seemingly insuperable barriers of climate and disease. Fate seemed to bar the way to the gold-producing regions of Africa, while in Bambouk and Boure the elaborate, complicated system of barter impeded direct access. The importance of the gold trade influenced Mali's relationship with Ghana. Mali did not resort to war to absorb Ghana but instead settled for an informal entente to contain Ghana and to safeguard continued access to Ghana's precious metal. One symbol of Mali's unrivaled power was the control of the important trans-Saharan trade routes, with Walata in Mali's northwestern region the principal terminus. Walata eclipsed the declining Awdaghast as well as Koumbi-Saleh, once the seat of Ghana's power, and became a symbol of the success of African state-building: it assimilated adjoining desert-dwellers (*ahl al-qafr*) and Berber groups into organized institutions of state and society. The affected Berbers ceased to be seasonal migrants and *rentiers* of watering holes and formed settled communities in states and kingdoms. Situated some hundred kilometers northeast of Ghana's old capital, Walata flourished as a cosmopolitan center. Berbers and blacks coexisted, a self-reinforcing social admixture of Arab and Berber traders and scholars comingling with the indigenous African population.

Oral traditions describe how the rise of Mali in the early thirteenth century under its founding pagan king, Sumanguru Kante of the Susu tribe, precipitated a dispersal of Muslims of Ghana, who then sought refuge in Bíru (Berber for Walata). In time, Mali incorporated Walata within its sphere of influence by appointing a governor there, and the resulting sense of order and security encouraged several Berber groups to migrate to the town. Prominent among them were the Mesúfa Berber nomads. The governor of Walata was African. When the Arab traveler Ibn Battuta visited the town, he reported that most of Walata's inhabitants were Mesúfa Berbers. Trade was brisk and well-regulated. The governor appointed a *mushrif* (overseer) as a putative local sheriff, who acted as market inspector and commercial agent. The local name for him was *mansa-jong* (royal slave), indicating that he was recruited from the royal slave household. He was not given free rein, however, lest he misuse his power to take advantage of unprotected visiting traders. On one occasion, following a complaint of ill treatment by a trader that the *mushrif* had paid him a hundred *mithqáls* of gold instead of the six hundred he was due, the *mushrif* was dismissed.[13] The dismissal of the *mushrif* might have served as a deterrent to such misconduct and an assurance to would-be future traders. The governor calculated that fair and just treatment of traders and strangers was a policy that would repay in increased traffic to Walata.

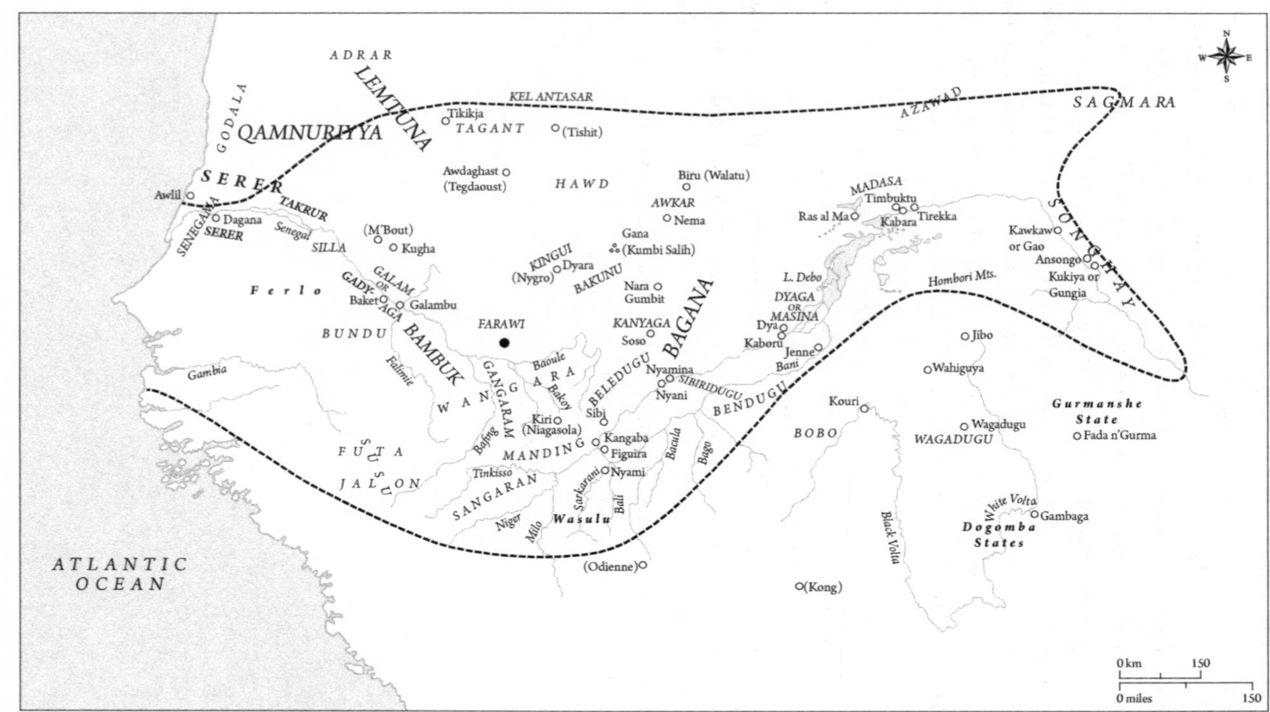

Figure 2.1 Empire of Mali. Adapted from *A History of Islam in West Africa* by J. Spencer Trimingham (Oxford: Oxford University Press, 1962), 38–39. By permission of Oxford University Press.

4

Beyond Routes and Kingdoms

New Frontiers, Old Hinterlands

> Praise to God who created the earth as a couch, the mountains as tent pegs, and from thence spread out the highlands and lowlands, deserts and fertile countries. Then in the midst thereof He opened up watercourses, causing rivers and seas to flow; and guided His servants to make for themselves dwellings, to erect buildings and homes. Thus they raised edifices and cultivated the fields, hewed out houses from the mountains and dug wells and cisterns. He made their zeal, for the erection of their edifices and for the construction of all that they built and strengthened, a lesson to the heedless and an enlightenment to men throughout history.
>
> —Yáqút (d. 1229) in A. F. L. Beeston, *Samples of Arabic Prose in its Historical Development*, 36.

Expanding Islamic influence in Ghana and Mali overlapped soon enough with old customs and traditions. Conversion was an organic social process more than a matter of force. Eye-catching Muslim dress, mosque architecture, the influx of strangers from Muslim lands, the circulation of books of religion and law, and the public rituals staged in the lunar rather than solar calendar reoriented society over time in the direction of Islamic influence. This gradual process can be observed in subtle, incremental changes in customs, practices, and relationships. The index of conversion is a sliding scale, with movement in both directions until a decision is made one way or the other.

A fountainhead of tradition and custom, the king and court act in this process more as registers than as drivers. Routes and kingdoms facilitated the introduction of Islam without becoming pathways of conquest, settlement, and domination. A regular and relatively secure pattern of trade and commerce developed, thriving more or less unhindered in a mixed social and religious environment. Accommodation characterized the practice of Islam in society, and in contemporary accounts, rulers stood out not by their aggressive promotion of Islam but by their lenient attitude toward religious and social diversity.

After noting that paganism is the religion of the people and king of Ghana, al-Bakrí commends the king because "he loved justice and was friendly to the Muslims." At this stage, the attitude of Islam toward custom and tradition was one of leave well enough alone. Even when devout converts took to the pilgrimage trail, it was not to burn bridges with the old hinterland, and in no way did that weaken their attachment to Islam. Commitment and tolerance went hand in hand.

In most Arabic and Portuguese accounts, Ghana and Mali figure significantly as states connected with the spread of Islam in West Africa. References are made to specific African populations—the Malinke (people of Mali) and those whom some scholars prefer to call Soninke (founders of the empire of Ghana)—as the major social groups responsible for the creation of Mali and Ghana before it. The identity of the social groups that embraced Islam when the religion was first introduced, and how these early converts practiced and propagated it, is a central issue of historical understanding. Local appropriation offers insight into the transmission and impact of Islam.

Mansa Músá: Pilgrim-King

The pilgrimage of Mansa Músá (known also as Kankan Músá), the king of Mali, in 1324 caught the imagination of the wider Muslim world and spawned a prolific industry of stories, legend, and theories. His pilgrimage increased the pace of Islamization in Mali. A contemporary account was written by al-'Umarí, who obtained his information from Abú 'l-Hasan 'Alí b. Amír Hájib, the Emir of Cairo, who hosted Mansa Músá in the city: "A friendship grew up between them and this sultan Músá told him a great deal about himself and his country and the people of the Súdán who were his neighbors."[1] This friendly side of Mansa Músá offers a glimpse into his personal temperament. Mansa Músá was a sensation in Cairo, where he halted briefly but conspicuously on his way to Mecca.[2] With the pomp and ceremony of his royal retinue, he dazzled the people of Cairo including the governor and host Ibn Amír Hájib. He flooded the city with lavish benefactions, bestowing on officials extravagant gifts of gold. Al-'Ujrumí, a guide who accompanied Mansa Músá on the pilgrimage, reported that the king gave him 200 *mithqáls* of gold for his troubles. The guide testified that the king was very open-handed towards his fellow-pilgrims and the inhabitants of Mecca and Medina. He and his retinue observed great pomp and appeared in public dressed in all their finery. "He gave away much wealth in alms," al-'Umarí was told. On returning to Mali, the king sent back to the governor of Cairo 5,000 *mithqáls* of gold as a gift. Mansa Músá's similarly lavish generosity to the people caused a great quantity of gold to be released into general circulation, which "depressed its value in Egypt and caused its price to fall." The high price of 25 *dirhams* and more for gold before the royal visit fell to 22 *dirhams* and fewer afterward. The price had not recovered by the time of Ibn Khaldun's report some fifty years later. The merchants of Cairo boasted of huge profits from the spending habits of the Africans. It was easy to dupe the Africans due to their gullibility, the merchants gloated. Al-'Umari explained that it painted a poor image of the Egyptians as swindlers.

Demonstrating his wealth in gold was not the real object of Mansa Músá's well-advertised trip. The Mamluk official who had responsibility for looking after important visitors and ensuring their safe passage in the city noted that after the king had sent many loads of raw gold to the government treasury—all indicating Mansa Músá's good will—he had difficulty persuading Mansa Músá to agree to an in-person meeting with the sultan of Cairo at the Citadel. The reason for Mansa Músá's unwillingness seemed hard to fathom. Mansa Músá declared, "I came for the Pilgrimage and for nothing else. I do not wish to mix anything with my Pilgrimage." Drawing on Ibn Khaldun, among others, al-Maqrízí is similarly explicit when he reports Mansa Músá as saying, "I am a man of the Malikite school and do not prostrate myself before any but God."[3] This explanation indicates that religious scruples made the king hesitate about meeting the sultan since that would involve the king having to prostrate and kiss the ground and the hand of the sultan as required by political protocol.[4] An acceptable compromise was worked out in which the king made prostration with the words, "I make obeisance to God who created me!" The sultan reciprocated when he half-rose and greeted him, sitting by his side. It was a cordial audience. Mansa Músá received many presents from the sultan, including suits of honor for himself and his attendants, a robe of Alexandrian open-fronted cloak (*muftaraj*) embellished with gold thread and miniver fur, bordered with beaver fur and ornamented with metallic thread, along with golden fastenings, a silken skull cap with caliphal emblems, a gold-inlaid belt, a damascened sword, a kerchief decorated with pure gold, standards, and two horses bridled and equipped with decorated mule-type saddles. He left for Mecca weighed down with additional gifts of camels complete with saddles and equipment to serve as mounts and provisions for his party.

The king's legendary wealth and lavish generosity notwithstanding, Mansa Músá's hosts in Cairo were eager to evaluate his religious credentials. Al-'Umarí records Ibn Amír Hájib's engagement with the king on the subject of marriage and family life. On learning of the custom of Mali dictating that the king's subjects give a beautiful daughter to him as a concubine, without the marriage rite, Ibn Amír Hájib expressed consternation. "I said to him that this was not permissible for a Muslim whether in law or reason (*wa-lá yahalla li-l'muslimin shar'an wa lá 'aqlan*). And he said, 'Not even for kings?' I replied, "No, not even for kings! Ask the scholars!' He replied, 'By God, I did not know that. I hereby leave it and abandon it utterly.' " Some modern historians have cited this incident as proof that Islam was a syncretistic religion in Mali. Despite the ceremony and fanfare with which he set out for the pilgrimage, Mansa Músá, critics charge, was ignorant of one of the most elementary rules of Muslim family life: that a man can marry no more than four wives at any one time. Critics made no allowance for the rule of taking an unrestricted number of concubines. They accused him of setting out for the holy city of Mecca with only a fragmentary grasp of what Islam required of ordinary Muslims.

Yet Ibn Amír Hájib and others who met Mansa Músá were impressed by his faith and sincerity. "I saw," said Ibn Amír Hájib, "that this sultan Músá loved virtue and people of virtue. He left his kingdom and appointed as his deputy there his son Muhammad and emigrated to God and His Messenger." His appetite for religion thus awakened, Mansa Músá resolved to return to Mecca in order to adopt a life of prayer and devotion and relinquish power for that purpose. He would return to his country and arrange for an orderly transfer of power before making good on his vow. He had every intention of retiring to Mecca "as a dweller near the sanctuary (*mujáwir*)" but died trying to do so.

Regarding royal concubines, Ibn Amír Hájib was assured by the king's response to his censure and offered a ringing endorsement of Mansa Músá's religious standing. He extolled the king as "a godly man who is diligent in worship, Qur'an study, and in devotional exercises on the name of God (*mutadayyanan muhafizan 'alá al-salát wa al-qirá'ah wa al-dhikr*)."[5] It is likely from Mansa Músá's response that, rather than showing he had only a superficial knowledge of Islam , he was following the prevailing lenient interpretation of Máliki law, in accordance with the principle of *qiyás* (analogy). The king was a student of the Maliki legal tradition. Like the codes of the other three legal schools (Hanafí, Sháfi'í, and Hanbalí), the Máliki code imposed a limit of four wives at any one time, though legal reforms in modern times have trimmed that number to conform to the growing pressure for monogamous marriage.[6] In any case, the assumption of Mansa Músá that concubinage (*istisrár*) was permissible was more than an ignorant misunderstanding; rather, it relied on a generous interpretation of Islamic jurisprudence, combined with a not-so-inconvenient indulgence in local custom.[7] But his conscience gave him no quarter.

Notwithstanding Mansa Músá's kingly indulgences, there is little question that he possessed Islamic scruples.[8] He seems to have felt an anguish of conscience when he learned that he was expected to kiss the hand of the Sultan, and he kept his distance until a compromise was made. In his hesitance to visit the sultan, Mansa Músá protested against the suggestion, considered idolatrous and also unfitting for a king, that we should yield our will to anyone but

God and thus made his declaration of "I make obeisance to God who created me!" on entering into the sultan's presence.

Even if Mansa Músá's motive for unwillingness was a disinclination to humble himself, the Mamluk sultan could not disagree with the king's affirmation of God as the only one entitled to our obeisance, though he must have wished that it had not been necessary for an African leader to remind him of it.[9] Mansa Músá's affirmation echoes the sentiment of religious teaching that the ruler is a caretaker of his people for the Supreme Ruler, not the replacement or alternative. In meeting the king halfway in this minefield of contending loyalties and disregarding the king's delay in coming to pay courtesies, the sultan avoided any awkward differences with his guest. Mansa Músá had by this time become something of a living legend in Cairo and beyond, and it was to the sultan's political advantage to be hospitable to him, as his appropriately generous reception of the king demonstrated.

Mansa Músá's reputation was that of a seasoned, well-instructed (*muháfizan*) Muslim according to al-'Umari, who was predisposed to subordinate the prerogatives of high office to the demands and austerities imposed by the Islamic code on king and commoner alike. Despite his possessing considerable authority, there is not the slightest indication that Mansa Músá had any concept of being anointed by the eternal law, à la Charlemagne, and for that reason he could magnify his Creator, not himself. This devout attitude curbed any temptation to ego. It is hard "to hunger after tyranny" when conscience reduces one to one's knees in humble supplication.

Ibn Amír Hájib was taken aback by the un-Islamic practices of court life in Mali mainly because, as he confessed, Mansa Músá had demonstrated such knowledge of Islam. In other words, Ibn Amír Hájib was impressed by what he saw of the king's unquestionable sincerity and applauded it on his own conviction: *wa-aná ra'aitu hádháhu bi al-masháhadah wa al-'ayán . . . hádhá sultán músá muhabban lil-khayr wa ahlihi* (I have seen with my own eyes and can vouchsafe to the truth that this sultan Músá loved virtue and the people of virtue). Mansa Músá, Ibn Amír Hájib continues, "maintained a uniform attitude and turning towards God. It was as though he were standing before Him because of His continual presence in his mind." Ibn Amír Hájib observed that the actions of the king in taking so many women were "in spite of the fact that Islam has triumphed among them [i.e., the people of Mali]," that his Muslim subjects followed the Máliki school of law, and that Mansa Músá was "a godly man who is diligent in worship, Qur'anic study, and in devotional exercises." Ibn Amír Hájib was trying, apparently with a generous view, to reconcile Mansa Músá's lavish display of taking many women and his sincere pilgrimage vows. He gives the king high praise for his religious sincerity. Back in Mali, similarly, custom would make being lavish in wealth and women an attribute of power and status and, accordingly, marks of a successful religion.[10]

In the course of his pilgrimage, Mansa Músá made the acquaintance of Abú Isháq al-Sáhilí (d. 1346), an Andalusian poet. Al-Sáhilí accompanied the king back to Mali, where he established himself as scholar, royal confidant, diplomat, and architect. He constructed a palace, called in Manding "Madugu," for the king, as well as the famous Grand Mosque of Timbuktu, an oft-threatened but still surviving landmark, subjected to many centuries of renovations and alterations.[11] A contemporary admirer described al-Sáhilí as a man of letters "with wide acquaintance with the various branches of knowledge," having "a generous nature and an ability to overcome every circumstance."[12] Ibn Khaldun reports that al-Sáhilí quickly got to work for his royal patron

> making something novel for him by erecting a square building with a dome. He had a good knowledge of handicrafts and lavished all his skill on it. He plastered it over and covered it with coloured patterns so that it turned out to be the most elegant of buildings. It caused the sultan great astonishment because of the ignorance of the art of building in their land[,] and he rewarded Abú Isháq for it with 12,000 mithqals of gold dust apart from the preference, favour (*al-mayl ilayhi*) and splendid gifts which he enjoyed.[13]

Al-Sáhilí traveled to the Maghrib from Timbuktu on a diplomatic mission for Mali and was warmly received by the Marinid sultan, Abú al-Hasan (r. 1331–1348). He presented the sultan with some rare gifts and received in return the favor of a handsome reward. On what appears to be his own initiative, al-Sáhilí addressed a poem to Abú 'l-Hasan that urged him to attack Abú Táshfín, the Zayyanid ruler of Tlemcen. In the attack that took place in 1337, Abú al-Hasan was victorious, and when the news reached Mali, an embassy was dispatched to Fez to congratulate the sultan. The good relations Mali enjoyed with the Maghrib increased al-Sáhilí's standing in the esteem of both rulers. Abú al-Hasan offered al-Sáhilí a position in his chancellery. The Marinid sultan reciprocated Mansa Músá's friendly gestures by sending out a high-ranking embassy of his own, along with magnificent gifts, bound for Mali. The exchange cemented an enduring relationship between the two states. Mansa Sulayman in 1346–1347 sent an embassy of his own to congratulate Abú al-Hasan on the occasion of his conquest of the Hafsid domains of Ifriqiyah[14], and in 1360–1361 Mali's Mansa Mari Jata authorized an embassy to Sultan Abú Salím to celebrate his accession with gifts that included a giraffe.[15]

Ibn Battuta gives an eyewitness account of special ceremonies conducted at the Mali court in 1352 to commemorate the death of Sultan Abú al-Hasan, who had died four years earlier.[16] A story circulated in Mali about an act of kindness to Mansa Músá when he was a boy. It concerned Ibn Shakyh al-Laban of Tlemcen, who made a gift of 7 *mithqals* of gold to the young boy. Mansa Músá later recognized him in an audience and instructed his officials to repay the kindness tenfold, which was done.[17] Trans-Saharan relations were cordial as well as highly fruitful, sustained by enduring ties of mutual respect. The relations were fostered in a culture of tolerance, enriched by a cosmopolitan outlook made possible by the fact that Mansa Músá and the leaders of Tlemcen shared a common faith as Muslims. Tlemcen appears to have had well-known connections with West Africa, for the scholar-jurist, ʻAbd al-Karím al-Maghili (d. 1505), a contemporary of al-Suyuti, hailed from Tlemcen to take residence in the court of Askiya Muhammad of Songhay.

Qayrawán, seat of the eminent jurist Ibn Abí Zayd (d. 996) and nicknamed the "Little Málik" (*málik al-saghíir*), was the fountainhead of the Málikí legal tradition for West Africa and elsewhere. [18] Given the extensive impact of this tradition and the reported pervasiveness of Islam in Mali, Muslim Africans must have been trained in the subject, operating a viable network of learning in Mali and in surrounding districts. It would be consistent with what we know of the independent standing of law schools operating in North Africa to assume that in Mali, too, however much political patronage helped the growth of centers of learning, Islamic scholarship maintained its institutional autonomy: the curriculum of learning and the intellectual unity of Islam did not come by state directive.[19] Mansa Músá told his hosts in Cairo that he followed the Málikí rite in Mali and as king was its promoter in the kingdom.[20] Independent scholars and traveling clerics helped circulate manuals of law and ethics that were used in teaching and organized community life. As Mahmúd Kaʻtí reported of Diakha-Bambukhu and Gunjur, and as corroborated by Ahmad Baba and Richard Jobson, this tradition of autonomy and sanctuary for scholars and scholarship thrived in the districts of Mali, to be followed by Timbuktu, where Elias Saad points to the tradition being established there too. Our main concern in this study is with the specific role of pacifist clerics and their Sufi counterparts in religious and ethical scholarship and how the network of settlements they founded helped in the dissemination of scholarly materials and ideas. The references indicated describe precisely this pacifist outreach.

Ibn Amír Hájib's statement to Mansa Músá that certain customs and practices, however hallowed and prevalent, are simply "not permissible for a Muslim, whether in law or reason," is a clear assertion of the tradition of autonomy and independence enjoyed by the Islamic religious code. No arguments of political or economic expedience can override a Muslim's religious obligations, and Mansa Músá was reminded that his power was not unlimited.

As is evident in the structure of religious obligations, equality before God without regard to one's station in life is a fundamental rule of the canon, and it demands that Muslims embrace society as a matter of the common good. Religion places all human beings on the same level: it subjects the wise and the ignorant, the geniuses and the common crowd, to the details of one and the same creed; it imposes the same observances upon the rich and the needy, the same austerities and burdens on the strong and the weak; it listens to no compromise with mortal men and women but, reducing all the human race to the same standard, confounds all the distinctions of society with submission to one God and in the duties we owe Him and one another as members of society. A saying attributed to Muhammad dwells on this principle of equality: "The white man is not above the black nor the black above the yellow; all men are equal before their Maker." "Equal before God, members of a great family in which there is neither noble nor villein, but only believers, Muslims are equal before the civil law; and this equality was proclaimed at a time when it was practically unknown throughout Christian society."[21] Race or pedigree has no ritual or moral merit in the canon; the *ummah* has a religious rather than a political character.

It can be inferred from Mansa Músá's understanding of his kingly office that religion qualified the exercise of power rather than power qualifying religious obligation, which would open the way to despotism.[22] Everyone involved—Ibn Amír Hájib, Mansa Músá, and the Mamluk sultan—seemed to accept that implicit truth. It is deeply instructive that in all this high-minded discussion about the imperative of prescriptive religion there is not a murmur about establishing theocratic rule in Mali or in Egypt. Radical extremism need not be a corollary to faithful religion.

It is also worth noting that the founder of the Málikí school of law, Imám Málik ibn Anas (d. 795) of Medina, personally bore the brunt of the displeasure of caliphal powers. For his refusal to cease withholding the oath of loyalty from the 'Abbásid rulers, Málik was bastinadoed and his arms stretched until his shoulder was dislocated.[23] It is interesting, given the implied refusal of the African Muslim authorities to surrender religious authority to political power, that this story was recounted in an abbreviated handbook of Málikí law designed for use in courts in Britain's colonial territories in West Africa.[24] The British went on to adopt and apply Islamic law in their African colonies, in part to win the hearts and minds of Muslim populations and in part in recognition of the limitations administrators faced with scarce resources and personnel.

PART TWO

CLERICAL EMERGENCE

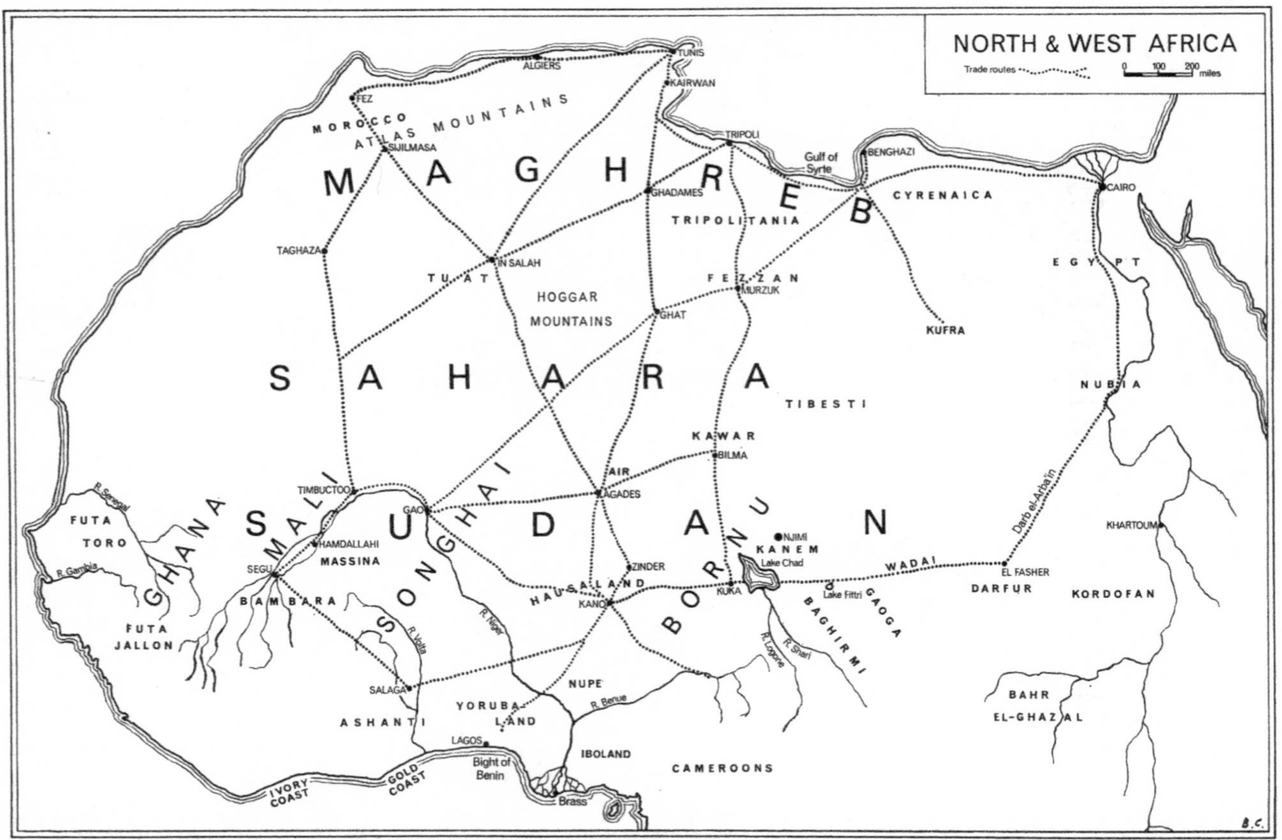

Figure 3.1 North and West Africa. In *The Fulani Empire of Sokoto* by H. A. S. Johnson (London: Oxford University Press, 1967), 241. By permission of Oxford University Press.

5

Beyond Trade and Markets

Community and Vocation

In temples God has allowed to be raised up,
and His name to be commemorated therein;
therein glorifying Him, in the mornings and evenings,
are men whom neither commerce nor trafficking
diverts from the remembrance of God
and to perform the prayer, and to pay the alms,
fearing a day when hearts and eyes shall be turned about,
that God may recompense them for their fairest works
and give them increase of His bounty.

Qur'an 24:36–38

Ibn Battuta in Mali

In the preceding chapters, attention has been drawn to the significance of al-Bakrí's way of framing the issue of the spread of Islam in West Africa, focusing on channels of trade and commerce as well as on organized political states where the religion could take shelter and establish itself through political patronage. It would be hard to overestimate the importance of this schema for our understanding of early Muslim West Africa: the society of the day would be largely unrecognizable without that framework and the accounts of it.

The veteran Arab traveler whose amanuensis described him as "the traveler of the age," Ibn Battuta visited West Africa from February of 1352 to December of 1353, and his remains the classic expression of this schema, this dual process of the spread of Islam via trade routes and organized institutions. He traveled the routes of caravans, traders, and pilgrims and found hospitality in kingdoms, towns, cities, and oases. Ibn Battuta was born at Tangier in 1304 and died in Marrakech in 1368. He collaborated on his travel account, known as the *Rihlah* (*Journey*), with his editor, Ibn Juzayy, who survived him. Ibn Juzayy's father, Muhammad b. Ahmad al-Kalbí (1294–1340), was a Málikí jurist and Qur'an scholar of Granada. Using his extensive travel experience and network of contacts and connections, Ibn Battuta not only reported on the presence of Islam but also observed and evaluated its impact on rulers and on the wider society. Ibn Battuta addressed directly and with authority this book's fundamental question—namely, the role of indigenous communities and individuals originating in the Mali Empire who were carriers and custodians of Islam. His work established the field on which this book's inquiry into the internal workings of Islam in African society is based.

Ibn Battuta set out for West Africa from Morocco, of which he gives a memorable description. He speaks of entering a mosque in Marrakech and climbing the minaret "to obtain a view of the whole town from it." That motif of using detail to grasp the whole is characteristic of Ibn Battuta's approach and style and allows him at once to engage and to compare, to experience and to generalize, while avoiding the pitfalls of using personal anecdotes as exotic stimulus and the unfamiliar as license for invention. He notes the exchange of the salt of Walata for the gold of Mali without making a caricature of the seemingly absurd idea of exchanging common salt for precious gold. After all, the trade was not simply a matter of commodities of unequal value; trade in them created a balance of economic benefits. Walata, Ibn Battuta says, "is the northernmost province of the blacks," with a representative posted by the ruler of Mali. About halfway to Mali from Walata, Ibn Battuta entered the town of Zágharí, describing its inhabitants as *wanjaráta*, a name used in numerous variations of the Manding people. From there the journey brought him to towns on the Niger that lay within Mali's jurisdiction. The people of these towns, particularly those of Jakha (Zágha), "are of old standing in Islam; they show great devotion and zeal for study."[1]

As he journeyed deep into Mali, Ibn Battuta found himself in a strongly Muslim environment. He had written beforehand and requested lodgings. He met the qádí, 'Abd al-Rahmán, whom he describes as "a pilgrim, and a man of fine character." The king at the time was Mansa Sulayman, for whose tight-fisted hospitality Ibn Battuta reserved special criticism. He complained personally to the sultan in the same terms. Although Islam had clearly taken hold in Mali, the old pre-Islamic customs remained prominent in court ritual, and here the poet-troubadours occupied a favored place. On feast days each of them would get inside a figure resembling a thrush, made of feathers and with a wooden head with a red beak. These figures stood in front of the sultan and recited poems, addressing the sultan: "This *pempi* [dais] which you occupy was that whereon sat this king and that king, and such and such were this one's noble actions and such and such the other's. So do you too do good deeds whose memory will outlive you." "I was told," Ibn Battuta continued, "that this practice is a very old custom amongst them, prior to the introduction of Islam, and that they have kept it up."[2] This describes rather well the role the *jeli* played in Manding history, as Niane and others have made clear, and shows that in the royal ceremonies the ancient ways had not been obliterated by the coming of Islam. It is one example of Islamization and Africanization proceeding as parallel currents, or the gradual interpenetration of the Islamic ritual system by African ceremonial culture. Muslims were present in the court where they witnessed traditional rituals being observed. Ibn Battuta could only sigh in befuddlement, declaring it "a ridiculous make-up," and otherwise held his fire.

What he witnessed of the lively nature of African custom left Ibn Battuta somewhat incredulous, but his incredulity was followed by the equally strong impression he had of the Islamization drive among the people. Muslim Africans, he testified, possessed admirable qualities: they were seldom unjust and had a greater abhorrence of injustice than any other people he had met. The ruler was ruthless with anyone who was guilty of the least act of injustice. There was complete security in the country, and visitors had little to fear from robbers or men of violence. The property of deceased foreigners was secured and placed in trust until its rightful heirs could claim it. The people were regular at prayer and assiduous in attending occasions of congregational devotion. They raised their children in the same spirit.

> On Fridays [the day of congregational worship], if a man does not go early to the mosque, he cannot find a corner to pray in, on account of the crowd. It is a custom of theirs to send each man a boy [to the mosque] with his prayer-mat; the boy spreads it out for his master in a place fitting him [and remains on it] until he comes to the mosque.
>
> Another of their good qualities is their habit of wearing clean white garments on Fridays. Even if a man has nothing but an old worn shirt, he washes it and cleans it, and wears it to the Friday service. Yet another is their zeal for learning the Qur'an by heart. They put their children in chains if they show any backwardness in memorizing it, and they are not set free until they have it by heart. I visited the qádí in his house on the day of the festival. His children were chained up, so I said to him, "Will you not let them loose?" He replied, "I will not do so until they learn the Qur'an by heart.[3]

This picture is consistent with this book's argument that in both Ghana and Mali there was a class of religious professionals dedicated to the propagation of Islam in study, teaching, devotion, scholarship, and public observance. Commenting on the "city" of Ghana as consisting of two towns divided between Muslims and pagans (idolaters), al-Bakrí notes that in the Muslim town there lived "salaried imams and muezzins, as well as jurists and scholars." The king lived in the pagan section some 6 miles away, enabling the coming of Islam without necessarily converting to it himself. The role of receiving the religion and cultivating it, while presiding over its diffusion in society to complete the conversion process, fell to religious professionals. The history of the expansion of Islam in Africa bears this out. "The missionaries of Islam in West Africa were clerics, not traders. Through their magico-religious services to non-Muslims, first and foremost to chiefs, they inculcated Islamic elements [in] the local society as an initial step in a long process of islamization."[4] Two distinct traditions developed: the secular establishment in towns and capital cities opened the way for the coming of Islam, and religious and clerical groups, who were often based in the countryside or in separate residential sections in towns, oversaw the training and formation necessary for providing religious services. Historians have pointed out that "all the leaders of the jihad movements in West Africa came from the countryside and not from commercial or capital towns." The call to faith "came mostly from the autonomous rural and pastoral enclaves."[5] This does not mean there was no Islam in the towns, only that the pastoral initiative lay elsewhere.

The Jakhanke and Peaceful Islam

Arabic sources on Islam in Ghana do not offer much precise detail about the relationship between the class of political rulers and the indigenous roots of the clerical tradition, pursued as a discrete, recognized instrument of Islam. By the time Arabic and other sources turn their attention to this clerical tradition, it had grown and spread, which leaves us in the dark about the origin and identity of the clerics involved. We need sources that bridge the gap between the early and the later periods. Oral traditions are indispensable when handled judiciously, both in their adopted forms in Arabic sources and in their diverse local forms. Oral traditions are valuable not as an uncritical, subjective insider's view but as an expression of the people's own sense of what they value and consider important to hand down. As with standard documentary sources, we should apply critical methods to oral traditions to obtain worthwhile information. The scholar's detached approach is not the only perspective to consider; local communities also have a stake in the interpretation of historical events.

Among the people Islamized in that early period were schoolmasters, teachers, marabouts, itinerant holy men, diviners, and pilgrims, who formed a professional guild as clerics that gave them social standing in the hierarchy of religious authority. Among the Manding of Ghana and Mali these clerics are referred to as *karamokho*, "master of *qara'ah*" (scholar). Among the Hausa they are called *malams*, among the Fulbe the *tcherno* (plural *sérnábé*), and among the Wolof of Senegal *seringe*. The tradition abounds among the Yoruba where the equivalent is the *babalawo*, the Muslim counterpart being the *alfa*. The term *alfa* (or *alufa*) is also widely used among the Manding, where it has a social meaning as elder or head of household. The term was used commonly in nineteenth-century Freetown, a free settlement for emancipated slaves and rescued captives, to designate the Muslim religious master and was adopted by the colonial administration as the Muslim counterpart to the pastor who was also schoolteacher and community superintendent. With his knowledge of the Qur'an as revealed oracle, the *alfa* acquired a mystical status as diviner, which added to his social standing.[6] As a colony for freed slaves and recaptive Africans skimmed off the high seas from slave ships, Freetown was home to a mixed population of Nova Scotian and Caribbean blacks as well as local ethnic groups. Many of those groups were Muslims escaping bondage. It is likely that the Freetown Yoruba Muslim community, significant in numbers and in influence, was the means by which the term was introduced in Nigeria, where the Yoruba mission and repatriation established a close link with Freetown.

We know from sources of later periods that the Muslim Manding and adjacent populations made a distinction among religious masters, the warrior class, and the political class, a distinction that prepared society for a class of specialist clerics to assume responsibility for religion. Clerics emerged as a religious guild alongside other local guilds. Muslims and pagans living in the same town would divide responsibility for affairs between the imam of the Muslims and the warriors and rulers from the pagan side. This was the case in the area that became the Ivory Coast. J. H. Saint-Père made similar observations for Guidimakha, where Muslim families maintained traditions distinct from those of the warrior class. Muslim religious masters provided services to the warrior/ruling families.[7] Anne Raffenel saw something similar in Senegal, Bundu, and the Galam region. Their roles were divided between the warrior group, called the Bakiri, who took charge of secular affairs, and the Muslim group, called the Saybobé (Ar. *sáhib*), devoted entirely to religion.[8] Levtzion's research in northern Ghana showed much the same pattern. Among the Gonja, the Manding warriors who invaded the area were not Muslim, but their descendants who converted to Islam became religious masters, leaving military and political affairs in the hands of the warrior class.[9] Relations between the two groups were not always cordial, with reports speaking of Muslims suffering harsh treatment at the hands of the warriors.[10] Religious persecution did little to diminish the sense of special calling for the clerics.

African Muslim sources, both documentary and oral, describe the clerical tradition as well established in society, indicating that the tradition existed contemporaneously with the first wave of Islamization of Ghana. Ibn Battuta reported that the Muslims of Jakha (Zágha) he met "are of old standing in Islam; they show great devotion and zeal for study." Scholars accept that the Zágha in question is the Diakha-Masina on the Niger. As we shall see, the trail extends across the centuries to emerge strong and vigorous in the nineteenth and twentieth. The "people of Jakha" may hold the key to understanding how an Africanized Islam was maintained and propagated in the empires of Ghana and Mali and in succeeding ages.

Historical and ethnographic investigations by several scholars have helped identify the "people of Jakha" as the Jakhanke, *ahl Zágha* in Arabic sources, "Diakhanké" or "Dyakhanké" in French accounts.[11] The Arabic *ahl Zágha* simply means "people of Jagha," although in that form it is easy to miss the professional connotations of the name. That pitfall is avoided with the name "Jakhanke" for the simple reason that it is not location-bound. Instead, it carries a distinctive religious professional meaning, though in the Jakhanke's scattered diaspora their name assumed the distinction of an ethnic status. This led historians and other scholars into claiming, inaccurately, that there is such a thing as a Jakhanke language, which is like saying that there is such a thing as a Jesuit language. No one has documented a separate Jakhanke language because no such language exists. The language spoken by the people is the same as that spoken by Serakhullé, the Soninke of other sources. The Jakhanke are Serakhulé who chose the religious vocation as clerics; it is their professional reputation alone that distinguishes them. Although historians have said that the people of Ghana were Soninke, relevant Arabic sources do not call them by that name, and this has obscured both the identity of the Jakhanke and our understanding of their professional life as religious specialists.

Clerical Prototype: Al-Hájj Sálim Suware

The origin of the name Serakhullé in relation to Soninke is discussed in the next section of this chapter. For now, we must track the history of the Jakhanke and its parallels with the history of Ghana. Recent research on the Jakhanke has revealed that the network of clerical settlements they created served as necessary institutions for their vocation. The tradition of the religious network is maintained by the chain of transmission connected to an obscure figure known in written and oral accounts as al-Hájj Sálim Suware, the founder and ancestor of that branch of the Serakhullé that broke off to pursue a missionary course. There is little doubt that Sálim Suware was a person of great charisma. His influence was felt across the whole Jakhanke diaspora; we can infer from reverence for his name that he was an outstanding leader. Oral traditions maintained among the clerics affirm him as "Mbemba Laye Suware." "Mbemba" means "patriarch" or "ancestor" in Mandinka and Serakhulle. The narrative of his early career shows him going on pilgrimage seven times. He returned to Diakha-Masina after his last pilgrimage, at which point his admiring entourage gave him the *laqab* (nickname) "su-waré" because he was mounted on a piebald horse.[12] He acquired the mystique of a towering, charismatic personality who emerged centuries later encrusted with the honor and devotion of the communities established to promote his mission. Over the long centuries and in diaspora settlements, al-Hájj Sálim Suware is regarded with high reverence as the epitome of peaceful Islam, shaped by his admirers no less than he shaped them. According to the clerical traditions, in the course of his seventh and last pilgrimage he received a dream commanding him to abandon his intention of settling in the holy precincts of Mecca as a *mjuáwir* (caretaker of a religious building) and to return to his people as standard-bearer of peaceful Islam.

The chronology for al-Hájj Sálim Suware is difficult to pin down with any degree of certainty. The chronicles and genealogies maintained by the clerics place him somewhere in the twelfth or thirteenth century, in the age of the ascendancy of Mali. Historians bring him forward as a fifteenth-century figure to help fill the gaps in their construction of the stages of Islamization of West Africa. The historian Ivor Wilks undertook a detailed reconstruction of al-Hajj Salim Suware's chronology only to conclude that it must be tied to the introduction from Egypt of a popular commentary, *Tafsír al-Jalálayn* ("Commentary of the Two Eminent Jaláls"), completed in Cairo in 1485 and allegedly brought by al-Hajj Salim Suware to West Africa on his way back from Mecca.[13] But this claim has no corroboration in contemporary sources. In his autobiography, the Egyptian scholar jurist Jalal al-Din al-Suyuti (1445–1505) spoke of al-Suyuti's works being circulated in West Africa from 1477 to 1478 and that unidentified students, including an unknown sultan and his entourage from West Africa, came to Cairo to study under him. This indicates a well-established scholarly trail from West Africa by the time of the *Tafsír al-Jalálayn*.[14]

As we describe here, the introduction in Kano from Cairo of the Maliki legal text, the *Mukhtasar* of Khalíl,[15] reputedly coincided with the visit of 'Abd al-Rahman Jakhite, a Jakhanke cleric, who arrived in Kano during the reign of Muhammad Rumfa (r. 1463–1499). It is most improbable that the Sutukho Jakhanke settlement cited in a Portuguese report in the 1450s predated al-Hajj Salim Suware who founded the vocation. Although by no means definitive, it is not implausible to suggest that the best evidence places him in the thirteenth century. Still, although by now dated, Wilks's work is the first detailed attempt at an exposition of the clerical network as a vehicle of peaceful Islamization. Leaving aside his method of dating, Wilks's description fits well with what is known of the fuller history of the tradition presented here and elsewhere.

Oral traditions claim al-Hájj Sálim as a relative, or at any rate as the religious counterpart to Magham Jabi (Diabé) Sisé, the "Soninke" founder of Wagadou between 750 and 800, the precursor of Ghana. In accounts collected and edited by Maurice Delafosse, a French colonial administrator and scholar with unusually developed anticolonial views,[16] al-Hájj Sálim is the half-brother of Magham Jabi, as befits his designation in tradition as "Diakhaba-Founé" (twin of Diakhaba).[17] We need to stress here the value of oral traditions, especially where we also have parallel written sources for comparison. The idea of Diakhaba-Founé is rooted in the tradition of parallel social institutions where the secular and the clerical sides are represented respectively by Magham Jabi and al-Hájj Sálim. We may say that just as Magham Jabi Sisé represents the state-forming political impulse of Soninke history, al-Hájj Sálim Suware represents the religious professional impulse of the Soninke. This picture of a two-prong development in Soninke history, in which the clerical vocation took hold without conflicting with Soninke political interests, is backed by sources depicting Ghana as a state in which Muslims and pagans lived peacefully in separate distinct communities.

The separation of Islam and power indicated by that arrangement is precisely what the Suwarian clerical tradition fostered; in the Soninke view, the religious vocation need not carry the obligation of jihad to be valid or feasible. Such an arrangement happens also to be conducive to trade and commerce. Spencer Trimingham, a pioneer scholar of Islam in Africa, noted the peaceful nature of the spread of Islam in this early period, aware that something like the Suwarian tradition must account for its success. He identified the dispersion character of the network of centers devoted to the spread of the religion, noting that

> Islam continued to spread by peaceful means and the Soninke of Gána have been of great significance in its propagation; the history of their dispersion, if it could be unravelled, would clear up many historical obscurities. Its acceptance by the peoples of the Sahil and Másina is due primarily to their efforts. Their traders converted and blended with the commercial and industrious Mande Dyula who carried it to the edge of the equatorial forest. By the beginning of the twelfth century, less than fifty years after the preaching of 'Abd Alláh ibn Yásín, Islamic traders had reached the south Sudan savanna and were on the verge of the routeless impenetrable forest. These Mande Dyula converted by the Soninke of Dyákha became accustomed to penetrate to the edge of the forest to buy kola-nuts, and their settlements often

became little states in the heart of the southern savanna among pagan peoples.[18]

This picture, connecting the peaceful propagation of Islam with groups originating in Jagha-Masina and the model religious communities they established, pinpoints the subject with which this study is concerned. That Islam came within close range of the "routeless impenetrable forest" requires us to move beyond al-Bakrí's model of "routes" and "kingdoms" as the framework of the introduction of Islam. The work of clerics and their social networks made the old system of dependence on rulers and caravan routes quite dispensable. As religious professionals, the clerics applied Islamic teachings in response to the opportunities and challenges of the African environment and thus helped the religion take root. The contribution of these clerics to Islam's impact on society is significant in specific ways and is discussed in depth. But first, some linguistic clarification is in order.

"Soninke" and "Serakhulle": What's in a Name?

The case for adopting the name "Soninke" for the founders of Ghana is one that modern Western scholars have made and is followed fairly consistently in French and other sources. Before proceeding with the history of the Jakhanke pacifist tradition, we review the history of the names "Soninke" and "Serakhulle." To my knowledge, early Arabic sources do not use the name "Soninke," nor do local traditions until about the eighteenth century. At that time, the first use of the name applied to pagans, who were the targets of Muslim religious wars. The *Ta'ríkh al-Súdán* ("The Chronicle of the Blacks"), a seventeenth-century history of Songhay, identifies Askiya Muhammad Ture as "Sillankí," from which translators have deduced the name "Soninke," even though that is not what the Arabic text says. [19] The same is true of the individual Mori Sálih Jawara, identified by the *Ta'ríkh al-Súdán* as a "Wa'koré" by origin but as Soninke by Hunwick in his translation.[20]

With variant spelling, the name "Serakhullé" first appeared in a sixteenth-century account by João de Barros, who says that the people so-called were engaged in long-distance trade with Cairo from the towns of Jenne and Timbuktu.[21] De Barros locates the Serakhulle (Çaragoles) in a region between the Senegal and Gambia rivers, with the Mandinka, Wolof, and the Tokolor as neighboring peoples.[22] Gaspard Mollien, the early nineteenth century French explorer, confirms this account by reporting extensively on the Serakhulle of Senegambia, saying they are prominent for their wealth and flair for trade.[23] Writing from Hausaland, Muhammad Bello (in Fula, "Billo") in his *Infáq al-Maysúr* ("Expending the Treasure"), makes reference to the "Sarankulí," giving an Arabic confirmation of the name.[24] These very different sources suggest in the first case that the name is not a nineteenth-century invention, as scholars have claimed, or that, in the second, it originated in ethnic ignorance in Senegambia, as has been contended.[25]

Initial cursory review of the sources does not reveal either a comparable early date or a corresponding geographical range for the use of the name "Soninké." Without questioning that the name has been in use among and with reference to the people known as Serakhullé in the sources, one may note the ambivalent sense it carries of non-Muslim, pagan groups. Controversy surrounds the use of the name, as Mungo Park testifies. He says that "Sonakies" are "men who drink strong liquors" (i.e., pagans). In his travels in Futa Jallon, Park reports that he came upon a community of Soninkees devoted to trade and commerce as Juula (*juula* in Manding means trader; *juulaya* is trade) and that the Muslim Fulbe went to war to compel them to convert to Islam.[26] Charlotte Quinn also discusses the confusion surrounding the name.[27] According to these sources, "Soninke" and "Muslim" are at variance, whereas the Serakhulle are Muslim. In his study of the origins of Mali, French scholar Charles Monteil speaks of the people as "Soninke" and in that setting refers to "Fode al-Hájj Suware." "Fode" is the local title for "cleric."[28] In his assessment of the origins of the Soninke, Monteil stumbled unwittingly on the tradition that it was clerical families who took charge of religion.

Although some scholars have claimed otherwise, the Serakhullé language is the same as Soninké, as I was able to determine in field interviews.[29] The close association between the name "Serakhullé" and the Islamization process underway in Ghana may have elevated the religious profile of the Serakhullé to separate them from adjacent non-Muslim Soninke populations. References to the Serakhulle go back nearly six centuries. Among the Mandinka of Senegambia, to say that someone is a Soninke is to indicate that he or she is non-Muslim, and that is how the name is used in nineteenth-century British colonial sources. The ethnic meaning was defused in the religious milieu. Writing more than two centuries ago, Mungo Park reflects that historical and common usage. Religion and history have combined to reinforce the prominence the name "Serakhullé" acquired in West Africa, from Senegambia, Jenne, and Timbuktu to nineteenth-century Hausaland. This does not, however, close the case.

Not unlike the Almoravid hypothesis, the Soninke ethnic theory, based on the idea of there being a Soninke language, is by now so routine and familiar that the uneven, speculative evidence of its historical origin has not been sufficient to dislodge it. But the theory cannot be preserved without a caveat. With that in mind, I adopt the name "Serakhulle" for reasons that have to do with the sources of its provenance, though that does not imply any intention of being final or definitive about the matter. The literature is already too saturated with the use of Soninke to justify wholesale reversion to Serakhulle, yet Serakhulle also is too well anchored in documents and usage to be overlooked in the discussion.[30] On this question, we should be flexible.

Jakhanke Pacifist Development

Ibn Battuta describes practices in the court of Mali as very old customs that existed prior to the introduction of Islam, kept up by the people. He writes as an eyewitness of the extensive, centuries-long Islamization process that had been underway in the kingdom. Rulers covered their flanks on one side with *mori-ké* (clerics) and on the other with *fina-ké* (chartered bards), an arrangement that recognized a course charted between rigid conformity to Muslim dogma and unyielding attachment to traditional religion. The resulting peaceful coexistence was a stimulus of trade, of the comingling of peoples, and of the religious vocation generally. The Jakhanke pacifist tradition originated in that kind of environment and developed with cumulative strength to serve successive generations of Muslim Africans.

Local Chronicles

The family chronicles that surfaced in site investigations offer a detailed account of the emergence of Jakhanke pacifism, and when those sources are supplemented with relevant materials in Arabic and European reports, they provide a strong picture of who the Jakhanke are and what accounts for their distinctive form of Islam. It is easy to miss this pacifist note by failing to credit the self-understanding of the clerics; the conventional historical approach had not given enough credit to that self-understanding.

In the widely disseminated chronicle *Ta'ríkh on Suware and Karamokhoba* (*TSK*), al-Hájj Sálim and his community were settled in Diakha-Masina prior to unspecified political upheavals. Due to what *TSK* defines as al-Hájj Sálim's aversion to warfare and political involvement, he and his community abandoned Diakha. *TSK* thus introduces the twin pillars of the clerical vocation: dispersion, in this case because of war, and opposition to war and politics considered repugnant to conscience. When Curtin stumbles on this dual theme in the sources and assigns economic activity as the reason, he is being unduly distracting. The standard historical approach does not give much credence to arguments of local Muslim initiative.[31] In this case, the evidence should be allowed to speak for itself. Diakha-Masina holds an important place in traditions about the wanderings of the clerics. The town "enjoyed the privileges of an inviolable centre of learning and commerce. Its early importance and its tradition of Islamic learning are confirmed by external Arabic sources as well as by Soninke and Fulani traditions."[32] The removal from Diakha is described as *hijrah* (emigration), in the same spirit as the *hijrah* of the first Muslims of Mecca. The Diakha exodus is also described by Charles Monteil, who gives what looks like the remnant of a once much longer list of al-Hájj Sálim's disciples and dependants: Salla Kébé, Baba Kamara, also called Wagé, an ancestor of the Kamara-Wagé of Kagoro, and Fa Abdullahi Marega, whose descendants dispersed to Mulline, near Kunyakari.[33] Monteil's account reads like fragments of a remembered history worn by time and confinement, much like al-Bakrí's description of the isolated Hunayhín of Ghana and the tenuous, drifting nature of memory of their Umayyad origins.

The information contained in *TSK*, on the other hand, is better organized and much more confident about detail and general outline. The list of family members and students in the Suwarian traveling entourage is far too long to include here, but it is important to note that migration and itinerancy are infused with religious meaning. Such activities are a critical component in the professional formation of the clerics. Supplemented with lists obtained in field inquiries from the leading clerics themselves, the account of al-Hájj Sálim's emigration assumes the scope of a full-scale strategic mobilization. The major dislocation it implies would be on the order of an epochal historical event, perhaps even a revolution. We return to this issue presently with evidence from an account originating from the far eastern end of the dispersion trail.

Traditional accounts trace al-Hájj Sálim's migration from Diakha-Masina to Jafunu, which was a well-established Muslim center situated on the strategic caravan route linking the Sahel with the Maghrib and beyond. We have discussed Jafunu's connection with the Almoravid Lemtúna as reported by Yáqút in the thirteenth century. The traditions say that al-Hájj Sálim spent thirty years in Jafunu. We can only speculate on al-Hájj Sálim's life and work there, but on the basis of details available for Karamokhoba and others (to be considered in chapter 8), it seems that he followed the clerical vocation of teaching, itinerancy, and devotion.

This is confirmed by what transpired in the next phase of al-Hájj Sálim's career, when he left Jafunu to found Diakha-Bambukhu on the Bafing River. The accounts of the founding of Diakha-Bambukhu may be interpreted to mean that al-Hájj Sálim was connected with the town if not as a founder then at least in the symbolic sense of anointing it as a new clerical center. Both Delafosse and Monteil, however, say that al-Hájj Sálim founded the town.[34] *TSK* is equally explicit, using the verb *assa* (to found) with respect to the relation of al-Hájj Sálim and his community to the center: *wa annahum al-mu'assisina balad zaghába al-qadím* (they founded the ancient town of Diakhaba). The "-ba" in Diakhaba is a Manding suffix and maybe an abbreviation of Bambukhu, or a word in the language meaning "great" or "ancient." It works both ways.

There is little question that Diakhaba was a Serakhulle settlement devoted to religion and to the clerical vocation. In that sense, it represents the emergence of the Jakhanke/Diakhanke (people of Jakha/Diakha) as a distinct community of religious specialists. The sources are unanimous with regard to the religious nature of the settlement, which does not mean that Diakhaba was not an important trading town as well. Clerical pacifism, we noted, was unquestionably conducive to trade and stability. *TSK* makes a similar point when it says that the community of Diakhaba was occupied with what may be called the triad of clerical life: *al-qirá'ah* (Qur'an study), *al-harth* (farming), and *al-safar* (travel or itinerancy). These domains of activity would cover a broad range of themes that together gave shape and range to the Suwarian initiative. In that connection, *safar,* for example, would include pilgrimage, diplomatic missions, educational recruitment, commercial journeys, and setting up new clerical centers, called *majális* (singular: *majlis*). Similarly, *harth* would include the acquisition and employment of slaves on farms. Slavery was a major source of labor for the clerical centers, even though it constitutes a challenge to the pacifist reputation of the clerics, as we shall see in chapters 6 and 9.

Qur'an study would include various forms of teaching and scholarship organized around religious practices prescribed in the standard curriculum, along with practices fixed in the religious calendar. Because Islam's lunar calendar diverges from the solar calendar by being shorter, the quotidian rituals and annual festivals, as well as the prescriptions of the law, are unaligned with the seasonal cycle of cultivation. "Adoption of the Islamic calendar is an important factor in breaking the link with animist cults and in the consolidation of Islam."[35] For traders and townspeople, adopting the lunar calendar involves no disruption of the normal pattern of activities. For rural Muslims, however, the choice is not so simple. They would adopt the two calendar systems, the lunar calendar for Islamic rituals and observances in civil society and the solar calendar for duties and practices in the agricultural year. Having to live life on the basis of two different calendar systems necessitates making choices because Islam's lunar obligations—the Ramadan fast, the New Year observance, and the pilgrimage to Mecca—pay no heed to the agricultural cycle. Choice involves awareness and its importance, which is where clerical leadership and guidance would factor in. Reform in this perspective would include changing values that depended on observing agrarian rites of the seasonal cycle.[36] Furnished with Scripture, daily discipline, sartorial style, and ethical rules, clerical Islam offered a persuasive religious option upheld by the values of knowledge of Scripture, tradition, regular public observance, education, and cosmopolitan advantage. This turned the initiative over to the countryside as a foyer of religious influence and practice. Edward Blyden describes the process as follows:

> The Pagan village possessing a Mussulman teacher is always found to be in advance of its neighbours in all elements of civilization. The people pay great deference to him. He instructs their children, and professes to be the medium between them and Heaven, either for securing a supply of their necessities, or for warding off or removing calamities . . . The Mohammedan, then, who enters a Pagan village with his books, and papers, and rosaries, his frequent ablutions and regularly-recurring times of prayers and prostrations, in which he appears to be conversing with some invisible being, soon acquires a controlling influence over the people. He secures their moral confidence and respect, and they bring to him all their difficulties for solution, and all their grievances for redress.[37]

The reforms at Diakhaba provided renewal and impetus of the clerical vocation. The community was divided into four main segments under the pastoral leadership of al-Hájj Sálim. The first segment was Suwarekunda, followed by Daramekunda, Fofana-Girasikunda, and Fadigakunda. Each section was assigned its own responsibility. Suwarekunda had general oversight of the clerical office, presiding over the maintenance of the vocation and supervising the day-to-day affairs of the community. Al-Hájj Sálim functioned as *imám ratti* (religious superior). Handling political relations with the rulers of Mali was also the prerogative of the Suware leaders. The Darame leaders were treated as the heirs-apparent of al-Hájj Sálim. The Fofana clan was responsible for trade and commerce and for community property. The Fadiga were responsible for student affairs: welfare, discipline, recruitment, alumni relations, student deployment, and follow-up. *TSK*, our only source on this matter, describes the heads of the four sections as *rijál al-sálihína* (the upright leaders), who, because of their devotion and sincere desire for al-Hájj Sálim's *barakah* (blessing), for themselves and their posterity, set the future course of Suwarian Islam.

As is evident in the lists, one of the major clerical lineages is the Kaba *qabílah* (clan lineage), which also takes the name of Jakhite (Zaghíte), normally combined as Kaba-Jakhite or Jakhite-Kaba. Such double-barrel assignation is common in other lineages too. The lineage originated in Bakhunu and reconstituted in Jafunu. The Kaba were part of the nucleus of al-Hájj Sálim's community in Diakhaba. They eventually spread in many different directions, with a major stream heading to Guidimakha, Gajaga, Didecoto, Bundu in Senegal, Dalafing in Mali, and Kankan in Guinea, among other places.[38] In that respect, Diakha-Madina in Dentilia was established as a result of the influx of immigrants from Diakhaba, with the Suware and the Kaba clerics assuming leadership of the center that included the Fofana-Girasi, the Jabi-Gassama, and the Jakhabi families.[39] As will be shown presently, a significant branch of the Kaba-Jakhite *qabílah* traveled eastward from Diakhaba, settling down eventually in Kano in Hausa country. In that case, the date of the Kano dispersion, which occurred in the reign of Muhammad Rumfa (d. 1499), points to a fifteenth-century timeline for the break-up of Diakhaba.

Under various designations, the profile of Diakhaba in the sources is as that of a major religious center that played an important role in the spread of Islam to the surrounding areas. The range and scope of clerics and students who left Diakhaba to settle in other areas suggest that the town was a pivotal supply link in the communication system. That it was itself a dispersion point for immigrants from Diakha-Masina means that Diakhaba was set up to foster the itinerant vocation, which is what seems to have happened. Al-Hájj Sálim was the model itinerant cleric, his legendary seven-fold pilgrimage to Mecca setting a pious record of mythic proportions. He undertook a *tournée pastorale* from Diakhaba to attend local need, and his example took hold and spread. Others followed in his footsteps as new centers and cells were established in the adjacent countryside, all of them distinguished by their adherence to the tradition of pacifist teaching. The specter of disagreement, say, over succession and inheritance among the clerics themselves, what the clerics call *wálio* (to be distinguished from *walío*, which means "saint") and what the Wolof call *werente seringe,* would precipitate removal and relocation, with the expanding trail conveying the values of religious moderation and devotion. Ivor Wilks focuses on the missionary implications of the *tournée pastorale,* saying that in a general way it allowed al-Hájj Sálim to strike out into pagan territory *(bilád al-kufr)*.[40] Everywhere he went, al-Hájj Sálim enjoined the repudiation of arms in favor of peaceful witness and moral example. He stressed the necessity of solidarity for effective pastoral work. What is clear in all this is that his emphasis on the dual heritage of Jakhanke practice—pacifist commitment and education and teaching as tools of renewal (*tajdíd*)—were among al-Hájj Sálim's most original and far-reaching contributions to African Islam. As far as we know, no one else had ever pursued this dual heritage as a desirable and viable vocation or elevated it to a self-sustaining level of communal identity, practice, and faithfulness.

Subsuming the clerical vocation of the Jakhanke under the omnibus term of "cleric" or "marabout," as has been the practice, has obscured the diverse character of the religious vocation and blurred key aspects of its particular professional application. The eclectic individual styles of an *alfa*, a *babalawo*, a *malam*, a *seringe*, a *tcherno*, and, for the Jakhanke and the Manding, a *karamokho*, are merged together with the catch-all term of "marabout." The titles typically refer to individual specialists who achieve their position by training and personal flair and, particularly in the Sufi environment, for their charismatic reputation. Even then the titles do not connote inheritance from a professional lineage, which is the sense in which in one community of Manding/Juula, Muslims understood the term. Being a *karamokho* is an achievement role. "A man is a *karamoko* (*sic*) because of his chain (*isnád*) for learning, not [because of] his chain for birth."[41]

Sometimes clerics by reputation may find themselves at the mercy of competing demands. That was the situation of Mammadu Maraamu at Sunokunda in the Gambia. Niumi and Jokadu, two districts, were on the verge of war, and Jokadu made it to the cleric first asking for protective amulets. The request came at night, and one of the cleric's wives who had conjugal rights that night took the payment for the amulets as compensation for her husband's lost company. When subsequently the messengers of Niumi arrived asking for the cleric's aid in their conflict with Jokadu, he told them, "I have exhausted all my powers on behalf of the people of Jokadu." The next of his wives whose turn it was to sleep with him that night and who saw the chance of receiving the payment of Niumi told the cleric, "it's either work for these people, or our marriage is finished!" The cleric acquiesced.[42]

The example shows how the clerical craft can create a predicament when it is made available to anyone who asks for it. But the clerical profession with its scholarly credentials suggests that there is much more to the craft than arcane prowess or conjugal interest alone. In their respective contexts, the *tcherno*, the *alfa*, the *seringe*, and the *malam* are what the Hausa would call "friars of the cowhide," those personages who take to the road lugging their goat-skin prayer rug, ablution jug, some Arabic manuscripts, and pen case, cutting the figure of a pious mendicant plying his peripatetic craft for personal gain.[43]

For the Juula Muslims, however, a *karamokho* still draws his legitimacy from being a member of Juula society: to be recognized he adopts a Manding *jamu* (salutation name), preferably that of his teacher, and takes a wife from the community. In other words, his being a *karamokho* draws him deeper into a close society of fellow *karamokhos* on the basis of a clerical vocation that is defined as much by individual achievement as by social affiliation. While the *malam* or the *seringe* is a practitioner by virtue of individual ability and personal choice, what the Wolof of Senegal call *borom bayré, borom barké*, in Mandinka *daraja-tio* and *baraka-tio*, "master of charisma, master of *barakah*," the *karamokho* is a guild member; his is the privilege of belonging, and his is the duty of promoting the tradition of *karamokhoya*. His wife and children share vicariously in the honor the guild confers (and, by conferring, sustains). The ethnic element is swallowed up in the religious profession and handed down as such. The *karamokho* becomes a *jamu*, a professional predicate: his ethnic origin notwithstanding, a *karamokho* is of the Juula.

Defined by the history of dispersion, the clerical system was al-Hájj Sálim's creation, and it represents one of his most notable contributions to Islam's pacifist impact in West Africa. The standard curriculum for training a *karamokho* includes proficiency in advanced scriptural exegesis, ethics, and religious law. Upon the completion of this course of study, students are handed a diploma and invested with a turban. At that stage the title of *karamokho* is conferred with license to establish a *majlis*. Those who wish to pursue advanced scholarship embark on a schedule of shaykh-seeking to add more links to the chain of learning. "At the completion of such further studies the *karamokho* becomes entitled to carry a staff and to wear the *burnús*, a highly decorative hooded gown. He may still choose to teach, but is likely to acquire a position as *imám, qádí* or *mufti*."[44] In this system of learning, religious solidarity had an intellectual foundation, evoking Ibn Khaldun's theory of ethnic solidarity, *'asabiyáh*. "No religious movement can succeed unless based on solidarity."[45] The assessment of al-Hájj Sálim's legacy paid tribute to him by noting that "over a large part of West Africa the institutional framework within which teaching has been organized seems largely his work, and the high esteem in which learning is held . . . must be attributed in no small part to the existence of regulations which militate against charlatanism and venality."[46]

The Clerics Move West

Diakhaba was the center and inspiration of this tradition, which was introduced by immigrants from Diakha-Masina. Monteil describes the town as an influx point for Wangara/Manding Muslims known as Jakhanke.[47] Drawing on local sources, Monteil writes that Diakhaba, what he calls Diakha-sur-Bafing, was established and run as a self-contained clerical settlement much as the first Muslim towns were established in the Upper Senegal River. He notes that Diakhaba's influence radiated out toward the Gambia River and countries to the south.[48] This observation is consistent with Jakhanke accounts claiming that under al-Hájj Sálim's leadership, the center of gravity of the clerical vocation shifted westward toward Bundu, Khasso, Senegambia, and Futa Jallon in Guinea—areas that received a large influx of people following the fall of Mali (see Figure 4.1).

Writing with respectful hindsight long after the community had dispersed, the *Ta'ríkh al-Fattásh* (*TF; Chronicle of Inquiry*) confirms the clerical influence of Diakhaba (*Ja'ba*), saying the rulers of Mali deferred to the town's independent standing. It underscores the center's religious prestige as a place of asylum for those escaping political oppression. Written at a time when the town had apparently long lost ceased to exist, *TF* continues:

> There was . . . at the time of the supremacy of Mali, a town called Diakha-Ba, a center of jurisconsults situated in the interior of the kingdom of Mali. The king of Mali never entered it and no one exercised authority there outside the *qádí*. Whoever entered the town had automatic sanctuary from harm or interference from the king. Even if he had killed one of the children of the king, the king could not exact recompense. They gave it the epithet "the city of God" (*yaqál lahu balad Alláh*).[49]

Clerical sources emphasize the fact that, thanks to al-Hájj Sálim's *barakah*, certain branches of the community emerged in Diakhaba to found the tradition as self-replenishing, self-reliant, and self-propagating. That is the reason given for how the Jakhite-Kaba *qabílah* were renowned as patrons of personal prayer (*mustajíbú al-da'wah*).[50] They produced notable *'ulamá* (scholars) and *fuqahá* (jurists). In the same vein, the Darame *qabílah* was favored with an untold number of saints, jurists, religious devotees, and scholars. They settled in the revered town of Gunjúr (Kunjúru), situated on the periphery of Bundu in Khasso in the region of Kaniaga (sometimes Kanyaga). The town at one time boasted some forty learned divines, turning it into a major intellectual center.

TF incorporated a summary of oral traditions collected from a local informant called Muhammad Siré, who appeared to belong to the Gunjúr clerical community. The character of the town as a republic seems cut out of the same pattern as Diakhaba, with which it shares the Suwarian tradition. In the description given of Gunjúr, the settlement's supreme authority is vested in the *qádí*, assisted by a council of *'ulamá*. The ruler's authority over the town was restricted to the performance of religious duties as prescribed in the calendar of rites. Each year in the month of Ramadan, the ruler of Kaniaga visited the town as the guest of the *qádí*, taking with him gifts and offerings. On the night of 26–27 of Ramadán, called "Night of Power," *laylatu-l-qadar* (Qur'an xcvii), the king ordered cooked food to be prepared, which he carried in a dish or calabash perched on his head before distributing the food to Qur'an school children assembled for the purpose. In return, the children called down blessings on the king before dispersing. The prayers of innocent children, according to tradition, are considered especially efficacious for being guileless. *TF* says this is the only occasion on which the king could enter the town.[51] This precaution of restricting the ruler to observing humble rituals brings to mind what the Qur'an says about "Kings, when they enter a city, disorder it and make the mighty ones of its inhabitants abased" (Qur'an 27:34).

Roused to defend the honor of his fellow Muslim Africans against the stigma of enslavement by Muslim raiders, Ahmad Baba (1556–1627) of Timbuktu, who was charged with sedition by the invading Moroccan forces and taken into captivity from 1594 until 1608, pointed to Diakha-Bambukhu as a leading Islamic settlement with oversight of "twenty villages, all of them Muslim unmixed with any unbeliever." Ahmad Baba's description is reminiscent of the clerical cells examined in this book; the fact that Ahmad Baba identified Diakha-Bambukhu indicates that he was familiar with the clerical tradition that developed there. The family names Ahmad Baba listed for these religious enclaves are Jakhanke. He highlighted Jafunu and Gunjúr as exemplary Muslim centers.[52] His list of eminent African Muslim patronymics draws explicitly on the clerical communities of our description. In the first tier of leading Islamic families were the Suware, the Darame, Fofana, Fadiga, Kaba, Silla, Sise, Jakhite, Jaghu, Sisokho, and Gassama, among others. His second tier comprised a longer list of Islamized patronymics.[53] This list is virtually identical to that of *TSK* noted earlier and *TBI* later, with the difference that *TSK* expands on the names on the list.

If we place Ahmad Baba's list in the broader context of the Suwarian tradition, it fits into a recognizable historical pattern. We should again stress that clerical separation from politics is not sectarian. The clerics did not condemn others, religious or secular, as corrupt and illegitimate. The clerical practice is not the radical politics of the infallible conscience that claims immunity from lawful authority on the grounds that the individual's saved status bestows the right to repudiate society. The clerics avoid the irony of virtue feeding off the vice it deplores by demonstrating that the peace they seek is not for pronouncing an anathema on others but for showing that commitment to tolerance is commitment, too, to the community. Their professional vocation is grounded in a shared tradition, not in a pretext to break fellowship with others.

For the clerics, the religious life and the affairs of the world are not separate, which is not to suggest that they are identical. The state cannot afford to ignore religion as a moral force or to co-opt it as a mere instrument of policy. At Gunjúr, this complex relationship was affirmed and ratified when once a year the ruler came as a pilgrim, indicating how the clerics acknowledged the connection with power without surrendering the pastoral initiative; in turn, the ruler recognized the religious constraint on power without giving up his title. Religion acted as a shield to prevent power from turning tyrannical and in other ways extending its reach without moral challenge. Contact with rulers should not, and did not, involve ingratiating oneself with them. The legal instruments needed to institutionalize this complex arrangement did not exist, which must qualify our judgment here. That notwithstanding, the Suwarian clerical teaching that the duties believers owed to God were not a matter of political concession or favor, nor a justification for sectarian separation, represents an important step in the cause of moderation. As *imán*, faith is not political calculation but an attribute of conscience.

Sutukho and the Jabi Gassama Revival

The Jabi-Gassama clerical segment developed in similar circumstances, assuming a major role in the Suwarian tradition. Oral traditions and the clerical chronicles claim that the founder of the Jabi-Gassama clerics, Mama Sambu Gassama ("Sambu" is the Jola corruption of "Shu'aybu"), eventually brought his community into agreement with al-Hájj Sálim's peaceful way when they both lived in Jafunu. When al-Hájj Sálim left for Diakhaba, Mama Sambu moved his community to northern Senegambia, where he founded a center at Sutukho in the district of Wuli; his grave is preserved there. Wuli on the north bank and the neighboring state of Kantora on the south bank, situated some 300 miles from the mouth of the River Gambia, are described in fifteenth-century Portuguese sources. Diogo Gomes (d. 1500), the Portuguese navigator, explorer, and writer, was the first European to visit the region in the 1450s, and his account indicates that Wuli at the time had ascendancy over Kantora. Gomes visited Sutukho, reporting that the area was under the suzerainty of the king of Mali.[54] Writing in 1508, Duarte Pacheco Pereira noted that Sutukho was the principal town of the district, with a population of some four thousand inhabitants. A trade fair was held in the town "to which the Mandinguas [Mandinkas] bring many asses."[55] A brisk trade in European goods takes place there, where five to six thousand "doubloons of good gold are brought from there to Portugal." The language spoken is Mandinka.[56]

The account of André Álvares de Almada, written in 1594, is the first to pay close attention to the distinctive clerical character of certain towns. Almada describes the class of traveling clerics known as "devout *bixirins*" (Ar. *bashírún*, evangelists), who live in secluded "large major establishments," corresponding, he says, to monasteries, "which arouse great religious feeling and devotion in the blacks, and in which these 'monks' live, and (also) those who are studying to become *bixirins*." One of these "large major establishments" is Sutukho (Sutuco) whose leading cleric assumes the position of an abbot or provincial.[57]

Almada describes the work of the clerics: writing in bound books "which they make themselves." The clerics are worn thin

> by their abstinencies, their fasts and their dieting . . . They wear long clothes, and over these capes and tippets of baize or leather, with large black and white hats, which are brought them by our traders. They make their ritual prayers with their faces turned towards the east. . . . They recite their prayers all together.

Almada concludes by saying that the clerical centers are separated from the general population, despite the fact that as Muslims they have certain practices and observances in common with the general population.[58]

Sutukho's clerical standing is described in considerable detail by Richard Jobson, the English adventurer, who traveled up the Gambia River in 1620. The hands-on observations of the Portuguese navigator, explorer, and writer Diogo Gomes (d. 1500) have never been appropriately introduced into discussion because, until now, scholars (myself included) have not understood that his report offers a breakthrough on the history of clericalism. This in spite of Jobson's explicit statement that he had come upon a very well-defined tradition of Islamic clerical practice quite distinct from what is evident in conventional Muslim communities. I had to consult field notes obtained in the investigations for this book to appreciate the significance of Jobson's report. The structure of the religious life of the clerics that Jobson describes appears too deeply entrenched to be a case merely of local idiosyncrasy, and it is fortunate that Jobson stayed close and long enough with the subject to give us details consistent with what we know of similar centers from other sources across the centuries.

Jobson describes the public authority of Sutukho as the "high Priesthood" that presides over fellow clerics, Jobson's "Mary-buckes" (marabout).[59] The Sutukho clerics and their families are separated from the general population not by religion but by the professional clerical style. Jobson notes what he called "the habitations and course of lives" of the clerics

> concerning whom I have with diligence observed, that in their whole proceeding they have a wonderous reference, to the leviticall law, as it is in our holy Bible related; the principals whereof they are not ignorant in, for they do report concerning Adam and Eve . . . talking of Noahs flood, and of Moses . . . their houses or dwellings are separated from the common people, having their Townes and lands set out in severall within themselves, wherein no common people have dwelling, except such as are their slaves, that worke and labour for them, which slaves they suffer to marry and cherish the race that comes of them, which race remains to them, and their heires or posterity as perpetuall bondmen; they marry likewise in their owne tribe or kindred,

> taking no wives, but the daughters of Mary-buckes, and all the children they have, are nourished and bred up, unto to the ceremonies of their fathers.[60]
>
> But for the number of their wives and women, they have selfe course, that I described before among the Kings, and temporall people, in the like manner amongst them, every man in his dignity, and precedence having more or lesse: wherein there is no severed towne but hath a principall, for better relation whereof, I will declare unto you the towne and place, where there especiall, or, as I may say, high Priest doth dwell.
>
> The Towne is called Setico, lying from the River side some three miles: to this Towne I went, having occasion in following of our Trade, lye with my boate so neere as I could come, my Guide or Conductor, was one of my blacke people I hired, called Fodee Careere, who in his profession was a Mary-bucke.[61]

Jobson goes on to describe in detail his meeting with the town's leading cleric, Fode Bram (Ibrahim?), offering observations on religion, education, learning, and the social life and customs of the people. Illness had at the time confined Fode Bram to bed, but Jobson's guide insisted that he go and meet him, for courtesy demanded no less. Upon arriving at the compound, Jobson found a concourse of clerics at the house waiting on their dying leader. After the presentation of gifts, the order was given for Jobson to be introduced to the leader, who

> caused himself to be lifted up from his bed, or mat whereon he lay, sitting on the side whereof, supported and helde up by three of his wives, he sent out to have me brought unto to him, and after our salutations past, he held me fast by the hand, giving me many thankes, for that present he had received, bemoneing much his sicknesse hindered him, he could not accompany me, thereby to show his respect unto me, during our conference he cause a dinner to be made ready.[62]

After dinner, Jobson decided to embark on a tour of the town that he described as "the greatest Towne, or place, that I had seene, and the manner thereof in my opinion, was worthy the observation."[63] The town had a large street that joined the houses, the walls of their compounds, and their barns close together. Jobson said the diameter of the town was about a mile and that the clerics possessed cattle and asses, the latter put to much use in their work.

The company seemed to stir in Jobson a current of contemplation concerning the role religion played in the life and work of the clerics, for he concluded that attachment to religion accounted for his gracious reception as a non-Muslim by these gentle vicars of the spiritual life. About that hospitality he singled out an elderly cleric, Muhammad, "who was ever a faithful and loving neighbour unto us . . . and did diverse times lodge and entertaine strangers, that came, especially of his owne profession."[64] The clerics, Jobson said, worship the one and true God much as the English do; they pray to this God and call on His name constantly; they harbor no images or pictures of God or of any divine beings, which they regard as abhorrent; they profess faith in Muhammad and circumcise their children; they observe Friday as their Sabbath; and they divide the days of the week by name. While they observe the special religious obligation of Friday, they do not, however, treat it as a day of rest but instead "on that day will they follow any Trade, they will have with us, and their owne occasions: without any intermission."[65]

They instruct their children in religion, Jobson adds, teaching them to read and write. For this purpose, because paper is too scarce and perishable for routine consumption, they use "a small smooth board, fit to hold in their hands, on [which] the childrens lessons are written with a kinde of blacke incke they make, and the pen is in a manner of a pensill." The language of instruction is Arabic, and much effort goes into inculcating Arabic learning in the clerics' children, though not so much in the children of ordinary Muslim families, Jobson observed.[66]

The ailing cleric died the day after Jobson visited him, and Jobson describes the steps taken for the elaborate funeral and for the succession. The details, including the rules of hereditary succession, show the clerical community to be a tightly knit guild, with families united in support and continuity of the pastoral profession. The entire community mobilized for the funeral; the network was used to spread the news and to organize the events connected with the obsequies. The clerical dispersion trail linked those clusters of minor cells lodged in remote districts and sustained by periodic visits, gifts, and donations. An event like the funeral of a *majlis* leader (*majlis* signifies a clerical center) reverberates throughout the network of interconnected cells to alert and convene the community in mourning, tribute, and rededication. In this case, mourners came from near and far, lugging "beeves, others goates, and cockes and hennes, with rice, and all sort of graine the country yielded, so as there came in a wonderfull deale of provision, my Mary-bucke entreated mee, to send something of sweet savour, to be cast upon his body, which the people much esteeme of."[67] "This assembly held," Jobson continues,

> for the space of ten days, with a continuall recourse, of coming and going, but not altogether for the burial of the dead; for after certayne days were spent in the celebrating of his Obsequies, then beganne a great solemnitie, for the establishing and investing of his eldest sonne in his place and dignities: whereunto came agayne many gifts and presents.[68]

Jobson commented on people bringing valuable and expensive gifts for the occasion, including rams considered special. The sacrifice of a ram was deemed appropriate on the occasion of the investiture of a *majlis*, as was the case this time. "I understood likewise, that in their high Priesthood, the sonne succeeded the father, & this of course is held amongst their Religious orders, wherein they differ from the temporall governments."[69]

Evidence of such a strong religious culture ensconced in remote Africa inspired Jobson to make comparisons, first with parallel arrangements of political authority and secular culture, and second with the influence of religion in his own home country. The approval of his Muslim African hosts regarding his religious standing among them, he said, was proof that the clerics would not dismiss his religion and that of his kind. Jobson was deeply moved by what he saw of the Sutukho *majlis* and the center's paths of learning and devotion. It is clear from Jobson's account that the standard was set by his Muslim hosts, and he responded accordingly.

The spectacle detained him. He writes in one place that although he must attend to necessary matters of trade and commerce for the benefit of his sponsors, he was constrained, nevertheless, to beg his readers' indulgence to be allowed to record his admiration for the intellectual commitment of the clerics, the evidence for which lay about him like the clear light of day. He pleads:

> onely it is necessary, I part not obruptly (*sic*) from my religious company, and to acquaint you that they have great books, all manuscripts of their Religion, and that we have seene, when companies of Marybuckes have travelled by us, some of their people laden therewith, many of them being very great, and of a large volume, which travel of theirs, it is most necessary I acquaint you withal, in regard from then proceedes, a great deale of intelligence we have, and I may not passe one virtue of theirs, the narration whereof, may make their intelligence more respected, and in my poore opinion carry alongst a better esteeme.[70]

This kind of admiration for the clerics by travelers and other observers, dating back that early, parallels that of the Arabic chronicles in descriptions of similar clerical centers, including Diakhaba. Remarkably, Jobson's admiration echoes that of chronicles with their own Islamic outlook, showing the vitality of the tradition on its own terms.

Other travelers have commented in similar terms on the pervasive influence of religion among Muslim Africans and the care taken to inculcate religious knowledge, which is consistent with the deep roots as well as the extent of the spread of Islam. The African manifestation presented Europeans with a kinder, gentler face of the religion than the controversial image handed down from the era of the Crusades and revived under colonial rule.[71] During his travels in the same region as Jobson, Mungo Park comments on the leading cleric in the context of local hospitality.

> The schoolmaster, to whose care I was entrusted . . . was a man of mild disposition and gentle manners . . . although he himself adhered strictly to the religion of Mahomet, he was by no means intolerant in his principles towards others who differed from him. He spent much of his time in reading; and teaching appeared to be his pleasure, as well as employment.[72]

The schoolmaster in question possessed in his library a variety of manuscripts purchased from Moors and others copied by hand with great care. Gauging from their knowledge of Scripture, the Muslim teachers were in possession of Arabic versions of the Old Testament and could speak knowledgeably about "our first parents [Adam and Eve]; the death of Abel; the deluge; the lives of Abraham, Isaac, and Jacob; the story of Joseph and his brethren; the history of Moses, David, and Solomon, etc. All these have been related to me in the Mandingo language, with tolerable exactness, by different people."[73] Edward Blyden observed hospitality and peacefulness during his field inquiries in West Africa in the nineteenth century.

> The Mandingoes are an exceedingly polite and hospitable people. The restraints of their religion regulate their manners and control their behavior. Both in speech and demeanour, they appear always solicitous to be *en regle*—anxious to maintain the strictest propriety; and they succeed in conforming to the natural laws of etiquette, of which they seem to have an instinctive and agreeable appreciation.[74]

It struck Park, as it had struck Jobson, that although Africans had an appreciation for the wealth and power of Europeans, Muslims among them "think but very lightly of our superior attainments in religious knowledge."[75] White traders, Park added dishearteningly, did not help the cause by keeping aloof from the people, a suggestion that trade by itself would not narrow the cultural gap—it might even widen it.

Jobson reported on evidence of trade with the Portuguese on the coast and with Berber Arabs to the north. Jobson received information in Sutukho about the custom of dumb barter, salt for gold, which was practiced inland. When Jobson pressed for the cause of the prickly secrecy surrounding the trade, his informant "made a signe unto his lippe, and could receive no farther answer." Even if Jobson were able to barge his way up river, he would be prevented from tracking the source of the gold, he was told.[76]

From Sutukho to Didecoto

Jobson's picture of life at Sutukho captures some of the salient features and rhythms of a clerical center and the prominent place occupied there by education and learning. His account also confirms the role of the Jabi *qabílah* in the transmission of al-Hájj Salim's legacy. It was, however, under the leadership of the seventh-generation descendent of Mama Sambu, who presided over the expansion of the Jabi-Gassama *qabílah* from Sutukho to Didecoto in Bundu, that the initiative faltered in Sutukho. (In the time of my visit to Sutukho the town had been under the pastoral care of al-Hájj Ba Jakhite. The town was in decline, and, complaining of the neglect of the heritage by the authorities, Ba Jakhite made no reference to the possible revival of Sutukho. His resignation was a measure of how far the center had declined.) Under Muhammad Fátuma the community expanded and flourished in Didecoto, where their fortunes became intertwined with the career of Malik Sy, the seventeenth-century Tokolor leader of Futa Toro.[77] Critics of Jabi-Gassama's bid for a share in al-Hájj Sálim's clerical prestige are quick to pounce on this political association as evidence of the compromise that can be traced to Mama Sambu's warrior days. The most important development since the founding of Diakhaba emerged from the Didecoto Jabi-Gassama community. Assuming the initiative once held by Sutukho, Didecoto became the nerve center of missionary initiatives in many of the surrounding districts and beyond, in a trail cutting across to Senegal and the Casamance. As is discussed later in some detail, the sequel to Didecoto was the deployment of the mobile pacific vocation in one of its most brilliant phases and the long-delayed fulfillment of the promise made to al-Hájj Sálim in the dream he had at Mecca bidding him to return to Africa.

Oral traditions are ambivalent on the subject of the claim that the Jabi-Gassama *qabílah* embraced the pacifist way at the same time as al-Hajj Salim Suware, indicating that the pacific commitment was not a universal cause among the Serakhulle at this time. The ambivalence may also be for reasons of professional rivalry, with the Suware *qabílah* unwilling to concede equality with the Jabi-Gassama whose star was set to rise. Even as late as the 1970s, I found evidence in the field of lingering suspicion about the legitimacy of claims that Mama Sambou was al-Hájj Sálim's companion with respect to his role in establishing the tradition. For their part, the Jabi-Gassama clerics are unwilling to retreat from the moral argument for the pacifist calling, which inclines them to bring the career of the founder of their lineage into congruity with the emergence of Suwarian clericalism.[78] All of that concedes al-Hájj Sálim's primacy for the tradition, but equally also the jealousy for the tradition. The question is how soon or how wholeheartedly other branches of the Diakha community joined the pacifist community of clerics, not whether the cause was just and tenable.

The sources are candid about this, as they would be, since the Suwarian prescription is by no means the generally accepted way of following Islam. That is what makes Jakhanke Islam so remarkable—and, in retrospect, its preservation over the centuries so impressive. Instead of thinning the ranks, dispersion mobilized and expanded the clerical vocation, spreading the founder's public teaching that peace and moderation best express the vocation of religion, not strife and violence. The Muslim *ummah,* the Qur'an stipulates, is the community of the middle course, not that of extremism (2:137). The *ummah* is the moral community subject to renewal by pastoral instruction and mediation. Pacifist teaching contends that warfare does not spare religion; it is a contradiction to make warfare necessary for religion. Spilling blood as a holy cause will turn converts into stained trophies and worldlings. Scripture affirms that understanding when it declares, "there is no compulsion in religion." (Qur'an 2: 257) Pacifist clerics are invested in religion, they testify, but not in coercive means of pursuing religion.

Examples in abundance include the Kunta Arabs and certain Berber tribes. These tribes are cells of Sufi-leaning devotion, eschewing the common path and worldly affairs; however, as Jamil Abun Nasr has shown, they are not model pacifist communities. They often competed with men of power to be regarded as the legitimate inheritors of the legacy of the Prophet and his religious ideals.[79] As we know from the history of the Qádiríyah and the Tíjániíyah, among others, the Sufi orders figured prominently in militant movements of change and resistance. The Qádiríyáh was founded in the name of 'Abd al-Qádir al-Jíláni of Baghdad of the eleventh century and became one of the most successful widespread Sufi orders in Islam. Through Ahmad al-Bakka'i al-Kunti (d. 1504) of the Kunta Arabs of the western Sahara, the tradition came to West Africa in the sixteenth century to emerge as the preeminent order until later in the nineteenth century when the Tíjániíyáh, an eighteenth-century North Africa order, arrived to challenge it in the hands of al-Hajj 'Umar al-Fútí, the architect of the order in West Africa. The Tíjániíyah order stresses a stricter code of conduct than the Qádiríyah, such as a prohibition on smoking, drinking alcohol, lying, corruption, and, in north Nigeria, a ban on *bōri,* the cult of spirit possession among the Hausa.[80] What distinguishes Suwarian Islam is that it mostly succeeded in securing the respect and acceptance of political rulers without compromise of its pacifist tenets. Many rulers were not averse to adopting or backing jihad yet conceded the legitimacy of the Suwarian pacifist counter-narrative.

A severe test awaited the clerics in the form of colonial penetration, but what emerged from the ashes of that historic debacle would vindicate al-Hájj Sálim's memory as vicar of peace and moderation. The history of clerical dispersion is marked by cycles of settlement and dispersion, a pattern in which domicile and exile help equally to maintain consolidation and transmission. It is not a negligible achievement that al-Hájj Sálim's teachings endured through them both.

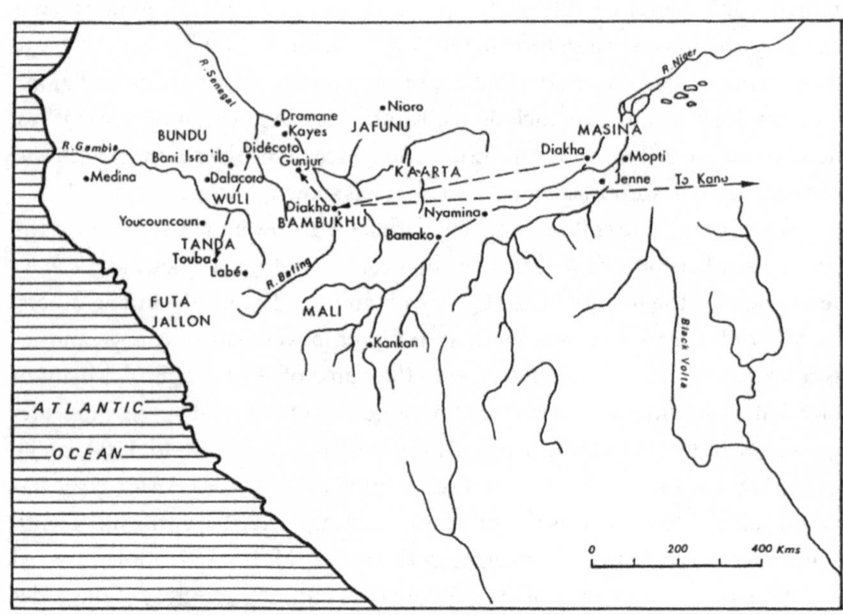

Figure 4.1 Jakhanke Dispersions. Created by the author.

6

Beyond Homeland

Religious Formation and Expansion

> All men are truly said to be tenants at will and it may as truly be said that all have a lease of their lives, some longer, some shorter, as it pleases the great Landlord to let. All have their bounds set, over which they cannot pass. . . . The certainty that that time will come, together with the uncertainty, how, where, and when, should make us to number our days as to apply our hearts to wisdom, that when we are put out of these houses of clay we may be sure of an everlasting habitation that fades not away.
>
> —Anne Bradstreet (d. 1672)

ʿAbd al-Rahmán Jakhite in Kano

A recently discovered Arabic chronicle dating back to the seventeenth century has revealed a hitherto unknown expansion of the clerical movement from Diakhaba bearing east to Kano, and it confirms the greater West African scope of the Suwarian tradition. The chronicle, *Asl al-Wanqarayín* ("The Origin of the Wangara"), is significant because it describes a fairly large-scale, long-range dispersion for reasons that are ostensibly entirely religious. This lends support to the idea that the leaders concerned were involved in a religious mission: Why else would a group of Wangara (Manding) strangers uproot and head for a foreign land with no apparent ethnic or economic appeal? Once we factor in the Suwarian tradition of dispersion as a religious vocation, we can shed light on the community and events described by the *Asl al-Wanqarayín* (*AW*).

According to *AW*, the dispersion originated in Bambukhu with a community of emigrants descended from an unnamed shaykh—the religious basis of their identity. All signs point to al-Hájj Sálim as the shaykh in question, as the identity of the leader of the dispersion makes clear: he is ʿAbd al-Rahmán Jakhite of the Kaba lineage (Ar. "Zaite" or "Zaghite"). He and his followers left Mali in the year AH 835 (1431–1432 AD) purportedly for the pilgrimage, though the size of the immigration party indicated plans to resettle in a place well short of Mecca. *AW* describes the company of the Wangara pilgrims as 3,636 erudite scholars (*al-'ulamá al-mutafannin bi-kulli fannin*).[1]

The scale of the mobilization alarmed the ruler of Mali. Fearing a brain drain from the flight of scholars from his kingdom,[2] he pressed 'Abd al-Rahmán to delay or to abort his plans and arranged for a barrier at the river crossing to prevent the pilgrims from proceeding. 'Abd al-Rahmán and his party made it to Kano nonetheless. The scholarly nature of the traveling party and the fact that they tarried in Kano indicate that the Mecca pilgrimage idea was a ruse: a whole community of family and dependents does not set out for *hajj* in this fashion. The real intention was to embark on *hijrah*, not to undertake the *hajj*. From the large-scale removal from Bambukhu, we can only infer that Bambukhu had peaked and was fragmenting, a notion further substantiated by reports of dispersions from Bambukhu to areas in Khasso, Bundu, and adjoining regions.

Accompanied by his community, including his wives, Sise and Kebe, four sons, three daughters, and three brothers, 'Abd al-Rahmán took up residence in Kano at about the same time 'Abd al-Karím al-Maghílí (d. 1505) visited the city, though this is difficult to reconcile with the chronology of *AW*. At any rate, al-Maghílí recognized 'Abd al-Rahmán as an outstanding scholar. 'Abd al-Rahmán had learned by heart the Málikí jurisprudential work of al-Tanúkhí (d. 854 AD), *al-Mudawwana al-Kubrá*, and his scholarly reputation brought him to the favorable attention of the ruler of Kano, Muhammad Rumfa (r. 1463–1499). [3] Sultan Rumfa interceded with 'Abd al-Rahmán to abandon his pilgrimage vows and stay in Kano under royal patronage, which 'Abd al-Rahmán agreed to do.[4] By then, 'Abd al-Rahmán could have been in no doubt about Rumfa's sincerity as a host, if that was ever in question.

'Abd al-Rahmán's decision to accept political patronage hints at a departure from the Suwarian tradition of political neutrality, but it was consistent with Suwarian adherence to the religious vocation without a separatist stigmatization of politics. He resumed pastoral oversight of his community in a social setting that put much store in his moral leadership. By all indications, Islam had penetrated Kano by this stage. According to the *Kano Chronicle*, the religion was brought there in the reign of Yájí (1349–1385), though the *Kano Chronicle* conflictingly states that the person who brought Islam was the same 'Abd al-Rahmán Jakhite. [5] This conflict may have arisen from scribal conflation; the older *AW* tradition was circulating in fragments, but the author of the *Kano Chronicle* had no access to it and incorporated other sources instead. Alternatively, the *Chronicle* may be indicating the general idea that it was elements from Mali who introduced Islam in the city, which does not conflict with *AW*. Be that as it may, the Islamic impact in Kano was far from complete by the time of 'Abd al-Rahmán, and Rumfa claimed him to strengthen the royal hand. 'Abd al-Rahmán spawned a charismatic reputation in Kano based on devotion to Qur'an study and related religious exercises. The accounts tell us that he was commissioned to cut down a tamarind tree on the site of a pagan cult. To seal the Islamic triumph, he built a mosque for Friday worship on the site.

His sojourn in the city coincided with the introduction of the standard Máliki legal text, the *Mukhtaṣar* of Khalíl, thanks to a visiting shaykh from Cairo. A blind old man by this time, 'Abd al-Rahmán asked to meet the shaykh for what turned out to be an intellectual duel. Perhaps 'Abd al-Rahmán wanted to preempt any challenge to his moral authority and so requested a public meeting to confirm his standing in the eyes of the people. Elaborate preparations were made for the meeting, advance notice was given, and the visiting shaykh was told to roll up his sleeves for the task at hand. The *AW* says that he passed a sleepless night in study. The following day, 'Abd al-Rahmán arrived in the compound of the visitor. The Cairene recited from memory a portion of *al-Mukhtasar.* 'Abd al-Rahmán listened attentively, interrupting the recitation at one point to allege a deviation from the text. He was found to be correct. His claim to superior knowledge appropriately vindicated, 'Abd al-Rahmán rose to mount his horse, assisted by the humbled Cairene.

Under all this public display is a pattern that runs through the story of Islam's influence in society: scholarship, teaching, and the transmission of learning. This scholarship has a propensity for localization, far more stabilizing and enduring than the all-or-nothing, muscular way of jihad. Islamic classical writers place education at the center of Muslim society and for that reason see it an obligation of religion. Burhán al-Dín az-Zarnújí (d. 1223), a scholar from Turkistan, cited a poet in saying that knowledge requires of the one who serves it that he should make everyone the servants of knowledge.[6] The Qur'an declares that those who surround the throne of God cry out: "Our Lord, Thou embracest everything in mercy and knowledge" (Qur'an 40:7) Regarded as the most authoritative writer on the philosophy of Islamic education, al-Ghazali wrote in his *Ayyuha al-Walad* ("O Son!") that the sum total of learning is to know the meaning of obedience and service to God.[7] Standing firmly in that tradition, 'Abd al-Rahmán was a model of scholarship and devotion, and he showed how law and devotion could challenge and invigorate commitment to Islam's spiritual heritage. His presence in Kano along with the Egyptian visitor showed how the religious trail connected Muslims across vast distances, a reminder that travel had a long-standing association with religion and scholarship. On the threshold of Islam's breakthrough in Kano, and without political prescription, two scholars met as religious masters to spar and to spur the process of conversion. In African hands, Islam would rise by learning and devotion, not by fire and the sword.

'Abd al-Rahmán died in Kano, though we do not know in what year. We do know that he predeceased Muhammad Rumfa, who died in 1499 after expressing a pious wish for burial at the side of 'Abd al-Rahmán "so that I might obtain his *barakah*" (*la'allí ajidu barakátuhu*).[8] After so many revolutions in the fortunes of the city, it is equally difficult to say how much of the Suwarian tradition Kano was able to conserve. An epicenter of the nineteenth-century jihad of 'Uthmán ibn Fúdí, better known as Shehu Usuman dan Fodio (d. 1817), Kano emerged as an intellectual center under British colonial rule. In time Kano was host to several different Islamic influences, including the Tijániyáh brotherhood from Senegal, and Wahhabi ideas that caused considerable friction with Sufi notions and practices.[9]

Kano in Hausaland lies well outside the orbit of ancient Mali, so we would not expect Hausaland to be affected directly by the fallout from events in Mali. The fifteenth-century dispersion of the Suwarian community of 'Abd al-Rahmán is one of the few indications of known contact. The size of the clerical dispersion is also a sign of the scale of the breakup of Diakhaba and an indicator of similar dispersions to areas much closer to the town.

Bundu Interlude: The Silla *Qabílah*

The Suwarian legacy in Kano has more or less faded into obscurity, but that is not the case in other areas. The region of Jafunu and the adjacent country of Bundu were among the most prominent for the Suwarian tradition. A major carrier of this tradition is the Silla *qabílah* whose center, called Baní Israíla (children of Israel), hints at an ancient Semitic connection. It is past time to test this perplexing Semitic hypothesis definitively, but this is not the occasion.[10] The Silla chronicle, *Ta'ríkh Baní Isrá'ila* ("Chronicle of the Silla Community of Baní Isrá'ila") tells the story of the founder of the lineage, Fode al-Hasan, present at Diakhaba where "our ancestor al-Hájj [Sálim] Suware brought together all the lineages (*ansáb*), among them the Silla, the Suware, the Darame, Jakhabi, Gassama, Sise, Kaba, Fadiga, Ture, and Fofana and others" (folio 1).

Under their leader, the Silla clerics left Diakhaba and arrived in Bundu, where they founded the new settlement of Baní Isráila, probably at the same time 'Abd al-Rahmán Jakhite and his community were settling in Kano. Sources on the contemporary history of the settlement are scarce, and by the time any firm records emerged, Baní Isráila had become a major artery of the regional trade. Mungo Park visited Baní Isráila for two days and described it as a "Serawoolli" town and as the principal town of the district. He noted slave traffic passing through it. The trader with whom he traveled was a native of Baní Isráila but had for three years been seeking his fortune abroad. Park comments on the trader's homecoming welcome as well as how traders used information on slave price fluctuation to time their commercial journeys. Yet the country in which Park was traveling was not a commercial corridor in the usual sense of the term. It was agricultural country and had the commensurate concentration of population. Traded goods included native iron and shea butter, both regional commodities in the agricultural economy, native iron for making farm implements, and shea butter. There was in the same area a town Park called Kirwani (Qayrawán), where agriculture was the principal occupation. Park describes it thus:

> This town stands in a valley, and the country, for more than a mile round it, is cleared of wood, and well cultivated. The inhabitants appear to be very active and industrious, and seemed to have carried the system of agriculture to some degree of perfection, for they collect the dung of their cattle into large heaps during the dry season, for the purpose of manuring their land with it at the proper time. I saw nothing like this in any other part of Africa. Near the town are several smelting furnaces from which the natives obtain very good iron. They afterwards hammer the metal into small bars, about a foot in length and two inches in breadth, one of which bars is sufficient to make two Mandingo hoes.[11]

In the 1720s Pierre Labat reports traversing the country Park would later cross, describing the neighboring town Gunjúr as "a republic of clerics." The contiguity of these clerical centers indicates active communication among them in the sense that the Daramé religious family of Gunjúr, the Silla of Baní Isrá'ila, and the Jabi-Gassama of Didecoto shared the pacifist teaching that created their common and shared vocation. The *Ta'ríkh al-Fattásh* (*TF; Chronicle of Inquiry*) mentions a Baní Isráila in Masina with horticultural traces of a once-flourishing but by then defunct Jewish community.[12] Whatever the connection with its namesake in Bundu, the name of this Masina settlement suggests that its associated memories were familiar in clerical circles, regardless of a possible racial designation. The country setting of these centers was given to subsistence agriculture, augmented with some trading activity. According to Jobson's description, the grain barns of Sutukho are evidence of the practice of crop husbandry in an environment able to support it. The soils of the riverain alluvial plains of Senegambia continue to be prime farmlands.

This was the attraction of Bundu: a climate enabling agriculture and prosperous settlements. If Bambukhu can be considered "the Peru of Africa," because of its gold, Bundu can be reckoned its granary.[13] "The soil in the valleys of the river banks is extremely fertile, and the regions of Tiali and Nieri are considered by the Almamys of Bundu as a storehouse of abundance."[14] The dimensions of Bundu are given as 90 miles east to west and 60 miles north to south (see Figure 6.1). The region produced corn in four varieties, rice, pumpkins, watermelons, gourds, sorrel (*Rumex acetosa*), onions, tobacco, red pepper, pistachios, cotton, and indigo.[15] Park describes Bundu's geography and location as follows:

> Bondou is bounded on the east by Bambouk; on the south-east and south by Tenda, and the Simbani wilderness; on the south-west by Woolli; on the west by Foota Torra, and north by Kajaaga.
>
> The country, like that of Woolli, is very generally covered with woods, but the land is more elevated, and towards the Falemé river, rises into considerable hills. In native fertility the soil is not surpassed, I believe, by any part of Africa.[16]

On the religious status of Bundu Park makes some cogent observations, corroborated by others and pertinent to the tradition of clerical moderation. He says the people are Muslim,

> and the authority and laws of the Prophet are everywhere looked upon as sacred and decisive. In the exercise of their faith, however, they are not very intolerant towards such of their country-men as still retain their ancient superstitions. Religious persecution is not known among them, nor is it necessary; for the system of Mahomet is made to extend itself by means abundantly more efficacious. By establishing small schools in the different towns, where many of the Pagan as well as Mahomedan children are taught to read the Koran, and instructed in the tenets of the Prophet, the Mahomedan priests fix a bias on the minds, and form the character of their young disciples, which no accidents of life can ever afterwards remove or alter.[17]

Other travelers have testified to the influence of Islam in similar terms, commenting on the religion's clerical character. Travelers' reports characterize the government as "theocratic," loosely defined, with Sharí'ah-based law and jurists presiding over the implementation of the religious code. The population was scrupulous in following the tenets and prescriptions of Islam, and Qur'an schools were established in every town to teach children the rudiments of the faith and the Qur'an in Arabic. The religious leaders were distinguished by their cavalry, dress, and white turbans surmounted by red or blue cone shapes.[18] This prominence of religion evoked the "theocratic" sentiment.

After the breakup of Diakhaba, a branch of the Suware clerics emigrated to Dentilia in Bundu where they established Diakha-Madina.[19] Dentilia was still a flourishing district when Park's traveling party passed through it, though Madina, the capital of Wuli district, showed evidence of decline as a *majlis*. Yet, in keeping with itinerant character of clerical life, the contraction of Madina was offset by expansion in other centers.

At the time of Park's second voyage to Africa in 1805, the leading cleric of Baní Isráila in Bundu was Fode Ibrahima. Park described him as "one of the most friendly men I have met with. I gave him a copy of the New Testament in Arabic, with which he seemed very much pleased."[20] Park and his traveling party struck east from Baní Isráila, and after several days of trekking through open country they came upon the gold fields of Bambouk. Though he reported in detail on the method of mining the gold, with women doing the washing and sifting, Park took care not to betray his eagerness to learn the location of the gold fields. He found it "necessary for me to be cautious not to incur the suspicion of the natives, by examining too far into the riches of their country."[21] He said he could imagine that the quantity of gold produced in one year would be considerable even though "they wash only during the beginning and end of the rains," about three or four months altogether.[22] Park then described the trade in ivory and the toll it took on elephants in the interior. Gold and ivory, however, were not his main objects at this stage, and he went on to describe with urgency his plans to reach the Niger against the sapping effects of the seasonal rains—it was mid-June, and the rains had set in. Several members of his party had fallen ill with what may have been malaria. Eventually the toll on the expedition reached tragic proportions. Of the forty-four Europeans who left the Gambia in good health, there remained only Park and three soldiers, one of whom had become delirious and unhinged. Park said he would persevere until he discovered the estuary of the Niger, "or perish in the attempt," which, indeed, came to pass.[23]

Perhaps the most pertinent clue to the breakup of Diakhaba comes from a report by João de Barros about the military career of Koli Tengella, whose adopted father was killed by the forces of Songhay. Koli Tengella regrouped and launched an assault on the towns on the Faleme River and attacked Bambouk in 1534. The attack foreshadowed the ultimate fate of Mali and forced the king in 1530 to call on the Portuguese for help. John III, or John II according to Trimingham[24], dispatched an embassy to Mali in response. Koli was defeated and died in 1537, but his successors continued the struggle against Mali. The collapse of the Songhay empire in 1591 emboldened their efforts to bring down what remained of the Mali empire. In about 1600 the Fulbe arrived on the scene to assert control of a large area from the Sahel to Futa Jallon and the Upper Senegal, including Diakhaba—a strike at the heart of Mali's economic power.[25]

Mali lost the goldfields of Bambouk at this time. This effectively ended the rule of the last king, Niani Mansa Mamudu (Mahmúd), who was finally defeated at the gates of Jenne at about the same time. It is clear from all the evidence that Koli Tengella's military threat to the security of Mali did not spare Bambouk and its lucrative gold fields, and Diakhaba did not escape the fate of the empire because of the military events described by João de Barros. The dates certainly fit well with the internal evidence in *TF* and *AW* of the town's decline. The *Ta'ríkh al-Súdán* fixes the date of the disintegration of Mali to the rule of Niani Mansa Mamudu. According to the account, Mali's over-extended power was precariously balanced between two independent-minded commanders, one in north and the other in the south. "This led to tyranny, highhandedness and the violation of people's rights in the latter days of their rule." The inevitable followed, and Mali disintegrated "into three groups, each under a leader ruling a particular area with his supporters and claiming to be the sultan."[26] This chronology seems reasonable in light of subsequent developments. It conforms fairly closely to Jobson's witness to developments in Sutukhu consistent with a western shift toward Senegambia of Mali's religious equilibrium.

Profuse references to Bundu in the sources point to it as a key to the mystery of the sequel to Diakhaba. Bundu was the destination of the most important clerical clans from Bambouk, and this is proved by the presence of representatives of all the main *qabílah* segments. The accidents of geography and trade alone cannot explain this wholesale influx into Bundu or what appears to be a sudden mass exodus from the region of Bambukhu. Park's report was based on traditions available in Bundu, which was the western point of the Bambukhu refugee trail. His report confirms the pattern of movement of earlier immigrants from the eastern and central regions of Mali as described by João. Profiting from duties and levies imposed on trade in the region, the king of Bundu established himself as a formidable ruler in the eyes of the neighboring states. After a short and bloody campaign, his army defeated Sambu, the king of Bambouk, who was obliged to sue for peace and to surrender all the important towns on the eastern bank of the Falemé.[27] Those events caused waves of immigrants to stream into Bundu, the new clerical hub. After Diakhaba, Suwarian clericalism, upheld by its supporting Serakhulle and Manding cultural structures, was nowhere more successfully established than in Bundu and adjoining areas.

The date for the breakup of Diakhaba can now be fixed somewhere near the events associated with Koli Tengella. It is safe to assume that the settlement had ceased to exist at the time of the composition of *TF* and, in all probability, of Ahmad Bábá's *Mi'ráj al-Su'úd* ("The Ladder of Ascent towards Grasping the Law Concerning Transported Blacks"[28]) noted earlier. Jobson in 1620 reports no information about whether or not Diakhaba still existed. Even if we assume that his informants would have been aware of its breakup and reported it, we cannot conclude anything definite from Jobson's silence. João de Barros and the *Ta'ríkh al-Súdán* independently fill the vacuum and elucidate Park's observations. The substantial body of oral tradition Park was able to gather, and his report on the concentration of clerical cells in Bundu, point to a gravitational shift in the clerical profession from Bambouk to Bundu and the adjoining country. No account after João de Barros refers to Diakhaba except to recall its once distinguished past. *TF* says the town flourished "at the time of the supremacy of Mali," implying it was no longer active at the time the chronicle was being produced in the seventeenth century.

The clerical community emerged in Didecoto in Bundu with all the vigor the tradition once enjoyed at Diakhaba and Sutukho. Muhammad Fatuma's leadership of the community was strengthened by the proximity of adjacent centers, with the pathways of travel channeling news, ideas, gifts, teaching materials, students, and disciples. Today the dispersion trail is as much a foyer of support and renewal as it is of retreat and security. Dispersion gives the clerics the option of removal and relocation in response to prevailing threats or unrest, and it relieves the pressure of confinement by offering the clerics new starts in more promising settings. Clerical cells form a network united by the energy and rythm of regular traffic and the stimulus of periodic relocation. Intermarriage among clerical families is standard practice, giving the clerical communities the double advantage of family bonds and professional solidarity. In field interviews in the religious settlement of Nibras (described in chapter 10), the leading cleric emphasized that intermarriage alone could not sustain the pacifist vocation. Commitment and knowledge of the pacifist tradition were also necessary. Responding to the repeated charge that the clerical reputation could be acquired from nothing deeper than looking the part,[29] a leading cleric responded that principle and vocation are not accidents of birth. The clerical tradition is a moral vocation, and the consecrated vow is more meaningful than blood—it hallows the family bond.[30] The clerics maintain close family genealogies in which lineages, preserved in *barakah,* are set down as ethical exemplars.

Where even two or three clerical centers are gathered, there abides a living tradition. A celebration, a funeral, or an emergency in one center will move the interconnected clusters into action for mutual support and collective commitment. Delegations bearing gifts are regularly dispatched to visit clerical establishments whose leaders share not only family ties but a common scholarly profession. This cultural ethos has allowed isolated communities to endure and, where necessary, to move into new territory with fresh leadership. The clerics are very mindful about not duplicating their work among themselves, and moving to found new centers is a proven way to solve the problem of overcrowding, especially since contact is maintained.

Devotion and Obedience

Its professional vocation gives the clerical community the distinct character of a religious order, much like a Sufi brotherhood but without collective subjection to the mystical initiation or adoption of a *wird* (litany). Clerical practice is not committed to mystical exercises, nor does it practice the *bay'ah* (pledge of obedience) to a *murshid* (guide). Rather, clerical practice confines itself within the bounds of teaching the religious code. There is very little speculative output or theosophic writing in the work of the clerics and little theological production. This is no different from the Islam of the Sunni canon, wherein devotion and obedience are focused on the obligations of the religious canon and on its missionary mandate, not on the charisma of the mystic. The clerics deviated from standard Islam—or, at least, from common preconceptions of it—in their rejection of war and political office, a position that placed them under tremendous pressure in relations with jihad leaders and, later, colonial administrators.

Mobile clerical communities dedicated to teaching and instruction, as seen in Jobson's account, is a defining feature of the Jakhanke way of life. We shall see this with respect to Karamokhoba of Touba in Guinea. The clerics, Jobson said, are a people given to travel "in whole families together, and carrying along their books, and manuscripts," with their young "whom they teach, and instruct in any place they rest." They earn their living by providing religious services and use the knowledge acquired in travel as well as their reputation for peace to secure concessions from their hosts and neighbors. Consequently, they are allowed safe passage even in countries where wars are raging. The cleric in this way "is a privileged person, and may follow his trade, or course of travelling, without any let or interruption of either side."[31] Religious reputation formed an important safeguard against political sequestration.

It is appropriate at this point to examine briefly how Muslim scholars tracked developments in pagan societies. The scholars' proximity to events on the ground by virtue of educating the children of the community and giving advice to family heads gave them a front-row seat without political ties or obligations. A fifteenth-century document from West Africa indicates that Muslims, including the scholars, were a minority with little prospect of assuming power. The scholars watched the intermixture of Islamic and traditional customs with close attention and increasing wariness, caught between preserving peaceful coexistence, which might require problematic compromise, and upholding Islamic standards even at the risk of conflict. The scholars decided to seek guidance and assurance in Islamic sources. For them, jihad was not even a remote option, which left them with the middle course: tolerating acts considered reprehensible or even forbidden without endorsing unbelief. One horn of this dilemma was much less damaging than the other, and so a supple conscience served Muslims far better than rigid principle.

Jurists and the Religious Code

The scholars found in the Islamic religious code contingencies and remedies for life in a mixed society. They therefore had to possess the sound knowledge of the code or, failing that, consult eminent jurists. The middle course of co-existence fits well with the classical Orthodox view that for Muslims living in "the sphere of mixing" (*dár al-khalṭ*), compromise, flexibility, and accommodation are necessary and permissible.[32]

The document offering that tidy solution came of the inquiries of a local scholar seeking answers from the Egyptian jurist al-Suyúṭí, a familiar name in learned circles in West Africa and beyond. Al-Suyúṭí's responses to the scholar's detailed list of questions compose part of the document. The questions arose out of conditions of fifteenth-century society in an unidentified region of the Sahel, probably around Aïr in Niger, in which a minority Muslim community was obliged to participate in activities of dubious merit. Muslims were unable to maintain spatial separation and exemption from the more objectionable aspects of customary practices, such as worshiping and offering meat to idols and prostrating before rulers. Proximity made compromise unavoidable. It became urgent to consult scholars, who could interpret the legal code with regard to actions deemed reprehensible in ways that did not oblige Muslims to reject society entirely. In the vast majority of cases, al-Suyúṭí instructs, Muslims are under no obligation to repudiate society even if they suffer discrimination and unjust treatment as a minority. Muslims may be blameworthy and even commit sins, but that in no way makes them guilty of the condemnation of *takfír* (anathema).[33] Clerical centers answered a need to be publicly religious without the requirement to impose Shariʻah as public law. Even the ambivalent conditions of *convivencia* are valid enough to suspend the obligation of jihad, which is categorized then as an extreme and exceptional undertaking. Jihad does not merely happen; it has to be created. The justification for it is exceptional and, for the clerics, unsupported.

Expansion of the Clerics

Oral sources and clerical family chronicles hint at one of the possible causes for the eventual decline of Didecoto when they claim that the establishment of the Didecoto community coincided in the 1690s with the rule of the Tokolor, Malik Sy (c. 1637–1699). History credits Malik Sy with founding the Bundu state. The Bundu trails of Jobson's description, at the time thick with traffic of books, manuscripts, scholars, and visitors, thinned out as fortunes changed. It is a safe guess that the events of the Bundu jihad of Malik Sy helped to uproot the clerical community, and the historical trail of that community opened the next chapter of the Suwarian course in African Islam.

There are no grounds for doubting that the clerics had close personal connections with Malik Sy. Malik Sy's chaplain was Shaykh Muhammad Fode of the Jabi lineage or, according to reliable clerical sources, Shaykh Muhammad Fode's grandfather, 'Abdallah. In any case, the Jabi clerical family maintained close political ties with the Sy dynasty.[34] Shaykh Muhammad Fode married Fatumata Sy, a daughter of Malik Sy, and it was from that union that Muhammad Fatuma (d c. 1772) was born, as his uterine appelation shows. Tradition maintains that Muhammad Fatuma was the spiritual founder of Didecoto where, while presiding over a growing community of students and disciples, he raised a large family.

Ensuing political unrest in eighteenth-century Bundu prompted a reassessment of clerical options. The community at Didecoto had grown enough under Muhammad Fatuma to make geographical expansion a natural development. This inevitably meant further dispersion and resettlement, a replication of the clerical pattern. This pattern increases our understanding of the tradition's progression from its origins; practices today carry memories of earlier religious communities. A son of Muhammad Fatuma carried forward the momentum of Didecoto and ensured the continuity of the Suwarian clerical heritage. The long-range effects of the achievement of al-Hajj Salim Suware are seen clearly in this representative clerical lineage, to be examined more extensively in due course.

The clerical families interviewed in this study (including leaders of the charismatic Suwarian community at Jarra-Barrokunda on the Gambia River, once a force in the region), as well as an Arabic chronicle authored by Maliki mufti of Bobo-Dioulaso in Burkina Fasso, are unanimous in their view that Muhammad Fatuma's lineage carried forward the most important and enduring extension of the clerical endeavor in the early modern period. [35] Clerical chronicles are handed down as the intellectual property of their communities of origin and serve not only as a source of historical information but as an instructive guide and a rule of organization. Both *TF* and the *Ta'ríkh al-Súdán* show aspects of the social nature of handing down history with suitable advice for future generations. The preface of *TKB* cited in chapter 10 shows a similar goal of preserving and handing down tradition. "Soundness" applied to clerical sources means not only the accurate recording of facts but the didactic purpose to be served. Historical veracity and community interest strengthen trust in the value of the original Suwarian covenant; as the clerics undertook dispersion to other places, either because of external pressure or internal reasons, they maintained communication and contact with other settlements. This is a point made with great eloquence by a descendant of Muhammad Fatuma when his life and the community's survival were at stake. Nothing stood between the summary expropriation of the clerical tradition and advancing French colonial power except the clerics' pacifist reputation.

With war come dislocation and uncertainty, as well as expansion and consolidation. The fall of Mali and the dispersion from Bambukhu in turn created dispersion trails and the establishment of new communities in Bundu from where fresh trails developed to Fouta Jallon and beyond. In the Sufi life, the rigors of travel and exposure are used to develop self-control and to pursue inward renewal. As will be explained in further detail in chapter 13, Sufism is Islam's version of mystical religion, but because of its focus on the subjective and the emotional as valid criteria of religion, Sufism came under suspicion and persecution in Sunni Islam. Some Sufis were considered antinomian heretics because of their willingness to regard the religious code as dispensable for salvation. But, as is true of mainstream Sunni Sufis in general, the clerical subjects of this book have kept a wide berth from such antinomian tendencies. Sidi Mahmud, Sufi master of Niger, advised his disciples: "Know that the books and the *sunna* are the source which the saints of Allah Almighty have shown to [His] servants. Whoever forsakes both of them is in error, but he who follows them will be happy and fortunate. He who spurns them will perish and he who makes use of them will be saved."[36] This view echoes the teaching of al-Junayd of Baghdad (d. 909–910), from whose work al-Ghazali sought guidance. Al-Junayd wrote: "This path (of Sufism) is for him who has taken the Book of God in his right hand and the *sunnah* of Muhammad in his left and walks by their light so that he falls not into the pit of doubt or the darkness of heresy."[37]

A thirteenth-century Sufi manual of the Suhrawardiyah ţaríqah claims exile and adversity as metaphors of the discipline and refining work necessary for personal devotion and inward trust.

> The being separated from one's native land, from friends and familiar things, and the exercising of patience in calamities cause lust and nature to rest from pursuing their way; and take up from hearts the effect of hardness. In subduing lusts, the effect of *safar* [travel] is no less than the effect of *nawáfil* [supererogatory devotions], fasting, and

> praying. On dead skins, by tanning, the effects of purity, of softness, and of delicacy of texture appear; even so, by the tanning of *safar*, and by the departure of natural corruption and innate roughness, appear the purifying softness of devotion and change from obstinacy to faith.[38]

The effects of alternating expansion and regrouping, of surges followed by retractions, with perseverance and devotion promote "the tanning of travel." The pastoral impulse is strengthened as much by historical circumstances as by religious practice and observance in the community; wayfaring is no less spiritually rejuvenating than settled life. Its underlying religious intention (*niyah*) distinguishes the pastoral journey from migration as a demographic phenomenon. Under the right conditions, the hazards of travel—potential loss of possessions, security, and even life—are risks worth taking to attain safe refuge and a fresh start. The clerics had no homeland, no territory to promote as a promised land. They were thus free to embrace any foreign country as a motherland, and the dispersion network could energize the vocation by expansion. Itinerancy was one more effective way to bypass and transcend jihad.

Criticism of Mungo Park's *Travels*

Despite the fact that Park witnessed firsthand events in the clerical centers on which he reported, a brief word is in order about the historical merit of his book. Much controversy followed its publication. Park's employer, Bryan Edwards, was the editor of the manuscript as well as the owner of a West Indian slave plantation. He wrote a fifty-page abstract of Park's *Travels* and is thought to have manipulated the text of the book before publication. Edwards campaigned actively against Wilberforce and Parliamentary abolition, and his association with Park created grounds for distrust of Park's book. Proslavery circles cited evidence Park gave of the deep African roots of slavery as proof that he had set out to discredit impending Parliamentary legislation aimed at eradicating the slave trade. Abolitionists drew on the same evidence to argue for enlightened intervention to address the dire African need for moral supervision. Park declined to enter the debate, content to let his book stand. Critics took that reluctance as proof of Edwards's influence.

Critics claim that Park's book betrays too much studied cultivation and contrived rumination to be acceptable as a faithful, authentic transcript of his African journey.[39] While exposed to the challenging, makeshift conditions of the African bush, opponents charge, travelers simply did not have the luxury of indulgence in reflexive discourse. Edwards's boast that he served Park editorially as much as Dr. John Hawkesworth had served Captain Cook confirmed suspicions that he had fiddled with the manuscript. Critics noted that the African Association appointed Park and paid him a stipend to write his book. Joseph Banks led the African Association that appointed Park; Banks was also president of the Royal Society and director of Kew Gardens, recently created by George III. In 1769 Banks had traveled to Tahiti with Captain Cook. As Banks's protégé, Park was beholden to Edwards, who led the African Association, particularly because the association voted to appoint Park to undertake a second expedition at government expense. Critics felt that this could not but affect the book's objectivity and credibility and good faith in Park's reputation with it. Paradoxically, Park's *Travels* was defended by both sides of the abolition debate, the attacks of which eventually turned against each other rather than entirely against Park.

According to an account Sir Walter Scott wrote after a fishing trip with Park on the River Yarrow, Park talked freely about his first expedition but would not consent to include a great deal of that information in his *Travels* or to disclose it to the public, because he did not want to offend his readers' credulity or make his book sound like a tale of marvels. The public, Park felt, should not be exposed to matters of his own personal experience.[40] Critics wondered if that was an implied admission that the book was doctored, if not invented. Fuel was added to the contention of some historians that the *Travels* was an unreliable, tendentious work designed to damage the antiabolition Planters' lobby in the British Parliament, at a crucial time for the slave trade debate. Despite attempts to use Park for their cause, in the end, judging that Park's work was not as useful as they initially thought, the abolitionists distrusted the book as a subversive influence whose circulation could not but hurt their efforts.[41]

The final objection grew out of the controversial nature of Park's second expedition of 1805. The image of a swashbuckling buccaneer shooting down hostile natives to secure the prize of discovering the course and endpoint of the Niger cast Park as a self-interested adventurer rather than as a scientific explorer—an image not much improved by his mysterious death. None of that boosted Park's stock with the influential humanitarian movement.

Whatever the justice of these strictures, readers should remember that abolitionist sentiment was changing the political climate in Britain in a profound way; that Park's publication coincided with a lobbying campaign that spared few knowledgeable or influential people from the imperative to take sides; and that Park refused to do so. As his information is corroborated by other sources where appropriate and does not openly contradict evidence in comparable sources, Park remains a valuable original source. His forays into the Mandinka language, long before cultural anthropology was a recognized field, show an effort to understand the societies he encountered and for which he retained respect and even admiration. The controversy surrounding him is extrinsic to his book.

7

Beyond Tribe and Tongue in Futa Jallon

Religion and Ethnicity

> Love what God loves. Love God with all your hearts, and weary not of the word of God and its mention. Harden not your hearts from it. Out of everything that God creates He chooses and selects; the actions He chooses he calls *khíra*; the people He chooses He calls *muṣṭafá*; and the speech He chooses He calls *ṣálih*. From everything that is brought to man there is the lawful and unlawful. Worship God and associate naught with Him; fear Him as He ought to be feared; Carry out loyally towards God what you say with your mouths. Love one another in the spirit of God. Verily God is angry when His covenant is broken.
>
> —The Prophet Muhammad in Ibn Isháq's *Sírat Rasúl Alláh*, 231.

Ethnic Tension in Futa Jallon

In the course of the nineteenth century, Futa Jallon became the new frontline of the clerical encounter with the French. Islam had been introduced in the area through a reform movement led by a local Fula cleric trained in Kankan, but Fulbe ascendancy over the local non-Muslim populations provoked ethnic tensions that impeded the progress of Islam and led to an inconclusive social truce. The Jakhanke dispersion to the area was a response to Islam's unfinished mission there. In time, French colonial forces would penetrate the region and aggravate the underlying ethnic tensions. The cousins of the Sy dynasty of Bundu moved into Futa Jallon to bolster Fulbe ascendancy, a process interrupted by the fateful arrival of the French. Accounts of traditions maintained by the Fulbe themselves speak of their origins in Masina, where they encountered al-Hajj Salim Suware and were directed by him to settle in Futa Jallon. It is hard to know what truth there is in these accounts, but they indicate a Suwarian motif in Fulbe sources. In any case, the Bundu clerical immigration to Futa Jallon took place under the leadership of al-Hajj Salim Gassama, son of Muhammad Fatuma and scion of the Sikunda Tukolor family. Named after al-Hajj Salim Suware, al-Hajj Salim Gassama is better known to history as Karamokhoba, the great scholar, a title by which he is honored in the clerical community to this day. The story of his life was a major force for the Suwarian tradition as it faced external danger and internal dissension. It is necessary to fill in the historical background before resuming with the subject of the clerics.

The earliest penetration of Islam into Futa Jallon is tied to the influx of Muslims from Mali in the first half of the thirteenth century, including elements of Fulbe.[1] The steady influx of immigrants led to the gradual displacement of the indigenous populations and, eventually, to the virtual extinction of two of the three major ethnic groups, the Bassari and the Baga peoples. The admixture of the Manding and the sedentary Susu population resulted in the emergence of the Jallonke people. The name means simply "the people of Jallon," a designation initially with no ethnic implication.[2] The Jallonke are no more than a function of the circumstances of their origin; they have no legends or myths about their past.

The arrival of the first Fulbe in the area was into stranger quarters known as *zangos*.[3] The date for their arrival cannot be fixed with any precision, although Fulbe traditions claim that al-Hajj Salim Suware directed them to Futa Jallon after meeting them in Masina.[4] Tradition claims that a major stream of Fulbe immigration stemmed from the career of Koli Tengella, whose adopted father, as we saw earlier, was killed in Dyara by the troops of the *askiya* (ruler) of Songhay in 1512–1513 after he revolted.[5] Koli Tengella unified the disaffected Fulbe and Manding and led them to Futa Toro, which he conquered before setting up the Denianke dynasty.[6] João de Barros's report about Koli Tengella's rebellion against Mali is a little garbled, trailing off into ranging estimates of the bounds of Mali's power, but it does help to date the Fulbe's arrival in Futa.[7]

Fulbe relations with the Jallonke were based on trade in cattle, hides, milk, cheese, and butter. As a people under scutage, the Fulbe paid taxes to their Jallonke landlords, including the much-abused levy of *jangali* (cattle tax). The region's political structure consisted of clusters of independent chiefdoms to which the Fulakundas (the Fulbe of the *zangos*) owed tribute and fealty. United by a common ethnic bond and rising resentment of the taxes, the Fulbe nursed a simmering sense of injustice. With the increase in Fulbe immigration, and with it the sense of national feeling, Fulbe grievances hardened into a defining ideology. In search of grazing pasture, freewheeling Fulbe cattle pastoralists called the *wodadbé* (sing. *bódadò*) moved into the country, where their numbers were increased by roaming bands of Fulbe nomads, the *bórorò* (sing. *wororbé*).

The cattle pastoralists deeply resented having to sell their cattle to pay the *jangali* tax. Selling cattle as a mere commodity was a hateful betrayal of pastoral values with respect to the symbolic worth of their herd; it amounted to violation of a religious interdiction. But the very nature of Fulbe society, stratified as it was along lines of group loyalty and occupational specialization, provided little sense of solidarity in Ibn Khaldun's sense of the term. The Fula language was not a unifying ethnic force, a fact acknowledged by the Fulbe when they refer to themselves simply as *hál pulár'en* (speakers of Pular). Although they were Fulbe, the *bororo* nomadic pastoralists kept to themselves and to their cattle. As just indicated, speakers of the language are stratified into groups, with different groups defined by occupational and residential characteristics.[8] As John Ralph Willis has shown, the *sernabé* Torodbé (i.e., Fulbe clerics of Futa Toro in Senegal) developed as a distinct social class.[9] They called themselves *Pular,* whence the French *Peuhl.* The role of language in Fulbe ethnic self-understanding can be illustrated by the Fulani who settled among the Hausa: they maintained their ethnic identity long after they became Muslims and shed the Fula language, adopting Hausa instead but retaining their racial identity. It is an interesting example of how, on adopting Islam, the Fulani chose ethnic designation over language and in the process embraced Islam in its Hausa cultural assimilation.

Economic grievance and social discrimination combined to provoke the Futa Jallon Fulbe into something like a national awakening. Fulbe began to feel themselves increasingly as other than their Jallonke neighbors. Waves of immigration (*fergo* in Fula) from the eastern flank of Masina and the western from Futa Toro increased the population dramatically. By the eighteenth century, the Islamic elements in Fulbe immigration brought about the need for the Fulbe to demand a strategic reordering of social relationships with the Jallonke and neighboring ethnic groups. The defining experience of a discriminated people became an identity issue, with Fulbe national feeling ratcheted up to become a mobilizing cause with Islam as fuel.

The critical point for the political rise of the Fulbe came in the late seventeenth century with the arrival in Labé of a wandering band of Fula immigrants from the greater Bundu region under their leader Kalidou.[10] These immigrants were called the Irlabe or Jallo (the French Diallo) Fulbe. Irlabe remains even today one of the most important clans of the Fulbe. In the ensuing friction with their Jallonke landlords, the Irlabe fell into line behind Kalidou, whose role was transformed into a political one through alliance with the largely non-Muslim Susu population. There is evidence to suggest that Kalidou's profession of Islam lacked the ideological severity required for jihad, and the more fervent Muslims among his people murmured in their camps against him. Yet, given the political prize at stake in Fulbe relations with the Jallonke, religious criticism was muted as Kalidou took charge of the cause of Fulbe political interests.[11] Islam was a factor; jihad was not. It was the Irlabe Fulbe who later toppled Jallonke power in Futa Jallon and opened the way for the eventual ascendancy of the Fulbe in the region.

Possessed of an astute sense of timing and the support needed to displace the Jallonke and assert Fulbe political dominance, Kalidou showed himself to be a gifted organizer. He summoned the Fulbe, scattered at the time in uncoordinated settlements, united them in a common purpose by articulating their grievances in a galvanizing message, and offered a strategy for overcoming oppression and taking power. Kalidou's achievement was strengthened by the arrival of a clerical personage called Almamy Umaru, of the prominent Ba Fulbe lineage. Almamy Umaru pointed the Irlabe political agenda in a religious direction by citing Islam as the moral advantage of Fulbe ascendancy. Yet Kalidou's secular achievement survived in a group identifying itself as the Hal Pular party, which differentiated itself from the religious platform of Almamy Umaru. The Hal Pular party joined with the Hubbúbé party; *hubbu* is derived from the Arabic phrase *hubbú rasúli-lláh* (those who love God's Messenger and wish to follow his *sunnah*). The Hubbúbé rebelled against the old Almamy establishment structure, and, together with the Hal Pular, pursued parallel secular and religious paths with the unified goal of advancing Fulbe power. Accordingly, they adopted a political formula in which ethnicity would neither impede Islamization nor be subsumed by it. Over the centuries, Muslim Fulbe and their secular compatriots went on to live cheek by jowl quite successfully, taking turns running affairs.

Eventually, however, the Hubbúbé Fulbe were forced to choose between religious interest and the Hal Pular secular heritage. This was occasioned by the career of Alfa Ibrahima Sambegou, who made a bid at the first theocracy of Futa Jallon in 1727. He is better known in history by his *laqab* (sobriquet) Karamokho Alfa, the "Karamokho" evidence that his scholastic career included tutelage under Jakhanke clerical masters.

Karamokho Alfa received part of his education from Shakykh Qadiri Sanunu of Kankan, head of the Jakhite-Kaba family and of Jakhanke origin.[12] Karamokho Alfa continued with his studies in Fugumba, Futa Jallon, under the highly revered Tcherno Samba.[13] It was at Fugumba that Karamokho Alfa claimed to have had an epiphany in which the Prophet appeared to him with a promise that if he spent time in prayer in seclusion (whether of the *khalwah* [devotional retreat] or *istikhárah* [secluded prayer of guidance] variety is not clear), he would be rewarded with leadership of the country. In his prayer retreat, which lasted seven years, seven months, and seven days—a figure with obvious apocalyptic overtones—he called for God's aid in converting the pagan Jallonke. When he emerged from his seclusion, his disciples proclaimed him ruler of all Fulbe. He was greeted with the words: "Your prayers have been answered, and all Futa claim you as their leader against the pagans."[14] It is significant that the Jallonke's conversion was deemed a prerequisite for Karamokho Alfa's success. Any tendency toward jihad in his political campaign had to be adapted to appeal across ethnicities.

Paul Marty, a French colonial official with a North African background who served as a senior advisor on Muslim affairs in West Africa, proclaimed Karamokho Alfa the grand exemplar of his epoch. The Old Testament and the records of the early of days of Islam, Marty said, offer many examples of the characteristic figure of an age. "Karamokho Alfa is the prophet of Israel come to rouse his people from their slumber, to awaken their soporific faith, and to launch them on their grand destiny."[15] By 1766, however, Karamokho Alfa had gone insane and had to be replaced by his nephew, Ibrahim Yoro Pate, who adopted the name Ibrahima Sori. Sori died in 1791.[16] It would be rash to conclude that jihad was the principal force behind the rise of the Fulbe. Ibrahima Sori gave the signal for the commencement of hostilities against the Jallonke; his challenge to the authority of Djam Yero, the Jallonke chief, struck at the core of the indigenous political status quo. Convincing himself that coexistence would not serve his interests, Djam Yero rejected offers of compromise with the Muslims and banned Muslim public prayers, abandoning a long-standing pact and driving Islam underground. In response, Ibrahima Sori split the sacred drums used by the Jallonke people at religious ceremonies.[17] His Irlabe-Bororo Fulbe forces went on to target Jallonke chiefs and instigate defections by offering immunity to Jallonke collaborators, mostly impoverished peasants, economic insolvents, and rootless migrants. In effect, the Fulbe fought a class war with a pious veneer.[18]

The Jallonke countered with full-scale mobilization, prompting the Fulbe *mawubé* (political elite) to convene a war council at Fugumba. There they adopted the name "Futa Jallon," "to indicate the unification of the different Fulbe tribes and Jallonke converts to Islam."[19] Even in the heady milieu of jihad mobilization, Ibrahima Sori found it necessary to rein in theocratic impulses. He took extreme measures by curtailing the power of Fugumba, the first city of Muslim Futa and a holy center consecrated by the revered holy figure Tcherno Samba. Fugumba blessed and consecrated kings, judged and settled civil disputes, and reserved for itself the power to review and arbitrate political disputes. Karamokho Alfa had claimed to receive a vision there, convincing all Futa to embrace association with the town's moral reputation.

Now that religion was no longer a reliable unifier even for the Fulbe, Fugumba as a religious town was vulnerable. Jihad faltered by exposing interethnic tensions and forcing pragmatic social relationships into permanent alignments. That the Fulbe campaign was patched together with the help of unemployed and discontented social elements revealed the basic weakness. News of revolts among the Jallonke reached the Sulimana populations, who were allied with the jihad in operations in Sankaran and the upper Faleme. The revolts showed that the jihad was very much a patchwork of diverse ethnic groups. The Muslim forces became pinned down in wars of fending off revolts within the ranks that impeded the work of consolidation.[20] In the new *entente* between religion and political power, Ibrahima Sori concluded that Fugumba must be converted into a shared legacy rather than be allowed to remain as a religious asylum. He forced his way into the town and, in a reversal of jihad, put his religious rivals to the sword.[21]

At Timbo, the new secular stronghold of the Hal Pular party about 30 miles southeast of Fugumba, Sori created in 1780 a forum of political elders (*kautital mawubé*), signaling the end of Fugumba's mystique. Sori thus became the guarantor of the secular Hal Pular cause. Under his leadership the Fulbe triumphed, and Futa Jallon reassembled under their dominance. Sori was succeeded by his son, Sadou, who was murdered five years later by members of the rival Alfaya religious party. The Alfaya backed Salihou, the son of Karamokho Alfa. Sadou's murder threatened the intricate mesh of Fulbe hegemony, opening the way for an all-too-certain Jallonke backlash and a revolt of the autochthones. Distressed by the sad turn of affairs and unwilling to inherit a costly family blood feud, Salihou declined the succession. His brother, Abdoulaye Bademba, assumed power in 1799.[22]

Clearly the use of Islam in the revolution was something of a gamble. It did not prevent necessary concessions to indigenous ethnic interests and to the Hal Pular secular sentiment. Fulbe national feeling came of a contrived interethnic coalition that accepted religious *entente* with the Hal Pular'en pragmatists. Despite this *entente*, there was still the risk that the Fulbe political momentum could dissipate in an inconclusive intraethnic stalemate.

Over the course of the Fulbe's rise to power, Islam was adjusted to achieve a delicate ideological balance within the Muslim community and in its relations with non-Muslims. Fulbe communities continued to exist in many areas, including Futa Toro, Masina, Niger, north Nigeria, Adamawa, and north Cameroun. Yet, in terms of successful ethnic alliances, nowhere had their impact been greater and more enduring, despite its mixed outcome, than in Futa Jallon. In precolonial no less than in colonial Futa Jallon, religion and ethnicity remained an unstable mix. Jihad raised the religious stakes without resolving ethnic secular claims.

Ensuring stability and the preservation of Fulbe dominance required fostering a mutual understanding between the Alfaya and the Soriya parties, who supported the successors of Karamokho Alfa and Ibrahima Sori, respectively. The national interests of the Fulbe were well served by the forces of Islamic awakening and vice versa. The Fulbe rescinded ethnic claims for being Muslim; Muslim Mandinka and Jallonke had a guaranteed place in the new Fulbe dispensation alongside non-Muslims. This establishment of equal standing ruled out jihad as political choice and ethnic chauvinism as a viable ideological motivation. The resulting compromise created remarkable long-term stability. Nearly a hundred years later, Surgeon-Major Dr. Valesius Gouldsbury, the administrator of the Gambia whose 1881 trip to Futa Jallon provoked the French to move into the area, confirmed this tradition of mutual recognition.[23] He noted that political power alternated between the Alfaya and the Soriya. The Soriya party was represented by Abdul Qadir and the Alfaya by Abdoulaye Bademba. It was around 1804 that Karamokhoba (the subject of the next chapter) met both leaders, who hailed him as a scholar and paid him high homage.

It is relevant to the nature of inter-ethnic unity that the Fulbe trade caravans enjoyed mutual protection with Serakhulle caravans at a time of internal civil war, leading Gaspard Mollien, the French explorer (referred to in chapter 5) to note enviously that the two groups "were not even subjected to those searches which with us expose traders to so much inconvenience. Relying on the probity of the merchants, the two governments protect them, and they could not adduce a single instance of a caravan having been pillaged by either of the armies."[24]

The prevailing political culture in Futa Jallon was not uncongenial to the Suwarian tradition of accommodation and moderation. Paul Marty writes of a continuing influx of Serakhulle immigrants into the area from points on the Niger bend, Jafunu, and surrounding areas, well into the nineteenth century.[25] The story of Jubba Almamy illustrates this. A Serakhulle, he emigrated from Jafunu to Bissikrima in the district of Dinguiray where he settled and raised a family. His eldest son, Kankan Fode, founded a new settlement named after himself. Two of Jubba's grandchildren, Fode Yaya and Fode Baba, were spiritual protégés of the Jakhanke, who conferred on them the Qadiri Sufi mantle in 1907.

Islam Through Colonial Eyes

The French colonial authorities regarded ethnicity as the means of defining Islam in Africa. The administrators subjected Islam to surveillance and sequestration, tracking prominent Islamic figures such as local *walís* and karamokhos. Their logic was cockeyed. Jihad Islam—what the French called Islam *arabe* and perceived as the purportedly true Islam—was dangerous, they reasoned, while ethnic or folk Islam, Islam *noir,* was bogus, though equally

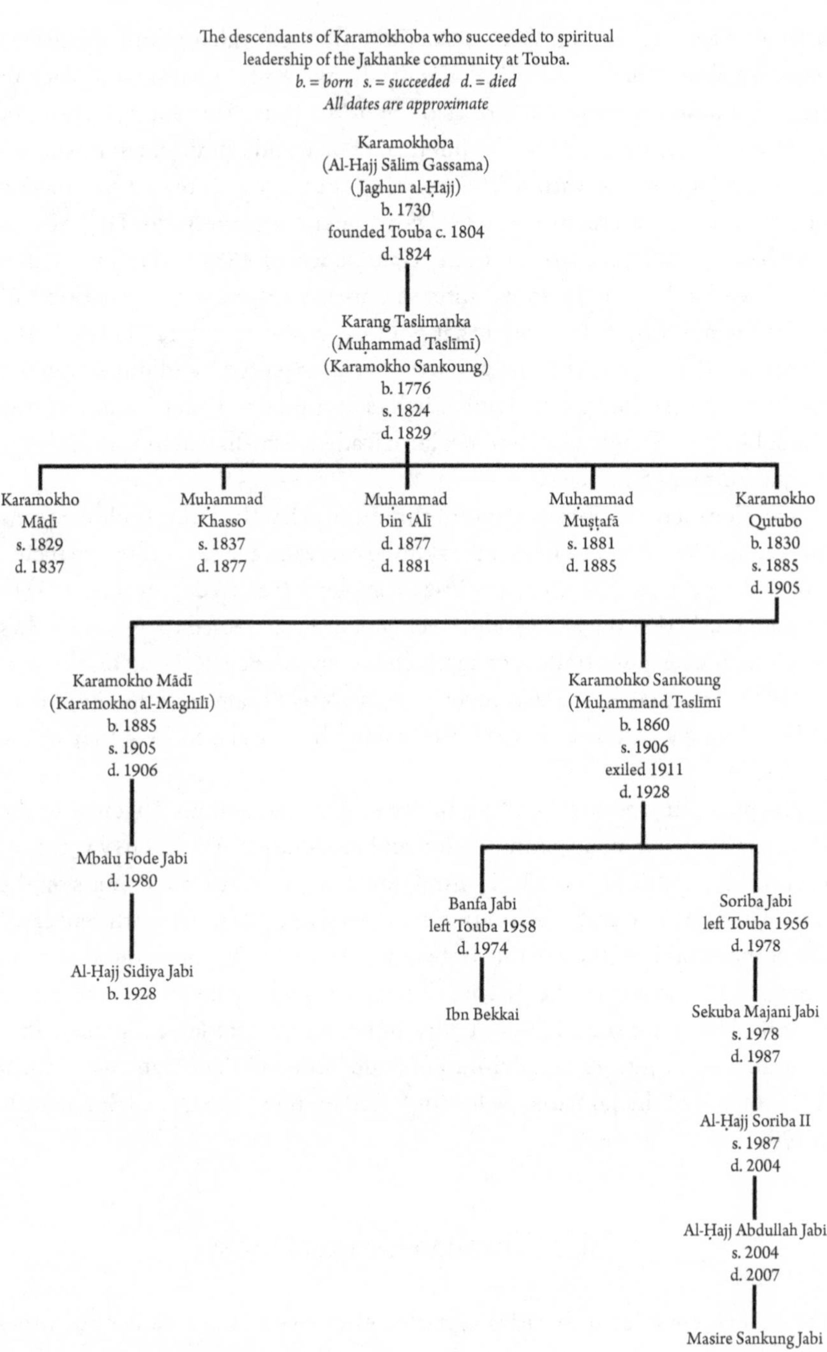

Figure 5.1 Clerical genealogy list. Created by the author.

dangerous in its capacity to disguise conspiracy. Administrators sought to drive a wedge between devotees of the two types of Islam.

By definition Islam *noir* was unstable, anthropolatrous as a personality cult, superstitious, stoked with ethnic pretension and naïveté, and too consumed by the exigencies of daily subsistence to engage in metaphysical thought or intellectual reflection. Islam *noir* was said to offer the African peasant a present divinity and a faith that "are contained in this natural world which feeds him, which supplies all his needs, and whose magnificence and mysterious power are sufficient for his spiritual aspirations."[26] Islam *noir* made West Africa look like a chessboard of mingling ethnic groups, where maraboutic jealousies and polemics attached themselves to secular rivalries of peoples, tribes, and races. Islam *noir* thus inhibited a general indigenous political awakening. It perpetuated ignorance of Islam's unifying power, and to enable unification of its inchoate fragments would be "to prepare with our own hands the means of our eventual ruin," which would "exceed all the limits of possible madness."[27]

A fickle Islam *noir* was easy prey for mischief-makers and their ambition to challenge colonial supremacy. The capricious African "bought one day with the price of gold will declare himself against us the following day if the white rats, the kolas, or other oracles give an unfavourable opinion."[28] In this view, religious conversion was a process wherein the infantile *joie de vivre* of the indigenous fetishist was checked, only to turn into morbid brooding and disgust for his previous life and frustration at being barred from the celestial delights of his new religion. The convert "walks, bent under the weight of a nagging obsession, his fevered fingers telling his beads. As if chewing in his sleep he constantly mouths his prayer *La illah ill'Allah,* which he repeats at first with a stubborn wish and then mechanically in the torpor of his vacant brain."[29] He is a fanatic waiting for a call to arms. This was how fingering the rosary came to be equated with saber rattling.

Conversely, Islam *arabe* threw down the gauntlet to the colonizers, fomenting sentiments of Pan-Islam. It owed allegiance to the worldwide Muslim society as the universal *jama'ah* (community) that rejected colonial rule's global ambitions as well as its context-specific methods. The pilgrimage was a potent force of Islam *arabe,* leading Africans on a Pan-Islamic course and fostering anti-Western animus. In a communication to his superiors in Paris, the French governor of the Ivory Coast warned of plans under review to track Muslim African contacts with Mecca, for

> it is to be feared that [the Muslim African leaders] will bring back cherifian directives from Mecca intended to unify the present diverse groups of AOF [French West Africa], the multiplicity and contrary tendencies of which make it easy for us at the moment to restrict and

> to supervise Islam, whereas anything which favors unification inevitably creates a danger for us.[30]

Admitting they lacked the power to control "the rallying slogans at their source" in Mecca, officials tried to stop the momentum at its impressionable local stage.

Islam *arabe* was calculated to obstruct "the fertile influences of [Western] civilization" and was disposed to plot revenge on the French. The more the administrators could keep the two types of Islam in mutual ignorance of each other, the better. A senior official tipped his hand in this divide-and-rule strategy. "I am aware of the fact," he wrote bluntly, "that in religion as in any political affair we have an interest in dividing rather than unifying."[31] Such categorizations often had undesirable consequences for the administrators. Administrator Clozel of the Ivory Coast found himself contemplating the unsettling prospects of the breakdown of "fetishist society," saying how, as a direct result of French conquest, Muslim groups would be left as beneficiaries of the defeat of pagan Africa.[32]

In its wider usage, "folk Islam" implies denigration of local reception and appropriation. Illiterate peasant society offered fertile soil for it. This is how the Islam of the desert nomads (*fellahin*) is characterized: it lacks the intrinsic capacity to produce religious values of consequence for society. Folk Islam reveals its primal limitations in the encounter with science and modern amenities, disposed to believe that "the man in white coat with the stethoscope may be the high priest of the divine inscrutable will." This attitude is described in Richard Critchfield's novel *Shahhat: An Egyptian*. With the instincts of a hardened member of the *fellahín*, Shahhat decries the inexorable march of modernity set to sweep away the landmarks of a familiar and cherished way of life. Things are what they are because they are predestined and part of Allah's plan. "Everything is from Alláh. . . . I cannot decide anything. Everything we are is from Him."[33]

The superstition of folk Islam lacks the sting of radical religion. Islam remains, but no longer as a dangerous force in politics or the modern world. One observer contends, perhaps too sanguinely, that, as "with Christianity in the West, Islamic civilization is being gradually detached from its religious roots, and the gulf between the spiritual and secular spheres of life is widening." He predicts that in Africa, "it is questionable whether Islam can be expected in the future to exercise the profound political effect it has had in earlier periods of African history."[34] This complacent view does not reckon with Boko Haram and Ash-Shabbat as a future likely challenge. At any rate, in the colonial estimation Islam *noir* was by no means a spent force, and measures would be taken to guard against the proliferation of its nefarious influence.[35]

In the end, colonial intervention in the affairs of Africa would not spare anyone: Africans, Muslims, whether *arabe* or *noir,* or even the French themselves. Cheikh Hamidou Kane, the Senegalese writer, aptly summed up the issue of colonial hegemony for all concerned. A character in his novel *Ambiguous Adventure* declares: "We have not had the same past, you and ourselves, but we shall have, strictly, the same future. The era of separate destinies has run its course. In that sense, the end of the world has indeed come for everyone of us, because no one can any longer live by the simple carrying out of what he himself is."[36]

The colonial policy of direct intervention and supervised assimilation, well articulated by Jules Ferry of the French Third Republic, demanded more than the cooperation of amenable religious leaders; it demanded collaboration and assimilation as the sequel to capitulation. The ubiquitous ethnic conundrum became an instrument of policy. Administrators were inclined to regard ethnicity as by nature prone to conspiracy, considering native culture too fickle to resist being exploited. Ethnic ill will, accordingly, loomed large in colonial fears of local antipathy to foreign rule, and it provided the rationale for confrontation and subjugation. Colonial powers assumed the moral authority to rule without the consent of local populations, whose new status as colonial subjects conflicted with ethnic interests. The imperial order created an acute dilemma for the Suwarian tradition; ethnicity and religion collided with foreign rule to compound the problem of the clerics.

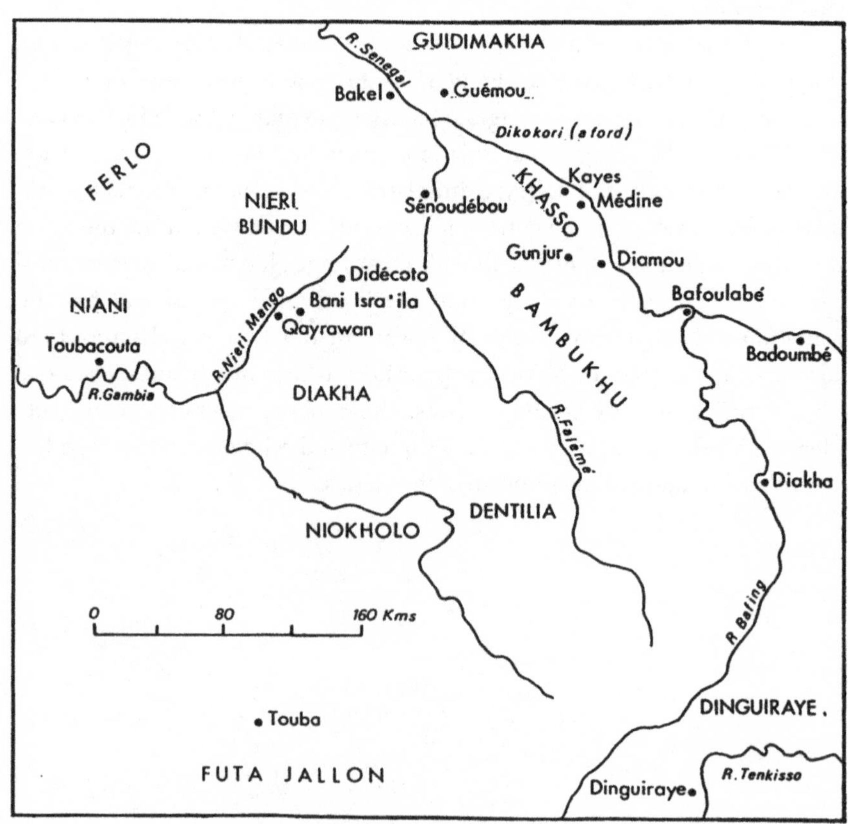

Figure 6.1 Jakhanke in Bundu. Created by the author.

8

Beyond Consolidation

Rejuvenating the Heritage

Thucydides does not seem to have grasped fully that in estimating the action of an individual in history his whole character must be taken into account; he is a psychical unity, and it is not possible to detach and isolate certain qualities. Psychological reconstruction is one of the most important as well as [most] delicate problems which encounter the historian, and Thucydides failed to realize all that it means. In his impatience of biographical trivialities, he went to the extreme of neglecting biography altogether.

—J. B. Bury, *The Ancient Greek Historians*, 146–147

New Beginnings in Futa Jallon

Yves Person (1925–1982), who taught African history at the Sorbonne and whose father took active part in the 1908 French colonial takeover of the Ivory Coast, attributes special significance to the role of the Jakhanke clerics in a Futa Jallon scarred by war and political upheaval. Futa Jallon, Person writes, "had exhausted its conquering strength but its cultural and religious prestige remained enormous. This was due largely to the Dyakhanke minority, whose main centre was Tuba, west of the Labé."[1] There was wide recognition among the Fulbe that the theocratic experiment was a failure. This is acknowledged in a Fula proverb to the effect that "the cleric (*tcherno*) begets a chief (*lamdo*), the chief begets an infidel (*kefero*)." We now explore the Jakhanke clerical role in Futa Jallon's religious and cultural fortunes.[2]

The reconstruction of religious life in Futa Jallon was instigated by al-Hajj Salim Gassama. Also known as Jaghun al-Hajj, he was the son of Muhammad Fatuma by his wife, Jaghun Ba, "the senior Jaghun." His name was adopted from al-Hajj Salim Suware, but he is known as Karamokhoba (eminent scholar), the *laqab* (honorific) given him by his admiring Fulbe hosts. Karamokhoba's family intended him to follow in the footsteps of al-Hajj Salim Suware, the prototypical cleric who brought about a watershed in the religious history of his people. History would vindicate the faith of Karamokhoba's parents. He became known for two great undertakings: he took long educational journeys, during which he gathered a large retinue of students and disciples, and he founded a clerical center and established there a reputation of learning and holiness.

The pursuit of prestige and *barakah* through scholarship and devotion is a recurring motif of the clerical life, and Karamokhoba stands as its exemplar. His biography gives us insight into how he was perceived by the clerical community. The community valued his faithful devotion and promotion of clerical heritage, rather than any bold personal actions he might have taken outside or against the canon. Despite his conservative outlook, Karamokhoba found ways to apply the Suwarian tradition to contemporary political and social problems, giving clerical teaching a new purpose and a new appeal for generations to come.

Biography of Karamokhoba

Karamokhoba was born around 1730 at Didecoto. He began his studies under Muhammad Fatuma, who left instructions for his son's further education before dying in 1750. Accordingly, Karamokhoba transferred his studies to Kounti in the Gambia, where a leading *tafsir* (exegesis) scholar of the Qur'an, Shaykh 'Uthman Derri, called Kounti *moro,* "the spiritual guide of Kounti," was established. Shaykh Derri had been a student of Muhammad Fatuma. Professional connections of this type provide important clues about the transmission of learning in Muslim Africa as well as about the network that supports it.

It is worth pausing here to describe the clerical atmosphere in the Kounti *majlis*. On a field trip to Kounti, a modern-day visitor would quickly notice the pastoral role of the presiding head of the *majlis,* who on the occasion in question was Shaykh Muhammad Khalifa Silla, who depended on the structure of consultation and delegation that held the community together. Under him were *qabílah* leaders who presided over family compounds. Around him were senior advisors who directed the professional affairs of the *majlis* and formed a consistory to adjudicate cases; the clerics did not take the oath or take part in civil suits. These advisors also received news and visitors. Schoolmasters and their assistants, with the aid of senior students, took charge of instruction and of organizing the means of it.

In the course of the visit, Shaykh Silla arrived at the town center after everyone had gathered, having just emerged from his prayers. After receiving reports from the *qabílah* leaders on the purpose of the meeting, including a verbatim account of the visitor's self-introduction, Shaykh Silla pronounced blessing on the gathering and directed his assistants to lead the assembly to the mosque where the grave of the founder of the *majlis* was located. This was Shaykh Silla's way of expressing the sincere good will of the *majlis* toward the pursuit of scholarship that occasioned the visit. He surprised the visiting party by appearing unannounced at the entrance of the mosque, where he led prayers of supplication and thanksgiving. He was said not to have missed a single *salat* in all the decades he led the community, deserving the title *dhu ath-thafínát* (the one with the callosities) by reason of the deep prostration marks on his forehead.[3]

Shaykh Derri conferred on Karamokhoba the award of a *khirqah* to recognize his outstanding scholarly merit. At the conclusion of his studies in Kounti, Karamokhoba returned to Didecoto, then proceeded to Gunjúr. The account of his life says that he resolved to adopt the path of shaykh-seeking to acquire knowledge: *nahadat bihi al-hammah al-'aliyah ilá maqámát rijál 'lláh ta'álá fa-'amala al-rihlah.*[4] It recalls the exhortation of the classical rule that the seeker after knowledge "should not become sated from the length of discipleship, for the teacher is like a date palm: you wait for something to fall on you from it."[5]

Karamokhoba's return to Didecoto opened a new chapter in his life, and the career of shaykh-seeking henceforth placed him on the path of learning and study. After his move to Gunjúr, his teacher was Fode Ibrahim Jané, known by the *laqab* Gunjúruba: "the great scholar of Gunjúr." Under Fode Jané, Karamokhoba studied the *Mukhtaşir* ("Abridgement") of Shaykh Khalil, a standard Málikí work. Then, under Fode Hasan Gakou, he studied the *Maqámát* ("Assemblies") of al-Harírí, followed by a *fanna* (branch) of *tafsír* under Fode Muhammad Jawara. After his studies in Bundu he went to Khasso, where he studied *nahw* (grammar) and resumed study of *tafsír* under Fode 'Amar Ture. From there he traveled to Bakhunu, where under Fode al-Hasan Fulání he studied the two-volume commentary *al-Makíkí*, a work on *tawhíd* (theology). At Bakhunu, his teachers included Fode Bakari Jabaghate, with whom he studied the works of al-Sanúsí in five volumes and who reportedly greatly impressed him. Karamokhoba went on to Jenne with the intention of studying Islamic jurisprudence, *li-qasdi ta'allam al-shifá*. While in Jenne he made the acquaintance of numerous scholars, including Alfa Núhí, the Fulani. Alfa Núhí is represented in the account as a man with a prodigious memory, a master of forty branches of learning (*hafiz 'arba'ina fanna min funún*).

Karamokhoba's other teachers included Alfa Hátib, with whom he continued study of jurisprudence based on the work *Shifá* by Abí al-Fadl 'Iyád bin Músá.[6] He proceeded to more advanced studies (*fanna al-awfáq*) under Alfa Ráha and then, under the guidance of 'Umar Nahawí, commenced study of philology through *al-Fiyah,* the work of Andalusian jurist Ibn Málik (d. 1274).[7] Muhmmad Nahawí taught him more *taşríf* and *lúghah* (linguistics). He also studied under Muhammad Tumáju, Muhammad Kharáshí, Muhammad Ghullí, and Muhammad Kamisátu, all still much loved among the clerics. This lengthy list of Karamokhoba's teachers shows how "his competence has become complete, his preeminence apparent," having "studied, reviewed, and perused" the sources necessary for his scholarly career.[8]

That the clerics preserved such detailed records of Karamokhoba's scholastic career shows the great value they placed on learning, travel, and mastering the religious canon. That such a rich store of intellectual resources was available to Karamokhoba is a clear indication of the thriving state of Islamic learning in precolonial West Africa.[9] To the clerics, study was a more natural companion to religion than jihad. Knowledge of the divine law did not compel a call to arms and power, as the standard theory of jihad has long maintained.

Among Karamokhoba's many teachers, no star shines brighter than that of Alfa Núhí. The accounts testify that it was Alfa Núhí who brought Karamokhoba to full intellectual stature by initiating him into the Qadiriyah *wird,* the *wird* Alfa Núhí had received from Shaykh Mukhtár al-Kuntí of the Kunta Arabs. The practical effect of this spiritual investiture was to license Karamokhoba to undertake a fresh clerical initiative on his own authority. He had completed his studies and obtained the commendation of his teachers. His seventeen-year association with Alfa Núhí signaled his passage from an itinerant life to one of residential leadership. From this time on, when Karamokhoba traveled to meet religious masters, it was to confirm his scholarly standing and to receive affirmation in their company.

From Jenne Karamokhoba traveled to Masina. There he made the acquaintance of a charismatic scholar, Muhammad Taslimi Saghanogho (d. 1825–1826), who left a lasting impression on him. [10] At this point the chronology becomes rather shaky, but it is known that Karamokhoba's meeting with Saghanogho inspired him to found a settlement. He named his new center Taslimi, after Saghanogho. He lived there for three years, then took a number of short trips.

An important journey took him to what would become Sierra Leone, to a place called "Mfailo" (sometimes "Failung"). This journey is memorialized by a miracle he is reported to have performed there. Before he reached the town, he received a prophecy from a man he met on the road, who told him that in a forthcoming visit he would marry a princess who would bear him his spiritual heir and successor. Once in the town, he was told that a large piece of rock was obstructing passage in an unidentified nearby river. Using the prayer ritual called *'ilm al-asrár,* resulting in *ru'yá al-şálihah* (a dream fulfilled subsequently—a sound dream is so-called because it is clear enough not to require interpretation, *ta'bír al- ru'yá*), Karamokhoba caused the blockage to be removed. The town's chief, Isháq Kamara, offered a reward in form of the hand of his daughter, Aisatu ('Ā'isha) Kamara. Karamokhoba paid a large dowry (*mahr*) in gold, which some accounts say Chief Kamara returned to Karamokhoba to distribute as a votive offering—a sign of the latter's high religious esteem. With Aisatu ('Ā'isha) Kamara, Karamokhoba had a son, Muhammad Taslimi, also known as Karamokho Taslimi. He then went to Kankan where he lived for three years before moving to Konya.

According to the *Ta'ríkh on Suware and Karamokhoba* (*TKB*) and *Kitáb al-Bushrá,* the miracle Karamokhoba performed in Sierra Leone began his public career. It is worth noting that Islamic religious scholars did not dismiss the power of dreams and spirits. They included the subject of dreams in the rules of orthodox practice. One popular work on dreams is the *Ta'bír al-Ru'yá,* attributed to Muhammad bin Sírín (d. 728), who is cited as the author of another work on the subject that is widely circulated in Muslim Africa.[11] The magisterial authority is al-Nábulsí (d. 1731), who authored a two-volume study of dreams.[12] Like Ibn Khaldun, these authorities consider dreams one-forty-sixth part of the qualifications of prophecy and dream interpretation (*ta'bír*) one of the religious sciences.[13] The clerics use the term *dabara* (cabbalistic technique) in their therapeutic work of prescribing remedies for afflictions of evil spirits, sparing the arcane and spirit power from stigma or condemnation.[14] Certain Qur'anic passages, copied out on wooden slates and washed, with the water collected in a receptacle, are employed as protection against evil spirits. Dream work has a place in respectable scholarship and should not be dismissed as religious ignorance or associated only with naïve folk Islam. The clerics who study and employ it take part in a venerable tradition.[15] Cabalistic learning is steeped in study of Scripture; in Islam "magic is legitimized by religion."[16] The metaphysics of Islam overlapped well with the primal African worldview; indeed, this aspect of Islam has attracted such populations as the Maguzawa people of north Nigeria, who continued to resist full-scale conversion despite adopting the Islamic religious vocabulary.[17]

Karamokhoba arrived in Kankan shortly after performing the miracle, accompanied by his community of family members, students, and disciples: essentially a fledgling clerical community. *TSK* lists the names of the leading members of this traveling party as well as their places of origin.[18] The extensive detail here shows great pride in the clerical vocation as a calling elevated above the political: any town or country could be a destination without being a homeland, and settling down did not mean that a cleric was relinquishing the vocation of the itinerant pastoral life.

Karamokhoba received a warm welcome in Kankan. Despite his announced intention of pressing on, leading citizens prevailed on him to settle among them. His visit coincided with the visit of Muslim notables from Jenne, who gifted him a cow to honor him and as a plea that he accede to the wish of the Muslim leaders and adopt Kankan as his home. Karamokhoba relented, accepting their plea and their gift. He gave the cow to one of his senior students, Karang Dawda Suware, for slaughter (*yadhbahuhá*). Not to be outdone by the Muslims from Jenne, the people of Kankan assigned to Karamokhoba four men as his personal assistants: Karamokho Khadijata Madi, grandfather of Muhammad Sharíf (better known as Sharif Fanta Madi, d. 1955); Karang Talib Silla; Karang ʻUthman Kamara; and a son of Alfa Mahmud Kaba. Karamokhoba stayed three years in Kankan operating a school and receiving visitors. He made a deep impact on Islamic teaching and learning in the town; clerical sources extol him as "the founder of Qur'anic teaching" in Kankan.[19] There is little doubt that Karamokhoba found an eager, receptive audience in Kankan and that Kankan's clerics felt that his presence there elevated their profession. The descendants of Mahmud Kaba, a member of al-Hajj Salim Suware's Diakhaba community who immigrated to Kankan, were glad to reassemble under Karamokhoba's guidance. We read in the *Kitáb al-Bushrá*, written by a descendant, a cogent epitaph for Karamokhoba's influence in Kankan: *wa baqí fíha áthára ʻilmihi ilá zamániná hadha* (he bequeathed there his scholarly heritage that has endured into our own time).[20] Published in Tunis (no date) and out of print, the *Kitáb al-Bushrá* is authored by al-Hajj Soriba (d. 1978) and is one of the very few works we have on the Sufi connections of the clerics of Touba. The book also shows how close the clerics kept to the Qur'an and *hadíth* as standard authorities of Muslim religious life.

In the 1770s, around the time of Karamokhoba's visit, local warrior Condé Brahima launched an attack on Baté on the Milo River. Baté was an important political center and an immigration point of the Jakhite-Kaba clerics. Attacks there and elsewhere failed, and the clerics regrouped under leader Alfa Kabiné Kaba to resume life in the Milo valley.[21] Not much more is known about Alfa Kabiné Kaba apart from the fact that clerical chronicles consider him important enough to include in the list of religious leaders.

The Kankan sojourn was of personal as well as spiritual significance to Karamokhoba. While there, Aisatou Kamara gave birth to his sixth son, whom he named after his clerical patron, Muhammad Taslimi of Jenne. From Kankan, Karamokhoba traveled to Lako in the canton of Oualada, a strong Mandinka center, where he lived for a year. It was while practicing in Lako that he made wide-ranging contact with Fulbe leaders, including, as previously noted, Imam Abdoulaye Bademba, a son and heir of Karamokho Alfa. Bademba lavished honors on Karamokhoba, including a special burnous that cost 100 dinars. Karamokhoba prudently decided to meet also with ʻAbd al-Qádir of the Soriya, who presented him with gifts, including seven slaves and a thoroughbred horse ("*fa'akramahu wa a'aṭáhu sab'ah 'abíd wa farsan a'tíqan*").[22]

At Lako, Karamokhoba met Alfa Muhammad Woinké, a respected erudite scholar versed in several disciplines (*'álim mutafannin*) with whom he rehearsed (*tadhákara*) his earlier studies in theology. In the meantime, students and disciples from Timbo were flocking to him. He was pressured to accept political office in Futa Jallon but resisted, invoking his clerical vows. The offer of the position of a paramount chief at a place of his own choosing he turned down firmly. He made his reasons clear: political offices had never belonged to the clerical heritage he was raised in, and he had never entertained the possibility of assuming one under any circumstances.

Karamokhoba's sentiments are echoed by Ahmad al-Bakka'í, the Tuareg scholar-warrior, when he wrote to his mortal foe, the *mujahid* al-Hajj 'Umar al-Fútí (d. 1864). Ahmad al-Bakka'í explained his rejection of jihad.

> "My conditions," he declared, "are the conditions of my forefathers. We teach the ignorant, put right those who have deviated, and meet the needs of those who seek our help. We do not master anyone, nor will be mastered by anyone . . . I replied to these people [the followers of Muhammad Bello who wrote to him], 'I am fully aware of the merits of jihad, but jihad leads to *mulk* (political office and kingship)—and *mulk* leads to *zalm* (tyranny). Our present condition as it is is more suitable to us for not having indulged in jihad, and more assuring to us for not having indulged in unlawful things which jihad would entail.' "[23]

Al-Bakka'í appealed to the teaching of his grandfather, Sidi Mukhtár al-Kabir al-Kunti (d. 1811) on the separation of religious authority from political authority. [24] Pacifist practice actively prohibits involvement in jihad or political life, the point made by Karamokhoba to the Futa Jallon *mawubé*. Yet in his confrontation with al-Hajj 'Umar, al-Bakka'í hypocritically resorted to violence for his cause. Earlier al-Hajj 'Umar saw fit to mock a local ruler whose grandfather was a highly respected man of religion and learning who, upon obtaining power, promptly lost his sanity, the point being that learning and, in this case, political power, did not mix well.[25] Al-Hajj 'Umar seems to have violated his own rule about not mixing religion and power.

This charge that al-Bakka'í initially made is virtually identical to one made against al-Hajj 'Umar al-Fútí by his own *shaykh* in Mecca, Muhammad al-Ghálí. While initiating al-Hajj 'Umar al-Fútí into the Tijániíyáh *wird* and conferring on him the status of most favored disciple, al-Ghálí demanded that 'Umar should "cease associating with kings or sultans" and that he should never seek temporal power lest al-Ghálí should cease "sustaining him in his prayers and intercessions." Al-Ghálí pressed upon 'Umar the necessity of abjuring temporal power, reminding him of the words of the prophet: "the best emírs are those who comply with the wishes of the 'ulamá, and the worst 'ulamá are those who comply with the wishes of the emirs" and "the 'ulamá have the security of the Messenger of God as long as they spurn association with sultans. But if they associate themselves with sultans, they are unfaithful to the Messengers."[26]

The Decision to Settle

Encouraged by official cooperation and popular demand, Karamokhoba decided to establish his *majlis* in Futa Jallon, which he subsequently did in 1804. He convened a council to spell out his terms: unrestricted movement; full control over his personal destiny; peace and tranquility for his community; an agreement that the clerics would be subject to the authority of the *majlis* rather than secular jurisdiction; and renunciation by the people of jihad, strife, and divisiveness. He underlined the pastoral role he saw for himself by citing a *hadíth* from the Prophet, to the effect that every Muslim is a shepherd of the flock entrusted to him. He obtained from the political leadership a pledge of good faith on these terms, confirming clerical independence and political neutrality.

Karamokhoba's decision to establish his *majlis* in Futa Jallon was a watershed decision in clerical history, and it opened a new and brilliant chapter on his pastoral career. The ruler of southern Futa Jallon, where Karamokhoba traveled, was the vassal chief (*al-amír al-mutawallí*) Modi 'Abdullah Wura. Like so many before him, Modi 'Abdullah Wura was impressed by Karamokhoba, so much so that he apprenticed his son, Alfa Salihu, to him. Karamokhoba met several scholars in Futa Jallon: Bakari Bote and Sa'd b. Ibrahim al-Dalmi, from whom he sought *barakah*. At Labé, Karamokhoba convened a town meeting where he taught the merits of pacifist Islam, exploring many *hadíths* for this purpose and impressing on those present the importance of the pacifist vocation. He took his pacifist message directly to the people, leaving them in no doubt that he was proposing a radical alternative to jihad. He proposed exchanging the sword of war for the rosary and the inkpot, the rules of extraction for the arts of peaceful persuasion and principle. He proclaimed that struggle in the path of God (*jihad fi sabil li-llah*) as enjoined in the Qur'an (ii:190–193) was ultimately about embarking on the path of the higher life, what al-Ghazali calls *sálik sabíl 'l-haqq* ("the traveler in search of truth"), not merely the mindless observance of rituals.[27]

> It is not piety, that you turn your faces
> To the East and to the West.
> True piety is this:
> To believe in God, and the Last Day,
> the angels, the Book, and the Prophets,
> to give of one's substance, however cherished,
> to kinsmen, and orphans,
> the needy, the traveller, beggars,
> and to ransom the slave,
> to perform the prayer, to pay the alms.
>
> Qur'an ii:177 (Arberry's translation)

According to Karamokhoba, religion practiced with a focus on ethical obligation was the pacifist path. He pleaded for the support of the wider Muslim public. It was in pursuit of looking to the support of Muslims in general that, after reaching an understanding with the Fulbe *mawubé*, Karamokhoba took his campaign directly to the people.

Chiefs in Fouta Jallon vied to host him. Modi 'Abdallah Wura's symbolic gift (*tawallá*) of his son, Alfa Salihu, was intended to woo Karamokhoba to Wura. Karamokhoba dwelled there briefly. Age and his demanding travel schedule had started to take their toll, and the obstacles of fame were making travel increasingly difficult. He was more than seventy years old, his reputation and his community were growing, and a younger generation was ready to take its turn. The saying of Sa'id ibn Jubayr that "a man remains a scholar as long as he learns" could be practiced in a sedentary lifestyle as well as in wayfaring.[28] Karamokhoba left Wura for Touba-coto (old Touba) in Bakoni, where he would stay for eleven years. He founded a *majlis* between 1804 and 1805, constructing some four hundred compounds. The size of the community was an indication of how impracticable a roaming life had become. As the community expanded, neighboring populations began to take notice. Their alarm increased when the influx did not slow down with time. In the end, trouble broke out. The threatened Bassari of Tanda made sorties on Touba-coto. In one fatal assault, the settlement was sacked, heavy casualties inflicted, and many captives taken. These captives included a son of Karamokhoba, Muhammad al-Kabir, who was able to escape to safety. The attack signaled strongly that the clerics were in unfriendly, non-Muslim country (*bilád al-kufr*) and unwelcome. The clerics, well accustomed to dispersion, relocated. The attack had been more or less the last gasp of the already endangered Bassari, who, like the neighboring Baga, went into decline thenceforth as a result of conflict with their neighbors.

A warm welcome awaited the unsettled community in the district of Binani. There they were received by Modi al-Husayn, the reigning ruler. His welcome persuaded Karamokhoba to make a second attempt at founding a *majlis* in Futa Jallon. He was an octogenarian by now, and his assistants encouraged him to make one more effort to find a permanent place for his people. Following the guidance of his senior wife, Nana Ba, who received a message in an assuring dream (*ru'yá al-ṣálihah*), he founded Touba-Binani. Touba-Binani was an especially significant achievement after the disastrous Touba-coto. The clerics saw auspicious signs in their second attempt at settlement.

It is remarkable that Islam faced and survived political challenges of so many kinds; that so many states and kingdoms emerged and vanished; that diverse populations had embraced, deferred, or resisted the call to faith; and that through all these changes the religious canon remained recognizably itself. Once preponderant in the Mali empire, Islam survived past Mali and did not fade out of subsequent communities despite centuries of collapsing political structures. Religious practices offered a sustained moral vision for society and continuity for succeeding generations.

Whatever material profit there may be in religion is hardly evident, if evident at all, in the clerics' nomadic careers and self-exclusion from power. For clerics, nation-building was not their calling. For political elites, the pursuit of power is its own justification and aggrandizing power—what Tocqueville calls the "hunger for tyranny"—its fuel cell. For this reason, as Voltaire noted, governments must have both shepherds and butchers, one for moral guidance and the other for self-serving ends. Confining themselves to the religious sphere in Muslim society, the clerics shunned political power to devote themselves to scholarship and pastoral care. They did not reject authority; they rejected power. Voluntary exiles and yet at home everywhere, clerics broadened the idea of religion beyond the local and the temporal. The pacifist tradition created new boundaries when clerics established settlements in new pastures. Their observance of Islam connected them with other Muslims, while their pacifist teaching set them apart.

Settling at Touba: Diakhaba Reaffirmed

> And though it in the centre sit,
> Yet when the other far doth roam,
> It leans, and hearkens after it,
> And grows erect, as that comes home.

> Such wilt thou be to me, who must
> Like th' other foot, obliquely run;
> Thy firmness makes my circle just,
> And makes me end, where I begun.
>
> —John Donne

When setting up a new *majlis,* the clerics typically planned to build a community mosque as a symbol and sign of professional commitment. At the new Touba, circumstances were different. Building a mosque there took some time to accomplish. Painful memories of old Touba were still fresh, and it seemed possible that events might take another sour turn and compel further relocation. It took seven years for Karamokhoba, now nearly ninety, to approve the design and construction of a mosque. In a ceremony to mark the completion of the mosque, he was installed as *imám ratti* (presiding imam). He remained in that position for another seven years before dying in 1824.

It is important to note that Karamokhoba was viewed by his community as the holder of a religious rather than a political office, and in this the clerics were in step with several examples of religious distancing from politics. The example of al-Qábisí, a Málikí jurist of Tunisia, was cited earlier, and in Songhay we saw several instances of the scholars turning their backs on offers of political appointment and favor. When he surveyed the structure of Muslim life and government, Ibn Khaldun looked to religion for ultimate authority. "This is because the purpose of human beings is not only their worldly welfare. This entire world is trifling and futile." This is why the Qur'an challenges, "Do you think we created you triflingly?" Ibn Khaldun continues: "The purpose of human beings is their religion," concluding that the imám holds a position of the highest moral leadership.

> The leadership of the prayer (*imámat al-ṣalát*) is the highest of all these functions [listed as prayer, the office of judge, the office of mufti, the holy war, and market supervision (*hisbah*)] and higher than [kingship] (*al-mulk*) as such, which, like [prayer] falls under the Caliphate. . . . If this is established, know then that mosques in a city are of two kinds: the great and spacious mosques devoted to public prayers, and the smaller ones which belong to a particular group or quarter.[29]

The backing of the Fulbe political leadership and the support of neighboring populations allowed the clerics to establish Touba on solid foundations. The model for Touba was Diakhaba. In that model, the clerical population was apportioned into four principal wards or sections, each assigned with specific tasks and functions. [30] The mosque was the focal point of pastoral life and community affairs. The first section (*al-qasm al-awwal*) was the Karambaya, composed of the families of Kaba, Silla, Darame, Ture, Suware, Fadiga, Dabo, and Jallo. Attached to them were members of the *nyamakala*, what social scientists call ascriptive occupational groups: tanners (*garanké*), goldsmiths (*numu foro*), and blacksmiths (*numu jong*).[31] The second section was Gassamakunda Temoto (Middle Gassama-kunda) and Gassamakunda Santo (Upper Gassama-kunda), both with affiliates from the caste groups and their families. The third was Fofana-Girasi, Sise, Dumbuya, Jawara, and Kamara; they also had caste groups assigned to them. The final ward included families of the Fofana-Jula, Bajo, Dansokho, and Minte. At the head of the whole community was the Karambaya *qasm* (ward) under the pastoral office of Karamokhoba, the office Jobson terms the "high Priesthood." Karamokhoba's jurisdiction extended over the entire community, except for the dependent castes (including slaves), which were under the authority of their respective landlords and masters. The slave population was fairly large and a source of labor.

True to type, Karamokhoba had a large family, and the accounts pay close attention to the subject. He had twelve sons and eight daughters, of whom nine sons survived and had families of their own. We do not have any information about the daughters on that score. Eventually the families of Karamokhoba's sons subdivided into five sections, and only one son, Muhammad Khasso, went away to establish his own *majlis* at Kanjalong in the Casamance.[32] The blessings of family had their counterpart in the spiritual gifts bestowed on Karamokhoba.

Touba and the Clerical Network

Touba remained out of bounds to political leaders. The clerics ran their own affairs and maintained a network of contacts with other clerical centers and with outside powers. As was intended, the town became a magnet for visitors and students. The clerics went on periodic pastoral tours (*tournées pastorals*) to rally support, mobilize resources, establish connections, and expand the clerical range. An endowment was created to build a granary to host guests, stage ceremonies, and assist the needy in the community. Karamokhoba traversed a large geographical area in his educational career, and his influence was strong on his disciples and successors who followed in their turn. The centers offered support, encouragement, and protection in times of danger.

Composed of the leaders of the four *qabílah* sections with Karamokhoba at the head, a consistorial council laid down procedures, handled disputes and disagreements, and made rulings. The presiding head of the community was responsible for setting standards of educational performance, establishing and implementing the curriculum, and enforcing discipline. Marriage, naming ceremonies, property, succession, inheritance, funerals, trade, security, and the acquisition and deployment of slaves all came under the responsibility of the consistorial council. The forms and practices were based on the tradition created by al-Hajj Salim Suware, another way in which Touba was consciously designed on the pattern of Diakhaba. Touba's clerics were determined to repeat the professional endeavor that was the heritage of the pacifist clerical life.

Touba's reputation for learning and sanctity spread throughout Futa Jallon and beyond, and such an active network is the lifeblood of a clerical establishment. The clerics began a recruitment drive in the surrounding country. Continuity with the legacy of Mali was maintained, in that Touba emerged as the preeminent center of teaching and scholarship for Mandinka populations across the diaspora, including the Bambara, Jallonke, Kuranko, and Fulbe. The clerics used pacifist teaching to refocus ethnic allegiance by building diversity and tolerance into the structure of religious life. In so doing, they neither ignored nor fomented ethnic distinctions; rather, their pacifist commitment offered a peaceful outlet for ethnic distrust. Trusted by their neighbors for their religious reputation and political neutrality, the clerics were accepted as honest brokers of moderation and reconciliation. They showed that one could be religious without ethnic qualification—after all, faith does not come of ethnic entitlement.

The Clerical Withdrawal From Politics

The clerics are a taciturn people. Their religious modesty discourages them from seeking the political limelight. At several clerical centers, clerics are inclined to much diffidence in matters of personal attainment or material possessions. This modesty is institutional as well as personal; size does not determine the importance of a center. Of real importance is that political rulers respect the autonomous standing of these settlements, usually established in clusters. This is how Ahmad Baba described Diakhaba and its satellite villages: the town was a leading Islamic settlement with oversight of "twenty villages, all of them Muslim unmixed with any unbeliever."[33] As we have seen, Jobson describes a similar setup at Sutukho where what he called "the habitations and course of lives" separated the clerics from standard Muslim towns. The *TF*, Labat, Park, Delafosse, Monteil, and others made similar observations about the residential separation of the clerics, and this clerical pattern was also seen in Timbuktu.[34] Residential separation, with the clerics living off the beaten track, created a favorable environment in which to practice moderation and modesty. The clerics took great care to avoid becoming entangled in contentious state disputes. Having abandoned the idea of possessing the earth for a homeland, they were free to stake their reputation on religion as a calling without partisan borders. They were too religious to use religion as a bone of contention or as an instrument of expedience, and they did not need a fixed benefice to be viable. Exchanging the rosary for the gun and taking the prayer rug as pledge and security, they embarked on their mission of travel and education, walking the earth with meekness and bearing patiently the swings and arrows of misfortune (Qur'an 31:15).

Miracles in Islam

The miracle stories of the clerics have strong social resonance. Their underlying premise is that miracles are not rewards or tokens of purity of life, strength of will, and singleness of heart. Instead, they are favors God bestows on those close to Him. Miracles, says Ibn Khaldun, "are not within the ability of men, but beyond their power," suggesting that men cannot claim credit for them. Those close to God in this sense are called the *awliyá* (saints; sing. *walí*). The difference as applies to prophets is that miracles "take the place of an explicit statement from God to the effect that a particular prophet is truthful, and they are proof of the truth. An evidential miracle is the combination of a 'wonder' and the 'advance challenge' (*tahhadí*) that [announces] it."[35]

In contrast, miracles in the Western tradition typically come of ascetic monastic feats of poverty, chastity, austerity, and obedience. From its roots in Egypt, the monastic movement did far more than any other single institution to spread the Christian faith to societies and cultures as widespread as Axum and Iceland. Monks flung themselves into spiritual combat in remarkable defiance of human frailty. Those who live in the flesh cannot please God—or, in this case, their human superiors—and so war against the flesh was unremitting, with solitary physical deprivation a constant theme. [36] Monastic virtue was achieved through self-mortification with stoic disregard for worldly comfort. Marcarius of Alexandria (d. 391 AD) subsisted for seven years on scraps of cabbage leaves. Serapion of Antioch (d. 211 AD) lived in a cave at the bottom of an abyss, shocking intrepid visitors with his physical state, which they described as haggard and depleted beyond recognition. Serapion had abandoned his life in the Roman aristocracy for the grueling discipline of monastic sequestration.

Monastic obedience was as often taken to extremes. At the command of his superior, a novice would plunge into a raging furnace and emerge unscathed at the other end—worthy reward of his obedience. One monk was set the task of watering his abbot's walking stick until it flowered, which necessitated two-mile daily trips to the Nile for the purpose. In his third year of watering, God took pity on him and caused the stick to bloom. The cult of martyrdom in which zealots provoke attacks to earn martyrs' rewards is a familiar example of the extreme lengths to which ascetic severity would go. These acts in themselves have no intrinsic social merit. They are valued only as feats of faith and unquestioning obedience. Monks seldom washed, because cleanliness was considered antithetical to godliness. The rewards for such feats of personal obedience and endurance were marvels and miracles, the proliferation of which brought prestige and influence to the institutions and individuals concerned. The reputation for thaumaturgy was coveted, as demonstrated in the life of St. Gregory Thaumaturgus (d. c. 270 AD). He was the wonder worker whose ideas were formative in the development of the Nicene Creed. As his *jamu* indicates, it was his reputation for healing and exorcism that lifted him in the eyes of his contemporaries.

While it is true that Muslim ascetics (*zuhhád*) indulged in corresponding feats of personal endurance, the theology and social context are fundamentally different. The Muslim religious code "suppresses the austerities and the numerous interdictions imposed upon the Jews by the Mosaic law, abolishes the macerations of Christianity, and declares its willingness to comply with the weakness and frailty of man, and the practical necessities of life. 'Alláh lays upon each man only what he can fulfil.' "[37]

There were exceptions for individuals who were themselves exceptional, such as Hasan al-Baṣrí (d. 728 AD) and Ibráhim b. Adham, prince of Balkh (d. 777 AD). In the Muslim religious canon, however, attending to the desires of the flesh is not a shameful contradiction of virtue; bodily cleanliness is an obligation of religious practice, as is raising a family. The example of Rábi'ah of Basra (d. 801 AD), a Sufi poetess who rejected marriage to devote herself to the mystical quest of divine love, is recognized as the exception that proves the rule. She once said, "I will not serve God like a laborer, in expectation of my wages." Rábi'ah was a pivotal figure in the transition of asceticism to mysticism (*taṣawwuf*). By the tenth century, Islamic mysticism had become a social institution that, not unlike the monasteries, profoundly influenced Muslim life.

Not wholly devoid of worldliness, Sufi brotherhoods used their organizational strength and popular appeal to compete with political rulers for religious authority over the Prophet's heritage. The *faqíh* (jurist), called *fode* by the clerics, and the *faqír* (mendicant, dervish) may be "strangers" to the world, subsisting on acacia pods and water while guests around them feast on sumptuous food, but such self-denial and defiance of convention have their limits. For one thing, making a spectacle of self-mortification might be criticized for trying to "force the hand of God," and for another, the obligation of Scripture to "command the good and forbid the wrong" stipulates paying attention to the affairs of the world. Spiritual devotion cannot replace the responsibility of earning a livelihood and meeting the demands of organized society. Withdrawal on that basis is not permanent or complete seclusion. After all, the *walí,* as "the friend of God," is also the intercessor and advocate of the needs of the people. The *walí* is such because his prayers are answered, typically in tangible manifestations of healing, success, protection, and power.[38] He "has charge of rain, of harvests, of troops, and of sickness. He intervenes in disputes. He is protector of the weak and the oppressed. He instructs children in the rudiments of the faith. He takes a wife from among the leading families, and becomes a *shaykh* or *muqaddam.*"[39]

The Jakhanke clerics have not seen fit to promote their work dressed in rags, eating peanut shells, and drinking rain water—all grist to the mill of hagiography. On the contrary, clerical *barakah* is distinguished by the success and prosperity it cultivates in building family, students, disciples, dependents, supporters, and community well-wishers. The social order is fitting background of religious biography. The lives of the clerics never rose to the level of the medieval *Lives of the Saints*[40] or to that of the legends of the Greek gods. In the case of the clerics, biography is not deification or civic glorification. Biography here is a model of fidelity and modesty, prized for the spiritual blessings it brings.

Accounts and field investigation reveal the cleric to be a sedate, sober, and self-possessed professional, painted in the grey, measured proportions of Maliki legal constraints rather than in the vivid colors of ecstatic fervor. The miracles of Karamokhoba show this respect for restraint and for the religious status quo. The miracles create no new precedents for faith and practice, nor do they establish the cleric as a contending authority. The purpose of reporting miracles is to inculcate confidence in the religious code. The devotion and trust they inspire in disciples and sympathizers bind those worshipers more firmly to canonical teaching. By nature, miracles call for devotion to the revealed canon.

The miracle stories of Karamokhoba demonstrate this. In one story, Karamokhoba is said to appear distressed for no ostensible reason. Upon inquiry, it was discovered that he had learned by miraculous means of the plight of a former student, who was in danger of dying in an accident at sea. The student had fallen off a capsized boat and in his distress cried to Karamokhoba to save him. "The shaykh then rescued him from the sea safe and sound. The shaykh was not absent from Touba for more than half an hour or thereabouts. When he reappeared, someone asked him and he explained."[41] Oral accounts embellish this story. It is said that Karamokhoba sat among his astonished students, dripping with water from the rescue mission. He explained that he had just saved a drowning student. In the written account, his physical appearance revealed what he had done.

A variation on the theme is offered in another account. Karamokhoba set out to lead the *'asr* (afternoon) prayer at the main mosque. He opened the prayer with the standard *takbír* ("*Alláh-u-akbar*") and had completed one standing position (*rak'ah*) when, contrary to the stipulated rules, he broke off with the *taslím*, the greeting that closes the worship. He explained that he had just been brought news that Shaykh Muhktár al-Kuntí (d. 1811) had died in the early part of the afternoon, and the *'asr* prayer just interrupted was joined by the unseen prayers of the saints in mourning for al-Kuntí. This happened on Wednesday, the fifteenth of Jumáda al-Ākhiratu in the year AH 1226.[42] He had not received the news, it is claimed, from any person until that point in the prayer when he had miraculous intimation of it. Students and observers drew from this the lesson that devotion to worship will bring manifest blessings. A miracle in this sense is not proof of personal sanctity but rather the reward of a life of service and devotion to the religious canon, without any implications of sainthood.

One miracle attends to the prestige of the clerical vocation and its vindication against secular power. Bakari Tamba, a Jallonke ruler, took a dislike to and arrested Muhammad (al-Kabir), not knowing Muhammad to be a son of Karamokhoba was miraculously made aware of the incident during the night of the arrest when he prayed and called to God (*fa'ibtahala ilá-lláh*) to intercede for his son's welfare. Immediately, Bakari Tamba appeared in Karamokhoba's house, where he faced a barrage of questions: Did he know where he was? Did he know before whom he was now standing? Tamba answered in the negative in both instances. Karamokhoba told him he was in Touba and that the one asking him questions was the father of the man Tamba had arrested and intended to harm. Tamba became completely discomfited and bewildered. Karamokhoba demanded the immediate and unconditional release of his son, threatening to bring down the wrath of God on Tamba should he fail to do as commanded. Tamba was allowed to return home to carry out Karamokhoba's wishes. Shaken by the experience, he went even further. After releasing Muhammad, he made him a gift of the hand of his daughter, Sukhurung Sakho, as well as annual handsome presents.[43]

There is some question that Bakari Tamba's kidnapping of Muhammad and the Bassari's capture of Muhammad al-Kabír might be the same event, though another account exists suggesting that they are separate incidents. Be that as it may, the matter of secular subordination to the moral authority of religion is an overwhelming theme in the sources.

The Sacred and the Secular

The clerics did not require miracles to secure the acknowledgment from political rulers of Islam's spiritual power. That power was enshrined in a potent

Qur'an. Baba of Karo, a woman of the Muslim Hausa, testifies that a man became insane for swearing a lie on the Qur'an. A British colonial magistrate reported that a highly educated Muslim legal scholar requested a fresh copy of the Qur'an for the court because "the old one had lost its punishing power."[44] The king of Songhay, Askiya Ismá'íl (r. 1537–1539), attributed his affliction with a serious illness to the fact that, after he had sworn an oath of allegiance to his predecessor on the Qur'an, "It is that book that has afflicted me and executed its judgment upon me. I shall not long retain my authority."[45]

Both the *Ta'ríkh al-Fattásh* and the *Ta'ríkh al-Súdán* contain specific anecdotes concerned with the distinction between the "sacred" and the "secular," between the cleric and the prince. This can be seen in the narratives on Diakhaba, Timbuktu, and other places. The examples of the Ta'ríkhs show the cleric attaining the upper hand over the ruler. After many attempts to assert his authority over Timbuktu, the Askiya Muhammad Turé, king of Songhay, visited the city in person and summoned the *qádí,* Mahmúd b. 'Umar, to an audience. In the ensuing discussion, the *askiya* demanded to know why the *qádí* resisted his orders and turned away his message-bearers. After a flurry of short questions and answers, the *qádí* threw down the gauntlet:

> Have you forgotten, or are you feigning ignorance, how one day you came to my house and, crawling up to me, you took me by the feet and held on to my garments and said, "I have come so that you may place yourself in safety between me and the fire of damnation. Help me and hold me by the hand lest I stumble into hell fire. I entrust myself in safe-keeping to you." It is for this reason that I have chased away your message-bearers and resisted your commands.[46]

By any measure, this is a stinging reprimand, and yet the king, equally remarkably, left the gauntlet where the *qádí* dropped it, pleading abjectly,

> By God, it is true that I have forgotten this, but you have now reminded me and you are absolutely right. By God, you deserve great reward for you have saved me from harm. May God exalt your rank and make you my security against the fire. What I have done has provoked the wrath of the All-Powerful, but I beg His forgiveness and turn in penitence to Him. In spite of what I have done I still invoke your protection and attach myself to you. Confirm me in this position under you and God will confirm you (and through you) defend me.[47]

It is just possible that the chronicler may in this passage have been attempting to paint an exaggeratedly pious image of the *askiya*. Even so, he is employing a strategy that shows his royal patron upstaged by a subordinate official, a risk he would be unlikely to take if the story were not true and familiar. That such an encounter took place, perhaps in less dramatic circumstances, seems safe to accept. It is credible in the context of other evidence of the separation of religion from political authority and shows the esteem in which religion is regarded by Africans, king and commoner alike.

The chronicles report many incidents in which political rulers tried to render religion politically serviceable. A well-known example is the king of Songhay, Askiya Da'wúd (r. 1549–1582), who attempted to appoint the *qádí* of Timbuktu. The appointee, revered scholar Muhammad Baghayogho, refused the post. The city's leading jurists interceded with him on the king's behalf, but even that failed. Baghayogho agreed to be *qádí* only after the king threatened to offer the job to an ignoramus. The stand-off lasted over a year, with the king forced to find a stop gap—al-Sa'dí does not say whom.[48] In another incident, the king is said to have felt slighted when the prestigious Sankore mosque was being built in Timbuktu because he was not informed of it until the project neared completion. Undeterred, he sent a generous donation. The clerics used it not for the mosque but for repairs to an adjoining cemetery. [49] The king could not have missed the pointed symbolism: his contribution should be considered a goodwill offering toward the repose of faithful souls rather than a bid for the merits of the faith community. The clerics were determined to show that religion was too important to be ignored or co-opted by the state.

In an essay written while he was in exile in Morocco, Ahmad Baba recalled a well-established injunction warning religious scholars "against being close to tyrants and befriending them or seeking them out and entertaining companionship with them. Such quest after the rulers of this passing world and its lowly and waning rewards is reprehensible."[50] Ahmad Baba's view is consistent with the pacifist argument. It represents an impressive moral achievement, showing the penetrating clarity of clerical views about the limits and hazards of the political co-option of religion.

Perspective is necessary here, however. As a matter of strict constitutional separation, the distinction drawn here between the Islamization of the state and the Islamization of society was never institutionalized as public policy, though it is relevant to note that scholarship was not a state function nor religion a political office. Jihad seeks the Islamization of the state; pacifist teaching, on the other hand, seeks Islamization of society. Jihad binds religion as a political instrument; pacifist teaching makes it a choice of civil society. This distinction was not, however, formalized into institutional separation. It is still significant that the distinction was maintained as a matter of principle rather than by political prescription.

It shows that professional clerics did not regard religion as a derivative of state authority.

Sainthood (*Wiláyah*) Without Saintship (*Waláyah*)

In Islamic religious practice, "holiness" is not dependent on the idea of political adoption. This is because the state of sainthood (*wiláyah*), unlike saintship (*waláyah*), is not a matter of institutional jurisdiction and territorial allegiance. Sainthood is an attribute of personal spiritual attainment and cannot be transferred by heredity; saintship, on the other hand, is a system based on cultivating a following.[51]

In one account of a miracle in Kankan, Karamokhoba was mysteriously surrounded by a company of *jinn* (spiritual beings) who interrogated him closely. The *jinn* were joined by a gallery of orthodox Muslim saints (*awliyá al-ummah al-muhammadiyah*), including Shaykh 'Abd al-Qádir al-Jílí (d. 1410 AD), Abú Isháq 'Umar al-Suhrawardí (d. 1234 AD), al-Shádhilí (d. 1258 AD), Ahmad al-Badawí (d. 1276 AD), al-Sha'rání (d. 1565 AD), Muhammad Riqqád, Mukhtár al-Kuntí (d. 1811), and his son, Muhammad Khalífa (d. 1825).[52] Al-Sha'rání held the *jinn* at bay, offering answers drawn from the sanctioned opinions of the saints; Muhammad Khalífa remarked on the impressively numerous *jinn* and on al-Sha'rání's effective handling of the interrogation. In order to disconcert Karamokhoba, the *jinn* disguised themselves sequentially as Jews, Christians, Magians (Zoroastrians), idol worshippers (*'ibádah al-asnám*), and heterodox figures. The company of Muslim saints prevailed over the *jinn*; the attempt to cast doubt on Islamic teaching failed. According to the *Kitáb al-Bushrá*, this illustrates a verse in the Qur'an about how the spirit world is divided against itself: "And some of us have surrendered, and some of us have deviated" (lxxii:14).[53] Thus Karamokhoba received the *barakah* of the saints without being elevated either to sainthood or saintship.

That Sufi masters appeared shows the importance of Sufism to Suwarian Islam. Abú Isháq 'Umar al-Suhrawardí was head of an influential ribát in Baghdad and a jurist of Sháfi'ite law. He was a charismatic preacher with a large popular following. Among his admirers was the Caliph al-Náṣir, who came to hear him preach and adopted him as his spiritual guide. His thirteenth-century manual *'Awárif al-Ma'árif* gave no standing to political authority in religious teaching and training.

Abú Hasan 'Alí al-Shádhilí was born in Ghumára in northern Morocco. He went shaykh-seeking in Iraq, where he wanted to attach himself to a *murshid* (guide), and eventually returned to Morocco where he was initiated into the Sufi way by Abú 'Abdalláh Muhammad b. Harázim (d. 1236). He was adopted as a disciple by the charismatic *murshid* 'Abd al-Salám b. Mashísh, who elevated him to the rank of *qutb* (pole) and directed him to settle in Shádhila, whence his *nisbah*, "al-Shádhilí." He left the town and went to settle in Tunis. His sojourn in Tunis coincided with a crisis in Almohad (*al-muwahhid*) power. The Caliph al-Ma'mún repudiated the stringent doctrine of Ibn Tumart, precipitating agitation in the Andalus against the Caliph al-'Ādil, and in Marrakesh, where the sultan was toppled with the help of the largely Christian Castile. Castile's interference did not sit well with the intrepid supporters of Almohad doctrine. They perceived it as further illegitimatization of the repudiation of their doctrine. In the ensuing backlash against Caliph al-Ma'mún, al-Shádhilí came under suspicion, and he left to settle in Egypt. He died in 1258 on the Red Sea coast while returning from one of his many annual pilgrimages to Mecca. In time, the Shádhiliyah order took firm hold among the Jakhanke clerics of Futa Jallon in a remarkable renaissance from the eighteenth century.

Ahmad al-Badawí was an Egyptian Sufi whose tomb at Ṭanṭa became a famous and popular local pilgrimage (*ziyárah*) site. His order, the Badawiyya, spawned a number of branches that spread beyond Egypt to the Hijaz, Turkey, Syria, Tripolitania, and Tunisia.[54]

The inclusion of al-Sha'rání in the list indicates the broad orthodox Sunni leanings of the clerics, for al-Sha'rání was not a conventional Sufi. Though he defended Ibn al-'Arabí (d. 1240), who was widely suspected of pantheistic tendencies, al-Sha'rání was openly critical of theosophic elements in Sufism.[55] Reared in Shádhilí doctrine, he tried to harmonize *fiqh* and *taṣawwuf* with his strict view; he was intent on defending the *sharí'ah* code against syncretist corruption. He demonstrated his independence of mind by criticizing both the jurists for their fastidious obtuseness and the Sufi orders for exploitation and for harboring corruption in their midst. This endeared him to neither side. The middle course he steered between legalism and subjectivism aligned him with 'Asharite moderate thought and its influence on Sunni theology concerning the difference (*mukhálafah*) between God and His creation, a position consistent with the separation of religion and politics. Al-Sha'rání's social criticism also aligns with the mainstream Sunni tradition and its 'Asharite aversion to speculative, systematic theology.[56] He left his mark on society by way of his highly influential *záwiyá* (hostel) in Cairo. The hostel consisted of a mosque, a *madrasah* (educational establishment) for law students—of whom there were two hundred at one time, with twenty-nine blind—and a place for migrants. Al-Sha'rání and his large family resided in the *záwiyá*.

Al-Sha'rání championed the cause of social justice, focusing on aiding *felláhin* who suffered chronic economic and social disabilities. He held the *'ulama* accountable for their detachment from the life of the people, their deference to the Ottoman authorities after the conquest of 1517, and their venal, self-serving opportunism. For Al-Sha'rání, the ethical obligations of religion had first claim on the attention of Muslim leaders, so that religion could exert a wholesome influence on society. In defense of Islamic teaching about an inscrutable God that Sufis tended to disregard, al-Sha'rání insisted that mystical illumination (*ilhám*) and the two successive stages it can lead to—annihilation involving abnegation of the self (*faná*) and subsistence, the state of consummation in the divine (*baqá*)—do not absolve the Sufi from the observance of the religious code. Annihilation here involves the effacing of all consciousness of the self ("I, being self-confined/True self did not merit,/Till leaving self behind/Did self inherit," wrote Rumi); subsistence means unity with the real "in which he [the mystic] was before he was."[57] No reciprocity with God is implied in being a *walí* (friend) or a *muqarrib* (near-one) of God. Ultimately, whatever his or her station or attainment, the Sufi remains only a protégé. We see this in the *Kitáb al-Bushrá*, where communion with the *awliyá*, however heady, never breaches the barrier of communion with God. Nothing is more crucial for appreciating why Jakhanke clerics never perceived Sufism as irreconcilable with the religious code or with the need for society. They never challenged the theistic desideratum of al-Ghazálí's teaching of God as the only creator, revealer, and judge at the last day or the necessity of the community of faith.

The following summary of al-Sha'rání's Sufi habit shows the extent to which Sufis might go without flouting the obligations of faith, and in that regard it points to an affinity with the latitude given to popular clerical religious practice. Clerics prided themselves on hewing close to the code for faith and practice. Since no *ijmá'* (consensus) existed for canonization in Islam, the *walí* was such only in the eye of the beholder: popular acclaim typically established who was a saint.

> Al-Sha'rání has all the *walí* material in profusion, a hierarchy of saints, a wonder-world of visions and miracles, a spirit-world inhabited by *jinn* (who, he tells us, attended his lectures with open ears) as well as the spirits of saints and their archetype, al-Khadir; all these intensely real in their relationship with mankind. He was an assiduous tomb visitor, the Qaráfa [city of the dead] must have seen him every week, and he records his conversations with their inhabitants. "If one visits a *walí* at his grave," he was asked, "how is one to know whether he is present or absent?" "Most *walís*," he replied, "are roamers, and not restricted to their graves, they come and go." Then he gives information as to when one can find certain *walís* at their tombs. That of Abú 'l-'Abbás al-Mursí, for instance, has to be visited on a Saturday before sunrise to be sure of finding him in residence.[58]

The social nature of *barakah* qualified it as a worthy subject of pacifist teaching. Precisely because *barakah* was much more a quality of the religious quest than a measure of political advantage, the clerics employed it in their work. An attribute of personal trust and faithfulness, *barakah* as personal blessing presumed membership of the *ummah* without respect to privilege, rank, or status; indeed, it reflected Islam's disregard of cultural, national, or political prerequisites. Even as a protégé, the *walí* was such not because of a political ordinance or by reason of national origin, and the Qaráfa as a final resting place was also for the bidding of the *barakah*-bound initiate. Saintly veneration was different from political popularity—*daraja* in Mandinka, *bayré* in Wolof; both carried the sense of charismatic favor bestowed by God, not by a political ruler. The pacifist approach transcended and, when necessary, rejected political bids for the office of religious teaching. To present *barakah* as other than a moral virtue of exemplary biographical anecdotes, without compulsion or coercion, is to violate its nature. *Barakah* is not loose or wild; it is not intrusive or assertive. It belongs with all that is true, merciful, and hopeful and not with what is disruptive, sectarian, strident, or stubborn; it abounds with the virtues of patience, forbearance, modesty, trust, and generosity. *Barakah* enhances and dignifies; it does not diminish or trivialize; and it is solicitous and winsome rather than threatening or overweening. Biography is its human embodiment.

The doctrine of *mukhálafah*—the distinction between God's sovereign power and worldly prerogative—could therefore be interpreted as intellectual justification of the clerics. The clerics possessed authority by practicing religion as a safeguard against political intrusion and by keeping religion out of politics, though somewhat asymmetrically. The admonition to al-Hajj 'Umar demonstrates this asymmetry: "the best emírs are those who comply with the wishes of the *'ulamá*, and the worst *'ulamá* are those who comply with the wishes of the emírs." It would seem that the religious qualification of power has positive advantages, while the political qualification of religion does not: the expansive state diminishes religion, while religion acts as a brake on political overreach.[59]

Islam and Civil Society

The religious calling is not about withdrawing from life, nor is it about creating a theocratic state. Inspired by religion, civic ethics is the binding element of the civil order and its stability. Religious oversight of the civil domain is vested in the institution of the *hisbah*, in the mandate to command right and forbid wrong.

> The practices of our ancestors regarding *hisbah* over rulers were undertaken on the basis of the general agreement that specific authorization to do so was unnecessary. If the ruler approved of whoever was ordering good, then this was fine, but if the ruler disapproved of him, this disapproval was an evil which had to be forbidden.[60]

The Ghazálían view of civil society and public life assumes an elevated status for religion. God's commandments are binding on believers without exception, and no one is above being answerable to God. The weight of moral responsibility is not lessened by the office, status, or rank one occupies, and this applies even to the caliph, as the following anecdote demonstrates. On pilgrimage to Mecca, the caliph al-Mahdi was pushing other pilgrims out of his way during the circumambulations. 'Abd Alláh b. Marzuq "sprang forward, grabbed him by his robe and shook him. 'What do you think you're doing?' 'Abd Alláh said, 'What gives you more right to the Ka'ba than those who have come from far away, so that when they get here you stop them from reaching it?' "[61] The source of the freedom and authority to challenge the caliph, al-Ghazálí insists, resides with God, who presides over the common life. Al-Ghazálí sets standards for the office of the *muhtasib,* who also acts as market inspector, stressing the point that religious scrutiny, like rulership, is not itself above the law or without qualification. The *muhtasib's* role was to ensure "that the religious and moral precepts of Islam are obeyed."[62] According to Maqrizi, "only the principal men in Islam should be appointed to the *hisbah* because it is a religious duty."[63]

For al-Ghazálí, the ethics of *hisbah* concerning lawful and unlawful acts cannot be reduced to a secular administrative function; *hisbah* is a duty God has laid on individual Muslims without regard to their position and rank in society. Not unusually, views differ on the extent to which one may carry out the duty. Some authorities say that exhortation may be given only when an unlawful act is committed or is about to be committed and when compliance with the advice is likely (*innamá ta'mur man yaqbal minka*). Otherwise, prudence dictates that the exhortation is not a duty. Sufyan al-Thawri (d. 772 AD), the early Iraqi jurist-scholar who defended the right of *hisbah,* was horrified at reports that, under the pretext of *hisbah,* people's walls were scaled and their homes raided in an attempt to catch them off guard.[64] British scholar Michael Cook argues that al-Ghazálí's adoption of the term *hisbah* for commanding right and forbidding wrong was its first usage in the specific religious sense. Al-Ghazali wished to emphasize the importance of doing something for God's sake "without personal or worldly motives of any kind."[65]

Worldly affairs undergo constant change and transformation; religion is similarly affected by the historical process. Ibn Khaldun has drawn attention to this.[66] No matter how unified the faith and practice of Muslims, we cannot necessarily infer from the religion alone the reasons for its spread or appeal. Nor can we distill the teachings of the faith solely from the customs of the societies embracing the religion. There is a distinction to be drawn between belief and practice, between rule and conduct. As Carl Becker rightly noted,

> The religion now known as Islam is as near to the preaching of Muhammed [*sic*] or as remote from it, as modern Catholicism or Protestant Christianity is at variance or in harmony with the teaching of Jesus. The simple beliefs of the prophet and his contemporaries are separated by a long course of development from the complicated religious system in its unity and diversity which Islam now presents to us.[67]

The reality of Islam is found in the styles and patterns of Muslim life. Islam is not merely a facimile of practice. This suggests a fluid nexus between belief and practice, between creed and action. There is both unity and diversity in Muslim faith and practice, which we can see in the way Muslims responded to encounters with the West in the colonial and postcolonial periods. Undergoing cycles of resistance, ambivalence, co-option, collaboration, and acquiescence, Muslim society emerged from colonial rule battered and bruised but generally wiser and more realistic. Its claims regarding territorial boundaries were more favorable and religious practices better organized for it: the Sharí'ah civil code was reformed and systematized, the *zakát* levy more consistently applied, and the Mecca pilgrimage more organized and better supported. Lord Cromer, as governor-general of Sudan, said that administrative policy of patronage strengthened Islam. In an address to the *'ulama* at the outbreak of the First World War he said the government had facilitated the pilgrimage to Mecca, subsidized and assisted the men of religion, built and encouraged the construction of new mosques, modernized Islamic law, and trained Muslim magistrates to preside over Islamic courts.[68] British officials pursued a similar policy in Nigeria where H. R. Palmer, the senior administrator of north Nigeria,

> argued that the former Fulani states and Bornu drew their culture from the "civilized East," rather than [from] the "barbarous" West African coast [of Western influences]. This culture, of which Arabic and Islamic learning in general were vital parts, enabled the Emirs to rule effectively. If the next generation of Emirs were to be equally efficient collaborators the British had to preserve this cultural heritage.[69]

In a general way, as Trimingham pointed out, "the diffusion of Western influences accompanied the diffusion of Islam."[70] Sometimes, though, Islamic resistance can persist against the pressure. In 1961, a year after Nigeria gained its independence, there were 27,600 Qur'an schools with a total student population of 423,000, compared to 2,490 primary schools with 320,000 pupils of which 36,000 were girls.[71] The disparity prompted Muslim leaders to request making girls' education a priority despite opposition from traditional rulers.

We must, however, take a step back here. It would be yielding too much to Western notions to imply that either Islamic scholars or clerics set out to separate the sphere of religion and "the wilderness of the world," to recall Roger Williams. The concept of "church" as an institutional machine maintained by a system of ordained, salaried officials was virtually nonexistent among Sunni Muslims. This lasted until the colonial powers and a secular Turkey, bowing to Islam's influence, created a class of salaried clergy. Shi'i Islam, by contrast, does maintain a clerical hierarchy. At any rate, none of the clerical centers was a diocesan province or a magistracy in the European sense. Muhammad was his own Constantine, except in the establishment of a subordinate clergy. For all that, the centers did represent a singular and original tradition of fostering a nuanced distinction between the spiritual and temporal spheres. The centers promoted a tradition of moderation that did a great deal over the centuries to inhibit the growth of radical ideas in society, if not to complicate notions of a monolithic Islam.

Karamokhoba's Legacy

Karamokhoba lived to a very old age—ninety-nine according to the Muslim lunar calendar[72] and ninety-six according to the Western calendar. What he created in Touba remained one of the most notable of his many contributions to Jakhanke Islam. The influx of students and disciples into the center confirmed his appeal and authority. Students were recruited from among the Manding populations, the Fulbe, the Jallonke, the Susu, and the Bambara, among others. The different ethnic affiliations of Karamokhoba's own teachers reveal the same diversity. The name of Alfa Nuhi the Fulani stands out in that list, as does that of Muhammad Taslimi, whom Karamokhba honored by naming a son and a clerical center after him. Karamokhoba led recruiting drives among adjacent populations, in one case dispatching his son Muhammad Khaira on such a mission. A growing clerical center places commensurate pressure on its leaders to secure resources and provide for the needs of the expanding community. When and where appropriate, satellite settlements spring up to relieve the pressure and also to cash in on accrued social capital. The process has created the clustering that is so well described in the accounts. This clustering has three advantages: (a) it follows a demand-and-supply rule by reassigning clerical personnel and resources where and as the need arises, (b) it preserves the principle of mobility, and (c) it creates a widening circle of mutual support among the centers, with immunity from political interference a guiding rule.

This process is a legacy of Karamokhoba. A life of travel and mobility could be justified by the standard style of itinerancy to strengthen social links but for the clerics includes a more explicit religious motive. Karamokhoba traveled constantly "from town to town and from one country to another because of his aversion to civil strife (*fitnah*) and to political oppression and because of his desire for a safe place to live."[73] A *hadíth* is cited in support: "a person of religion is one who flees from trouble spot to trouble spot until he reaches the pinnacle of a mountain of security," because his only purpose is to teach, search after knowledge, and work with his hands to farm and labor. His aim is never to seek a political kingdom (*mulk*) or to harbor a desire for worldly preeminence (*riyásah dunyawiyah*).

Karamokhoba left as his personal bequest a large number of offspring. His sons brought their own contribution to the clerical life. They participated actively in the teaching and pastoral functions of the community and maintained regular contact with each other and with the clerical centers in which they operated. Their families recognized their special bond to Karamokhoba and to fellow clerics. Their names were added to the roll of honor to maintain the tradition.

After his death, Karamokhoba was buried within the mosque precincts. This was a tradition followed by the clerics to show reverence for their deceased founders and to remind the community that all are sojourners bound for another city, whose builder and maker is the Ruler of the universe. According to tradition, Karamokhoba died in bed peacefully on the second or third of Şafar al-Khayri, the second month of the Muslim calendar.[74] He was succeeded by his sixth son, Muhammad Taslimi (Karang Taslimanka), thus fulfilling the prophecy that the princess Aisatou Kamara would bear his son and heir (for the successors of Karamokhoba see Figure 5.1).

Clerical Consolidation and Expansion

Touba was conceived in fidelity, in that it was designed after the venerable precedent of Diakhaba, "the city of God." The town stood for a dream fulfilled, a symbol of moderation and conciliation, and a reward of faith and endurance. The physical size of the settlement bore little relationship to its wide influence. Writing of his pilgrimage to Mecca in 1184 AD, Ibn Jubayr of Valencia, Spain describes the hardships, vulnerability, unjust treatment, and continuous peril of wayfarers at the hands of unscrupulous swindlers. The pilgrim finally arrived at the destination with a sense of gratitude for a mission accomplished. He affirms,

> A manifest miracle is that this Safe City [Mecca], which lies in a valley bed that is a bow-shot or less in width, can contain this vast host; a host, such that, were it brought into the greatest of cities, could not be contained. This venerated city, in what concerns it of manifest miracles, namely, its expansion for multitudes beyond count, is described only by the true analogy of the *'ulamá*, that its enlargement for newcomers is that of a uterus for the fetus.[75]

The mother city of the Jabi-Gassama clerics, conceived in a dream of guidance and tested by trial and fortitude, Touba's modest beginnings gave little hint of the future magnitude of its moral and intellectual heritage. For nearly a hundred years it remained the beacon of Suwarian Islam, a reminder of the impulse of the pacifist dream he was given on his own pilgrimage to Mecca, and a testament of endurance and triumph in a time of great change. The town became the preeminent educational center of the region. Disciples and students flocked to it with gathering strength, within a generation raising its profile to that of a pilgrimage site. As the pacifist record is prone to show, time would not forget Touba's achievement. The question was no longer whether the pacifist clerical vocation had any future in Futa Jallon; it was how and when the consolidation and expansion would start.

The leadership of the Jabi-Gassama was an integral part of the life of the center, as well as in the overall structure of Suwarian Islam. Karang Taslimanka acquired a reputation for devotion and piety, and his leadership of Touba was greeted as a welcome and fitting tribute to Karamokhoba. Taslimanka was endowed with pastoral gifts, signs of solicitude and intimacy. He traveled only once, when he journeyed to the Sahel to be inducted into the Qadiriyah *wird*, first at the hands of Shaykh 'Abd al-Latíf of the Kunta and then under the cure of Muhammad Khalífa, son of Shaykh Sidiya al-Kabír, of the Walad Biri of Trarza.[76]

The accounts of Taslimanka's connections with the Qádiriyah emphasize the importance of the order to the clerical practice. The Qádiriyah's presence in important Muslim towns offered affiliates network support on their travels; it lent the religious personality interethnic range and social currency; it gave spiritual expression to patronage without political strings, so that religious influence could be exercised without regard for political gain; it gave structure for clerical training; and it supplied a charismatic link in the chain of transmission (*isnád*) of knowledge and *barakah*.

Events leading to the Touba clerics making contact with 'Abd al-Latif al-Kuntí began with the visit of one of al-Latif's students to Touba. Karang Taslimanka in turn dispatched one of his students, al-Hajj Kamara, more commonly known as N'dar Bambo, to obtain a copy of a book by Shaykh Mukhtár al-Kuntí on Qádirí litanies (*awrád*). Accompanied by another student, Sahil Binne, who hailed originally from Badibu Salikeni in the Gambia, al-Hajj Kamara set out on his errand. The visit was successful, and al-Hajj Kamara returned with the book, *Kawkab Waqqád*, which became the chief instrument for introducing members of the clerical community to Qádirí devotions and practices.[77] Karang Taslimanka did some writing, but his output was meager. Three works are known, two of which are a eulogy (*madíh*) of the Prophet (*Safínat al-Khalaṣ*, and *Dhakirat al-Muhibb fí Takhmís Ṣalát Rabbi*) and a third on literature (*adab*), *Tanbíh al-'Aṣif 'alá Mawárid al-Ta'líf*.[78]

For all the remarks extolling his virtues and deferring to his moral authority, Karang Taslimanka remains a figure of modest attainment. It must be conceded that Karamokhoba was a hard act to follow. Taslimanka has no explicit claim to miracles or wonders and for that reason fits the pattern of clerical modesty well. He died at age fifty-five in about 1829.[79]

Taslimanka was succeeded by his eldest son, Karamokhoba Madi, who presided over the community for eight years. Karamokhoba Madi died while on a journey in Dabola in central Guinea. His brother, Muhammad Khasso, succeeded him and headed the *majlis* for forty years. His long reign is remembered for his distinguished, outstanding pastoral leadership. He was referred to as "a servant and shepherd of the flock, godly and upright (*'ábidan wara'an*)." He died around 1877 and was succeeded by his brother, Muhammad bin 'Alí, and then by Muhammad Muṣṭafá ibn Muhammad Taslímí, each of whom died after ruling for four years. The French administration appeared in the land during the reign of Muhammad Muṣṭafá, who is particularly remembered for the numerous efficacious prayers he performed for individuals and for the community.

Muhammad Muṣṭafá was succeeded in about 1885 by his brother, Karamokho Qutubo (Quṭb), who was born in about 1830 and died in 1905. His name at birth was 'Abd al-Qádir. Unlike his brothers, he was born too late to have known his grandfather, Karamokhoba, but like all of them he was educated at Touba. Karamokho Qutubo achieved considerable renown in his lifetime. By contemporary standards his personal library was large, with a list of seven hundred books and small manuals. He wrote some fifteen books on grammar, law, theology, prosody, and eulogies on the Prophet.[80] In about 1860, Qutubo embarked on a traditional *tournée pastorale* that took him to Mauritania, where he met Shaykh Sidiya al-Kabír, a Qádirí leader. On this particular trip, he visited Futa Toro, Pakao in Casamance, Jarra, Badibu, Niani,

Wuli where Sutukho is located, Sandu, Bundu, and outlying regions. When he finally returned to Touba, his entourage of students, disciples, and slaves numbered 780. The epitaph to Qutubo includes this verdict on his life: *shaykh al-kabír wa al-ustádh al-shahír . . . wa kána mujaddid al-dín wa mujtahid fíhí* ("he was a great shaykh, a renowned teacher, a renewer of religion, and diligent and conscientious concerning it").[81]

The teaching activities of Qutubo receive a great deal of attention in the sources. A large number of students passed through his hands, many of whom he nurtured into eminent scholars in their own right. They traveled far and wide to take their message to the larger society. Paul Marty, whose main clerical informant, Banfa Jabi-Gassama (referred to as Alfa Oumarou), was a descendant of Karamokho Qutubo, cites a tradition that essentially describes the education and spiritual stature of Qutubo. Touba had become the new "city of God." Marty declares:

> The young marabout impressed everyone by his knowledge, his virtues, and his commanding qualities. Under his pontificate of half a century (1860–1905), Touba soared to unprecedented heights. Students flocked there from all parts; Juula-missionaries carried the good news to the three-countries of Guinea; and Islamic studies flourished there to a considerable degree. As never before, Touba became the holy city of the whole region.[82]

The sources pay special attention to Qutubo's influence on local political leaders. He intervened willingly in missions of political conciliation and was able in specific instances to alter the course of events. It confirmed the terms of the concordat into which the clerics entered with the Fulbe *mawubé*. Qutubo built on that understanding, enabling clerical reconstruction of the area's religious life and practice. The personal friendship Qutubo was able to cultivate with the political leaders enhanced Touba's stature as a center of religion and scholarship.

One particular friendship with political leaders was to place great strains on Touba's reputation. It was simply fortuitous that, at the time, the French happened to be leading a drive to subdue local political leaders. Qutubo was a personal friend of Alfa Yahya, the Fula Almamy of Labé, who refrained from assuming the title "Almamy" possibly for fear of opening the wounds of Futa Jallon's past religious and political conflicts. The two men first met in the 1890s. It appears that Alfa Yahya approached Qutubo to offer a personal vow of comity, which makes sense in light of the long-standing public concordat initiated by Karamokhoba. Such a pact would carry no mutual security undertaking, since the clerics reject political office for themselves, and certainly would involve no offer of military assets then or at any other time. But circumstances often ride roughshod over intentions, and such was the case here. Alfa Yahya traveled to meet Qutubo with his son Modi Aquibou by his side as token of his personal good faith. Alfa Yahya might not have been aware of the possibility that his son was on a personal mission too.

The mission soured when, to establish himself as heir apparent to his father, Aquibou assassinated his brother around 1897. The action brought condemnation from the Alfa Yahya, who in a fit of vengeance mobilized troops to pursue Aquibou. Alfa Yahya commenced operations from Kadé, taking personal charge of a column of troops. Aquibou organized in Toubandé and bore full tilt toward his father. It happened that Alfa Yahya's path of progress cut through Touba, where Qutubo was alerted as to what was afoot; he promptly intervened to defuse the conflict. He prevailed on Alfa Yahya to forgo his attack and secured the submission of Aquibou to his father's authority. As close to the events as he was, Paul Marty did not doubt that Qutubo's stature and influence prevented a major political crisis.[83]

It was during this period that the French doubled their efforts to assert control over Futa Jallon, and they took an active role in political developments of the area. There are two perspectives on how the Jakhanke, under Karamokho Qutubo, responded to the French presence among them. Representing the French point of view, Marty says that at first the Jakhanke were dismayed that the French were pressing into the community and adopted a wary, chilly attitude. Gradually, however, relations improved between them, and in 1903 Qutubo pledged the cooperation of the community.[84]

The second version is the Jakhanke view contained in *TKB*, and it differs from the French view in a rather fundamental way. According to *TKB*, when the French came to Labé, Alfa Yahya sent a message to Qutubo informing him of the fact and soliciting advice on how best to respond, suggesting that he felt threatened. Around the same time, the Jakhanke were themselves confronted by the French, who established an administrative post at Touba under the direction of Commandant Faye. Meanwhile, Qutubo had written to Alya Yahya counseling submission to the French (*fa amarahu bi-taslím*). Qutubo also sent secret word to the other leading citizens urging a similar act of submission, and the account says that all of them heeded Qutubo's message. It was a resounding vindication of the reputation of the Touba leadership.

How do we evaluate the discrepancy between the French and Jakhanke versions of this crucial event? Marty's account is surprising in light of the fact that he noted Qutubo's successful conciliation work between Alfa Yahya and Aquibou. Yet his version suggests an initial misgiving on the side of the clerics. There is little indication anywhere to suggest that the Jakhanke harbored or concealed an antipathy toward the French, at least not when the French settled in Touba, an act that obviously violated the principle of clerical immunity. The clerics responded with their usual equanimity. The mutual agreement they had with local leaders carried no sanctions or stipulations for enforcement, as Marty well knew. The clerical version maintained in *TKB* may not have been available to the French at the time, but it is a faithful representation of the public stance of the clerics, and they would have had no reason to conceal it from the French. It can be assumed that the Jakhanke would not welcome the French with open arms, not because they were complicit in a rival political cause but because it was not their role to play the part of a political faction. The French insinuated that the Touba leadership was disingenuous. The discrepancy in accounts would have far-reaching consequences for Franco–Jakhanke relations.

Qutubo established Franco–Jakhanke cooperation to guide Touba through the uncharted waters of colonial politics. This was not simply done on the whim of Qutubo but out of centuries of experience and practice. As Qutubo well knew, more was at stake than his leadership: the whole *raison d'être* of the clerical vocation. Marty confirmed that, by the time he died, Qutubo had established very sound relations with the French. Suret-Canale, a French scholar, concurred with this positive view of Franco–Jakhanke relations by citing a message Qutubo sent to Alfa Yahya explaining why cooperation with the French was not in conflict with the enjoinment of religion:

> The fact that the French are in our country is the will of God. You must avoid war. You have already spilt a great deal of blood and if you persevere in this fashion, you will not enter Paradise. . . . If you do not comply with the orders you have received, you are sure not to enter Paradise.[85]

The substance of this message can be accepted as genuine in spite of the abrupt change of tone from friendship to reprimand. It is not in character for someone who was a trusted friend to be at once abrupt and distant in this manner; given the episode of Qutubo's intervention in the rift between Alfa Yahya and his son, it is not implausible that Qutubo's patience had worn too thin for minced words. In the end, all Qutubo could do was appeal to Alfa Yahya's own sense of the moral peril he would face before his Creator. It was his only spiritual leverage, and he used it in a final attempt at reason and self-exculpation—self-exculpation was probably a major motivation.

All the accounts agree that Alfa Yahya complied with Qutubo's message when he received it and, accordingly, offered his surrender to the French. In 1897, along with Oumarou Bademba of the Alfaya, Alfa Ibrahima Sori Elely of the Soriya, Alfa Ibrahima, the grand marabout of Fugumba, and others,

Alfa Yahya signed a treaty of capitulation dictated by the French. The treaty secured for the French the right to nominate successors to political office as well as a guarantee of French monopoly on commerce in the area, among other things.[86]

A remarkable theory has been propounded that the "marabouts of Touba [with] certain malice on their part," were not "altogether displeased to see the king of Labé (Alfa Yahya) humbled."[87] It is hard to make sense of this claim, for it implies either that the clerics condoned a conspiracy to overthrow Alfa Yahya and the Fulbe elite, in which case there was no evidence for French suspicions of a nefarious marabout alliance with Alfa Yahya, or that the clerics were never part of such an alliance despite secretly wishing, as Suret-Canale says, for Alfa Yahya's downfall. There is no foundation in fact for this theory. Suret-Canale himself quotes a report to the effect that, after securing Alfa Yahya's compliance, Qutubo assured him continuance of his personal rule in Labé.[88] It is hard to imagine why, under no ostensible threat, Qutubo should make this assurance if his friendship with Alfa Yahya was not genuine. It would be *mala fide* of the type that would undercut clerical credibility and, the clerics would argue, incite history to judge them harshly for shirking their honor.

Not unlike colonial administrators before him, Suret-Canale cites the ethnic issue as the reason for Jakhanke antipathy to Alfa Yahya. He writes:

> One notes that the Jakhanke of Touba received pupils from all over West Africa with the exception of precisely the Peul [Fula] country surrounding them. . . . The religious and commercial vocation of the Jakhanke and their publicly expressed aversion to war hardly led them to find themselves in sympathy with the warlike and plundering ways that characterized the aristocracy of the Fouta, and that of Labé in particular.[89]

In point of fact, not only did the Jakhanke recruit students and disciples among the Fulbe; Fulbe political leaders were among their admiring supporters. After all, Karamokhoba settled in Touba only because of the entreaty and solicitude of the Fulbe *mawubé*. Ethnic chauvinism, as noted earlier, was mitigated by the terms of the bilateral *entente* between the Alfaya and the Soriya, though in the colonial calculation, ethnic sympathies still carried the stigma of indigenous untrustworthiness. Unknowingly, the clerics had reached the point where others would choose for them the political role they did not wish to play.

Qutubo died on July 6 or 7, 1905. He was seventy-eight by the Islamic calendar and seventy-five by the Christian one. Under his leadership, Touba had acquired a preeminent standing in West Africa. He imbued the clerical community with spirit and intellect that earned the respect and admiration of surrounding populations, Muslim and non-Muslim alike. The clerics kept well clear of political involvement while retaining a deep moral influence on society and public affairs. Whatever the complications in relations with Alfa Yahya and the French, the Touba clerics never departed from their principle of not taking up arms, whether in the cause of others or in self-defense. The reputation for neutrality allowed the clerics to act as valued, honest brokers in local politics and, when the time came, in relations with the French. The clerics took the sting out of ethnic chauvinism by helping to reconcile ethnic groups whose alienation as targets of raids and sorties had impeded the Muslim cause.

Edward Wilmot Blyden (1832–1912), who lived and worked in West Africa and became a prominent philosopher of Pan-African cultural nationalism, came upon evidence of the range and influence of Touba on meeting Fode Tarawali, a Susu.[90] Tarawali was educated at Touba but left to settle in the Kambia district in Sierra Leone at a place called Gbileh, where he founded a successful Qur'an school and clerical practice. Blyden visited Gbileh in 1872, calling it "the Oxford of this region—where are collected over 500 young men studying Arabic and Koranic literature." Conversion of the Susu remained an age-old challenge; to meet it, the clerics learned the language and adopted the gentle approach of peaceful persuasion. Knowing of Touba only through hearsay, Blyden described it as a center "of great literary repute," literary subjects being of great interest to Blyden himself. [91] Dr. Gouldsbury (described in chapter 7) traveled personally to Touba in June of 1881, during Qutubo's tenure. He gave an eyewitness description of the place, saying it was the largest town in the region with about eight hundred houses. Like Jobson centuries earlier, Gouldsbury was struck by the religious character of the clerical center, calling it "the Canterbury of the country. When the Foulahs are about to make war they send to Toobah to invoke the prayers of its priests for success in their enterprise."[92]

Qutubo's legacy survived the challenge of colonial intrusion and prospered with his family. His son, Muhammad Jabi, otherwise known to the community as Mbalu Fode Jabi, immigrated to Casamance in Senegal where he established his religious practice and served as Maliki mufti (see Figure 8.1). He was author of several works on Islamic religious law and ethics, much of it designed for use in teaching and study. Among his works are *Majmu'a Khuṭbah Díniiyah Islámiyah,* edited by his son, Shaykh Sidiya Jabi, who is the author of *al-Diwán al-Mashhún,* an anthology of select poems and prose texts, concluding with testimonies to Karamokhoba. Mbalu Fode died in 1980 at age seventy-eight. Sidiya Jabi, his eldest son who was born in 1928, took over the leadership of the community, and was still active in April 2015. He personally supplied information on the clerical lineage, including books from his library pertaining to his work and that of his father. One of his sons went on to earn a doctorate in Francophone literature. Sidiya Jabi wrote a book of exegesis and ethical principles drawn from Scripture and Hadith called *Irshád al-Sá'il* ("Guide to the Inquirer"). In recent times Sidiya Jabi founded three clerical centers: Taslimi, his clerical base (the name Taslimi was a favorite of the clerics ever since Karamokhoba met Muhammad Taslimi in Masina; the name was adopted for Karamokho Sankoung, among others); Dar ud-Din in 1985; and Jasling Touba in 2007. According to Sidiya Jabi's own account, in 2015 Taslimi was a religious settlement of some 750 inhabitants situated in Casamance on the Senegambia border. It forms part of a cluster of similar clerical settlements creating a network of active parish-style centers that offer a sense of stability and community in the midst of sporadic political disturbances of the region.

Karamokhoba created a community based on the power and prestige of religion, for which reason his tomb became a center of local pilgrimage (*ziyárah*), catering to a wide circle of pilgrims and visitors. Karamokho Qutubo inherited this tradition and built on it his own considerable influence. He carried out the first major renovation work on the mosque of Touba and in that way inscribed his personal imprint on the fabric of the clerical legacy.[93]

Figure 7.1 Some Islamic books from the library of Karang Sambu Lamin of Sutukung, stored away in large metal boxes. Photo by the author.

9

Beyond Confrontation and Crisis

Colonial Denouement

> The *old man* who had passed his simple and innocent life in the neighbourhood of Verona, was a stranger to the quarrels of kings and bishops; *his* pleasures, his desires, his knowledge, were confined within the little circle of his paternal farm; and a staff supported his aged steps on the same ground where he had sported in his infancy. Yet even this humble and rustic felicity (which Claudian describes with so much truth and feeling) was still exposed to the undistinguishing rage of war.
>
> —Edward Gibbon, *The Decline and Fall of the Roman Empire,* 99–100

The lives and work of Karamokhoba and his clerical heirs were rewarded with the thriving center at Touba, and everyone concerned took heart in what that promised for the future of the tradition. By the time of Qutubo's curacy, the pioneering work had been done, a system of handling the region's volatile religious and ethnic relations had been established, and the division of labor among clerical lineages settled. Touba had matured in its defining mission, and the necessary structures required for running its many functions had passed the test of time. There was a palpable sense of achievement and hope for a future of great promise and peace.

That was the intellectual climate in which Karamokho Sankoung, the most brilliant of Qutubo's heirs and successors, assumed the responsibilities of head of *majlis*. But before he finished taking stock of the heritage at his command, Sankoung found himself unable to evade a stubborn reality: there was no ignoring the fact that the French were in the country intending to be masters of the land and determined to "bind the people in [France's] furrows."[1] The question was whether that left any room for compromise and, if so, at what price.

Early Career and Leadership of Karamokho Sankoung

The majority of Karamokho Qutubo's numerous children established their own *majlis* outside Touba, maintaining regular contact with the mother *majlis*. But Qutubo's two eldest sons, Karamokho al-Maghílí (commonly referred to as Karamokho Madi) and Karamokho Sankoung (c. 1860–1928), stayed at Touba and assumed responsibility for the community.[2] It was at this time that the pastoral office (*majlis-tio*) was distinguished from the office of lay magistrate for which the alkaliship, a subchieftaincy office, was created. The community needed both offices: a canoe must be paddled on both sides to keep a straight course.

Named after his grandfather, Karang Taslimanka, Sankoung was called at birth Muhammad Taslimi, but the appellation "Sankoung," also a *laqab* of Karang Taslimanka, stuck. Meaning "rain cloud" in Mandinka, *sankoung* has the connotation of "head or source of blessing," which was the intended meaning of the clerics who adopted it. Sankoung's mother was Fatumata, known by her house name as Fanta. He was his mother's only son, but he had two sisters, Khadijatu and Aisatou, also called Mbinki, both of whom married at Touba.[3]

Sankoung had four wives. The first, Kadi, was the daughter of a Wolof father of Kakandi, in Casamance. She bore Sankoung two daughters: Mariama, named after the mother of Shaykh Sidiya Baba of Boutilimit (1862–1924), and Mahjúba, named in honor of the grandmother of Shaykh Sidiya. Sankoung's second wife was Jan-Kemba, daughter of Karamokho Dawda, the alkali of Touba. His third was Fanta Kaba, daughter of a Jakhanke cleric of Touba, and, finally, Umuna, another local girl, whom we discuss presently. Kadi and Fanta Kaba left Sankoung during his long internment by the French.

Sankoung had five sons: Banfa Jabi, Soriba, Ba Fode, Karam Ba Qutubo, and Sidiya. Qutubo and Sidiya continued to live in Touba after the community was broken up by the French in 1911. Banfa and Soriba were the heirs to the clerical title of their father. As the genealogical table of succession indicates, the legacy of clerical leadership passed into the hands of Soriba's descendants. Banfa ran errands for his father while Sankoung was in detention. I consulted both sons while writing this book.

Sankoung named his sons in recognition of the deep spiritual bond between the Jakhanke clerics and the Kunta Ṣúfí shaykhs. The French perceived Shaykh Sidiya as an important potential ally, believing that to control the leading personalities of African Islam meant controlling Muslim society.[4] For his part, Sankoung built on the foundation laid by previous generations of religious leaders, including Shaykh Sidiya al-Kabír of the Awlád Biri and Ahmad al-Bekka'i. It was Shaykh Mukhtár al-Kuntí who propagated the view among the Kunta Arabs that holding political office was incommensurate with the vocation of spiritual leadership, believing that political power was unethical since it involved taking advantage of the weak and innocent and risked confiscation and abuse of the religious law.[5] This helps to explain the close relationship between Jakhanke and the Kunta shaykhs, including the very personal expression of this relationship by Karamokho Sankoung who named his children after the Kunta religious leaders.

Sankoung's father assumed direct supervision of his early training, and presumably this included some teaching. Sankoung then transferred his studies to Karamokho Sakho, a cleric with a charismatic reputation for healing and divination. Karamokho Sakho died in 1895, while Sankoung was in the middle of his studies. With advanced training from leading scholars at Touba, including his father, Sankoung was able to establish his own Qur'an school, a stage widely recognized by the clerics as the passage to qualification as a scholar in one's own right. The Qur'an school was a huge success, attracting large numbers of students. It enhanced Sankoung's standing in the community, establishing him as heir apparent of his father. From about 1890 to 1905, when his father died, Sankoung's school was the magnet of aspiring students from the Casamance and Kaabou as well as from different areas of Futa Jallon. On those students who qualified for the part, Sankoung conferred the Qádirí *wird*, an office he received from his father. Touba became a center of Qádirí ideas, whose influence spread to different parts of West Africa.[6]

Sankoung's travel itinerary was of the characteristic *tournée pastorale* pattern; his was a familiar name to neighboring communities. On his travels, he rallied support for the work of the center, recruited students and disciples, received material gifts and endowments, and explored potential new sources of support. Sankoung visited several centers regarded by the clerics as significant religious establishments: Boké, Kakandé, Boffa, Kindia, and Conakry.[7] Sankoung's travel fits into the *tournée pastorale* model, in which the parish extends throughout the dispersion corridor. In this model, the chief purpose of travel is to strengthen existing clerical and personal bonds, to reinforce the sense of vocation, and to share in the promise and achievements of a common endeavor. The other common model of religious travel is the missionary plan, which involves venturing beyond the tried and proven. Here Sankoung's reputation was also strong. He made significant inroads in non-Muslim areas. Marty confirms this, saying Sankoung "is well known and very popular in all the surrounding country, equally among the disciples of rival centers as among Pagan populations."[8]

Sankoung engaged in a third kind of travel when he set out to attain personal profit and self-improvement. In 1909 he traveled to Mauritania to meet

Shaykh Sidiya Baba at Boutilimit. He seemed to have been preparing for this meeting for years, as evidenced by his naming his daughters after Shaykh Sidiya's mother and grandmother. As noted earlier, the Qadiriyah were a major force in the clerical vocation. Sankoung wanted to be inducted into the order by Shaykh Sidiya, just as Shaykh Sidiya's father initiated Sankoung's father in 1860. Accompanied by his brother Khairaba, Sankoung traveled to Conakry and then sailed to Dakar and up the Senegal River to Podor before arriving in Boutilimit. His month-long sojourn there was highly successful. He struck up a personal friendship with Shaykh Sidiya, who welcomed him with high honors and received him into the religious fraternity. Shaykh Sidiya presented Sankoung with a number of books before their cordial parting. Sankoung's visit strengthened the clerics' affiliation to the Qadiriyah brotherhood not only through personal ties but also through the vicarious merit of family association. Travel advances knowledge and *barakah* and gives concrete expression to the personal and social character of religious affiliation.

French Interference: 1908

A few years after the death of Qutubo and the succession of Sankoung, a dispute broke out in the community that attracted the unwelcome attention of the French. The episode was a portent of greater tribulation, beginning a drama that culminated in the defeat of the clerics at the hands of the French. The published sources covering the dispute are cautious about suggesting a logical connection with later events at Touba; the events recounted by Sankoung's sons, Banfa and Soriba, differ in details from the only extended published version, that of Suret-Canale.[9]

The principal characters in the drama were Ba Gassama and Karamokho Sankoung, cousins on the paternal side. Ba Gassama was known for his rising political ambition. Marty says Ba Gassama led a faction opposed to Sankoung's leadership.[10] His alliance with Alfa Yahya was well-known. According to Banfa and Soriba, Ba Gassama had a lurking ambition to assume the leadership of Touba and had relied on the tacit support of Alfa Yahya to achieve that. Committed to a pact of friendship and understanding with Qutubo and with his son Sankoung, Alfa Yahya had spent his power and could not feasibly back Ba Gassama. Furthermore, his relations with the French had deteriorated. He was arrested and exiled to Dahomey (Benin) in November of 1905. According to al-Hajj Soriba, Ba Gassama then turned to the French for help. It is clear from both Marty and Suret-Canale that he failed to obtain it. The French were not in the business of encouraging indigenous political ambitions.

In the meantime, conditions took a turn for the worse for the clerics but also, ironically, for the slaves. The French implemented a policy banning slavery in French West Africa. On December 12, 1905, a decree was issued prohibiting trade in slaves in hinterland Francophone West Africa. Until then, only trading in slaves by sea had been banned.[11] Touba became aware that enforcement of this decree was a heavy blow, as the clerical system was heavily dependent on the acquisition of slaves for agricultural and domestic work. "In the eighteenth and nineteenth centuries, with the abundant supply of slaves in West Africa, Muslims owned more slaves for farming than did their non-Muslim neighbors. Slave-farming gave Muslims the leisure to pursue learning and to teach. Hence the growth of a rural tradition of Islamic scholarship that complemented the older and better known urban tradition."[12] The economic consequences of abolition were immediate and critical, but equally critical was the impact on relations among the clerics with respect to their slaves. It is hard to imagine the *majlis* without the centuries-long institution of slavery. Slaves were crucial members of the community for religious, social, and economic reasons. They worked on farms, served as porters and ceremonial attendants, kept buildings in good repair, ran errands, acted as child-minders, and as slave women served as concubines.

Ba Gassama traded in slaves and made a great profit. He tried to use the wealth he amassed to gain political control, much to the alarm of his fellow clerics. In so doing, he was bound also to provoke the French. Converting slave capital into political leverage defied French colonial penetration, and in the all-too-certain resulting debacle, the clerics were not spared, whatever their role or excuse. According to the accounts, Ba Gassama felt antagonized by the slavery ban. For a while he conducted his trading activities underground to avoid conflict. Nervous about what adverse consequences might follow from Ba Gassama's noncompliance, the clerics kept an eye on him. Karamokhoba Gassama, the *alkali* and a protégé of Karamokho Sankoung, reported violations to the administration. Ba Gassama took his dispute with his fellow clerics to the *poste* at Touba for litigation. Playing into the hands of the French, Ba Gassama must have thought that an open dispute would damage the prestige of the Karambaya establishment and thus avenge his sense of grievance against Karambaya. In an interview at Macca-Kolibantang, al-Hajj Banfa Jabi indicated that as a motive, saying Ba Gassama thought that by establishing proof of internal dissension he would provide justification for the French depriving Karamokho Sankoung's ministry of its autonomy, and the French were only too willing to take advantage of it.

The precise details of the outcome of Ba Gassama's litigation are not known. That he subsequently took matters into his own hands indicates that he was unsuccessful in his complaint. As a direct challenge to the Touba clerical leadership, he intervened in the marriages of his daughters to members of the Karambaya *qabílah*, removing them along with other relatives to his side of the town. Karamokho Sankoung and his brothers Mukhtár and Karamokho Khairaba were at that time married to sisters of Ba Gassama.[13] By breaking up the marriage of his daughters, Ba Gassama fractured family relations with Karamokho Sankoung, husband of Ba Gassama's sister Umuna and head of the Karambaya *qabílah*. In his efforts to turn Umuna's children against their father, Ba Gassama threatened an escalating family feud. The shattered profile of the *majlis* thus began with a dispute inside the community, rather than with outside French intervention.

Not surprisingly, the dispute extended to property rights. A rice field partially owned by Umuna Ba Gassama was sequestered. The rights to it transferred from the Karambaya *qabílah* to the new settlement of Nata, a few miles south of Touba, where Ba Gassama and his family moved. The transfer was forced by an order from Karamokho Bambo Gassama in his role as intermediary of the French, and it only exacerbated Ba Gassama's ill will toward the Karambaya *qabílah*. He appealed to the French administrator Legeay, the *chef de poste*, for authorization to harvest the rice at Fofanakunda in Touba that had been planted before the separation. The *chef de poste* granted the request but neglected to inform the *chef de village*, Karamokho Bambo Gassama, who had acted on previous occasions as an intermediary between Touba and the French. The oversight would have serious consequences.

On October 28, 1908, Soriba, Kajali (Ghazálí), and Mbemba, three of Ba Gassama's brothers, turned up at the rice fields at Touba to harvest the crop. Their way was barred by the *chef de village*, who was acting under what he mistakenly believed was the standing order of the *chef de poste*.[14] Given the deteriorating relations between the principals in the dispute, too much need not be made of the oversight by the *chef de poste* in his failure to communicate with the *chef de village*. The issue, it is reasonable to infer, was not ignorance of the bad blood between Ba Gassama and the Karambaya but who might fill the role of peace-maker, a role not designed for the French to play. In the final analysis, the miscommunication compounded the issue of what role the *chef de village* was supposed to play. Whether or not he intended it, the confusion aided and abetted Ba Gassama's goal of making Karambaya a target of administrative intervention.

On being asked for clarification, the *chef de poste* confirmed that he had given permission for the harvesting of the rice to proceed. This led to a second attempt by Ba Gassama to enter the fields, which the *chef de village* of Karambaya interpreted as provocation. A fistfight broke out. Another account claims that Ba Gassama and his party were reminded of the ban on them when they were spotted loitering around Touba.[15] This led to an exchange of angry words, and fighting ensued. Soriba, a brother of Ba Gassama, had his arm broken in the fight, and others received saber wounds. In response, the French *commandant* dispatched a platoon of riflemen to arrest the belligerents. He next summoned the *chef de village* and reprimanded him.[16] The *chef de village* responded by reminding the *commandant* that it was the *commandant* who ordered the ban on Ba Gassama in the first place. Touba was no longer pristine, free of political conflict. It had been breached by the French.

In a subsequent incident, or perhaps in a different account of the same incident, members of the Karambaya ward ambushed Ba Gassama and his party as they were heeding a summons to return to Touba from Nata. The leaders of the ambush were Soriba, Sidina, Sidia, Bahio, Demba, and a tradesman named Sankoung.[17] They were spotted arriving at a gathering, and M. Legeay was informed of their presence. To avert trouble, he posted a guard, Mamadou Kourouma, to look after Ba Gassama and his companions. Despite the precaution, fighting broke out at Béréla, an intermediate point. Ba Gassama was badly mauled and left for dead. He was being abducted when his attackers were stopped, at which point he was rescued and taken to the *poste* to nurse his wounds.

Another account of the attack, possibly describing a third incident, claims that a party of Ba Gassama's supporters appeared one morning at the market in Touba. Because of the prevailing ban against them, local people challenged them. The supporters drew arms as a precaution, and a confrontation seemed imminent. Word reached the *chef de village*, who ordered that the intruders be apprehended. Ba Gassama arrived under summons, accompanied by three hundred slaves, which was perceived as a provocative gesture. In spite of guns being drawn, only one shot was fired, allegedly from Ba Gassama's side. It wounded a member of the Karambaya party on the leg, precipitating a confrontation in which Ba Gassama was rushed and overpowered.[18]

The French response to these incidents remains ambiguous in the sources, and the eyewitness testimonies of two of Karamokho Sankoung's sons do not clear up the confusion. Al-Hajj Soriba speaks in a generic way about the French intervening and resolving the dispute without suggesting that this interference was unwelcome. The opinion of M. Pobéguin, the administrator of the Cercle de Kadé (the jurisdiction in which Touba was located), indirectly confirms this benign interpretation, with the idea that the intervention on its own, while unwelcome, was not the cause of the breakdown of relations at Touba. He said that the troubles had "neither a religious nor a political character."[19] The clerics felt differently. Viewing this troubled period in hindsight, they persuaded themselves that there was all along a colonial design in the disputes and in their outcome.

French Action against the Clerics: 1911

Looking back, the clerics perceived the troubles of 1908 as a dress rehearsal for the events of March 1911. On March 30, M. Liurette, the commandant of the district of Kadé, sent a detachment of forty sharpshooters commanded by a Lieutenant Amberger to occupy Touba. Karamokho Sankoung, Ba Gassama, and Jamilatu Seku—a prominent name on the French blacklist—were apprehended. Ba Gassama was picked up at the *poste* where he had been held two days earlier, for fear that he might abscond to Portuguese Guinea-Bisão. With a presentiment of impending trouble, Karamokho Sankoung, accompanied by a small devotional party, decided on the day after Ba Gassama's arrest to make a pilgrimage of protection to the grave of Karamokho Qutubo. During the night, there was a related demonstration of religious feeling: the kettle-drum at the mosque was sounded though it was not this time a signal of the call to prayer.[20]

Jamilatu Seku, a resident of Touba and a prominent ally of Alfa Yahya, announced the imminent return of Alfa Yahya from banishment in Dahomey (Benin). He added that Alfa Yahya was set to recover the slaves forcibly emancipated by the French decree. This propaganda set the French on edge. Whatever the truth of the report, the prospect of Alfa Yahya nursing his grievances by feeding on residual Muslim discontent was too real a threat to be dismissed. It aroused French suspicions that there was, indeed, a nefarious network of support for Alfa Yahya in the clerical community, and they could not risk letting him loose in that volatile milieu. Alfa Yahya returned from Dahomey in November of 1910. He and his son Aguibou were arrested. They were interned at Conakry on February 9, at the same time the arrest and incarceration of the Touba leaders were ordered. Governor Camile Guy of Senegal, who had jurisdiction over Guinea and was the principal orchestrator of the administrative plan to deal with the threat of indigenous insurgency, sent a memorandum to the *commandant* of the district of Labé indicating definite information had reached him—he did not say how—about an underground religious conspiracy dedicated to promoting Alfa Yahya's political program. According to Guy, the principal architects of the plot were Sankoung and Tcherno Aliou, the *walí* of Goumba. The letter was dated February 25, 1911.[21] No evidence was produced to back this claim; the conclusion must be that the French "were moved by an irrational sentiment of fear," as Marty put it.[22]

Camile Guy brought to his office a pronounced spirit of anticlericalism. As lieutenant-governor of Senegal he put in place a policy of closing down Qur'an schools as well as mission schools. He drew up a decree in July of 1903 with the aim of widely restricting and controlling the number of Qur'an schools. The restrictions included prohibiting schools with fewer than twenty pupils, placing a ban on the tradition of pupils going around with begging bowls, making it unlawful to operate Qur'an schools during the period when French lessons were given, and requiring proof of pupils' attendance at a French school before a marabout was allowed to continue teaching them. In addition, marabouts were required to pass a competency test conducted by local Muslim scholars appointed by the administration. Although the French thought they had the power to control Islamic education, they did not have the resources to do so. The *arrêté* merely showed a disposition of distrust and disfavor toward traditional Muslim institutions. The French issued a warrant for the confiscation of arms throughout the district, convinced that a secret anticolonial plot was being hatched.

The campaign against the Touba clerics was coordinated with a drive to arrest Tcherno Aliou, the *walí* of Goumba, who was suspected of masterminding a Mahdist ring on the slavery issue. Administrators were extremely prickly about any hints of Mahdist insurgency, thanks to the widely publicized reports on the Mahdist uprising in Sudan, with rumors of religious discontent leading officials to fear an outbreak of trouble.[23] Military action against the *walí* was led by Captain Tallay and Lieutenant Bornand, who headed for Goumba in pursuit of their subject. Forewarned, the *walí* was secreted away to neighboring Sierra Leone, and the French detachment, comprised of Captain Tallay and twelve of his men, was cut down by the *walí's* supporters and sympathizers.[24]

Initially, William Ponty, the governor-general of Senegal, played down the incident and cautioned against overreacting. He observed sanguinely,

> The rivalry which exists between the religious chiefs forces them to act in isolation. There is no doubt that a suitable policy can win us the support of the least compromised. For if for the mass of the Foulahs only the religious question is at stake, for the marabouts it is really a question of ameliorating or at least maintaining their material situation which has inevitably been affected by our domination. We can furthermore count on the devotion of the Soussou population, the enemies of the Foulah.[25]

Yet there was overreaction. The French despatched a reprisal column, burning villages, confiscating cattle, and freeing slaves.[26] That the arrest of the *walí* was timed to coincide with the arrest of Sankoung suggests that the arrests were planned to be carried out simultaneously rather than that one was the cause of the other. Marty, however, believed that the arrest of Sankoung was a direct consequence of the misadventure at Goumba, arguing that the deteriorating relations with the *walí* pointed to Sankoung as a plausible accessory.[27] This would have to be corroborated if the theory is to stand.

Behind the military action was a policy of penetration of centers of traditional authority, a policy formulated by Camile Guy. Futa, he argued, should be occupied militarily and its leaders arrested without leniency:

> and when we have struck down the leaders . . . we should penetrate not just the country but the souls of the natives as well by means of the doctor, schoolteacher, roads and railways, and finally by means of a more numerous and active administration than exists today in this almost unknown country. In doing so, we will avoid the pain of having at a certain moment, perhaps not so far away, to repress a full-blooded revolt against our poorly understood and mistrusted authority.

Guy arrived in Goumba in the middle of the military operation and accompanied the bodies of the slain officers to Conakry for burial; the dead African troops were buried in Kindia. The burial in Conakry became a political event. The local paper published an opinion piece calling on the administration to adopt a more muscular policy toward Islam and Muslim leaders. The "whimsical and arbitrary administration in French Guinea," the writer protested, had been guilty of complicity with Tcherno Aliou.[28] Guy became the target of a no-confidence campaign. The campaign collapsed, but the disillusion persisted. The source of the threat to French power was deemed to be Islam in its essence, the clerical personality its embodiment, and "the hatred of the white man the unique aim" of religious activity. The French used this reasoning against a charismatic spiritual figure, Shaykh Hamallah of Nioro (1886–1943), hounding him from pillar to post in the course of trying to trip him. Their pretext was his disciples' use of the shortened eleven-bead prayer rosary, an intense, concentrated discipline officials believed could have only a sinister purpose. A worried governor-general warned that "the verses on which the 'abbreviators' based themselves must be considered as manifestly bearing the sign of combatant Islam," intended to produce in devotees an "anti-French orientation in the course of the exercise of their religious practices."[29]

Shaykh Hamallah was asked directly why he would not use his influence to turn his disciples into loyal, compliant subjects of the French. He responded that he paid his taxes as required and did not spread any propaganda and that he should be told if the French had any evidence to the contrary. To the demand that he turn his students over to the French, Shaykh Hamallah responded that he had neither the influence nor the power to enforce it; if he did, he would be a political authority, not a spiritual figure. The French, he said, "are the personification of authority which you exercise effectively, having at your disposal soldiers, police and an army. As for me, I have only my rosary."[30] The French were unpersuaded. In their eyes Shaykh Hamallah was using evasion to conceal anticolonial grudge.

As Marty noted, the *walí's* well-known cordial relations with Karamokho Sankoung acquired a sinister connotation, lending support to the theory of a grand maraboutic anti-French conspiracy. Following an order for his extradition, the *walí* was captured by the British and sent back to Guinea to face trial. The trial was for political show: the rules of evidence and procedure were disregarded to obtain the desired outcome.[31] The only sense in which the trial was more than "a mockery," more than "a mere exercise in cosmetic justice cooked up for metropolitan consumption," was through its dramatization of "the elaborate and civilized affair of the French judicial system," a none-too salutary example of how stereotype availed where empirical evidence was wanting. The trial demonstrated only that Tcherno Aliou's fate and that of his clerical allies was sealed solely by his being typecast.[32]

The meticulous search for arms did not yield any evidence of an arsenal. Only 30 guns were discovered in Touba and 733 in the whole district. Given the fact that the population of Guinea had never been disarmed and that religious ceremonies were accompanied by great consumption of gunpowder, the quantity of arms discovered was nothing out of the ordinary. There was no evidence of a coordinated plot. As for European arms, only two Portuguese carbines and four double-barreled hunting rifles turned up, and these were owned by Modi Oumar Binani, who engaged sporadically in petty trading.[33] The French troops found in Sankoung's house only a large quantity of religious objects: charms, amulets, and holy articles—nothing else.[34] Nor is there any indication that the clerics had removed the offending articles for safekeeping elsewhere.

Nevertheless, the French decided to strike. Several developments provided justification for action. The arrest of Alfa Yahya in February of 1911 following his return from Dahomey in 1910 signaled that the French were determined to force a reckoning with indigenous leaders and anyone of public standing. Looking to save himself, Abdoul Bakar, the Landouman chief of Boké, denounced Karamokho Sankoung as chief instigator and Ba Gassama as organizing genius of an alleged conspiracy. Ba Gassama, Abdoul Bakar continued, had convened a council of Landouman chiefs and notables to discuss plans to revolt.[35] Another accomplice of the plot was said to be Kalli Salifou, the son of the chief of the rival Nalou and at that time an interpreter for the French administration. Even the French found this a wild and absurd theory. Ba Gassama's relations with the Landouman chiefs concerned resistance to the suppression of slavery, not plans to lead a political insurrection. The notion that Ba Gassama and Karamokho Sankoung had allied in this way struck the

French as contrived spin. If the French were going to take action against either or both men with any justification besides the force of administrative fiat, they would require grounds more solid than the flimsy claims of Abdoul Bakar.

Karamokho Sankoung composed a letter, professing his innocence, which reached de Coutouly, the assistant administrator in Conakry, who was in charge of investigating the alleged plot. The letter was dismissed on the grounds of insincerity and guile: the French decided that it was designed to throw them off the scent.[36] The letter was consistent with Suwarian principles—neutrality and abstention from politics as the ground of commitment to pacifist norms—but in the repressive colonial milieu, consistency was regarded as deceptive and unresponsive.

> In the course of his cordial exchange, Sankoung sent [de Coutouly] a brief historical memoire describing with remarkable precision the rise and fall of the great marabouts and warriors of Senegal, Sudan, and Guinea. He formulated conclusions, stamped with loyalty, where he stressed that had his fidelity not been born of natural sympathy, it would have been a matter of the necessity of logic and of history.[37]

Despite a sense of deepening foreboding regarding imminent military action, the Touba clerics discountenanced any form of resistance, allowing French troops to have the run of the place. The arrests and earlier search for arms were carried out in an atmosphere of calm and orderliness. Even when faced with the humiliation of members of their High Priesthood, the Touba clerics conducted themselves quietly and with dignity. The only voice raised was that of a supporter of Ba Gassama, and even that was as much in consternation as in fear.[38] Taken to Conakry, the prisoners were eventually arraigned before the governor-general, who, on June 21, 1911, sentenced them to ten years' internment with hard labor, coupled with banishment to Port Etienne in Mauritania. The community reacted with stunned, incredulous silence. "At most there was a muffled tension expressing itself notably in prophecies of the imminent collapse of French domination. But it raised the alarm in some colonial circles, where it expressed itself in demands for repressive and punitive action."[39] The prisoners comported themselves well under French orders, and it appears that Karamokho Sankoung, as supreme cleric, accepted his personal misfortune with philosophical resignation. Sankoung's fate moved Marty to ask: "By what chain of circumstances did one manage to make of this sympathetic marabout and conciliatory magistrate the deportee of Port Etienne?" He followed the story of the prisoners to Mauritania and gives this account of Sankoung's detention, remorseful that he did not do enough to help:

> One was perhaps wrong not to indicate to the *commandant* of the Bay of Lévrier [the detention site in Mauritania] the situation of Karamokho [Sankoung], his past history as well as his future prospects. Condemned to the requirement of the painful schedule of breaking stones and digging ditches, it became immediately clear that he was incapable of following this regime, and his comrades in misfortune, moved and respectful, decided immediately and by common accord to abandon to him the task considered the least arduous in the camp: cleaning out toilet bins. The whole story is at the same time touching and painful to recount.[40]

The Issue of Slavery

One theory of the troubles in Touba is that the emancipation of slaves left the Jakhanke scrambling to avert the social and economic consequences for the town. In the process, supposedly, the clerics fell back on the support of old allies like Alfa Yahya, though it is not clear what form that support was to take. There is no denying that slavery was critical in the structure of the religious community and that the ban on it would have immediate and long-lasting repercussions, but there is no evidence that the clerics looked for a remedy outside or against the law. Furthermore, if slavery was as entrenched in the community as is claimed, a ban on it should have united the clerics instead of dividing them. The accounts agree that Touba's population plummeted with the freeing of captives. Suret-Canale estimates a drop from seven thousand slaves in 1908 to three thousand in 1911.[41] Other sources claim a much steeper decline, for in one day alone 4,800 slaves were freed on the orders of the French.[42] Ba Gassama and Sankoung, individually and together, stood to lose a great deal from sudden emancipation; they would have no reason to be pitted against each other under the circumstances. We can infer from the dispute between them that other things were more important than grievance over the freeing of slaves and captives.

The question of slavery touched on other aspects of the domestic life of the clerics. Following Muslim law, many Jakhanke patrons adopted slave women as concubines. When emancipation was ordered, slave women were accorded a notional freedom that allowed them to be taken back as legal wives. [43] As discussed earlier, this was the custom Mansa Músá invoked for his case; but he was told that this was taking unwarranted liberties with the law. Given the entrenched nature of this custom of concubine-turned-wife, emancipation and the mass evacuation of ex-slave families caused severe disruption of clerical domestic life. Slave children by clerical fathers were separated and expelled with their mothers to their places of origin—where, ironically, stigma against one-time slaves was more intractable than Islamic legal provisions for amelioration and manumission.

The Islamic code treats slavery, defined as "legal incapacitation," as a temporary condition and a freed slave as on a par with a free Muslim who has never been enslaved.[44] An eyewitness story speaks of emancipated slaves being afforded the considerations due to a free person despite the persistence of social prejudice. Writes W. G. Palgrave, an English traveler in the Middle East,

> These new possessors of civil libertie soon marry and are given in marriage. Now, although an emancipated negro or mulatto is not at once admitted to the higher circles of the aristocratic life, nor would an Arab chief of rank readily make over his daughter to a black, yet they are by no means under the ban of incapacity or exclusion which weighs on them among races of English blood.[45]

That facility did not obtain in non-Muslim areas of caste stigmatization. Evacuated freed slaves exchanged the Islamic contract status of a qualified slave with prospects of manumission for the harsh labor practices and the caste prejudice of traditional society. British administrators in Nigeria as well as in the Gambia were aware of this problem and consequently instituted emancipation in a phased program of labor reform.[46] Administrators discovered that, thanks to the depredations of slave raiders, the slave trade could be banned without much resistance from the chiefs, but it was a different matter with the slave status. That could not be abolished by the mere stroke of a pen due to the deep social roots of the institution.[47] The success of the gradual integration of slaves depended on whether the society into which they were integrated had a loose enough system of caste to permit gradual absorption. If not, caste would reinforce the slave stigma and, together with economic pressures, discourage integrating slaves back into society. As Martin Klein shows, the social stigma of being a slave in French West Africa persisted well beyond formal emancipation and removal from the control of slave masters.[48] Prevailing caste stigma encouraged many of the absconding slaves to maintain their attachment to Islam, thus becoming unwitting agents of the spread of the religion.[49] Whether as "bearers" or "agents," in Humphrey Fisher's distinction, [50] these ex-slaves' history of bondage terminated where the history of Islam became their personal cause. As carriers of religion, sometimes with political implications, ex-slaves have been a neglected element of Muslim Africa.[51]

Faced with the sudden burden of a slave-deprived society, the Jakhanke led a deputation to the governor in Conakry, asking for a lenient implementation of the emancipation decree. They asked that slaves would for a few years be partially free, working two or three days a week for their masters—a proposition that mixed the *mukátab* and *mudabbar* provisions. A *mukátab* is a slave whose master has signed a contract to say the slave can purchase his freedom—it means the slave cannot now be sold—whereas a *mudabbar* is a slave promised freedom after his master's death. The promise suspends the right for the slave to be sold or to be a bequest. This request shows the clerics' alignment with the presumption in Islamic law that slavery is not a universal or permanent negation of the idea of freedom and humanity and that legal and educational provisions for its amelioration are intended to lead to its abolition.[52] Quoting a verse in the Qur'an (90:14), a *hadith* from Bukhari reports that Muhammad was enjoined to discourage slavery: "Verily my friend Gabriel continued to enjoin on me kindness to slaves until I thought that people should never be taken as slaves or servants."[53] Bukhari adds the following: "Any man who has a slave girl and teaches her, instructing her well and instilling good manners in her, and then frees her and marries her, shall have two rewards."[54] The religious code offered options to help the clerics face the shock of sudden emancipation. In their approach to the governor, the clerics took handsome presents as tokens of good faith. But the administration would not back down.[55]

Fifteen years after the British Parliament enacted the emancipation of slaves, Governor Harris of Trinidad wrote to the Colonial Office in London in 1848, "A race has been freed but a society has not been formed."[56] That was true also for slaves freed in Muslim territories by French edict, except that Muslim society possessed ameliorative measures for integrating slaves once freed, and, for the clerics, the religious code made room for absorption at home, at worship, and in the *ummah*. This may explain in part why in the Muslim world, in general, separate free colonies, as distinct from separate quarters for slaves, called *jongkunda*, were not necessary.[57] Separation on the basis of religion was far easier to entertain than separation by race or caste—there is no assigned place at worship or at the *hajj* for race or caste distinction.

The clerics had by now shown their hands, and any further efforts on their part were limited to peaceful overtures, however remote the chances of success. It seems clear that the connection between Jakhanke grievances on the slavery issue and their complicity in a political plot of insurrection is mere speculation. The question remains as to what explanation the clerics gave for their mistreatment at the hands of the French, as they broke no laws and threatened no insurrection.

French Antipathy and Touba's Internal Unrest

The clerics designate the colonial antipathy to Islam as the motivation for the action taken against them. This explanation is best expressed with the words of Harrison, who writes that the French acted on "exaggerated fears and belief in the 'permanent conspiracy' of Islam."[58] When Camile Guy was newly appointed as the lieutenant-governor of Guinea, William Ponty urged him to bring the clerics to account: "We must put an end to this Islamic clericalism . . . it will cause a lot of damage if we leave it free. . . . Through the contagiousness of the fanaticism it inspires it could, if we don't take it seriously, cause numerous local troubles."[59] The French heard in "the sound of the muezzin and the recitation of prayers" subliminal calls to insurrection.[60] They could conceive of no other purpose for Muslim prayer. In April of 1911, the *chef de poste* of Touba declaimed: "The influence of the marabout is limitless. For us he is an irreducible enemy whom we must put in a position where he cannot possibly do us any harm."[61] The Interministerial Commission on Muslim Affairs concluded that "African Islam is never stable," insinuating that despite its ostensibly harmless profile "African Islam" was inclined to imbue fickle nativism with hatred for colonialists.[62] In this view, the African and the Muslim made a pernicious combination.

There were several factors in the decision to target Islam. The *mission civilisatrice* adopted by the French required a social revolution in Futa Jallon that would replace clerical power with colonial power. The French had to this point followed a policy of co-opting alliances and pacts, a means of inserting themselves into local political rivalries. For example, they exploited the Alfaya/Soriya distinction in order to gain a foothold. They decided, however, that this policy would be overhauled. They were occupying a country they did not govern and signing treaties they had no power to enforce, relying instead on traditional leaders and institutions as syndicates for trade. The advantage of co-opting a network of agents was that it dispensed with the need for takeover through white settlement or full-scale military conquest. On the other hand, it left considerable initiative in the hands of local rulers keen to foil foreign occupation of their country.[63] That concession would be replaced by the new *mission civilisatrice* to force a choice—what in the jihad tradition is called *intidhár*, as we saw with Ibn Yásín in chapter 1. *Mission civilisatrice* repudiated any compromise with the *ancien régime*. The events of 1908 to 1911 showed that the French had crossed the Rubicon with Islam. It was no longer sufficient for Muslim political and religious leaders to be allies and supporters, or for the clerics to be mere bystanders; they had to be collaborators and clients subject to French mandate.

Another factor in the French decision to take action against Islam was fear of a Mahdist revolt. This fear intensified into panic when Alfa Yahya returned from detention in Dahomey. His second arrest in 1911 was carried out amidst allegations that he was at the center of a clerical plot to stage a revolt. At the trial in September of 1911, Tcherno Aliou, the *walí* of Goumba, was interrogated on suspicions of heading a Mahdist conspiracy, which he denied. That made little difference to his fate, as Mariani, the French Inspector of Muslim Education, made clear. Mariani confided in the *commandant* of Kindia that Goumba was a hotbed of Islamic disaffection, despite the acknowledgment of officials describing the people as peaceful and amenable. What made the people undependable, Mariani wrote, is "when under the pretext of religion they are encouraged to wage Holy War against the infidel." He noted that as the *walí* left after being summoned to Mariani's residence in Goumba, he "didn't stop shouting 'Allah Akhbar [*sic*]' in a loud voice as if he was leaving for Holy War. . . . You must be careful of such a man agitating in such a fanatical environment where everyone obeys him blindly."[64]

The French policy shift meant taking political measures to suppress Fulbe ethnic ambition and yoke ethnic feeling of the different groups to the French chariot. The attraction of Islam was to be offset by proactive administrative action, including stopping the conversion of animist populations to Islam and replacing Qur'an schools with a *madrasah* educational system under colonial control and oversight. In such a system the French curriculum would include the teaching of Islam. William Ponty expressed the general colonial attitude of ambivalence when he wrote in 1910 that the French should avoid giving the impression of supporting Qur'an schools and of promoting a religion whose followers were by nature hostile to foreign rule and to the new French ideas of social reform. The French school was the weapon of choice in social reform, he said, and Qur'an schools could not be allowed to compete or to obstruct.

Effective control required breaking the perceived link between the political class and the clerical class. Clerics possessed moral influence over the chiefs, leaving administrators who wished to use Islam as moral leverage with the people unable to bypass the clerics. Officials pursued Qur'an schools to bring them under heel without provoking a backlash. The official view was that "to suppress the [Qur'an] schools would be dangerous, to abandon them to themselves would be folly."[65]

It left the administration with the option of co-option accompanied by measures to diminish sources of Qur'an school recruitment, including obtaining slaves for use on farms and in domestic chores. It was therefore necessary to dismantle the social institution of slavery, which was the lynchpin of political and religious power for rulers and clerics alike. With slavery gone, the old power structure would crumble, causing the fabric of clerical cohesion to unravel—at least that was the plan. French power would step in to organize a new structure and cement the pattern of the transforming society. Clozel made this argument, saying that ending slavery would strike at the heart of Islam's power to subjugate the population and "logically have the result of a regression of the Islamic faith."[66]

The French looked to other controlling measures as well, such as trade restriction. Camile Guy in Guinea regretted that press freedom prevented him from banning the sale of Islamic literature introduced via trade with Syrian, Moroccan, Libyan, and other merchants from the Arab world. In Senegal, Mauritanians called Nár dominated the convenience-store business in the local retail economy, but the Nár scarcely mingled with the people. They also left no incriminating paper trail. The French overlooked the Maronite Christian background of many of the Syrian traders, who became collateral victims of the prejudice and fear associated with Islam. Pressure mounted to curtail their activities.[67] The official religious policy was not merely clumsy; it was willful and tone-deaf. It should be pointed out, however, the French would later become the backers of the Maronites of the Levant when, under international mandate, they assumed control of Syria and, later, of Lebanon, following the dismantling of the Ottoman Empire in the 1920s.

Ponty did remind Guy that it would be imprudent to imply that the French were engaged in religious persecution of Muslims; Guy must make a distinction between religious and political activity. In theory it was sensible advice; in practice it was well-nigh impossible to implement, as time would tell. Only a porous boundary separated Islam from what the French defined as politics. For administrators the only politics acceptable was the one in which marabouts and other indigenous leaders assumed the status of a subject class. The remoteness of West Africa provided no assistance for the French in the event of fallout from any harsh policies pursued locally. Unless prevented, the Islam *arabe* of French designation would exploit local grievances by insinuating Pan-Islamic support. A Moroccan trader named Abdul Karim Mourad appeared to conform to this category of agent of Pan-Islam; his trail was followed when he left Abidjan for Dakar. Ponty suggested having him intercepted mid-journey on the pretext that his transit papers were not in order. It was suspected that "under the cover of commercial operations he has been taking part in active Muslim propaganda, very probably of an anti-European nature."[68] No evidence of such propaganda was produced.

In a clumsy, cart-before-horse style of policymaking, Ponty asked for dossiers on clerical personalities, compiling a watch list of family, ethnic, and religious leaders—anyone who purveyed religious ideas. Islam *noir* was seen as a matter of maraboutism, not of philosophical erudition and theological production, in keeping with the nature of a syncretistic culture. Thus marabouts and anyone who looked the part were trailed. The overall goal was to control Islam by means of cataloguing and tracking the footloose personalities propagating it. Relatively easy to assemble because of the small number of people involved, the dossier was an appropriate instrument of taming (*apprivoisement*). If the soft-footed approach failed, there was always the big stick.

The colonial conflict with Islam arises in part from the logic that jihad could be preempted only by an administrative resolve to effect a new moral dispensation—one that required the complete submission of Muslims. Colonial rule proposed an enlightened program in harmony with the true spirit of Islam. It included, among other things, eradicating superstition, improving communication with a railway and road system to sever the old trans-Saharan connections and link African Muslim hinterlands to the new coastal towns and ports, and creating an administrative system for education and for monitoring the pilgrimage, all of that without the obscurantist pitfalls of the literalism the French feared in an unreconstructed Islam. France, one official declares, is "the natural guardian of her Muslim subjects in Africa, [and] has always protected their doctrines and customs . . . Let us raise their children in sentiments of respect towards France . . . Let us make our collaboration serve the development of French influence."[69] The pacifist clerical rejection of violent jihad carries with it a none-too-subtle repudiation of the moral claims of colonialism, though that repudiation is no real threat to security.

The French were astute enough to understand this but too insecure not to misconstrue it as a cover for jihad. Even a cleric engaged in the ostensibly pious business of alms collection, one administrator noted, should be placed under surveillance. "Whether the marabout is a peaceable man or whether he is considered a dangerous individual, you should draw up a personal file, if possible with a photograph attached."[70] The officials found it hard to believe that Muslims might oppose colonial hegemony and its ideological secularism for religious reasons that had nothing to do with jihad. Administrators operated on the presumption that resistance to a new regime could only come of an incorrigible jihad mentality. They did not understand that the clerics rejected war and power in order to safeguard their professional reputation. The rosary must replace the gun. Yet to the French, the abbreviated rosary "was the rallying sign of Muslim xenophobia."[71]

French administrators had created too inflamed a situation to enable peaceful clerics to steer a middle course between religious seclusion and political conscription. In the precolonial era, the clerics could view their relations with rulers sanguinely, illustrated by the old adage "The king has asked us and given us a choice about whether we should build him a castle, or about whether we should take up arms and go to war. We have said, if he asks us to build him a castle, we shall build him a castle; if he asks us to take up arms and go to war, we shall build him a castle. We are entirely at his disposal." Political compliance need not be moral abdication to be genuine—a point wholly lost on officials requiring comprehensive colonial control. The meaning is well expressed in the observation that "Every subject's duty is the king's; but every subject's soul is his own."[72] This was not a distinction allowed to the clerics.

The clerics felt that, since they never conspired or used force in their opposition to the slavery ban, their opposition could not have been the reason for reprisal against them. There is evidence to support this position, including that of various French administrators. Paul Marty attested to the moderating influence of Karamokho Qutubo on Alfa Yahya in relation to grievances over slavery and other matters. There is also evidence of anti-Islamic bias by administrators as the reason for the invasion of Touba. Officials assiduously propagated the notion that the religious masters were ringleaders of a conspiracy. This belief took firm hold and dominated their thinking, determining the treatment they meted out to the clerics. Yet stories of a clerical plot exist only in the marabout files created for the purpose. It is true, as many have argued, that the perception had roots in colonial fear and suspicion, but the issue is not the psychology of administrators—it is the actions they took and the suffering they caused.

There was indeed a conspiracy, and abundant proof of it. Its conspirators were not the clerics, however, but the colonial administrators, with their dossiers and rumors. No imaginary clerical plot was as organized, sophisticated, and efficient as the very real administrative dragnet. The bureaucratic and military measures adopted by officials left the clerics virtually surrounded. On the basis of reputation alone, the marabout became the Amalekite "to be hewn hip and thigh" by Joshua's sword.[73] Scholars seeking to understand West African history would do well not to confine themselves to colonial rationalization.

It must be acknowledged, however, that Touba's internal troubles were also a factor. These troubles attracted the attention of a colonial administration that had not made cooperation with traditional political and religious elites a prerequisite of power and had by then forced its way into Touba and established a *poste* there as demonstration of new policy. The *poste* signaled a radical change of status for the *majlis*, a situation for which the clerics were little prepared. By the time they realized what was happening, the clerics had been snared into the dragnet of rising French power and become targets of military action. It is worth pondering what effect that was likely to have on the pacifist legacy as the *raison d'être* of the clerical profession.

Exile and Return of Karamokho Sankoung: 1911–1917

Thanks to the goodwill and intercession of numerous people, Karamokho Sankoung did not serve his full ten-year sentence. He was released in April of 1916 and placed under official surveillance at Dakar. There had been intense lobbying for a remission of his sentence. Even on the official level, an effort was mounted to prove Karamokho Sankoung's innocence. The governor-general wrote to the lieutenant-governor of Guinea to request a review of the case and to support a reconsideration of clemency. At the time, Sankoung had been living in Dakar for eighteen months since his release from Mauritania, and it had become clear that there were no grounds for continuing to hold him given that "his culpability in the affair of the walí was very limited," in the words of Paul Marty. This statement amounted to exoneration. The head of the Political Affairs Department minuted in a report to the Permanent Commission of the Council of Government that Shaykh Sidiya, whom Ponty once called "the pivot" of France's Islamic policy in West Africa, had given personal assurance of Sankoung's political intentions and his good faith. Shaykh Sidiya was commended in the report as a person "whose devotion to the French cause and high moral worth are indisputable."[74] These official assurances and entreaties achieved their end, and on September 10, 1917, Sankoung was granted remission of his sentence and allowed to return to Touba.

In the oral accounts of Banfa Jabi and Soriba Jabi we find a picture filled with the personal details of eyewitness. In this case, the testimony, inspired by filial devotion, adds a measure of pathos. According to the combined account of Sankoung's two eldest sons, after Sankoung was arrested at Touba he was brought to Conakry, then transferred to Gorée Island just off the coast of Dakar, then shipped to Mauritania. His comrades-in-misfortune were Alfa Yahya, his son Aguibou, and Ba Gassama. Alfa Yahya died at Port Etienne while under detention there. In about 1914, al-Hajj Banfa, Sankung's eldest son, left Touba on a mission to try to obtain his father's release. He traveled to Boké, Dakar, and then Boutilimit to see Shaykh Sidiya Baba, to appeal for intercession with the French authorities for his father's freedom. He then went to Port Etienne to see his father. The administrators had informed Port Etienne in general terms of al-Hajj Banfa's arrival without specifying its purpose.[75]

Al-Hajj Banfa spent two years with his father, during which time he was able to give fresh hope to the prisoners. He then returned to Boutilimit for one more visit with Shaykh Sidiya, before arriving in Dakar. Al-Hajj Banfa resumed his mission and approached a certain Captain Martin for help to obtain Sankoung's release. At about the same time, al-Hajj Banfa led a deputation to Blaise Diagne, who in time became a deputy in the French Assembly.[76] Diagne is reported to have promised help but at a price: al-Hajj Banfa was to write to both Shaykh Sidiya and Karamokho Sankoung soliciting their prayers for Diagne as he faced impending elections. Following the elections, in which Diagne was successful, fresh efforts were mounted to secure Sankoung's release. The efforts were successful, and Sankoung was granted his freedom. Sankoung was eventually transferred from Port Etienne to Dakar, where he spent two years under official observation. At this point, the oral account merges into the official reports and other written sources.

The fate of Ba Gassama, the other surviving prisoner, is somewhat unclear. One report says that he died at Port Etienne before the end of his ten-year prison sentence, but it does not give the date.[77] This conflicts with the eyewitness account of al-Hajj Banfa, according to whom Ba Gassama was released at the same time as Sankoung but on the way from Port Etienne took ill and died on the voyage. He was buried at sea. Alfa Yahya died at Port Etienne before he was granted a pardon, and al-Hajj Banfa said he performed the funeral rites there. All the accounts agreed, however, that neither Ba Gassama nor Alfa Yahya made the voyage back to Conakry. Ba Gassama's death did nothing to assuage the ill will he incurred at Touba, where Marty found much bitterness toward him and little following for his cause. "The Diakanké are still very cross with him, and his return from Port Etienne is not the object of anyone's desire. Ba Gassama is a man well educated and intelligent, but restless and meddlesome."[78]

The Jakhanke continued to trickle into Touba during the remaining eleven or so years of Karamokho Sankoung's tenure there, but the center never fully recovered from its troubles. Its ability to function as a clerical settlement was impaired with a loss of confidence and an accompanying decline in enrollment, and the natural sympathy for Sankoung was colored by the painful experience of invasion and arrest. The life of the *majlis*, conceived in fidelity, was made bitter with bondage. The existence of the *poste* was a reminder that Touba was the "kept city" of a foreign power, no longer complete master of its own affairs. Even long after his death, Ba Gassama remained a haunting symbol of mistrust. The plot of land that had been Ba Gassama's concession lay unforgotten and unoccupied, a standing curse of the feuding and division he had caused. Having tamed Touba, the French allowed it to languish in official obscurity. The *poste* was abandoned and administration transferred elsewhere in the district. All major communication networks bypassed the town. Its original spirit of dynamism was quenched, leaving behind scarred memories. Suret-Canale wrote the epitaph for Touba when he observed that the town

> remained scarred by the drama of 1911. The injustice then suffered broke the spirit of confident loyalty which had characterized it before this date. Touba remained faithful to its rule of political loyalty on principle, but now it stemmed from suspicion and distrust.[79]

The Qur'an school that once enjoyed such prestige and renown suffered serious attrition during Sankoung's 1911–1917 imprisonment, and its educational reputation fell to a low point. It had all the symptoms of fated decline.

> The University of Touba followed the decadence of the town. It has been a long time since the people of Touba could take pride in being able to count within their walls twenty-five eminent scholars and more than three hundred students hailing from all point of Guinea and Casamance. Today, if Qur'anic instruction, imparted to the children of the town, continues to be honored, instruction in higher studies has definitely fallen.[80]

Karamokho Sankoung died in 1928 or 1929, some eleven or twelve years after his return. His mantle fell on al-Hajj Banfa, who, with his younger brother, al-Hajj Soriba, assumed responsibility for the spiritual direction of the *majlis*. Al-Hajj Banfa became a traveling cleric, devoting himself to pastoral visits in order to support and mobilize the network, while al-Hajj Soriba remained at Touba, admired for his devotion to scholarship and study. As already indicated, his work *Kitáb al-Bushrá* has been an invaluable source for this study. The brothers together gathered the scattered debris from the fall of Touba and tended the flame of pacifist devotion, aware that they had reached a turning point, with dispersion as the logical next step.

The decision to uproot was not taken lightly. It was precipitated by the turbulent politics of the Marxist-inspired nationalism of Sekou Touré, the founding president of an independent Guinea. In 1955, a year before Guinea renounced its colonial ties with France, Banfa and Soriba took the decision to transfer the Karambaya *qabílah* to Upper Niani in Senegal Orientale. Guinea's new brand of nationalist politics did not seem an auspicious sign for the clerical practice, as the government asserted the right to require Islam to be interpreted in conformity with the ruling party's ideology of social development.[81] First under Soriba Jabi who immigrated in 1956 and then under Banfa Jabi who followed in 1958, the clerical community reestablished at Macca-Kolibantang, where students and disciples gathered once again to resume the clerical course set by al-Hajj Salim Suware. It is perhaps no coincidence that Macca-Kolibantang is situated within a relatively short distance from the Sutukho of Mama Sambu fame. The two places share a corridor for visitors, though Sutukho today sits somewhat overlooked in its faded glory.

The decision to relocate to Macca-Kolibantang proved a wise one. Students and clients began responding in large numbers. This success was acknowledged by an official appeal requesting the clerics return to Touba. While on a state visit to Senegal, President Sekou Toure asked permission to visit the clerics at Macca-Kolibantang. Accompanied by his host, President Léopold Sedar Senghor, President Toure pleaded with the *majlis* leaders to reconsider their decision and return to Touba. Speaking on behalf of the community, al-Hajj

Banfa politely but firmly declined the invitation. He had the undivided backing of the *majlis*.

Succession at the Macca-Kolibantang *majlis*, however, became contentious after the deaths of Banfa Jabi in 1974 and Soriba Jabi in 1978. Soriba Jabi's eldest son, al-Hajj Majani Sidia Jabi, relocated to Jarra Sikunda during his father's lifetime. His claim of the mantle of leadership from his father who died in 1978 was contested by Banfa Jabi's eldest son, al-Hajj Sekou [Shaykh] Jabi, who claimed the right to the family's patrimony at Macca-Kolibantang. The dispute was unsettled when Sekou Jabi died in 1987 and Majani Jabi in 2000. The bifurcated line of succession, one at Macca-Kolibantang and the other at Jarra Sikunda, persisted until 2004 when al-Hajj Abdullah Jabi was able to establish consensus in the community. He died in 2007 when his younger brother, al-Hajj MaSire Sankoung Jabi, took over as sole leader. By this time, it was clear that the descendants of Soriba Jabi, Banfa's younger sibling, had assumed a position of preeminence over the tradition. The leadership struggle shows that the pacifist practice is not immune to intramural tension and difference. Yet it also shows revival and momentum of the heritage of Karamokhoba in growing centers of pacifist profession.

Acknowledgment of the clerics' revival came from an additional direction. The popular local musician of Kankan, Oumou Dioubate, dedicated a song called "El Hadj" about the advancement of democracy and women's rights to the Jakhanke clerics of Macca-Kolibantang. She named al-Hajj Banfa's eldest son, al-Hajj Soriba, as someone who gave his support to her cause.[82] She had apparently visited Macca-Kolibantang to receive his blessing, and the lyrics of the song make clear that the meeting had a strong effect on her; the cleric's charisma seems to suffuse her confident feminist message. The al-Hajj Soriba in question is named after al-Hajj Banfa's younger brother, in a living tradition strengthened in filial acknowledgment and still bearing fruit in a new though not unfamiliar environment.

Figure 8.1 Al-Hajj Mbalu Fode, Mālikī maftī of Senegal, at his home in Marssasoum. Photo by the author.

Figure 9.1 Wooden slate used in Qur'an school. Photo by the author.

10

Beyond Confinement

Mobile Cells and the Clerical Web

> A [warrior] was no criminal if he followed local custom, if neighbours approved, if he was encouraged by official advisers or prompted by just authority, if he acted for the reason of state or [for] the pure love of religion, or if he sheltered himself behind the complicity of the Law. The depression of morality was flagrant; but the motives were those which have enabled us to contemplate with distressing complacency the secret of unhallowed lives.
>
> —Lord Acton, *Essays in the Study and Writing of History*, 546–547.

French officials believed that African Islam—Islam *noir*, as they called it—was encapsulated not in ideas, concepts, or institutions but in the native guise of a personality cult. They determined that this menace would be best handled through a focus on individual clerics and marabouts. "The influence of the marabout is limitless," they concluded. The marabout was "an irreducible enemy whom we must put in a position where he cannot possibly do us any harm."[1] Thus religion was used to justify aggressive measures. This left the clerics with hard choices: to become victims, to become colonial surrogates, or to disperse and become itinerants. When circumstances forced Karamokho Sankoung to come out of his pastoral seclusion and break his silence, he affirmed his fidelity to the pacifist cause—based, he said, not just on personal disposition but on logic and history. The logic was the rationale of clerical independence from politics and rejection of war, and the history was the centuries-long dedication of the Jakhanke to pacifist teaching.

In a prologue introducing the history of the community, the author of *TKB* reflects on the importance of faithful memory in upholding tradition for present and future generations. We cite that text here. The manuscript was compiled in 1915, with the incorporation at a later date of an addendum. It is undecipherable where the paper has disintegrated, thus the use of the square brackets in the translation here. The chronicle is titled *The Noble Account*

Concerning the Exalted History of the Doings of Karamokhoba and His Ancestors (May God Be Pleased With Them).

> In setting it forth we have relied upon the account of Karamokho Madi [Karamokho al-Maghílí] based on what he heard from his father, and in elaborating it, explaining it and giving weight [to one interpretation over another] [we have relied on] the interpretation of Karamokho Sankoung, sometimes also taking account, in such matters, of the view of one or another of the brethren. The Karamokhobaya community was in agreement over [the history] being written down and the writer of it is Karangba b. Jimmú (may God who is exalted have mercy on him).
>
> In the *hadíth* related from the Prophet (on whom be blessing and peace) [it is stated]: "Whoso records historical facts concerning a believer has, it were, brought him back to life."
>
> Now the Greeting [i.e., the laudatory preface] [which follows] is by Muhammad Taslímí ibn Shaykh Qutubo (may God be pleased with him):
>
> A genealogy derived from the most celebrated lineages, whose
> branches are clearly set out, like streams which [run] into a pool . . .
> a tall branching tree whose radiance spreads forth,
> For the branch thrives when the root is sound.
>
> They inherited leadership from generation to generation,
> through an authentic chain [of authority] and the worthiest link
> of reliability.
>
> May God preserve every lineage among them
> from evil in times of trouble
> through the Chosen one, the best of mankind,
> and his Companions for ever and ever.
> Peace.

The plaintive note in the supplication at the end reflects the somber mood of the clerics in the community crisis of 1915. This date happened to coincide with the First World War and its accompanying repercussions in the colonial territories in Africa. Yet the view in the Prologue that "the branch thrives when the root is sound" alludes to tradition's cumulative strength, which sustains hope in difficult times. Proof and vindication of that hope can be found in the string of clerical practices that developed elsewhere. In the immediate vicinity of Touba, a clerical center was created under the name "Toubanding," (Little Touba), home to a number of clerical families.[2] Students of Karamokho Dembo of Touba went to found a *majlis* at Kadé, and they included Karamokho Sitafa (b. c. 1875), Mamadou (b. c. 1880), Siré-Modi (b. c. 1870), and Shaykhu (b. c. 1862). Clerical centers were founded in Labé, one each at Touba-koto (Old Touba), Fetoyembi, and Summa, where the Jakhanke were warmly received by the Fulbe. Karamokho Alfa, the leading cleric whose namesake established Islam in Futa Jallon, was invited to assume political leadership of the town but declined. The invitation was a sign of the influence the clerics exercised over the town, as acknowledged by Alfa Alimou, the chief of the district, who proudly displayed on his chest an amulet Karamokho Alfa prescribed for him.[3] At Fetoyembi, the presiding cleric was Alfa Karamokho Sori, who, Marty reports, possessed a handsome library of Islamic books.

As noted earlier, a center was established in the district of Dinguiray at Bissikrima by the descendants of Jubba Almamy, a Serakhulle immigrant from Jafunu. Jubba Almamy's eldest son, Kankan Fode (cleric of Kankan), created the eponymous center of Kankan-Fodeya. The population there eventually merged with that of Bissikrima. Kankan Fode's two brothers, Mori Sallou and Bouba, raised their own families in the clerical tradition. Mori Sallou's sons, Fode Yaya and Fode Baba, were spiritual disciples of Touba. They did not belong to any of the clerical families though they came under clerical influence at Touba. A student of Karamokho Qutubo, Alfa Ibrahima Gassama, visited Bisskrima in 1907 during one of his pastoral tours. After numerous appeals by the leading clerics, he agreed to prolong his stay. During his sojourn, he conferred the Qádirí *wird* on Fode Yaya and Fode Baba, appointing them in the position of *muqaddam* for the whole region. "They in turn distributed the *wird* to their students from the region."[4] In 1910 Fode Yaya was appointed community head of a section of Bissikrima, and his tenure saw an increase in trade. The coming of the Conakry-Niger Railway in 1911, however, brought to Bissikrima unprecedented problems with new population groups different from the old trans-Saharan cargo, whose colonial orientation and growing numbers threatened the political interest of the older settled population. A collision seemed all but certain.

To avert conflict, Fode Yaya and his community followed clerical practice by relocating to Bissikrima-Koura (New Bissikrima). But the move did not help. Fode Yaya was denounced for his misrule as *chef de village* and as president of the provincial Tribunal at Dinguiray. He was stripped of his authority, tried, and convicted. In September of 1914, he was sentenced to two years' imprisonment. On January 8, 1915, his students and sympathizers, ostensibly on a recruitment drive, went on a rampage in Bissikrima. They targeted the new chief, Moukhtar Fall, who represented the new immigrant population. This was a sensitive period in colonial circles, thanks to events of World War I. Twenty-two of the demonstrators were arrested, including the sons, brothers, and principal disciples of Fode Yaya. All were incarcerated at Fotoba, Fode Yaya among them.[5] The Qur'an school was proscribed, amounting to a virtual shutdown of the clerical initiative in that part of Guinea. In one way, Fode Yaya's role in his political appointment brought disrepute to the clerical office and ensured his eventual failure. It should, however, be stressed that Fode Yaya was not a Jakhanke though they educated and trained him. The railway system compounded the situation by introducing a mobile population with little material investment and no clerical attachments to the old order.

The Jakhanke encounter with the Susu population revives a leftover issue from old Ghana, namely, the centuries-long negligible impact of Islam on the people. The clerics now set out to apply the peculiar power of the pacifist tradition. Missions were sent from Touba to the Susu population of Kindia. In about 1890, Karamokho Qutubo dispatched as his personal envoy Fode Seku to promote Islam among the Susu. When Fode Seku arrived in Kindia, he found one Fode Ansoumana in charge of a fledgling Qur'an school. Fode Ansoumana was also the *imám* of the local mosque. Fode Seku invested him with the Qádirí *wird* and designated him the personal representative of Karamokho Qutubo. As a consequence, Fode Ansoumana's sons, Fode Bokari (b. c. 1885) and Fode Musa (b. c. 1890), rose to positions of leadership in the clerical vocation. In their work among the Susu, the clerics used Mandinka in instruction, the Friday *khuṭbah*, and the *tafsír* of Scripture, as well as oral commentary. They refrained from employing the Susu language in religious work, however, even though they spoke it well.[6] As work among the Susu was still in its early stages, the clerics probably thought it prudent not to rush into employment of Susu before adequate curricular resources had been developed. Karamokho Qutubo sent missions to the Susu and Baga populations in the coastal Conakry region and to other places. There is evidence that the drive to take Islam to the Susu bore significant early fruit. One example is Dr. Edward Blyden's report on Fode Tarawali, a Susu convert who was trained under Karamokho Qutubo's leadership at Touba and who set up a school among his people in the Kambia district in Sierra Leone. At the time of Dr. Blyden's visit in 1872, Fode Tarawali had charge of five hundred students. This shows that the conversion of the Susu could not have been accomplished without the peaceful dissemination of Islam and should offer an instructive perspective on the appeal of religious moderation in Ghana and Mali.

The cleric Fode Amara Silla left Touba with seventy students to settle in Pakao in the Casamance, where he married the daughter of 'Uthmán Kaba. No date is given for the move to Pakao. He then traveled to Badibu-Kachang, where the Danso family with established connections in the area hosted him and provided him with a nucleus of students to start a school. He built a mosque there but was forced to leave by local opposition to his work. He returned to Pakao before continuing on to Básáfu and finally to Sonkodu, where he died. In the custom of the clerical tradition, he was succeeded by his eldest son, Karang (Karamokho) Ya. Karang Ya took to the trail but received notice in 1915 from French authorities seeking to conscript his students into the army. Moving to the Gambia under British jurisdiction, Karang Ya established a practice at Jarra-Sutukung, assisted by his brothers. The town was under the leadership of the non-Muslim Balanta, with whom the clerics maintained successful relations—another example of the effectiveness of the peaceful Islamization method. Jarra-Sutukung became a model success story, seeing generations of students and disciples pass through. It was at Jarra-Sutukung that I recorded an impassioned defense of pacifism as the morally right way for religion.

The career of Karang Sambu Lamin of the Jabi-Gassama *qabílah* illustrates Touba's widening influence in regions well beyond its borders. Karang Sambu left Touba during Karamokho Qutubo's leadership. In about 1894, he traveled through Manding country to the north bank of the Gambia. After fifteen years on the road, Karang Sambu came to Jarra-Sutukung on the south bank, where the *alkali* appealed to him to stay. Interviews I conducted with Karang Sambu's son and with a student-disciple revealed that his school at Sutukung had one hundred students and that the head student, Woinké Seidi, like Fode Yaya, happened to be non-Jakhanke (see Figure 7.1). One student was granted permission to undertake the pilgrimage to Mecca, which is unusual, and he returned to resume his studies—also unusual. Pilgrimage is not an aspect of student training, in part because it is undertaken much later in life and in part because one would have to have the means to perform it as required by Islamic teaching, which is not expected of students. At any rate, Karang Sambu's students went on to establish their own independent practices: al-Hajj Jali Samate at nearby Jappeni, Tankular Sise in Kiang district, Afang Sire Seidi at Kanikunda, al-Hajj Khousi (Ghawth) Faati and Afang Bakari Silla at Dankunku, and so on.

During his teaching career, Karang Sambu met Major Brooke. Major Brooke was the colonial district commissioner of Georgetown. The cleric made a striking impression on him: in respect of the cleric's ability, Major Brooke offered Karang Sambu official recognition in form of a subsidy or a regular stipend, which Karang Sambu politely declined on principle. Despite that, Karang Sambu remained on cordial terms with the commissioner. This was how a student of Karang Sambu, Ba Fode Jakhabi, came to settle in Georgetown and establish a modest Qur'an school, supplemented with peanut farming and income from acting as supply imám of the town. He had a hand in my own early education.

Another cleric who left Touba to settle in the Gambia was Karamokho Bakkai, the fourth son of Karamokho Qutubo. He had left Touba by the time

Marty wrote his study on Touba.[7] Family records, however, are able to fill in the details. Born in 1858, Karang Bakkai (as he preferred to be called) came to Kerewan-Dumbokono (the Kerewan [Qayrawan] panhandle) in 1928 in Fuladu district, where the *alkali* received him warmly and hosted him and his community. The clerical practice was successful: families, students, and disciples grew in number. This persuaded Karam Bakkai to contemplate moving the community to a new center. The *alkali* refused to grant permission for the move when he received the request because the clerical community had become so valuable. The *alkali* eventually yielded, realizing that Karang Bakkai's community needed more space to keep pace with its growth. The new center was established in the same vicinity, at Nibrás, as a concession to the *alkali* of Kerewan.

Karang Bakkai led his community until his death in 1949. He was succeeded by his eldest son, Sankoung Jabi, who was an informant for this book. Sankoung Jabi died in 1980, to be succeeded by his son Sanjally Jabi, who directed the community until his death in 1995. His brother, Bansi Jabi (d. 2005), took over the reins for ten years before the current leadership of Ataillah Jabi. The uninterrupted succession of clerical leadership at Nibras may stand as vindication of Karang Bekkai's decision to establish the pacifist vocation once again in Fulbe territory.

The name "Nibrás" was chosen deliberately. It means "light" or "lantern" in Arabic. I was told on a site visit that Karang Bakkai intended the center to serve as a point of diffusion of the light of religion to the surrounding area, where the majority Fulbe population had resisted conversion to Islam in spite of—in this case because of—aggressive efforts directed at them. The Fulbe were strongly attached to their ancient customs and rites, which made them targets of the jihad of Fode Kaba Dumbuya, a breakaway Jakhanke warlord.[8] Fulbe parents enrolled their children in the Qur'an school, where Bakkai offered fluent instruction in the Fula language.

No record of the Fulbe students has survived to enable us to follow their later careers, but it is clear that Karang Bakkai directed his labors to a major pocket of long-standing resistance to Islamization. The steady Islamic encirclement of the Fulbe closed any escape route from their shrinking pagan holdout. Time and the opportune intervention of bearers of Islam eventually overcame their resistance. The Fulbe in their defiance of Islam had only a finger in the dyke, and the tide won out when Mandinka and Fula clerics arrived from neighboring Casamance. The clerics had come seeking medical treatment at a Western mission dispensary set up to convert the people to Christianity. While sojourning there, the clerics preached Islam among their non-Muslim Fulbe hosts, with effect. Over time, the Fulbe villages embraced Islam, transforming their communities into Islamic centers.[9] It was not the intention of the mission dispensary to enable the expansion of Islam. Eventually, in the neighboring settlement of

Bansang-on-the-River, a commercial transit point, presiding Fula imam Shaykh Abu Bakr Saidy Jallow wrote a condensed version of Maliki law, *Bughyat al-Sá'il wa Ghunyat al'Aqil* ("The Desire of the Inquirer and the Wealth of the Wise"). He wished to convey "the true knowledge of the inner meanings and practices of Islam."[10] Shunning innovation, the book follows closely the format of similar abridgements of the religious code, indicating the importance of the continuing influence of the Málikí civil code on Muslim society.

The scattered Fulbe resistance to Islam after Fode Kaba Dumbuya's campaign demonstrates the inadequacy of violent jihad as guarantee of success. The effectiveness of the peaceful approach shows the potential of teaching and persuasion for Islam's mission, as seen in the clerical settlement of Nibrás. After all, Touba in Guinea was established as a peaceful effort to attract and reconcile to Islam the disaffected Fulbe of Futa Jallon and adjacent populations.

Nearby in Casamance, clerical centers were established for similar reasons. The work of Fode Kadiali (Ghazali) led to another center in this network founded under Jakhanke influence. Fode Kadiali was born in 1850 at N'Diama (Ar. *jámi'*), in the district of Yacine in Casamance. The name indicates the center's religious nature. His family originated in Futa Toro before uprooting and resettling in Casamance. His father, Mamadu Ousman, who was also born in N'Diama, participated in Muslim military action against the pagan populations of the region between 1860 and 1880. The Bagnouk ethnic group was a target of those attacks.[11]

Kadiali did his preliminary studies at Bidjini in Guinea-Bisão under Fode Amara. He traveled subsequently to Touba to study under Karamokho Qutubo, who taught him jurisprudence (*fiqh*), grammar (*nahw*), and literature (*adab*). Qutubo conferred on him the Qádirí *wird*. Kadiali thus followed in the footsteps of other clerics. He undertook a personal visit to Shaykh Sidiya Baba at Boutilimit, where he was confirmed in the order.

Kadiali opened a Qur'an school at N'Diama. It became a prominent educational center in the area. Kadiali combined his leadership of the school with pastoral journeys on which he was accompanied by a number of students and disciples. On his return from one of these pastoral journeys, he founded a village, called it Diakha, and moved his family and practice there.[12] At this time, religious and political unrest was spreading in the area, and Kadiali was constrained to move his community to safety. In 1890, he established a new center and called it Bakadaji (Baghdád). Fanned by the jihad of Fode Kaba, the flames of unrest spread to Diakha, forcing Kadiali once more to uproot and seek safety. He returned to N'Diama briefly. Then, under French aegis, he was again reinstated at Bakadaji. The French and Kadiali had a common foe in Fode Kaba. A measure of calm and normality returned, allowing Kadiali, with French support, to undertake the *hajj* in 1908. He used the occasion to acknowledge his indebtedness to his colonial allies by traveling to France before returning home.[13]

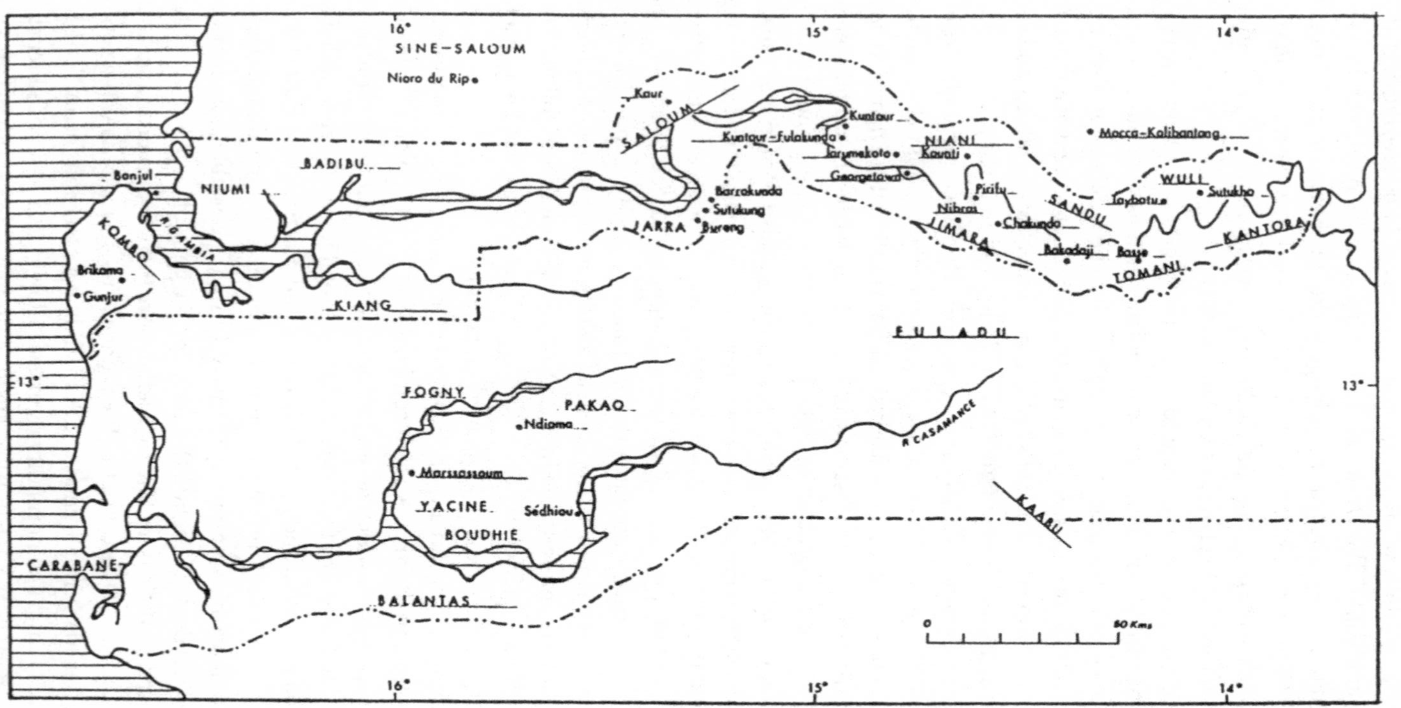

Figure 10.1 Jakhanke Centers in Senegambia. Created by the author.

11

Beyond Consensus

A House Divided

> Make not the calling of the Messenger
> among yourselves like your calling
> one another. God knows those of you
> who slip away surreptitiously; so let those
> who go against His command beware, lest
> a trial befall them.
>
> —Qur'an 24:63

To claim that pacifist clerics played a major role in the Islamization of West Africa is not to say that all clerics subscribed to pacifist teaching, or that they did so consistently, or even that militants did not achieve important victories. The jihadi perspective of religion as a moral sieve separating truth from error conflicts with the realities of routine Muslim life and practice. By choosing moderation, the clerics made sure that jihad could not be ordered with unanimous consent and that, furthermore, religious profession would be a matter of trust, not duress. Muslims do not lose their faith merely by breaking a canonical requirement any more than a cleric loses his credentials because of dissent. The clerical life has been subject to the circumstances of its time; it does not exist in a time capsule. Lines of allegiance have often been blurred and priorities mixed. But the basic clerical tenet has remained sound. Even under stress and strife, the clerics could regroup by recalling the memory of earlier pioneers and their loyalty to the vocation. As illustrated in the preface to *TKB* cited earlier, the list of clerics involved in its composition is meant to ensure reliability as well as continuity of the clerical practice. In addition, clerical pacifism thrives in a traditional environment of mixed religious practices, to which Islam arrives peaceably, with the intent to make gains incrementally. Clerical teaching adapts to this fluid religious situation, offering patronage in order to secure student recruits and converts to the cause.

Incremental gains over time produced more secure and more durable results in comparison to violent jihad. This gradual process secured the confidence and conversion of the people. The lesser jihad typically fell far short of its lofty goals and ideals and opened the way for unscrupulous leaders to exploit power for their own ends. The ensuing ethnic disaffection left the scholars wishing they had not opened Pandora's box. Religious militants and the dissident clerics who joined them pursued jihad only to find that they were set to achieve something very different from their original goal, and they left the surviving Muslim community to pick up the pieces. The prevailing religious wars in nineteenth-century Senegambia and elsewhere were object lessons in the foolhardy business of trying to make war serve religious ends—and vice versa, as pacifist teaching points out.

Pacifist clerics sometimes had to deal with militants in their own ranks. One such prominent dissident cleric was Fode Kaba, who hailed from a distinguished Jakhanke clerical lineage. His name first appeared in recorded history in a dispatch sent on June 14, 1855, from Colonel O'Connor in the Gambia to the colonial secretary Sir George Grey. Fode Kaba was emerging as the dominant religious personality of Kombo-Gunjúr, a clerical stronghold named after its ancient namesake in Bundu. Relations with the largely pagan chiefs of the surrounding country were deteriorating, while pressure was building from discontented Muslims to make a bid for power: state formation in the region preceded the establishment of Muslim communities there.[1] The colonial view was that agents from North Africa were disseminating their radical message in the Gambia and Senegal and that events in French Algeria in 1847 and 1848 had set off a pan-Islamic tidal wave that spread to West Africa, due to the work of "emissaries from the Mediterranean coast" who preached "jihad against all non-Islamic communities," including colonial officials and local pagan populations.[2]

The agents in question were two Berber religious figures, one named Haji Ismail and the other known only as Omar. Omar was reportedly involved in the uprising of 'Abd al-Qádir against the French in Algeria in the 1840s. Devout and ascetic, 'Abd al-Qádir was a charismatic and capable military strategist recognized as the architect of modern Algerian nationalism. His success in mobilizing tribal groups against the colonial administration earned him the fear and the respect of the French, who fought him in a draining campaign before coming to terms with him and signing a treaty.[3]

Omar arrived in Sabiji in coastal Gambia in the 1850s, at which point he joined the fledgling Islamic revolt against the British. Haji Ismail had disciples among the traders in Bathurst even though he did not visit the country. He confined his activities to French territory and was apprehended in the Casamance by the French, who deported him to Cayenne. Home to a volatile band of Adullamite rebels, the town of Sabiji was the northern front of the Muslim drive.[4] Buoyed by anticolonial sentiment and his military experience, Omar arrived in Senegambia. This alarmed both the British and the French. Eventually an Anglo-French force was assembled to suppress what turned out to be a desultory, elusive uprising, with serious cost of life and limb. Still, in keeping with their reputation as the reluctant empire[5] the British were disinclined to embrace the theory of a prevailing Pan-Islamic jihad. They preferred opportune withdrawal from the fray and so declined to pursue the Muslims to Gunjúr, which was well outside the sphere of British jurisdiction.

Sabiji was also outside of British jurisdiction before their military intervention in 1855. A treaty of capitulation was signed in 1856. Under the terms of the treaty, the British agreed to act as a buffer between the Muslims and their Soninke opponents, conceding that the two parties should be left to sort out their differences by means other than war. This cautious position was based on the view that the disturbances were desultory and ill-coordinated and the combatants a ragtag band of freebooters ready to sell their services to the highest bidder. The raids took the form of looting and reprisals rather than a conventional jihad campaign organized around a coherent reform program. In fact, no definite religious lines separated the sides; those involved "had no interest at all in the religious differences of the two factions."[6]

Aware of Islam's religious momentum in Sabiji, colonial authorities accepted the logical triumph of Muslims over their Soninke foes. Muslim leaders sometimes welcomed the intervention of the colonial administration in conflict with non-Muslim warlords, suspending in the meantime their distrust of infidel foreign power.[7] The authority of pagan chieftaincy lacked the ideological force and cumulative advantage, and therefore the rallying power, of Muslim teaching. Muslim teaching could inspire commitment and mobilize loyalty beyond the borders of geography, ethnicity, language, and race. The pagan chiefs lacked that intellectual advantage. Seeing this, the British drew on Islamic law and administration to set up Muslim religious institutions. Muslim magistrates were appointed to preside over civil cases and arbitration issues. There was no corresponding legal heritage on the pagan side, except as limited household corporations in the form of dynastic lineages.

The arrival in Sabiji of recaptives—Africans liberated from slave ships off the West African coast and brought ashore to communities on the Freetown peninsula—added a flammable element to the tension. Muslim leaders were upset by signs of mission activity among recaptive Africans. The recaptives were already Christian by the time they were relocated in the Gambia, but Muslims feared that they might be a ruse at attempts to convert them. Muslim hostility was aroused "by the activities of the Wesleyan missionaries among the liberated African settlers" despite the fact that the missionaries had scrupulously "confined their labours almost entirely to the new settlers, many of whom were already Christians when they arrived there."[8] Included in their number was a sizeable contingency of freed Muslim captives, called Aku-Marabouts, who took full advantage of Christian mission education without cost to their religious profession. Indeed, with colonial government financial support, both the Catholic and mainline Protestant missions followed a strict policy of nonconversion of Muslims, which standard practice.

The Methodists first arrived in the Gambia in the 1820s. They soon established schools for recaptive children, both boys and girls, in Bathurst and at Georgetown in the interior of the country. The influx of recaptives, many of them Christian, was suspected of being a harbinger of efforts at emancipation of Muslim slaves; Western abolitionists who led the movement to ban the slave trade and brought about emancipation sought to rehabilitate refugees from slavery and to resettle them in alternative, free communities for lawful enterprise seemed in Muslim eyes to be targeting them in their campaign to discredit the old slave-based and gender-biased social structure. Freetown in Sierra Leone and St. Louis in Senegal were established as colonies by the antislavery campaign. A similar fate appeared to be waiting slave-based Muslim societies. By the 1840s, the recaptive population and its influence had grown considerably. Lay Creole schoolteachers and class leaders of Freetown and Bathurst, now Banjul, including women, presided over education. ("Class leader" is a Methodist term that refers to lay leaders responsible for the midweek class meeting of members. These class leaders and lay preachers were important figures in civil society where they served as magistrates, justices of the peace, members of the Legislative Council, school principals, and merchants. One such lay Methodist leader was Sir Samuel Lewis of Freetown, who was acting Queen's Advocate and member of the Legislative Council. He was the first African to be knighted for his public service.[9])

In the final analysis, Muslims did not fear Christian proselytization as such, for they were in no way targets of it, at least in any meaningful sense. There are few, if any, cases of wholesale Muslim conversion to Christianity—the record shows the pattern to be the other way around. But Muslims did object to the related Christian policy of attacking the slave trade. Western influence was perceived as a threat to the social and economic interests of slavery. The antislavery movement was not a decoy of mission, however; it made no distinctions of a religious nature among the recaptives in the sense that a slave captive was worth rescuing, whatever the religion involved. In Freetown, a thriving community of Muslim Fulbe recaptives was settled in Fula Town, and a teacher of Arabic from Timbuktu set up school there successfully. In 1841 a contingent of Aku Muslims of Freetown went to Dinguiray to follow al-Hajj 'Umar, returning to Freetown with the Tijáníyah *wird*.[10] Freetown was the destination also of Fulbe caravans from Futa Jallon. Under the aegis of Governor Sir Samuel Rowe (d. 1888), a pro-Muslim colonial governor, an impressive mosque in the Middle Eastern style was constructed in the quarter.[11] The son of a Wesleyan minister, Rowe trained and qualified as a medical doctor at the University of Aberdeen before serving with distinction in several administrative positions in Lagos and Ghana and became governor of Sierra Leone and the Gambia. Rowe was admired for his skills in relations with Africans. Muslim schools were established to compete with Christian schools, with Dr. Edward Blyden an official promoter of Muslim education.[12] In 1892 a policy proposal of "concurrent endowment" to raise funds by public subscription for support of the churches was introduced in the Legislative Council and opposed by Samuel Lewis as a member of the Legislative Council. Lewis gave as reason "the presence in the colony of 9,000 sincere Muslims and 26,000 pagans."[13] He said the churches should rely on voluntary offerings by their members. In their African colonies the British pursued a policy of promoting Muslim interests in contrast to France's assimilation policy.[14]

Defined by the river, the Gambia's narrow boundaries are all too easy to scale, and effects of events in the country and in neighboring states tend to spill across the borders. The country's wide network of language, ethnic, and religious ties transcends the abstract notion of a boundary, of a line on a piece of paper. Like a river, Islam has followed its course across West Africa without regard to political or geographical boundaries, and when Muslim champions rallied disciples, they did so without regard to tribal and ethnic affiliation. The multiethnic factor in turn complicated the argument for the ascendancy of one group over another.

In general, Islam appealed by giving access to a broader set of connections, values, and interests: converts instantly became members of a community much larger, more prestigious, and richer in scholarly heritage than anything tribal society could muster. Islam offered a Scripture more potent than the oracles of fragile memory. With the five-times-daily prayer routine and its mandatory ablutions, Muslim rituals inscribed the religion into habits of personal discipline and tidiness. Dietary regulations and the prohibition of alcohol provided a social code more comprehensive than the traditional religions' sporadic sanctions and tribal taboos and more effective than the health-first, faith-later strategy of Christian missions. Healing and related therapeutic procedures are eclipsed in Islam by the idea of religion as a book of divine prescriptions with universal application. Furthermore, the Muslim dress code was an answer for nakedness that was a mark of tribal innocence; it clothed the convert in vestments suitable for worship, travel, and company.

The British observed that in the encounter with indigenous societies, time favored Islam. They saw that the Islamic advantage created a catch-22: when the old chieftaincy system worked, it provoked Muslim envy and challenge; when it did not, it offered an easy target. Unlike the French, the British faced Muslim agitators sanguinely. This was how they approached Fode Kaba and Maba Diakhou, a fiery Tokolor militant originally from Futa Toro, whose grandfather had converted to Islam and whose father was a marabout in Rip (Badibu). Maba received his Qur'an education in Cayor and taught briefly in the region. His brother, Mamour N'Dari, received his religious education in Mauritania.

Between 1840 and 1860, the two brothers settled in Badibu, where they operated a Qur'an school and raised disciples. As Martin Klein observes, Maba Diakhou achieved an unprecedented scale of Islamic militancy such as had not occurred before in the area. Adopting the path of "total war," he raised the standard for jihad and overran pagan strongholds in the area. His "battles were something new in Senegambia. The area had known revolts and plundering. It had not known revolution and total war. Ma Ba destroyed and pillaged, burned villages, sold slaves, killed pagans, not for greed, but for the power and glory of God."[15] It is that claim of warfare for the power and glory of God that pacifist teaching repudiated. The British intervened to halt the carnage, and Maba, settling for a truce, turned his fire on Sine-Saloum. His flag-bearers moved upstream to the banks of Georgetown on MacCarthy Island, close to the Jakhanke center of Kounti.

The attacks caused waves of refugees to flee for asylum in Georgetown. They settled in a quarter of the town called Morikunda, "the quarter of Muslims." Georgetown was home also to a recaptive Christian population, Catholic and Protestant, repatriated from Freetown. Peace was secured for the town in a treaty signed in 1864. The French caught up with Maba in Sine-Saloum, cornering and killing him in 1867.[16] The officials at Gorée Island received his head as a battle trophy, an appropriately gory symbol of his particularly bloody rampage of burnings, pillages, and raids—eyewitness reports describe the massacres of women and children. No one, including the British, seemed prepared for the scale or momentum of the violence. Maba reset the political magnetic field; this "resulted in the destruction of the old system of hereditary chieftainships."[17]

In an apparent continuation of the attacks, Fode Kaba took action in 1864 against the Soninke leaders in operations officials characterized with some skepticism as "so-called religious wars." Presumably this was a comment on their opportunistic nature. The attacks began with the staged conversion of a dishonest headman, who fled Sabiji upon the discovery that he had sold the inhabitants' gunpowder to the Muslim side. The town had purchased it for defense against their Muslim enemies. The headman fled to Gunjúr where he joined the Muslim enemies. From there Fode Kaba launched an attack. The attack was repulsed and British intervention stopped any further raids, forcing Fode Kaba to turn his attention for a while to nearby Casamance, a stone's throw from the border.

By 1875 Fode Kaba had made his presence known in Casamance by joining the rising tide of religious and political unrest there. He had battled the Fulbe of Fuladu and suffered losses. Now he turned to other targets. Aligning with local religious and political agitators, Fode Kaba declared war on the animist Balanta, then made a similar declaration against the Diola. By 1878 Fode Kaba was leading the Mandinka slave raids and the revolts they provoked. In the 1880s, however, the French began to exploit the fragmented nature of the revolts. By taking advantage of the opposition of Jakhanke, the French carved out an alliance against Fode Kaba. By 1881 many of the revolts had been put down. One reason for the rapid collapse was that his own Jakhanke community, led by Fode Jombo and Fode Landing, repudiated him: "Fode Kaba's methods were so brutal that even his co-religionists feared and detested him."[18] Fode Kaba's cruelty led to his downfall. His harsh policies drove the Diolas into the arms of the French, while the discovery of his secret alliance with Mamour N'dari, Maba's brother and successor, justified the French in declaring him an enemy.

In his correspondence with the British in the Gambia and with the French in the Casamance, Fode Kaba never referred to his wars as jihads. He lacked the credentials to do so. His wars could more appropriately be classed under the term *hirábah*, which is warfare that terrorizes society by targeting civilians. "In his military affairs, strategy and victory took precedence over faith and morals."[19] Technically, Fode Kaba's conflict with fellow Muslim leaders contained no elements of jihad or reform, as he was well aware. Because he considered the alliance essential to his short-term military interest, Fode Kaba's joint action with Musa Molo—the veteran leader of the Fulbe resistance to Islam—removed any religious pretense from his activities. The alliance with Molo collapsed, and the two men locked horns sometime in 1875.[20] Molo captured and carried off Fode Kaba's wives and children. The British then intervened to rescue the women and children and returned them to Fode Kaba. Officials were disappointed that "there was never the slightest expression of gratitude on Fodi Kabba's part to the Administrator or to anybody else, nor was there ever afterwards anything done by him to show that he appreciated this act of kindness."[21] In a letter he wrote to the administrator of the Gambia, Fode Kaba described himself as a warrior. "Ever since I knew myself to be a man, my occupation has been a warrior; and I make it my duty to fight the Soninkis, who profess no religion whatever."[22] In those words as well as in his actions Fode Kaba defied his own pacifist Jakhanke heritage; he became merely another worldly adventurer turning his back on his clerical background to wage war as a way of life.

By the time of his final defeat by the French in 1901, Fode Kaba was leading roaming bands of insurgents without any pretense of a strategy or coherent philosophy. The clerical repudiation he and his bands suffered denied them any reservoir of support or sympathy. The autochthones resented his violence, which prevented him from effecting their conversion to Islam, as was the case with the Diola and Balanta. In the Gambia, the British remained committed to a policy of neutrality by choice, involvement by necessity, and compromise by preference. Altogether this proved an effective containment of Fode Kaba.

Fode Kaba's Jakhanke Roots

Fode Kaba was something of an aberration in the clerical pacifist tradition. His family roots could be traced to Didecoto, Bundu. His mother was Hawa Gassama. Her father was Jaghun Fode (also known as Jagha Salimu), a brother of Karamokhoba. Jaghun Fode and his father, Bakari Dumbuya, left Bundu-Gumbaël and came to Niani-Tantukunda where Fode Kaba was placed under the tutorial supervision of Simoto-Kemo before Bakari Dumbuya's departure to engage in trade. At the port of Pirifu on the Gambia, Bakari Dumbuya set up a customs house that challenged the commercial position of neighboring Chakunda. Chakunda opposed Pirifu's right to the customs revenue and failed but did not drop the matter. In the next round of confrontation, Fode Kaba called on the prayer support of his fellow Jakhanke, who performed *salát al-istikhárah* (a ritual prayer of guidance).[23] The Jakhanke were adamant that they would not participate in war. War for self-defense was one thing; war for increased power was something else, the clerics explained. They confronted Fode Kaba with the prospect of collective repudiation should he persist.

On strictly pacifist grounds, the Jakhanke involvement with Fode Kaba muddies the water considerably. Like Ba Gassama's actions at Touba, Fode Kaba's actions amounted to a repudiation of pacifist teaching. That he could deviate so easily suggests that pacifism is not immune to dissent; of course, this is true of many traditions. Fode Kaba's fellow clerics' denouncement of him shows that the heritage could, on principle, disregard affinity. His sons, who scattered in the wake of their father's military setbacks, removed to clerical settlements in Casamance and the Gambia. In the final analysis, the pacifist vocation claimed family ties and religious affiliation to isolate Fode Kaba. Rejection by his people inflicted a serious blow on Fode Kaba's personal standing in the wider Muslim community and served as an object lesson to would-be religious adventurers. The clerics were clearly willing to reject making common cause with militants even from their own ranks and to present a united front in that regard. Fode Kaba's split with the Jakhanke showed that individual clerics might abandon the pacifist calling. It does not, however, cast doubt on the soundness of the tradition and the fidelity of the community. One bad apple does not spoil a harvest.

It should be noted that Fode Kaba did not attempt to create a rival order of his own, and he did not raise a hand against the Jakhanke; he left them alone. He also refrained from classing his operations as jihad. It was bad enough to engage in warfare; it would have been scandalous to appoint himself a jihad champion. He bequeathed no political cause, and whatever ideas he inspired ended with his life. He befriended enemies of Muslims only to break with them without any hope of recovering the support and respect of his community. His fickle relations with friend and foe alike, compounded by his controversial standing among the clerics, relegated him to the far periphery of the religious mainstream. Though much battered, the structure of pacifist commitment suffered no permanent damage as a result of Fode Kaba's activities.

The Jihad of Momodou-Lamin Darame

Momodou-Lamin's religious campaigns were as serious a challenge to the Jakhanke as that of Fode Kaba, his contemporary, and for the same reasons, Momodou-Lamin met with failure and defeat. French sources call him Mamadou-Lamine; in Arabic he is Muhammad al-Amin. I have adopted the form prevalent among the clerics of Touba and Senegambia.

The date of his birth is uncertain, but reasonable conjecture puts it around 1830, in Gunjúr. His mother came from Jafunu; according to Charles Monteil, his father was from Gunjúr. Momodou-Lamin began studies under his father before continuing to Bakel to study under Fode Muhammad Saloum. From an early age, he showed great intellectual promise. It was soon fulfilled. According to an eyewitness, "The persuasiveness of his speech, his ardent faith and his dignified attitude had already drawn to him the attention and respect of everyone."[24]

Sometime after 1850, probably when he was barely in his twenties, Momodou-Lamin undertook the pilgrimage to Mecca. The journey resulted in an extended period of absence from Bundu, as he explained in a letter to the French who were tracking him. Traveling to Mecca proved consequential for him. He spent at least seven years in Mecca and many more years sojourning in towns and cities. He visited Cairo, Istanbul, Borno, Waday, Hamdallahi (the center of al-Hajj 'Umar's jihad), and Segu. In the course of his pilgrimage, he affiliated with the Tijániyáh order in the *záwiyah* of Tíjání Sidi Soliman al-Kabír, a hospice established in Mecca for Africans.[25] His initiation into the

Tijániyáh order was a break with the long clerical tradition of affiliation with the much older Qádiriyáh order.

Momodou-Lamin left Segu sometime in 1885, crossing the Niger to Nyamina, about 150 kilometers northeast of Bamako. He was warmly welcomed in Gunjúr in July of 1885. Dioukha Samballa, the ruler of Khasso, greeted him, and a large cortège of people from the region formed to express their admiration and pride in him. They brought him numerous gifts to show their respect and support.[26] Before long, a spontaneous and growing popular movement begged Momodou-Lamin to assume the role of leader. It was impossible for him to resist. It was also impossible for the French to ignore the development. In his report on the situation, Henri Frey, an officer of the French colonial army, ascribed sinister motives to the man who seemed like a bolt from the blue. A tense situation already existed in the region because of colonial military operations against the population beginning in July of 1874. By the time Momodou-Lamin arrived, French operations in the area had heightened the tension.[27]

Momodou-Lamin immediately sought to assure the French of his good intentions. In a letter to the governor of Senegal in August of 1885, he announced that he returned to Gunjúr with a message only of peace: "I have come to inhabit the soil of my ancestors and my natal town, in order to follow the way of righteousness and of wisdom, and to counsel my people to follow my example and not to commit any acts of brigandage or theft, as is the custom of our neighbors and most other groups."[28] It is important to keep in mind that while Momodou-Lamin was expressing his peaceful intentions he was also busy amassing weapons and material resources, indicating he was preparing for military action. His allegations about bellicose neighbors shows that he had identified a threat there, though, for the time being, he would keep his powder dry.

It is not our purpose here to examine the religious and political components of Momdou-Lamin's revolution—how, for instance, his affiliation with the Tijaniyah order and his alleged grievances against the Tokolor helped to start him on a collision course with the advancing colonial power that was emerging from the throes of military confrontation with al-Hajj 'Umar, the arch-Tíjání of West Africa. Hiskett is skeptical about whether Momodou-Lamin's campaign had anything of an Islamic reform element in it, saying it did not display any of the characteristics "inspired by Islamic reform."[29] The central issue for us is the extent to which the clerical community of Gunjúr was involved in Momodou-Lamin's jihad when he launched it and what effect that involvement had on relations with him and on their pacifist reputation.

The social composition of Momodou-Lamin's followers suggests that he drew recruits from marginal groups and from a disparate assortment of unattached social elements, including ex-soldiers, porters, sailors, and unassimilated surplus individuals of the state, including, presumably, seasonal migrants, casual laborers, insolvent elements, and the long-term unemployed.[30] Detailed field inquiries show that the Serakhule populations gave Momodou-Lamin their strong backing. This is not surprising, given the ethnic composition of the towns where his influence was spreading.[31] Paul Marty gives a detailed list of some of the principal disciples from diverse array of ethnic backgrounds. Marty did identify a Jafunu Jakhanke cleric, Abdoulaye Kaba-Jakhite, as a close ally and supporter of Momodou-Lamin.[32] Among his followers and sympathizers were members of the Tijaniyah.

On the face of it, Momdou-Lamin's support from the Jakhanke clerics was tantamount to war at the gates. It conflicts with their pacifist reputation, as it did with Fode Kaba. Marty's explanation—that the clerics gave their support because of Momodou-Lamin's opposition to Tokolor power—is disjointed.[33] We have no evidence of a history of Jakhanke enmity toward the Tokolor and therefore no reason to assume that there would be a legitimate common cause with Momodou-Lamin against them. Furthermore, the particular issue of relations between Momodou-Lamin and the Tokolor was bound up with earlier French action in 1879 in Khasso, where they evicted the local rulers and replaced them with a more cooperative Mandinka leadership. When Gallieni, an officer of the French infantry, made a reconnaissance trip to Bafoulabé "the Mandinkas on both banks of the river were in arms against the Tokolors."[34] The children of the Mandinka and Bambara chiefs were given preferential treatment in French schools in St. Louis, to the further anger of the Tokolors. Although the issue was not connected to the Jakhanke clerics, it may be the background to Marty's ethnic analysis. The clerical split with Momdou-Lamin should logically have drawn the clerics closer to the Tokolor, showing ethnic calculations to be quite complex.

Also, the clerics did not adopt pacifist teaching because it was politically expedient or materially profitable. To suggest that the clerics abandoned pacifism to help settle old scores is to claim, without evidence, that the clerics were opportunists who paid only lip service to their principles. This is too serious a claim to make on the basis of mere supposition, especially when the available evidence seems to contradict it.[35] The Jakhanke achievement in Futa Jallon and their subsequent successful missionary forays into Fulbe and other communities show that the clerics had found a formula to overcome ethnic tension. References in both Jakhanke and Fulbe sources to al-Hajj Salim Suware as an inspiration indicate that the idea of interethnic harmony had a place in the self-understanding of the pacifist tradition. As we saw, the Fulbe *mawubé* were responsive to pacifist appeal.

Even after discounting interethnic grievances and Jakhanke refusal to support Momodou-Lamin, we have still to explain the ambivalence of the clerics. The evidence yields more than it seems to at first glance. Official French investigations offered a far-from-convincing account of clerical collaboration with the militants. What solid evidence there is backs the clerical view that Momodou-Lamin was mostly deserted by the Jakhanke, with a few individual exceptions. Indeed, there was an open rift. In a dispatch to Lieutenant-Colonel Galliéni, investigating French officer Lieutenant Bonaccorsi reported that the Jakhanke population of Bundu followed Momodou-Lamin to Bundu-Diakha only to break off relations with him. According to the dispatch, Momodou-Lamin sent a request for recruits and was rebuffed by the Jakhanke in no uncertain terms.[36]

The Jakhanke's rejection drew a sharp response from Momodou-Lamin. He threatened punitive reprisals, warning the people, allegedly for their own safety, "to evacuate the small villages and to reassemble in two or three well-fortified major centers so as to defend themselves in case of attack." This propaganda warfare was designed to spread fear to uproot and scatter the people, then strike them in flight. In a dispatch dated November 14, 1886, Lieutenant Guiguandon reported that Dianna (Janna), an early base of Momodou-Lamin's uprising, was the hub of a constellation of thirty-two villages in the Diakha region with an estimated total population of about 5,500 inhabitants. His search uncovered about six hundred guns but otherwise no evidence of an arms build-up. Though he suspected sympathy for Momodou-Lamin in the clerical community, he said he found and heard of none. He concluded categorically that the population would not respond to Momodou-Lamin's military mobilization because "the Diakhanké are not warriors."[37]

The Jakhanke found themselves under threat from Momodou-Lamin on one side and targets of French reprisals on the other. Jihad and colonial rule confronted the clerics with the same dilemma. After defeating Momodou-Lamin in 1887, the French turned their attention to the clerics. They enforced a ban on slavery to force the clerics' hand and to see if the grievances of the ban would expose any plans to resist it. As we saw in Touba, emancipation removed a critical source of labor; however, also as in Touba, emancipation created gaps in the social system that clients, the *nyamakala*, and other dependents could fill. This enabled the clerical community to absorb the shock of the ban.

The ban was followed by military action. In 1893 the French officer listed only as Hostains, accompanied by Malik Ture, the almamy of Bundu, laid siege to the three most important Jakhanke centers—Sillacounda, Laminia, and Samecouta—cutting them off from the clerical network. Not surprisingly, the centers offered no resistance. Nevertheless, they were not spared, and the clerics were severely punished "for reasons for which we are ignorant to this day and which no one is able to explain," confessed a remorseful official.[38] The clerics resumed their time-honored practices of dispersion and regrouping beyond attack and danger. As Belgian anthropologist Pierre Smith noted, the dispersion trail henceforth led to the Gambia, where students and disciples flocked for instruction.[39]

Momodou-Lamin's jihad presented the Jakhanke with an acute challenge, one they could not ignore. In line with clerical sources, archival records make this point. Perhaps the most serious setback Momodou-Lamin suffered was collective repudiation by his clerical *qabílah*; namely, the Darame clerics. The Darame *qabílah* fled from Bundu in the wake of Momodou-Lamin's military operations. The exodus was led by Safiatu Burema, Safiatu Madi, Safiatu Sanusi, and Safiatu Ma Sireng, all of them clerical leaders of the Darame *qabílah*. Eventually a section of the community settled at Bundu-Bakadaji under Fode Ansumana (al-Uthman) Darame. After the rift with Momodou-Lamin, Fode Ansumana removed the community once more to Jimara-Bakadaji, on the south bank of the Gambia, where he extracted a promise from local warlords to respect his pacifist commitment.

I visited the center at Jimara-Bakadaji in the 1970s, where in a public meeting the assembly had rehearsed its commitment to pacifist teaching. Fode Ansumana rejected siding with the warlords and decided instead to found an independent *majlis* in line with the clerical tradition. This was his condition for agreeing to settle in the vicinity. The accounts say that Musa Molo, the Fula warlord who was engaged in a tense deadlock with Fode Kaba, Momodou-Lamin, and other Muslim militants, agreed to meet Fode Ansumana on the cleric's terms. Attempts by the Muslim militants to force Fode Ansumana into taking sides in the conflict with Musa Molo failed, and Jimara-Bakadaji survived its tumultuous founding.[40]

The chronicle of the Kaba *qabílah, TKQ* (chronicle of the Jakhite-Kaba *qabílah*), describes Momodou-Lamin's split with another prominent Bundu cleric, Fode Mahmúd Jílání, who had several hundred students under him at one point. Fode Mahmúd Jílání had a mystical experience in which he encountered 'Abd al-Qádir Jílání, the founder of the *Qádiriyáh* order, and founded a center in Bundu that he named Jílání after 'Abd al-Qádir. As a consequence of the break with Momodou-Lamin, Fode Jílání removed to Pakeba in Senegal Orientale, where he lived until his death. His descendants, including his son Karamokho Batuo Kaba (who established a school at Jarumecoto), and a grandson, al-Hajj Kemoring Jakhite of Kuntaur-Fulakunda, founded clerical centers in surrounding areas.[41] Jarumecoto, Kuntaur-Fulakunda, and the older center of Kounti formed a clerical cluster in the region. Family traditions maintained by the clerics remember the split with Momodou-Lamin on grounds of pacifist teaching, indicating that principle, rather than expedience or pragmatism, was the basis of the disagreement.[42]

Toward the end of his career Momodou-Lamin took refuge at Tubakuta (New Touba), a clerical settlement in Niani district in the same region as Kunti. The presiding cleric there was Simotto Moro, described as "a well-known Fodi, or teacher" who came from Bundu in about 1870. "The fame of his teaching spread and he gathered a large following around him."[43] Tubakuta was able to survive several military attacks by warlords, including an attack by Musa Molo, and became a rallying point for Muslim refugees fleeing wars. Simotto Moro died in 1885, to be succeeded by his son, Dimbo. Fleeing the French, Momodou-Lamin sought refuge at Tubakuta. The presence of Momodou-Lamin at Tubakuta gave Musa Molo the pretext he needed to attack the town one more time, which he did. Momodou-Lamin escaped but was pursued and subsequently captured by Musa Molo, who beheaded him in 1887.[44] I visited the spot not far from Tubakuta at Lamin-Koto where Momodou-Lamin's remains are interred in a nondescript mud hut.

One important question is why the clerics refrained from declaring Fode Kaba and Momodou-Lamin renegades. Was their hesitation consistent with unambiguous pacifist commitment? Can that commitment survive compromise with jihad? Despite his public disagreement with Alfa Yahya, Karamokho Sankoung of Touba did not declare Alfa Yahya a renegade Muslim; yet this did not seem to weaken his attachment to pacifism. There is canonical support for this. Declaring a Muslim a renegade turns him or her into an apostate (*murtadid*) and a justified target of execution. This was the Khárijite position, but the clerics are not Khárijites. The clerics regard anathematization (*takfir*) as itself anathema. A Muslim scholar who witnessed firsthand the *reconquista* in Spain offered a stringent criticism of its religious policy, arguing that the Inquisition (*mihna*) is unnatural in Islam.[45] As Richard Bulliet of Columbia University points out, as a general matter "excommunication . . . is very nearly a meaningless concept in Islam."[46] That teaching is quite consistent with the standing of the clerics as Muslims and as pacifists; it also leaves the way open for future reconciliation with the community.

The clerics scattered widely after the defeat of Momodou-Lamin 1887 but did not lose the thread of their connected vocation. The pattern emerged once more as their wandering paths converged in camps and settlements dotted throughout the countryside, in farmsteads, and on river banks (see Figure 10.1). Dispersion offered safe passage and allowed the community to gain new footing in the countryside, enabling the network to expand and the vocation to strengthen. Clerical teaching continued to be the tried and proven means of mobilizing ethnic groups to rally to the pacifist religious standard. Summoning scattered memories in new settings enabled the clerics to relaunch the pacifist tradition. As Karamokho Sankoung testified on behalf of his fellow clerics at Touba, historical experience and moral reasoning offered instructive lessons of fidelity and perseverance in the face of opportunity and adversity; such faithfulness helped to strengthen the sense of collective solidarity and personal commitment. The new clerical centers that were being created showed that pacifist moderation remained a vital tradition.

PART THREE

WIDER HORIZONS

12

Beyond Jihad

Champions and Opponents

A stand can be made against invasion by an army; no stand can be made against invasion by an idea.

—Victor Hugo

The Case Against Jihad and Anathematization

To examine the pacifist tradition critically, we should weigh the strength of jihad against the arguments of its opponents. Few things vindicate pacifist teaching more than the fact that even jihad's most ardent promoters judge it to have produced mixed results. The jihad leaders of north Nigeria had foreboding feelings midway through a military campaign that their original moral goals had long been overtaken by the lust for power and gain. They saw the lines of believers breaking up and degenerating into nothing more than plundering forays. "'Abdullah, disheartened by these same corrupted motives and depressed by the loss of many of his friends, abandoned the community and set off in Sha'ban 1222/October 1807 intending to go to Mecca on pilgrimage."[1]

'Abdullah dan Fodio thought better of going to Mecca and tarried in Kano instead. He was a sensitive scholar, and the greed and worldliness of jihad continued to gnaw at him. When he returned to the fray, he did so a changed man. He bemoaned the state in which love of power had turned his fellow believers into rapacious mercenaries, whose purpose, he lamented, was none other than the desire to take land and lord it over the people, all for the sake of rank, status, and pleasure. The spectacle of jihad leaders jockeying for titles; appointing incompetent hangers-on to positions of authority; collecting concubines and fine clothes; riding horses that galloped for show in towns; devouring gifts of charity, booty, and bribes—and all this to the sound of lutes, flutes, and drums—was a mere rehearsal "of the customs of the unbelievers." The cause of jihad brought its champions to contemplate the moral "corruption brought about by worldly success, the loss of early ideals, the ebb of zeal, the decay of resolution, and the general decline in standards of conduct."[2] Jihad threatened to become the scandal it was launched to avert.

As the supreme architect of the jihad movement 'Uthman Dan Fodio was a scrupulous critic of the worldliness and corruption that could come—and did come—with jihad. Known to his community as Usuman Dan Fodio and in documents as 'Uthmán ibn Fúdí, Dan Fodio was the founder of the Sokoto caliphate as the culminating achievement of his jihad. But, seeing the greed that came with power, he came to regret the jihad and expressed himself forcefully on it. He issued sharp warnings about the slide into corruption and betrayal by unscrupulous leaders of the reform agenda he originally sponsored. He complained of the corruption of justice through the taking of bribes, the predatory practices of provincial officials who robbed the people of land and goods, the sale of offices, and the embezzlement of public funds. He accused officials of flouting the laws on marriage and concubinage and undertaking raids to seize women as slaves. The pleasures of power, he warned, were threatening to swamp the principles of religion, and all because jihad had opened the way for men of ambition to indulge their desires.

Growing dismay with how the jihad in north Nigeria turned out led to recriminations against Dan Fodio himself. He asserted his innocence in language that shows the depth and urgency of the crisis, invoking an oath in the name of God protesting his good name: "I give you proofs a thousandfold and more [that] I did not accept temporal office in any way. I have accepted nothing from the rule of temporal office."[3] A story is told of one of his nephews, Hamma Ali, bringing Dan Fodio gifts of gold and cowries to curry favor. Dan Fodio sternly rebuked Hamma Ali, telling him never to send him such "filth" again.[4] Dan Fodio is shown to be a person of unimpeachable integrity. The story also shows how close corruption had come to the centers of power. Lacking Dan Fodio's personal scruples, many leaders succumbed, fueling a growing sense of moral betrayal within the ranks.

Muhammad Bello, the son and heir of Usuman Dan Fodio, said that of the ten types of people in the *ummah,* he figured nine were not genuine members. There were those who, he said, regarded their ethnic identity as Fula to be sufficient criterion for membership. There were individuals even among the learned who espoused the cause of jihad because it was fashionable to do so. And then there were those who used jihad for personal gain an advantage.[5] Attracting fair-weather friends like these, jihad offered little protection against dissension within the community—a sign, arguably, that donning the mantle of jihad would not protect against corruption among Muslims themselves (Qur'an 6:42, 108). God's arrow has a built-in boomerang.

It was not long before a challenge to Dan Fodio from disappointed Muslims materialized. In his attempt to make suitable examples of the rebels, Dan Fodio took the unprecedented step of anathematizing the dissidents as infidels despite their Muslim standing. As we know from al-Baghdádí and al-Súyútí, cited earlier, Muslim theology is averse to applying the extreme sanction of *takfír* on fellow Muslims. Dan Fodio's anathematizations precipitated debate about his authority to do so. His studious response was his acknowledgment of the legitimacy of his critics. The criticism of learned Muslim scholars forced the combatants to turn their attention to scholarly sources about the legitimacy of jihad against other Muslims.[6] Dan Fodio felt the heavy responsibility of shedding Muslim blood, for he was all too aware of the fact that "the sanctity of Muslim blood is a point over which the Revealed Law is absolutely clear and binding."[7] Scripture states that anyone who "slays a believer willfully, his recompense is Gehenna, therein dwelling forever," stressing that God will not relent in enmity for that offense. (Qur'an 4:95.) This scriptural injunction made it unbearable for Dan Fodio to consider that he might even notionally be waging war against fellow Muslims, and he became all the more determined to convince himself that the people he was fighting were apostates.

This is illustrative of how even under the stress of war Muslim scholars made use of critical religious discourse to explain their actions. Jihad is more than a matter simply of gaining power; it can also bring scholarly credentials under stringent public scrutiny. The scholarly output of the jihad leaders was as great during the campaigns as it was before them, if not more so; waging jihad was no reason to take a rest from religion and learning. The jihadists had not been weaned on the cold-blooded doctrine of Clausewitz that war is a preferable method of doing politics—or, in this case, of doing religion. They paused to consider again why they were waging jihad: Was it necessary, as in self-defense, or was it for power and gain? Most of the scholarly exchange among jihadists occurred during military operations between 1810 and 1812.

Muhammad al-Kánemí (d. 1835) of Kanem-Borno was the Muslim leader who threw down the gauntlet on the jihad Dan Fodio and his followers were waging against fellow Muslims. He lived and studied in Cairo and Medina and had watched the spread of war in his state with increasing alarm. He wanted to know why, if jihad is what the rule-books say it is, his fellow Muslims should be targets. 'Uthman dan Fodio rejected the legitimacy of pagan jurisdiction altogether on the grounds that "the law of the country is the law of the ruler."[8] But that rule failed with respect to Kanem-Borno. Its ruler was Muslim, yet Dan Fodio repudiated him. This placed Dan Fodio in the untenable position of having to justify jihad against fellow Muslims, as John Hunwick noted.[9] Following Dan Fodio, Muhammad Bello insisted that Muslims who aided infidels had forfeited their faith and become themselves infidels in all but name. Bello's answer raises an equally urgent question about the true meaning of faith (*imán*) as a moral attribute—an attribute that, in the scholarly consensus, does not defer to human will.[10] To say, as the Fulani jihadists said, that choosing sides in war can render the faith of a Muslim null and void is to deem faith a temporal value and belief or unbelief a matter of the company one keeps. The Fulani jihadists were disposed to say that their opponents were unbelievers, though they included Muslim opponents, while their supporters and allies were believers when not all were Muslim. War is not a reliable way to sift believers from unbelievers.

In the Muslim canon, possessing faith is not merely a human transaction. Faith is grounded in a higher prerogative. The Qur'an declares that no one can believe except with God's permission (10:100). In his authority as sultan of Egypt, Saladin declared the faith of anyone who converted to Islam under duress to be null and void. With the backing of Saladin's prime minister, the renowned Jewish philosopher Moses Maimonides availed himself of this rule after fleeing to Cairo: he renounced the forced conversion he had undergone in Almohad-ruled Spain.

The view of Egyptian legal scholar Jalal al-Din al-Suyuti is tacit endorsement of Saladin's view. When asked whether anyone can be saved without duress simply by "loving the prophet though he be disobedient and neglect some of the obligatory acts," al-Suyuti responded that a person can.[11] He went further, stipulating that it is better not to fight even when loss of life and property are at stake. In al-Suyuti's hands, reform must proceed at the pace of a convoy. If one wants to walk fast, one walks alone, as a sectarian would; if one wants to walk far, one walks with others, as one would as a member of the *ummah*. Al-Qushayri (d. 1074) cited a story about self-centeredness and community merit. "This people has no protection save in the Prophet; everyone else on the Day of Resurrection will say: 'Me, Me,' but he will say: 'My people, my people.'"[12] This sentiment is expressed in the *Mishkat al-Masabih* ("A Niche of Lights"), a collection of *hadiths* by Muhammad ibn 'Abd Allah al-Tabrizi (d. 1340–1341), thus: "The hand of God is with the community (*jama'ah*). He who stands alone stands alone in hell."

These examples do not resolve the hard sayings of Scripture about dealing harshly with unbelievers (Qur'an 3:27–28; 5:43, 46, 49; 9:5, 29; 47:4; 60:8–9); the examples show that reading scripture is a matter of historical awareness, moral experience, and due regard for justice. A well-known case is one in which the Caliph 'Umar was about to amputate the left hand of a person who had committed a crime for the third time. 'Alí b. Abí Tálib, as the caliph's adviser, persuaded him to commute the sentence. 'Alí said he "would feel ashamed to face God" if the amputation went ahead and left the thief without a hand "by which he can eat and drink or clean himself when he wants to perform the obligatory prayer. [Similarly,] it would not be appropriate to cut off his foot leaving him with nothing on which he can walk."[13] Apostolic authority here recognizes that the intention of law is not to incapacitate but to uphold justice. Unless qualified in this way, a literal reading of the text will be arbitrary. It was this realization that made it impossible for the jihad leaders to ignore al-Kánemí's criticism. Bello and his fellow jihadists seemed to adopt the extremist position that deems faith to be alienable, contrary to al-Suyuti. This is why al-Kánemí's challenge rattled them.

The exigencies of war, al-Kánemí insisted, cannot decide who is or who is not a Muslim, nor can it decide our ultimate fate in the moral life. To mount his attack al-Kánemí had the considerable advantage of being able to appeal to sources also used by the jihadists. War, he challenged, was never intended to be the litmus test of religious faithfulness and certainly not the avenue for settling differences among Muslims. Tolerance and mutual acceptance were the only credible options for dealing with difference. Without tolerance, Muslims would be left to adopt force and intimidation in handling disagreements and before long would unleash a debilitating conflict that would exempt not even "Egypt, Syria and all the cities of Islam . . . in which acts of immorality and disobedience without number have long been committed."[14] In that regard, Egypt and Syria are like Borno, only worse.

> If praying and the giving of alms, knowledge of God, fasting in Ramadan and the building of mosques is paganism, what is Islam? These buildings in which you have been standing of a Friday, are they churches or synagogues or fire temples? If they were other than Muslim places of worship, then you would not pray in them when you capture them. Is this not a contradiction? [15]

Al-Kánemí contended that, presented with a society with varying degrees of religious adherence, to draw a line between true believers and the rest is an inflammatory act. This is why scholars agreed that leniency shown to an unbeliever is more acceptable than taking the life of a Muslim, even if one desires to preserve true religion from falsehood.[16] As ideologically difficult as it is for the jihadist to conceive of religion without the idea of war, it is similarly difficult for the Jakhanke cleric to think of Islam's mission without the idea of peaceful witness. The clerical view shrinks the role of jihad in the religious and moral life. Eusebius (d. 339 AD), the father of ecclesiastical history, set out to defend the pacifist cause in Christian history only to succumb to the idea, akin to jihad, that war can help religion. Accordingly, he defended the logic of "peaceful wars, fought for the very peace of the soul."[17] Eusebius built the cult of martyrdom on that contradiction, abetting the extremist view that the blood of the martyrs is the seed of the church, in the fighting words of Tertullian (d. c. 240 AD), a theologian of Carthage.

The offenses leveled by the jihadists were not sufficient to qualify the Muslims they targeted as unbelievers, because such Muslims made no attempt to deny the oneness of God, as the Qur'an enjoins (Qur'an 112).[18] Muslims might be guilty and blamed for acts deemed forbidden and disapproved, but that would not void their faith or justify jihad. Religious law is not the enemy of faith, nor does breaking it amount to *kufr* (unbelief). According to a *hadith,* when Muhammad was asked whether Muslims should not fight against bad rulers, he is reported to have responded, "No, not so long as they say their prayers."[19] This raises a larger issue concerning the premise of jihad. It is not reasonable to argue, al-Kánemí insisted, that the present age is created to be "more virtuous or stronger or more learned than the first Muslims," because that would impugn the faith of the early Muslims in light of their undeniable failings and would impose on later generations the liability of being heirs to a blemished heritage. Muslims would risk the reputation of Islam were they to press jihad into a handicap of faith in order to "force the hand of God." "No age and country," al-Kánemí continued, "is free from its share of heresy and sin," and to demand that would pack more bullets into the gun, making war for religion a routine matter. [20] Al-Ghazali noted that to demand freedom from sin is to make something like an act of criticism impossible.[21] It is a valid riposte to extremist sentiment, antinomian or jihadist.

Al-Ghazali's remark supports the pacifist view that jihad is not a sound way of being Muslim. In the name of religion, war is too extreme an instrument to purify religion or to make believers more ardent in their faith. Righteousness is not achieved or maintained through the pursuit of others as enemies. In an extensive study of Islam's roots in religious freedom, the Grand Imam of Al-Azhar cited Malik ibn Anas and other classical authorities in defense of the principle of moderation and tolerance, saying that it is preferred to err toward generosity in evaluating the faith of a fellow Muslim rather than toward condemnation. "If someone says something that might imply disbelief in a hundred ways, and might imply belief in one way, he shall be considered closer to belief, and shall not be considered closer to disbelief."[22] Ultimately, calculating the merits of belief and unbelief is not our prerogative. The virtuous city of the jihadists' quest remains hidden and unattainable to mere mortals, and to flout that truth is to reject sound religion.

Members of the *ummah* are such not by virtue of performing superhuman feats but through following religious teaching, with the understanding that this may require trial and error, rising and falling. The believer can take heart in knowing that religious injunctions were never intended to embitter the life of the Muslim through confinement in a stockade of legal restraints. Extremism occurs when the letter of the law undercuts the spirit of the law. Without the margin of discretion jurisprudence provides, and without the attribute of volition, religion would give way to rigid literalism that would harden the conscience and diminish freedom.[23] In addition to citing the Qur'an, al-Kánemí appeals to received tradition to mount his criticism of jihad. [24] "He who is versed in the books of *fiqh,*" he insisted, "and has paid attention to the talk of the imams in their disputation . . . will know the test of what we have said."[25]

Though the arguments and references in this section strongly oppose the waging of indiscriminate jihad, they fall short of the pacifist teaching of the clerics. Still, they show that jihad is embedded in a complex matrix of regulations, qualifications, safeguards, and conditions and that it requires serious advance contemplation.[26] The conventional notion of Islam as a religion of the sword is overly simplifying. Those who dream of Islam's dominance in the world might feel nostalgia for jihad, despite very limited historical encouragement for the sentiment. The circumspect way in which the religious militants in Senegambia declined to claim jihad for their particular campaigns, and the rejection they faced from the scholars, show that jihad is a matter of much contention within Muslim ranks. That the determined Fulani jihadists in north Nigeria felt compelled to pause and answer the criticism of fellow Muslims in careful, painstaking detail is their acknowledgment that waging jihad is a serious matter, subject to the most stringent intellectual scrutiny. Rules of war are secondary to the obligations of religion.

As demonstrated by al-Kánemí, al-Suyuti, as well as other religious scholars, together with the collective witness of the *ummah,* there are grounds for backing an approach to jihad that is far more nuanced and spiritual than a merely military or violent understanding. Muslim scholarship offers abundant support for pacifist teaching's call for patience and tolerance, in the form of religious injunctions, as well as what can reasonably be inferred by consensus and *ijtihád* (independent reasoning) from the text and tenor of the canon. As described in this study, the clerical tradition was developed in the congenial setting of social and religious pluralism, where the adoption of Islam was an asset for social tolerance.[27] Religious moderation and tolerance defined the character of the clerical communities, who used Sufi connections and materials to promote pacifist teaching. The link between belief and observance, between creed and practice, is not a matter of literal fact. Both are valid, whether or not they are aligned. The unity of faith and practice has not been a barrier to difference and diversity of Muslim life and practice; historically, it was often a framework and a stimulus of change and adaptation. As Hamilton Gibb has argued, the canon evolves in part from its capacity for adaptation to lived experience.[28] The Muslim code stimulates and expands as much as it defines and constrains and, in enjoining right and discouraging harm, helps believers to relate their spiritual understanding to the challenges of lived experience. As described later, the Qur'an enjoins Muslims to follow the middle path of moderation.

Clerical separation for the pursuit of the religious life is one way of acting upon the Scriptural rule of enjoining the good and discouraging wrong (*al-amar bi-ma'rúf wa nahy 'an al-munkar*). [29] In the competition for the most credible interpretation of the Scriptural injunction, the clerics faced challenges from militants within and outside of their own communities. Pacifist teaching was far from a universally observed rule, but by being bearers of peaceful Islam pacifist clerics blunted the appeal of jihad. The social diversity and religious pluralism characteristic of Ghana and of the Mali and Songhay empires shaped the clerics' leadership of their communities, strengthening their reputation as pillars of moderation. The circulation of Islamic books and writings on religion and law introduced the religion as a significant boost to intercultural exchange, gradually forming a cosmopolitan outlook among Muslims. Serakhulle, Mandinka, Susu, Berber, and Arab comingled in a culture of free exchange that Mali afforded them. "Islamic learning and its institutions made up a framework for different kinds of relations among Muslims themselves. They often brought together people from different ethnic and linguistic communities, as well as from different age groups and social layers. Institutions of Islamic learning became part of the prevailing social structure, in urban as well as rural and nomadic contexts."[30] The *ummah* is a spiritual community, not a national or racial society; it embraces without exception the whole human family.

Early Evidence of Pacifist Conversion

As we have seen, this peaceful theme and its pluralist ethos occur very early in Islam's African history. Travel routes and caravan centers opened channels of communication and brought into existence thriving diasporas at caravan and pilgrimage crossing points and in commercial towns and political centers. Among the earliest reports of the spread of Islam in Mali is the 1067 AD account of al-Bakrí, who introduces the subject in context of a ritual prayer for rain in a drought-stricken land. Al-Bakrí writes that when the ruler of Gao in Songhay assumed leadership, he was given as his insignia a sword, a shield, and a copy of the Qur'an from the Abbasid caliph at Baghdad. Though the king professed Islam at a time of growing traffic with the wider Muslim world, court rituals and protocol remained pagan.[31]

As discussed earlier, the claim that the Almoravid Berbers invaded and conquered Ghana in 1076 and imposed Islam on the people is not backed by sources contemporaneous with the event, and it gained support only many centuries after the fact. The Almoravid conquest is the basis on which scholars constructed the explanation for the rise and expansion of Islam in West Africa: caravans and trading centers created the pathway for the spread of Islam, and in time jihad arrived to reclaim the religion from pagan compromise. This explains the history of the Islamization of Ghana and Mali and accounts for the rise and expansion of Islam in West Africa in subsequent centuries. The theory has been a critical pillar of historical scholarship despite its lack of any material foundation.

Al-Bakrí devotes considerable space to the history of the Almoravid movement in North Africa, and his account has been supplemented by other writers. Yet nowhere does he indicate that there was any conquest of Ghana, or even an attempt at such a project. Rather, he perceives routes and kingdoms in sub-Saharan Africa as the means of spreading Islam and guiding its transmission in societies and communities, resulting in a mingling of Arab, Berber, and diverse African populations. Al-Bakrí's model has been followed by later writers but with the insertion of the Almoravid conquest. The plain sense of what he wrote leaves the religious initiative in African hands, however unsteady those hands might be.

The Almoravid claim obscured evidence of the pacifist impulse in the expansion of Islam but could not suppress it. Scholars remained preoccupied with jihad as the key to understanding the history of Muslim Africa, with trade and commerce as supporting factors. They overlooked evidence of the pacifist influence. Historians were distracted from the understated character of the cleric by the dramatic profile of the warrior. We have seen how writers have attributed the spread of Islam to jihad and economic factors even given evidence that clearly points to clerical teaching. Jobson's account of Muslim clerics has played that kind of secondary role in many studies, used merely as an example of traders looking for markets. The preoccupation with jihad distracted from any more significant use of Jobson's evidence. The common attitude has been that jihad explains the Islamization of Ghana and Mali, including establishing the standard of sound religion in subsequent centuries. In this reasoning, without jihad, converts to Islam are fated to syncretism. The pacifist paradigm rejects this reasoning without denying that jihad took place at other times and places.

The travel account of Ibn Battuta is a testament to the importance of local initiative in the transmission and appropriation of Islam. He found evidence of the existence of local Muslim communities that were distinctively inclusive and pluralist. Looking beyond the routes and kingdoms of al-Bakrí's description, Ibn Battuta documented examples of local practice and initiative that aided Islam's spread. His list of religious officials and their position in society proved that after Islam crossed the barrier of the Sahara, it took hold in the society and became a natural part of the mixed cultural landscape.[32] Ibn Battuta refers to reports of skirmishes and conflicts but nowhere gives credence to the theory that jihad maintained the faith among the people; how the Mali empire flourished without an accompanying jihad was the substance of his account. He described a high level of observance of local custom, some of which struck him as quaint; but he testified also to the peace and security Muslims enjoyed in Mali, commending the king for his scrupulous upholding of justice in his kingdom and his good treatment of Muslims. Ibn Battuta was confident enough of his welcome to complain that his own treatment fell just short of the expected high standard of hospitality.[33]

Mansa Músá's pilgrimage to Mecca in the early fourteenth century signaled a watershed in the fortunes of Islam in Mali. The journey opened a new chapter in trans-Saharan relationships and in the circulation of ideas and materials between Egypt and North Africa at one end, and Mali at the other end. Without an Atlantic sea route to provide links with the wider world, the trans-Saharan routes offered the only corridor of access to the wider Islamic world, and with that the stimulus of intercultural encounter.

It is true that slave traffic grew and expanded with the opening of the trans-Saharan routes, sometimes with substantial effect on political and social institutions in the states and societies of sub-Saharan Africa. In the Muslim canon, slaves were not considered merely a commodity. Islamic law surrounds slavery with a thicket of injunctions, qualifications, conditions, and stipulations for manumission. The force of these legal strictures was demonstrated not just by scholars who attacked the trade, but also by the measures adopted to ameliorate the condition of the slave. Ahmad Baba's stringent criticism of slavery as amounting to a violation of Islamic teaching is a well-known case in point.[34] Málikí law gives slaves qualified legal status that sets them on the path to eventual manumission. In response to Cardinal Lavigerie's 1888 address in Paris blaming Islam for the horrors of the African slave trade, Ahmad Shafiq countered that the Islamic code provides means to hasten "the release [of slaves] from the noose of slavery and to conduct them to the pathways of freedom."[35]

Muslim slavery fits into a complex framework of law whose religious underpinning infuses slavery with moral sentiments about the original humanity of the slave.[36] Not all slaves are the same or are alike in status or treatment. In contrast to transatlantic slavery, where economic motives and racial prejudice converged, the foundation of slavery in Islamic law—as distinct from the practice of it in Muslim societies—is not wholly racial, even if cultural views have affected racial attitudes.[37] Race may have social or cultural advantage, but has no religious or moral merit in the Islamic religious code. Slave communities in the Muslim world comprised individuals of diverse racial backgrounds.[38]

At any rate, besides being a conduit for slaves, the trans-Saharan connection assisted in the conveying of goods, materials, ideas, and personnel of numerous descriptions. It was in that context that Ibn Battuta offered his observations of the social and religious life of the people of Mali, often with respect and admiration. By this stage, the routes that would enable the formation of a clerical class were fairly well developed, as was the cumulative influence of Islam on society. Two great major influences responsible for the rise of religious clericalism are legal scholarship of the Málikí rite and Sufism; both exerted their influence on clerical principles without the state.

The example of Mansa Músá, a ruler who proceeded to Mecca as a humble, *barakah*-seeking pilgrim and returned with deepened appreciation of Islam as a religion without frontiers, was a great advantage to clerics promoting the religion in frontier society with no political qualifications. There was prestige in religion, but it was based on respect for Scripture as revealed teaching, not on political clout. No one—not even a king, as Mansa Músá was told in Cairo—was above the revealed law. It is an example of how criticism of a political ruler even that far back did not carry the idea of sedition as it did in much of the rest of Africa. Indeed, religious criticism of rulers appeared deeply entrenched in other religious traditions, including Judaism's classical prophetic tradition that inspired the other two monotheist traditions. In early Christianity the attitude was well expressed in Tertullian's provocative challenge: "Never will I call the emperor God. If he is not man, emperor he cannot be."[39]

This seminal idea of the primacy of the Muslim religious code prepared the ground for the clerical vocation to rise and flourish when and where it did. It began the process of distinguishing the peaceful impulse of the spread and practice of Islam from the jihad impulse and was a large part of the reason why jihad, if it was ever waged, was fated to such mixed results in the Mali empire and beyond.

Political, Civil, and Sufi Influences in Islam

Islam spawned three great spheres that defined its heritage. The political sphere emerged with the caliphate and the competing dynasties that sprang up across the 'Abbasid empire. When considering the political dimension of Islam, modern scholars dwelled too often on military conquest. The scholar Frederick Maurice claimed, for example, that Islam "can only thrive when it is aiming at conquest."[40] This alleged political heritage, weakened and fragmented by dynastic conflicts and sectarian strife, fell well short of Islam's spiritual ideal and, at critical points, was rather dysfunctional. When Hulagu (grandson of Chingis Khan) conquered Baghdad in 1257–1258, toppling the

'Abbasid caliphate in the process, he asked for a ruling from the city's scholars about which is better: a just infidel emperor or an unjust believing emperor. The answer he received, that a just infidel ruler is preferable to an unjust believing ruler, was an apt epitaph on Islam's moribund political heritage.[41] The practice adopted by the 'Abbasid caliphs of conscripting mercenaries instead of able-bodied Muslims indicated the real nature of "holy war" so-called. Mercenary armies were deployed for crass worldly reasons, including keeping Muslim subjects in line.

In time, the caliphate became nothing more than "the sinecure of the corrupt, despotic, and ignorant rulers that had been the bane of Islamic history," in the words of an Islamic scholar.[42] When in 1914 the Ottoman sultan declared a jihad against Great Britain, the Muslims of India, whom he expected to defect to his side in solidarity, ignored him. They preferred infidel imperial tutelage to waging war alongside a Muslim emperor. A British official saw fit to assure his Indian colleagues that Pan-Islam was "more a feeling than a force" and that that feeling could be widespread without amounting to a rallying power.[43] In 1894, shortly after the colonial takeover, the Muslims of Lagos were in correspondence with the Ottoman sultan, and in 1910 the sultan's name was being invoked in the sermon at the weekly Friday worship in Dar-es-Salaam (Tanzania). The idea of Pan-Islam, however, was only a romantic ideal; once attempts were undertaken to implement it, it crumbled into contention. The congresses held in the Middle East in 1924, 1926, and 1931 ended in disagreement and disappointment. It gradually dawned on Muslim leaders at these congresses that a caliphate was not a viable or required means of achieving Pan-Islam—Islam's cohesion rested with its spiritual power.

Centuries before the modern disenchantment with the idea of a caliphate, the medieval keepers of the conscience of Islam did not hesitate to pronounce the whole political system injurious to religious scholars. In his *Ayyuha Al-Walad,* al-Ghazali warns the scholars: "Neither associate with princes and kings nor even express an opinion about them, for thinking about them, attending their courts, and associating with them is very dangerous. . . . Do not accept presents and gifts from rulers . . . because coveting [anything] from them is to debase religion, since it leads one to sycophancy, compliance, and collusion in their acts of oppression."[44] There was a widespread desire among Muslims "for a religious guidance over which the holders of political office exercised no control."[45] 'Abdallah ibn al-Mubarak (d. 797) insisted that the scholar should reject political contact, including verbal admonition of rulers (*ii'tazalahum*).[46] Dhu al-Nun al-Misri (d. 860) of Egypt said that in matters relating to the Prophet's moral heritage, religious authority was superior to political authority. The saints, he said, were God's trustees (*umaná*) on earth, and God delegated guidance to them rather than "to the tyrannical, arrogant, and wealthy."[47] A modern Muslim scholar describes the role of jurists for the Islamic heritage as follows: they "were the purveyors of Islam, the guardians of its tradition, the depository of ancestral wisdom, and the moral tutors of the population."[48] As Carl Brown, the Princeton political scientist, has pointed out, "Muslim political history, in contrast with much of Christian history, has been characterized by a largely successful attempt to bar government from proclaiming (and then enforcing) religious orthodoxy."[49]

The second sphere—civil law and ethics—is distinct from the political heritage. Legal and ethical scholarship took hold and flourished in the heartlands and beyond, withstanding the vicissitudes of politics and geography. The civil system spawned a vigorous intellectual culture presided over by learned jurists, who "achieved by the pen far more than a warrior could achieve by the sword," as was said of the jurist Imam al-Shafi'í (d. 820 AD), who suffered much persecution at the hands of rulers.[50] Legal scholars in medieval North Africa argued convincingly for the validity of the Islamic laws of contract, property, and inheritance even when the lands in question were in sub-Saharan societies in the sphere of pagan jurisdiction. Legal stimulus led to religious expansion, and religious expansion stimulated legal scholarship. Across the centuries, legal and ethical scholarship left an enduring mark on the Muslim world, including sub-Saharan societies, and remains among the religion's greatest achievements.[51]

The third sphere is that of the Sufi orders, the engine of religious expansion. Sufism is a complex phenomenon, with variations ranging from the sternly ascetic to the judiciously antinomian,[52] from political quietism to political activism, and in either case paying minimal attention to law and worldly affairs.[53] As organized social institutions, the Sufi orders played a pivotal role in the mission and consolidation of Islam and stimulated the formation of the religious offices of teacher, scholar, imam, moral arbiter, spiritual guide, and counselor.

Michael Cook has comprehensively described the case for how, concerned with the mandate to command the right and forbid wrong, civil society maintained its role as the center of gravity of Islamic religious scholarship. It did so with conscious distinction from political authority, through physical separation, principled rejection of political actions, and sometimes direct challenge to the authority of rulers. 'Abdullah dan Fodio says that ordering right and forbidding wrong is a prerogative of religion in such matters as washing and ablution; alms-giving and fasting; buying and selling; teaching about what is exemplary, approved, or forbidden; "and how to be mindful of purpose in all these things."[54] In undertaking this exercise one should begin with oneself, he counsels. Abú Hanífa (d. 767 AD), a scholar-jurist of Kufa, Iraq, and founder of the Hanafí school of law, one of the four schools of law (*madháhib*) of the Sunni canon, is adamant that although commanding right and forbidding wrong is a duty imposed by God (*farida min Allah*) and is vested in each and every Muslim, it is not a call for rebellion against the community.[55]

The scholar-jurist Ibn Hanbal (d. 855 AD) cautions against reckless implementation of the mandate to command right and forbid wrong, for fear of causing greater harm: carrying out this duty is a matter of prudence. In difficult times, the injunction should be held in abeyance (*laysa hádhá zamán nahy* [suspended at this time]).[56] For Ibn Hanbal and others, the religious vocation has its roots in civil society apart from the state, a form of quietism that avoids both extremes of Erastrian supremacy of the state over religion and outright antinomian rejection of society. Ibn Hanbal considered the intrusion of the state on his work as a worldly ordeal (*fitnat al-dunyá*). He regarded with repugnance the favors showered upon him by the caliphal court, saying he wished he were dead. Circumspect in giving his obedience to the caliphs where it did not compromise his duty to God, he wished above all to be left alone. Like the other great jurists, Ibn Hanbal paid a high price for his refusal to accept state appointment or patronage. His wish to be left alone was violated in dramatic fashion when, at his funeral, the governor of Baghdad entered the mosque and pushed aside Ibn Hanbal's son in the leading of the prayers. This was a harbinger of things to come. Cultivated by Ibn Hanbal so assiduously, the tradition of religious quietism was sequestered by political rulers as a bureaucratic function of the state. This was a fundamental departure from the trail blazed by the jurists and a distortion of the religious genius of Islam.[57] Not for the first or last time, rulers became religious interlopers.

Abjuring involvement in the political sphere, the clerics and their network of centers belong to the religious, civil side of the heritage of Islam. As such, they aligned well with the preponderant religious disposition of Muslim thought. Religion assumed a leading role in the molding of society and in delineating a sphere of responsibility distinct from politics. Al-Hajj Salim Suware became the model of this religious heritage for the clerics, the anti-sultan par excellence of West African Islam. His peaceful style of religious propagation is key to understanding the distinction between the religious and political approaches to the Islamization of Ghana and Mali, as is evident in the founding Serakhulle traditions that refer to "Mbemba Laye Suware" in stories of the origins of the kingdom of Wagadou as a contemporary of Magham Diabe (Jabi) Sise, the kingdom's founder.[58] "Wagadou" is the old name for Ghana.[59] A parallel tradition developed among the Serakhulle, with one part given to trade and rulership and the other coalescing around the clerical religious line. The cleric as *karamokho* belongs to a centuries-long tradition of religion based on commitment and toleration, free of caliphal ambition.

Clerical Mediation

As previously discussed, the salutation name of *karamokho* spread from its Suwarian origin to ethnic groups other than the Serekhulle and Mandinka; the religious connotations of the title had supplanted any underlying ethnic significance. The Sufi link reinforced the pacifist commitment, while the challenge of ethnic diversity was met by social inclusion and religious moderation. Pilgrimage became a symbol of participation in a universal religious society of unity and purpose. Mecca and Medina became not just destinations of pilgrimage but metaphors of *barakah* and social prestige. Established in illiterate, rural communities, clerical cells exercised an influence that belied their size and number, offering organized services to their regions and making a cumulative impact on personal observance and social consolidation. Daily life was organized around school and mosque. Religious services were maintained, pastoral journeys undertaken, periodic assemblies of clerics convened, community celebrations observed, and the religious calendar, based on the lunar year, maintained. Islam's attractive elements are expressed in its outward appearance. "The formal prayers, the distinctive dress, the food regulations, the fasting—any of these features, or others, may attract attention, and stimulate imitation."[60] At its core the Muslim worship life is relatively easy to duplicate and to transplant.

> The interior of an Islamic mosque is simple and austere. There is no altar and no sanctuary, for Islam has no sacraments and no ordained priesthood. . . . Public prayer is a disciplined, communal act of submission to the One, remote, and immaterial God. . . . Islam has rejected dancing from among the devotional arts; it has rejected music and poetry, too, and confines its liturgy to the recitation of a few simple formulas of piety.[61]

It shows Islam as a religion of structure as well as being a religion of salvation, to amend the language of E. M. Zuesse.[62] The combined influence of religion and the Sharí'ah civil code shaped Muslim community life, along with the establishment of structures of accommodation for multiethnic, multiracial *convivencia*. Thus was assured a place of high prestige for Málikí law and jurisprudence. Through the daily practices of prayer, worship, study, as well as presiding at regular household ceremonies, the clerics and their Sufi allies inscribed the religious routine, including public reading of the Qur'an at the mosque and the staging of religious festivals, into cultural forms to give Muslim society its distinctive design, from the *adhán* (call) of the dawn prayer to the *tahajjud* (compline) of bedtime devotions.

Clerical Islam helped converts to satisfy the letter of Islamic law without foregoing traditional customs, thus contributing to the naturalization of the religion in Africa. The clerics played a major role in conversion and in its subsequent stages by providing religious instruction, leading worship and the Ramadan observance, and presiding at funerals and festival celebrations. These religious activities established a regular pattern in community life. Teaching, pilgrimage, trade, and travel opened Muslims to fresh resources, ideas, styles, and opportunities, bringing about corresponding changes in society. The standing of the clerics rose and fell with the demands for their expertise and services and with the depth of their roots in the community.

In his study of the holy men of the Blue Nile, cited earlier, Neil McHugh notes the immense prestige of Islamic scholarship, describing how that prestige was used by religious masters to solve social problems that might otherwise render religion insolvent. Society remains the crucible of spiritual power, and social fragmentation is more consequential than political failure. The severe personal style of the *faqíh,* who makes a spectacle of self-denial, is unknown in the Jakhanke clerical tradition. Elements of extreme self-mortification and ecstatic behavior are reported among the *Báy Fáll,* a splinter group of the Mourides of Senegal, but otherwise scarcely at all in the mainstream African Sufi orders.[63] Just as rare is the speculative monistic brand of mysticism identified with the pantheist leanings of Ibn al-ʿArabí and Rúmí, among others, in which devotees shun the religious code as irrelevant to salvation.[64]

The situation facing the clerics in Futa Jallon was how to bring the influence of Islamic scholarship to bear on issues in society. Leftover interethnic grievances from the inconclusive jihad were simmering. Ethnic feeling is a complex issue. The Fulbe *mawube* devised a system of political compromise to respond to ethnic political ambition, mollifying ethnic interest without being consumed by it. In the same situation, the colonial authorities were more hamfisted: they were disconcerted by the sheer complexity of ethnic groups. The colonial administration perceived ethnicity as the first line of explanation for local trouble and the incitement of anticolonial agitation. The uncompromising posture of the officials set them on a collision course with traditional leaders and institutions; the clerics and their schools came within the direct line of fire. Colonial administrators who welcomed ethnic allegiance as a barrier to the spread of Islam and its Pan-Islamic threat to imperial power found themselves becoming extremely wary of ethnic influence maintained in indigenous institutions without their oversight. The plot the administrators imagined indigenous leaders were hatching was met with robust action. Mere rumors of a maraboutic plot led to punitive force to mend or end the religious masters. For their reputation alone, the clerics paid the penalty of harassment, arrests, incarceration, and exile.

This experience had no precedent for the clerics nor, indeed, for most Muslims. Here was a civilization that, despite its foreign, infidel nature, challenged and conquered Muslims everywhere and went on to contest the idea that Islam was entitled to be left in charge of itself and of others. Religious masters who accepted this new imperial reality were co-opted as protégés and surrogates, as was the case of Shaykh Sidiya Baba of Boutilimit, the cornerstone of France's African Islamic strategy. Those who stood aloof, continuing to foster religion and attract students and disciples, were targeted and forced to choose between surrogacy and enmity, as happened with Tcherno Aliou of Goumba. Those who opted for pacifist neutrality were accused of temporizing and giving aid and comfort to plotters and malcontents. This was the fate that befell the clerics of Touba, as well as Shaykh Hamallah of Nioro.

Notwithstanding the fact that Islam nurtured the idea of territoriality in the preeminence of Mecca and Medina as an article of faith, in the clerical life territoriality had never been a motivation. Instead, dispersion and relocation offered a way of retreat and regrouping to promote the heritage. Family links were preserved as the clerics fanned out to establish settlements across new frontiers. The clerics' reputation for religious moderation made them welcome and valued neighbors. Many accounts show that local rulers pled with the clerics not to bypass a town but instead to settle there with their entourage, offering gifts and patronage for the purpose.

Dispersion and relocation alone could not solve all the problems of the pacifist vocation, as Karamokho Sankoung of Nibras explained. Family pedigree and itinerancy are not sufficient to ensure commitment to pacifist doctrine; for that, moral conviction is necessary and indispensable. The historical roots of pacifist identity may be sound, but the vocation's continuing credibility will thrive only when tended by devotion and experience. As Ivor Wilks was reminded, "A man is a *karamoko* [*sic*] because of his chain (*isnád*) for learning, not [because of] his chain for birth."[65]

Trouble found the clerics in their newly adopted homelands. Colonial penetration by new modes of communication, including Western schools and the railway, made complete sanctuary impossible. Increasing numbers of traders and wage-earners created a growing elite class. It was difficult for the clerics not to tangle with these elites in the course of religious retreat and regrouping. As potential clients, new elites gave clerical influence greater range and new sources of patronage and recruitment. The elites' newfound independence from custom and traditional observances, however, created a real risk of defection to alternative forms of identity, due to the advent of the West and modernization. Qur'an schools now faced strong competition from Western schools in education and employment. Despite this, it is important to remember that the Qur'an school was a social institution with communal roots, giving it credibility and influence with families. As such, it was quite effective at preventing the rise of the cultural dislocation that tended to result from the impact of the West.[66] Unlike their Christian and secular counterparts,[67] Muslim Africans did not rush to drop their Arab names in a bid to embrace native authenticity. This says something about the effectiveness of Islam's cultural integration.

Nineteenth- and early-twentieth-century religious wars in Senegambia, compounded by colonial intrusion, proved a severe test of the clerical pacifist commitment. Beginning in 1862, French officials in the area called the wars the "marabout wars," as between the Muslim clerics and their "Soninke" adversaries. This characterization conflated the specific facts of warlord uprisings with a sweeping generalization about holy war. With few exceptions, the marabout wars painted clerics with the same complicitous brush. Yet not all so-called marabouts were involved in war, nor were those involved committed to Islam or even were knowledgeable about it in any meaningful way. Nuance is critical in this milieu—critical for the reality on the ground and critical, too, for historical understanding. The work of the Jakhanke clerics helped to define the specific role of Islam in military campaigns, including the complex motives involved. Muslim involvement may be entirely for non-Islamic reasons or objectives. Despite Muslim involvement, warfare often impeded Islam.

The role of religion in the military conflicts of Senegambia is not straightforward. That most clerics opposed the wars indicates that Islam was not a consistent issue in the troubles. Similarly, the mediating role of the British demonstrates that not all colonial administrations played the same role. The British took limited part in the conflicts primarily because they feared overextending themselves. Their wariness afforded them the time and discretion necessary to understand the long-term balance of power between the traditional chiefs and their Muslim challengers.

Muslims enjoyed certain advantages as the followers of a Scripturally based faith with a worldwide audience and uniform practice. These advantages were denied traditional rulers, whose fortunes were bound with the temporal spoils of war and power. The promises of chiefs paled in comparison with the promises of religion. Islam was able to offer believers a future state of reward (*al-mawt wa má ba'dahu* [death and the afterlife]) when they sacrificed their possessions and lives in the cause (Qur'an 4:97; 57:10). Pagan dogma could not back such a claim with sacred text, which left it without competing intrinsic moral weight or intellectual scope. Unlike pagan traditions, Islam's God stands at both ends of human life, in this life and the next.

Furthermore, contrary to colonial allegations, Muslims assembled for prayer or at the mosque not only to prepare for war. The daily and weekly worship cycle represented order and discipline, first as a matter entirely of religious obligation and second as an organizing frame for society. The *Muwatta* ("The Beaten Path") of Imám Málik (d. 796) was the first compendium of law in Islam and the basis of several abridgements, including the *Risálah* of Ibn Abí Zayd al-Qayrawání. The *Muwatta* is concerned predominantly with matters of worship, ritual, liturgy, fasting, festivals, *zakat* (alms) and *sadaqa* (free-will offering), pilgrimage, vows and oaths, sartorial rules, the law of personal status, marriage, divorce, property, inheritance, rites of passage, wills, ritual sacrifice, debts, and, finally, the titles of the prophet.[68] Esteem for Khalil's *Mukhtaşar* was so great that some clerics considered it higher in status than the Qur'an.[69] As already indicated in chapter 10, this ethical template is faithfully reproduced in the *Bughyát al-Sá'il* ("The Desire of the Inquirer") of Shaykh Abu Bakr Jallow. Thus Islam gave structure to the regular cycle and rhythm of life. This role afforded it considerable advantage over traditional chiefs and colonial administrations in strengthening community identity. Before and beyond waging war, Islam provided a full prescription of how to account for one's life here and hereafter.

Islam's cumulative structural advantage is encapsulated in the universal reverence for the Qur'an. Particularly to the professional cleric, the Qur'an

> is all-sufficient for his moral, intellectual, social and political needs. It contains his whole religion, and a great deal besides . . . It is his code of laws, and his creed, his homily, and his liturgy. He consults it for direction on every possible subject; and his Pagan neighbor, seeing such veneration paid to the book, conceives even more exaggerated notions of its character.[70]

This point was conceded by a Dogon elder of Mali whose travels through the wider world exposed the limits of his traditional pagan religion and its ethnic fealty, making the contrast with Islam striking. He said that the crowded field of idols, proliferating to cater to the varied needs of clans and tribes and recognizable only to those who made them, "can only indicate error." By contrast, Muslim practices, places of worship, the call to prayer, and the art of amulet-making reassured their message of unity and showed where truth lay. "I conclude from all of this that Truth is one, and that its manifestation should not lack harmony. I want to practice Islam."[71] The Dogon elder converted by dispensing with an ethnic worldview he perceived as limited and embracing instead a large-scale worldview consistent with the injunctions of a universal deity.

The testimony of the Dogon elder shows the importance of the structural assets of Islam for societies undergoing change, particularly in the form of conflict or unrest. War is a force for change, and it is conducive to a heightened sense of religious awareness for individuals. As the French North African Army officer Charles de Foucauld (d. 1916) pointed out, the daily obligations of religious practice may suddenly loom large in the midst of the contingencies of battle. Foucauld was in the middle of a battle in Algeria when he realized that his Bedouin troops had stopped fighting and were

> prostrating themselves in prayer. . . . On the opposite hillside, too, the firing had stopped. At the risk of being shot like sitting ducks, the Uled Sidi Sheikh [snipers] had emerged from cover, turned their backs to the sunset and bowed down to the east . . . *Allahu akbar.* A strange silence filled the little wadi, a stillness that reminded Foucauld of the awesome quiet of Nancy Cathedral in his boyhood days when he still believed in God. That silence, in fact, had meant to the boy that he was indeed in the presence of God. He had laughed at himself since for such mawkish credulity, but he did not laugh now. These Arabs took God seriously. They had stopped fighting because it was time to pray. . . . They had exposed themselves to possible massacre to prostrate themselves before their god, refused to neglect prayer even in the face of the enemy.[72]

Under the orders of the French Army, the troops were waging war, not jihad. Undertaking their religious obligation in the midst of battle reminded them that their Muslim standing did not make their war a jihad. Waging war for the French meant a risk of life and limb but not of faith and spirit. The exigencies of the battlefield do not dispense with the duty to prostrate before God, though that is still short of jihad. Warfare might be undertaken on grounds other than jihad, but it cannot extinguish the flame fed by daily devotion. That habit of daily devotion seemed not to be interrupted on the battlefield nor to have turned into a jihad. Witnessing this example of religious commitment clearly had a dramatic personal effect on Charles de Foucauld.

In Senegambia we saw that the militants caused serious disruption of clerical life and routine but without religious decline. The attempt of the warlords like Fode Kaba and Maba to exploit unrest in pursuit of a political agenda ultimately failed. The leaders of the campaigns only rarely used the term "jihad," and even then the Muslim community failed to give them undivided support, with only sections of the community supporting the outbreaks in scattered fashion. The collective repudiation by the clerics undercut any pretense by combatants that religion was at stake and that believers would achieve spiritual gains by waging war.

When a jihadist rose from the ranks of the clerics, there was swift condemnation and a decision to cut off all relations—action in line with clerical teaching and carrying immediate force because of family ties. The jihad of Momodou-Lamin illustrates this: colonial officers confirmed that he stood alone against the interdiction of the Jakhanke people, despite family ties. With both Momodou-Lamin and Fode Kaba, pacifist teaching withstood a divisive episode within the ranks.

In an effort to bring moral reconciliation to the community, al-Hajj Banfa Jabi prepared to construct a memorial to Momodou-Lamin as his way of retrieving his memory from obloquy. The process was underway when Al-Hajj Banfa Jabi died in 1974. He was not unremorseful about the war within the gates but felt that the position of the clerics as defenders of the unfettered conscience needed to be restated once more. He played a similarly conciliatory role when he officiated at the funeral of Alfa Yahya, whose controversial political activities adversely affected the clerics but did not alienate them. Once more, Islam provided an answer to a problem of ethnic difference while promoting an inclusive view of the *ummah*. Difference was subsumed in religion, and religion was relieved of political entitlement. By honoring the principle of a free conscience in matters of faith, difference can even be advantageous in religion, as Jefferson observed.[73]

13

Beyond Politics

Comparative Perspectives

Cedant arma togae, concedant laurea laudi.
"Let war yield to peace, laurels to paeans."

—Cicero

Religion and Politics: Rules of Engagement

It is time now to examine aspects of pacifist teaching in light of the comparative Western experience. Jihad and colonial rule impinged directly on the pacifist tradition, challenging the age-old principle of abstention from war and politics. Colonial rule, both French and British, also challenged the religious rationale of clerical independence by requiring the clerics to submit to administrative directives. The clerics were regarded often with a mix of suspicion and fear by the authorities, in large measure because the clerics had followers across ethnic lines and had effectively reached pagan populations long resistant to Islam. Colonial authorities feared, quite irrationally, that the clerics dreamed of establishing a caliphate. The classical caliphate had long since been moribund. The golden age of the orthodox caliphate of the first four successors of Muhammad was, except for one of them, for the most part besmeared in blood and sectarian splits. It doomed attempts at trying to retrieve that golden age as a legacy of the worldwide *ummah*. Its sequel in the Ottoman Empire endured for centuries but without universal Muslim support, as Lawrence of Arabia was able to demonstrate. Islam's subsequent transnational expansion owed little to the caliphate as centralized power, and, as sovereign entities, the successor nation states of the nineteenth century were too fragmented to achieve Pan-Islamic cohesion. Under colonial rule jihad lost its rationale, its roots in Muslim tradition eroded by colonial modernization and, later, by the emergence of national jurisdictions that replaced the religious jurisdiction.

The intervening Western multilateral international system gave national jurisdiction universal legal legitimacy.

To establish power in Muslim society, colonial leaders looked outside of Islam for ideas: the French to their Revolution, with its anticlerical ethos, and the British to a combination of English common law tradition and pragmatism. Jean-Louis Triaud, a French scholar of Islam in Africa, noted that "the hostility to Islam in France also has roots . . . in the direct heritage of the French Revolution and [of] the republic."[1] One historical assessment argues that the "French Revolution aimed more at 'the regeneration of the human race' than [at] 'the freedom of France.'"[2] The French Revolution became an alternative religion.

With their twin aims of direct rule and assimilation, the French showed ambivalence in their Islamic policy. "Two parallel strands run through it, one pro-Muslim and the other, not so much pro-animist, as an attempt to hold the balance."[3] Pacifist clerics could reconcile themselves to the introduction of secular power as a matter of necessity, but they could also view its policy of tolerance of religion as a concession to conscience. Secular power was acceptable to the clerics if it involved no concerted attempt to repeal and replace the religious order and if separation of religious and political offices offered a place for religious conscience as sanctuary. Separation meant religion was neither prescribed nor proscribed; its free exercise was protected and supported. Mecca and Medina, Islam's territorial nerve centers, did not face a colonial takeover and remained free of the stigma of non-Muslim domination, indicating that administrators did acknowledge the autonomy of religion, whatever political twist they and others might give to it. Colonial provision for the pilgrimage gave the holy cities the seal of official recognition: "And in the [Muslim] cultural imagination, Mecca was far more important than Paris."[4]

The Civil Approach

The pattern of the development of clerical communities independent of political power goes back to the beginnings of the Islamization process. By the time of Ibn Battuta, and subsequently of Ahmad Baba and Richard Jobson, the clerical network had expanded and grown. The creation of the Bundu state in the seventeenth century and the dispersions that followed took over the Islamic impetus from the Mali Empire and opened new corridors of clerical penetration. The momentum carried the clerics into Futa Jallon, recently the center of the inconclusive jihad of Kamarokho Alfa. Under Kamarokho Alfa, Fula ethnic identity was split between the religious and the secular, resulting in a political stalemate, which, hampered by multiethnic differences, helped to immobilize Islam. The clerical penetration moved the religious vocation to new ground where the clerics presided over religious affairs without the burden of political ties. Political and ethnic representatives acknowledged the authority of the clerics and the wide influence they exercised, which strengthened the authority of the clerics. The clerics tried with mixed results to use that advantage to negotiate a truce with the advancing French, who were poised to take control of Futa Jallon. Despite the eventual breakdown in relations with the French, the clerics had by that stage refined and tempered the rationale for pacifist teaching, as Gouldsbury noted, and on that basis maintained their schools and farms.

The colonial disruption that followed coincided with a rash of military outbreaks seeking to fill the power vacuum left by the demise of the old Pagan order. It had been difficult to reconstitute a coherent jihad platform from the miscellany of local grievances and the surviving tensions of earlier inconclusive jihads. It was time to recognize that the last hope for saving anything of the area's political heritage long beset and enfeebled by corruption and incompetence lay with incoming influences. Muslim leaders decided to use colonial intervention to their advantage. They faced the necessity of an overhaul of the doctrinal case for jihad with sanguinity. Whatever the justifications sought for it in previous generations, jihad had become an unserviceable idea under modern conditions, no longer compatible with the norms of common citizenship as some leaders acknowledged. In the constitutional debates in 1947 before the establishment of Pakistan, Muhammad 'Ali Jinnah, a leader in the Constituent Assembly, backed the idea of a secular, nonreligious basis for the new nation. "You may belong to any religion or creed or caste—that has nothing to do with the business of the state. . . . You will find that in the course of time Hindus [will] cease to be Hindus and Muslims cease to be Muslims, not in the religious sense because that is the personal faith of each individual, but in a political sense as citizens of the state."[5]

Many Muslim leaders recognized the importance of engaging the moral arguments of such authorities as al-Ghazali and al-Suyuti that political leaders were not qualified to assume control of Islam's religious heritage and that the future of that heritage rested with leaders in civil society. Important Muslim African voices joined in this support for civil leadership. This line of thinking, if not precisely pacifist, was in keeping with increasing Islamic religious thought about the anachronism of jihad in the modern age. Religious autonomy and social pluralism would prosper by repudiating jihad, and those who pursued jihad despite evidence of dwindling support for it in the *ummah* acquired a reputation for fanaticism.

This development is not the sacrilegious betrayal radicals make it out to be. Tolerance and pluralism are not extrinsic to Islam's religious culture. At a minimum, Muslims recognized that the duties and obligations of religion were by no means perfectly and exactly reflected in observance and conduct. Few Muslims would claim that obligations and observance coincide always or with predictable regularity. That was the argument of Muhammad al-Kánimí, namely, that no Muslim could claim an unblemished record and that no age is "more virtuous or stronger or more learned than the first Muslims," who were not impeccable. No Muslim age or country, al-Kánimí challenged, is free of its share of sin and heresy.[6] The aberrations of practice and conduct that mark the lives of many Muslims do not render null and void the teachings of the religion. Turning a blind eye to the habitual failures and inadequacies of believers is the only way to redeem Islam from extremist blackmail. Islam allows Muslims to distinguish between good and bad or right and wrong without that fact requiring full and perfect compliance.

Islam has been widely accused of lacking tolerance, the stigma of jihad its religious birthmark. It is a short step from there to claim that tolerance and pluralism are alien to Islam, that democratic politics is necessary for remedy, and that religious euthanasia is needed for a successful democratic society. This book suggests that Islam is already well endowed with the capacity for both tolerance and democratic pluralism.

Conscience and Society

Michael Cook has argued with reason that exhorting what is good and discouraging what is wrong is described in Islam to a greater extent perhaps than anywhere else.[7] Promoting the good is part of general welfare as defined under Islamic law, in the concept of *maṣlahah mursala*: God's justice is in harmony with human well-being.[8] Duties based on the injunction are ultimately duties owed to God and thus a matter of conscience and the common good. Jurists recognize that the moral conscience has an affinity with revealed law, because the law does not command what is inhuman or morally repugnant. One jurist states *qiyás* (analogy, precedent) does not apply to natural functions, including gestation and accouchement. It is therefore reasonable for Muslims to accept Islamic religious teaching and the affairs of the world as not separate, even if they are not identical. Abú Hanífa's pithy definition of *fiqh* as "the self's knowledge of what is to its advantage and disadvantage" appeals to personal moral responsibility. Abú Hanífa gave great scope to *istihsán* (regarding as better), which gave discretion to qualified individual reason.[9]

The finer elements of social and cultural practices, such as modesty, truthfulness, cleanliness, hospitality, and respect, that permeate society have been assumed into Sharí'ah to revitalize the *ummah*. Such cultural adaptation falls under the rubric of *'ádát*, customs, or *'urf* (what is commonly known and accepted), not *'ibádát*, which are duties owed only to God.[10] A social good, such as the peaceful propagation of the faith, can be promoted under *'adát* as something good and desirable, endorsed by the religious code as commendable. In the clerical settlements, the understanding of religion as a matter of the free conscience was observed in an arrangement in which, once a year, the ruler entered the religious center as a pilgrim-guest to observe the rituals that occurred under pastoral supervision. In this arrangement the ruler yielded right-of-way to pastoral authority and to religion's moral primacy; however, political leadership shares with religious leadership mutual responsibility for promoting the good and restraining evil.

Public order exists to benefit and protect the common interest. It falls under God's jurisdiction, because God rules over the common interest. The Caliph 'Alí is cited to the effect that "All private matters belong to the human sphere, all concerns of society to the divine."[11] In this view, the sphere of the common good is a religious sphere and excludes all private interest. Anything owned by God belongs to one and all and must be administered by public authorities on God's behalf; it cannot be taken for individual possession. Al-'Āmirí (d. 992) stressed that religion is established only for collective welfare, never for private benefit or individual advantage.[12] In the words of Ibn Taymiyya, "Wherever there is a general need, there the obligation is to God."[13] "In short, it was by recourse to God that one created a public sphere."[14] Ahmad ibn Muhammad ibn Miskawayh (d. 1030), a Muslim philosopher of the Neoplatonic school, argues that human beings must live together in society in order to aid one another in the attainment of happiness and fulfillment of the end for which they were created. Every good and every happiness, he says, can be derived only from association. Each individual in the society helps the others as members of the body help one another. True morality, he claims, is a social virtue and is not to be attained by the solitary and the recluse.[15] The common good is a public norm and safeguard of collective security; the *mu'min* (believer) gives the common good its social character and human face.

Ibn Khaldun turned to religion to examine the nature of authority. He cited Qur'anic teaching to the effect that human purpose is not only worldly welfare; it is also religion. Therefore, the religious life is regarded as superior, not just incidental, to the functions of government: "The leadership of the prayer (*imámat al-ṣalát*) is the highest of all these functions, and higher than [kingship] (*al-mulk*)."[16] Ibn Khaldun's argument that the *imám* holds a position of the highest moral leadership does not conflict with the clerics' understanding of religion as a matter of pastoral jurisdiction, just as going to war is one of temporal jurisdiction under the ruler's authority. The principal of sanctuary that rulers observed for the clerical centers was adequate acknowledgment of the moral claim of religion. To defend that claim, the clerics relocated when sanctuary was denied them. Pacifist moral teaching prescribes moral restraint of political power. Without theocratic claims, religion in the public order should be important also for moderation in politics, which is implied in several statements referred to already, such as Suyan al-Thawri's opinion that uncritical mixing of religion and politics strips religion of its moral authority and politics of ethical safeguards. He stated: "The best of rulers is he who keeps company with men of learning ['ulama], and the worst of learned men is he who seeks the society of the king."[17] Suyan al-Thawri thus places religion in an autonomous moral sphere. God's rule of mercy over all life is valid without state or despite control (Qur'an 17:155).

Tolerance has value for religion as well as for politics. The clerics' abstention from politics is not a sectarian move to stigmatize rulers and public officials as unworthy of religious acknowledgment. Abstention is an attempt to distinguish between the spiritual and the temporal. The clerics hoped to avert both the politicization of religion and the sacralization of politics. Al-Maghílí observed that religion is not merely a contrived appurtenance on someone else's property. For the clerics, religion is an appeal neither to radical politics nor to rejection of society, in contrast to much of the history of pacifism in the West (examined in the next section). The celestial stairway (*kawkab waqqad*) that the clerics are encouraged to scale is designed to bring them closer to truth, rather than to power.[18] The clerics did not set out to reject society or to impugn the motives of other Muslims; they acknowledged with other Muslims a shared tradition.

Pacifism, East and West

For clarity's sake, it is necessary to pause to explain the nature of Jakhanke pacifism relative to the much better-established and better-known tradition of modern Western pacifism. The parallel is not exact. Pacifism has been a complex phenomenon in the West where pacifist groups fractured and multiplied, with the puritan clerical wing developing a sophisticated intellectual code for learning and society and a free-church wing that defied its roots in political secession to foster projects and programs of lasting benefit to society. In areas of conflict, these breakaway groups promoted with valiant resolve the cause of peace and reconciliation, often at much personal cost. Their work in antislavery, education, and humanitarian relief had a positive effect on marginal, hard-pressed populations around the world. The call in 1688 for abolition, issued by Francis Daniel Pastorius of Germantown with the support of three Mennonites, was the first such in America. Similarly, the pacifist ethics of hard work, discipline, honesty, and personal industry transformed many a wilderness into productive farmland and overcame dislocation and loss of homeland to produce shining examples of flourishing, peaceful communities. These achievements of recovery and regeneration belong proudly to the legacy of the West.

Pacifism also splintered church and society in the West and spawned a legacy of antinomian polemics against establishment structures and institutions. Pacifists repudiated church teaching and wrapped themselves in separatist colors, nursing their grievances in acts of defiance and isolation.[19] Anabaptist leaders Hans Denck and Ludwig Hätzer felt driven to deny the divinity of Christ, regarding him only as the most godly of men, who redeemed the human race not by his crucifixion but by his exemplary life. Called "the pope of the Anabaptists,"[20] Denck exalted the individual conscience above church, state, and Bible.[21] Pacifist groups broke up, their passion fueled by persecution. They rejected creeds and sacraments along with the institutional expressions of religion. Regarding Jesus as an ideal ethical model who is untrameled by creed and sacrament, pacifists shunned apostolic authority.[22] The founder of the Quakers, George Fox, embraced the pacifist ideal but only after he had defended military means: "To them that do well, the sword is a praise," he affirmed. As one scholar notes, "Most Quakers in the 1650s were not pacifists: Fox urged Cromwell to lead his armies to sack Rome."[23] This produced deep tension in the pacifist heritage. To deal with this tension and with the forces fueling it, pacifism turned narrow and unsparing. Pacifists rejected the sword and with it the idea of society providing means of defense for common security. The strife and division caused in the process left pacifist groups in a state of prickly agitation vis-à-vis establishment structures.

Focused on individual conscience of personal goodness, Philadelphia Quakers were in the forefront of the cause of social reform, as the example of John Woolman, the prominent Quaker antislavery activist, shows.[24] But Quakers did not excel at providing leadership for public life. Benjamin Franklin noted the ill fit between pacifist doctrine and practical politics, writing in 1730 that, in the Assembly in Philadelphia, he noted the awkwardness of the Quakers' position. Franklin wrote that he had many opportunities of "seeing the embarrassment given them by their principles against war."[25] They were unwilling to offend the government by refusing funds but also unwilling to offend fellow Quakers with compliance that violated pacifist ideals. They resorted to "using a variety of evasions to avoid complying, and modes of disguising the compliance when it became unavoidable."[26]

The pacifist rejection of the social order for its use of force resulted in the sequestration of their religion behind Roger Williams's "wall of separation," an enclave shut off from society as the sphere of the common good. [27] William

Penn's endorsement of government as an instrument to regulate morals, coupled with his repudiation of government as unfit "for distributing justice," left the door wide open for endless religious caviling and little consideration of society as a shared responsibility.

Penn was alert to this, and he eventually retreated from George Fox's idea of "keeping your own plantations in your hearts." "Government," Penn wrote, "seems to me a part of religion itself, a thing sacred in its institutions and purpose."[28] Capitulating to politics, Penn gave government the warrant he denied religion. In the end, the contradiction proved too much of a strain, and Quakerism broke up into factions. Penn's descendants, as the proprietors, defected to the Church of England, and the others found allies among the Scotch Presbyterians of western Pennsylvania. The split ended Quaker dominance in politics, though Quakerism survived to promote religious pluralism, as embodied in the 1740 founding of the University of Pennsylvania, America's first nonsectarian college. In time, "nonsectarian" came to mean protection not only for people of all beliefs but also for those who had no beliefs.[29]

Penn's pacifist position is instructive for study of the social effects of antinomian doctrine. He had conceived the colony he founded in 1682 on the west bank of the Delaware River as a "Holy Experiment." It would be free of Old World encumbrances, so that moral progress would occur by spiritual enlightenment and voluntary acceptance of salvation, not by moral regulation or ecclesiastical stipulation. In isolation, religious liberty combined with the sovereignty of the self to claim virtue as an individual attribute, rejecting religion as its social frame.[30] Penn seemed unable to conceive a public role for religion except when it was in contention with politics and the state. Here the pacifist and the puritan heritages diverged sharply or, rather, met as offsetting extremes.

Abraham Lincoln described how the logic of Quaker opposition to oppression of slaves left them with a hard choice when faced with the option of war to end oppression. In a letter to Eliza P. Gurney, a Quaker friend, Lincoln pointed to the thorny moral dilemma created for Quakers. "Your people—the Friends—have had, and are having, a very great trial. On principle, and faith, opposed to both war and oppression, they can only practically oppose oppression by war. In this hard dilemma, some have chosen one horn and some the other."[31]

Pacifists and puritans alike appealed to God's justice as something within reach of human reason without the mediation of inherited authority or institutions. For pacifists, this reason allowed the individual to be sovereign judge of himself or herself, while for Puritans reason was assumed to be commensurate and in harmony with the needs of society, making reason experimental in the sense of relying on changing needs and challenges for what was considered reasonable. The Puritan appeal to individual conscience, to personal experience, was, in effect, an appeal to changing social norms and values that reflected the interests and preferences of persons and society. As those interests and preferences changed, so must the reason for their necessity. The good of society did not exist in an ideal, pure form. What was good or bad could be determined within the scope of human reason and interest. On that ground, reason, like religion, is pragmatic. Society designed religion to meet its needs and promote its preferences, and those needs and preferences in turn framed the workings of individual conscience. Milton spoke for Puritans when he insisted that no religious teaching or requirement could justify anyone being cut off from the duties of human society.[32] John Winthrop was equally direct about the necessity of society, saying "mere Civil policy doth bind us; for it is a true rule that particular estates cannot subsist in the ruin of the public."[33] In this context "estates" are classes of people that form part of society. The pacifist, in contrast, chafes at assuming the duties of human society because serving society tarnishes the anointed self.

Lord Acton was critical of radicalism, whether religious or political, because of its potential for social disruption. Society, he said, exists for the protection of interests, while the state exists for the realization of rights. The state opposes the conversion of the social into the moral community, Acton argued, and social equality begot despotism, not democracy. The equality Acton had in mind restricted the role of religion in social change, with the suggestion that the freedom religion promotes is inimical to constituted power as an inherited office. Popular democracy, Acton claimed, is tainted with the same demagogic poison as individualist notions of religion.[34] Proof of such demagoguery may be seen in the garrulous authoritarian style of nonconformist preachers, of whom Hobbes wished a suitable example had been made.[35] Like Penn, Acton left unresolved the tension between religion or, for that matter, between individual freedom and democratic politics: How do we balance the sovereignty of the individual conscience—and consent—against the collective mandate of the majority? Is law greater than grace? Acton believed that there is a defined place in society for religion under license. Religion should be incorporated as a subject for private devotion, because without legal safeguard, religion is public nuisance and individual conscience insubordination. Acton was inclined to the view that government and society should place religion behind politics, where it can be patronized while being held in check. Religion should be regulated as a controlled substance.

William Barclay (d. 1978), a popular British Biblical theologian committed to making "the best biblical scholarship available to the general reader," took religion beyond politics, seeing it as a public gadfly. Speaking for his fellow pacifists, Barclay required unilateral disarmament and the renunciation of war as demonstration of religious activism, with the corollary that the mere existence of means of waging war—even for defense and deterrence—is reason to combat religion for being complicit in "war as mass murder." This view, as Acton feared, recast religion entirely as a single-minded, antistate and antiwar crusade.[36] That was how Bertrand Russell (d. 1970), a great "karamokho" in his own right, became a peace activist. Arnold Toynbee paid him lavish tribute as a leader in the campaign "for the survival of civilization and of the human race." Reviewing Russell's *Why I Am Not a Christian*, however, Russell's friend T. S. Eliot noted that Russell's support of freedom and other ethical causes was based on the same unreasoning prejudice as his aversion to tyranny and cruelty. Russell's pacifism had a strong anti-American twist to it, claiming in one place that the United States was responsible "whenever people are tortured and the masses left to rot under the weight of disease and starvation."[37] According to Russell, the history of democratic freedom would have to be written from a very different script. Russell was not merely the Good Samaritan; he regretted that the bleeding victim on the roadside was not better armed.

If diverging on the basis of opposing attitudes to society, the pacifist/Puritan positions on the sovereignty of conscience came together in promoting a culture of rational faith and lay activism. That culture penetrated the entire religious outlook of America, with worldwide consequence. Its characteristic political expression is self-reliance without the corrupting effects of public welfare, because being independent is the fuel of useful enterprise and a responsible life. It polarized society between makers and takers, with echoes of the moral distinction between hallowed and unhallowed lives.

In one respect, it would be logical to look upon the karamokho as embodiment of the Puritan maxim of being "blind in no one's cause, but best sighted in his own. He confines himself to the circle of his own affairs and thrusts not his fingers in endless fires."[38] Yet not all are hunters who blow the horn. Unlike the Puritan and the pacifist, the karamokho shares little of the radical political strains of religious thought, including the extreme idea that self-fulfillment can dispense with God's law and the faith community. For the Jakhanke clerics, ultimate merit is to be found in the sources of divine teaching, not in public reason. Truth does not lie in the eye of the beholder; it is not a question merely of perception.

The corpus of Islamic ethics is revealed ethics, with a conservative pull and a progressive inclination. The canon as revealed injunction could not be undone. But, on the other hand, interpretation and understanding must change and have changed with time and circumstances. It is on the fine balance between tradition and change that moderation depends, whence the *ummatan wasatan*. Although clerical work may seek and obtain economic rewards, it embraces society on religious terms and recognizes the sword and the ledger without making them a requirement of faith. Pacifist teaching was and remains an integral part of the *ummah*, upholding standards of ethics and conduct consistent with Islam's moral and ethical heritage. In contrast to the sovereign self of radical religious thought in the West, clerical moderation was a caution and a safeguard within the *ummah*, not outside or against it.

Religion: Origin and Civil Function

In the era of absolute monarchies in Europe and elsewhere, when religion and power were considered inseparable, the formula of religion as politics and politics as religion was fairly deadly. Neutralizing that combustible admixture as a general principle opened the way for the emergence of the modern world, though modern ideological fundamentalism means that the trouble is far from over. By repudiating jihad as a requirement of religion, Jakhanke pacifism frees Islam's ethical teaching from political directives. The Prophet of Islam, the clerics insist, never made war and partisanship a measure of religion; Muslims never had to be warriors to qualify as Muslims. In support of this view, the authors of the manual of Maliki law intended for use in West Africa as well as in Egypt affirmed: "If there is one quality distinguishing above all others the legislative work of the Prophet of Islam it is the quality of moderation. 'Truth lies in the middle (*khayr al-umúr awṣatiha*)."[39] Muslims are assured: "Thus have We made you a middle community" of moderation (*kadhálika ja'alnákum ummatan wasatan*) (Qu'ran 2:137). Believers are summoned to proclaim the faith "with wisdom and fair exhortation and to reason . . . in the better way" (16:126) and to be "securers of justice, witnesses for God. Let not detestation for a people move you not to be equitable" (2:11).

Muhammad is enjoined even in disagreements to give the assurance that "between us and you let there be no strife: God shall make us all one" (Qu'ran 42:14). God's witness is not to compel but to commend the message, and if people "turn their backs, thine it is only to deliver the Message" (3:19; also 22:66–67). In what amounts to granting asylum even to opponents, Muhammad is directed to extend to idolaters safe passage: "And if any of the idolaters seeks of thee protection, grant him protection till he hears the words of God; then do thou convey him to his place of security" (9:6). The peaceful way is upheld not because violence and coercion are impractical or untimely but because the peaceful way is the right way. "And bear thou patiently what they say, and forsake them graciously" (73:10). "Yet is there any other duty of the Messengers than to deliver the manifest Message?" (16:37). Even treachery deserves to be met with pardon and leniency because "God loves those who act generously" (5:16). In the pre-Islamic code, the ancient Arabs valued *muruwwa* (manliness) as brooking no compromise with leniency or forgiveness, both regarded as cowardly and ignominious.[40] Reuben Levy points out that in this regard Muhammad brought some of Islam's "most significant reforms." For Muhammad, "true nobility lay in forgiveness, that in Islam those who restrain their anger and pardon men shall receive Paradise as well-doers."[41] Islam was a revolution in the moral life of the Arabs; the legacy persisted into West African Islam as *sabr* (forbearance, restraint) and *yanfa* (letting go, forgiveness).

The observation of a seasoned French administrator with respect to Mauritania is evidence of the enduring pacifist influence there. He testified:

> A warrior is neither a trader nor a manufacturer, he can neither read nor write. He is the master of the gun, the representative of force. . . . The clergy is represented by veritable tribes of learned men . . . they never take part in war but rather dispense justice and are mediators of peace. Their rosary replaces the gun.[42]

For the clerics, as for other Muslims, the *shahádah* (creed) bears witness to the fact no instruments are prescribed or implied for the duty of testimony and submission only to the one God and to the Prophet as bearer of that message. The peaceful path is consonant with the spirit and letter of the religion, not warfare that risks compromise of *imán* (faith), when faith is understood as more than *islám* (in the lower case) and where *aslama* (surrender) is behavior motivated by gain (Qur'an 49:14).[43] The fact is, "Your Lord knows very well what is in your hearts" (17:26). Classical Muslim jurists, including Sufyán al-Thawrí (d. 778 AD) of Basra and al-Suyútí of Cairo, concur with this understanding of the discriminating relation between religion and politics rather than with their simplistic ideological conflation. Jakhanke teaching adopts the religious path without slipping into a political trap. The issue is not how politics (or war) may use religion for its own limited purposes but how religion is needed as a safeguard to constrain politics.[44]

Historian Jamil Abun Nasr suggests that where the influence of Islamic law on ownership and disposal of property is strong, the prospects of government intervention in the economy are correspondingly diminished. His examples include Nigeria, Morocco, and, after a brief spell, Egypt, among others. This correlation explains why in pastoralist societies such as Somalia, which is less influenced by Islamic law, the Marxist code found ready soil. Abun Nasr points out that attempts to establish socialist governments in Africa have had to adjust by directing their appeal to African culture, not to Islam.[45] (The appeal to African culture, not to Islam, appears to underlie the *Ujamaa* socialist program outlined in Tanzania's President Julius Nyerere's Arusha Declaration of 1967.) Thus, as a sphere of activity separate from the state, Islamic teaching contests the right of the state to religious anointing. In addition, religion is not just a staircase for gaining unimpeded power, to amend al-Maghiílí, the fifteenth-century godfather of the African reform tradition.[46] As Humphrey Fisher observed with respect to slaves and Muslim society, "we need to include, alongside secular and environmental elements, also religious standards, and the resonance which these call forth (or do not call forth, as the case may be) in the hearts and minds of local men and women."[47]

Religion and Tolerance

A retrospective view on Jakhanke Islam should clarify a general point about what can be called "the challenge of religion," which is the extent to which religious commitment is or is not compatible with tolerance. Jihad rejects any compatibility whatsoever, while clerical pacifism stakes its reputation and viability on it. For the clerics, tolerance is intrinsic to religion. On that basis, they set out to promote Islam by teaching, scholarship, devotion, and public witness. Splitting tolerance from religion is not far out of keeping with jihad. Jihad also cuts tolerance from religion, because tolerance allegedly weakens commitment. Jihad shares the secular view that tolerance is not compatible with religion. When tolerance excludes religion, it leaves only two contestants holding the field: the champions of tolerance who oppose religion and the jihadists who are at war with tolerance. The alternative clerical way offers another option. Jakhanke teaching views tolerance as vital for religion.

The clerics exhibit eminent good sense in teaching tolerance as a facet of commitment to religion. In so doing, they affirm a critical role for religion in society.[48] Coercion has no more a legitimate part in religion than in toleration. In the way the clerics have pursued their vocation, religion serves as a frame and guide of human behavior and conduct. The clerics are aware that up to a point law can compel compliance, but they know also that law cannot reconcile hearts or wash away grudges. Goodness to one another is not effected by the power of the law, and force cannot make us good. Yet society cannot flourish or long endure without goodness, making the moral endeavor important for individual and collective *faláh* (flourishing).[49]

Spiritual Versus Temporal Commitment

Important as the pacifist clerical tradition is for Muslim society in Africa, it does not amount to the legal instruments required for structural separation of church and state. Muslims of earlier times

> never acquired the sense of living in two distinct organizations, devoted to different aims, governed by different norms, and headed by different people, the king and his agents in the one case, the caliph (if any) and religious scholars in the other. In other words, one cannot speak of a separation of church and state such as that which developed in Europe from the great ecclesiastical reforms of the eleventh century onwards. Still less were the two domains separated to the point where religion was privatized and the sociopolitical order secularized, as was to happen in Europe in modern times.[50]

Times have changed, however, as have Muslim societies. The secular nation-state has taken hold in Africa as it has in most of the Muslim world, and with it a degree of necessary separation and privatization of religion. Such changes, even if ultimately irreversible, have left society with a distinct religious character. The Muslim canon is still recognizably itself and not something else. In various Africa societies, we have seen how rulers pursued a two-religion approach to foster a pluralist and diverse society. It was out of this pluralism, beginning in the Mali Empire, that the Suwarian tradition emerged to promote professional clericalism, building on the principle of separate spheres of responsibility.

Pacifist clerical teaching presents a genuine advance in local religious thought, showing how practicable it is to distinguish between the obligations (*'ibádát*) believers owe to their God and the fealty they owe to the ruler. The examples of the African kingdoms of Ghana, Mali, and Songhay demonstrate that it was kings and rulers who founded states—not the prophets, as early Muslim thinkers argued. These thinkers took as their premise Muhammad's founding of the first Islamic state in Medina, giving rise to the widely accepted (though also widely contested) view that the creation of political institutions resulted from the enthusiasm of a prophet or saint.[51] Ibn Khaldun pointed out in the fourteenth century, to the inexplicable consternation of many of the scholars, that prophets are not necessary to the founding of states. Abú Hátim al-Rází (d. 933), a famous Isma'ilí missionary who debated with the even more celebrated Abú Bakr al-Rází (d. 925), the physician and philosopher known to medieval Europe as "Rhazes," contended that all "the kingdoms of the world were governed in accordance with religion-based rules set by the prophets." The coming of the Qur'an, he declared, enabled this religion-based principle to "spread throughout the earth."[52] In Africa as well as elsewhere, however, it is easily demonstrated that states existed without the intervention or need of prophets. The clerics were all too aware of that.

With this inherited tradition, the clerics could develop the idea that religion is not a political construct or the state a religious construct. The clerics pressed the ethical argument that commitment to religion need not replace commitment to tolerance of others. Indeed, clerical practice abjured confrontation while pursuing the missionary mandate. Rather than putting the clerics at cross-purposes with the guardians of local shrines, the clerical mission was welcomed as added protection. Once established in the community, clerics could show if and how their religion would be more effective in addressing pre-Islamic needs and concerns. In the process, Islam penetrated society without conquest.

It is important to appreciate the power of organized religious activity for the advantage it gave clerics in supporting the pacifist case for separation from politics. There were no political strings attached to the call to conversion and little prospect of political dividends following it. In time, Islam's ethical teachings would offer a measure of personal fulfillment and the prestige and assets of a world religion. Fledgling Muslim communities that coexisted amicably with their non-Muslim neighbors before eventually winning them over are more representative of the pattern of the spread of Islam than jihad. Minority Muslims served as nonthreatening links with non-Muslim populations, becoming precursors of wider religious changes.

Today, the clerics cannot ignore that political participation has become a universal fact of life. Islam's religious heritage as expressed in the vocation of the clerics constitutes a legitimate sphere of modern society. This heritage belongs in civil society, not in the state. No one is exempt or barred from adherence to Islam on the basis of tribe, race, rank, influence, or wealth. Religious independence is a safeguard of moral integrity; it is also a check on power. Bernard Lewis writes, "Muslim law has never conceded absolute power to the sovereign, nor, with few exceptions, have Muslim sovereigns been able to exercise such power for any length of time . . . the authority of the ruler, though paramount, is subject to a very important limitation." In Islamic law, the state does not create the law; it is only entrusted with it. Religious independence is thus a check on absolute power, which rules out the idea of a theocracy, Lewis argues.[53] Recent manifestations of religious radicalism promoting theocracy as a response to the modern world have little precedent in the Muslim canon. Both are equally un-Islamic. Clerical moderation holds more promise for a flourishing democratic society than a lopsided move to a religious or secular extreme.

In the context of Western advances in political freedom, the clerical heritage has a recognizable place. For a culture of mutual tolerance, checks and balances are necessary but in themselves not sufficient. A shared cultural conviction of mutual forbearance, based on allegiance to a common Creator, is needed to make the safeguards at all effective. This idea was echoed in the Virginia Declaration of Rights (XVI), published in June of 1776, a month before the Declaration of Independence. The view of Muslim authorities that the state can reliably use patriotic virtue but cannot as reliably inspire or cultivate it aligns with the theocentric position of allegiance to a common Creator that goes beyond the utilitarian idea of virtue as a civic pride. Hobbes's insistence that the state pursues "no religious goals" and that "religiously defined goods have no place in the catalogue of the ends it promotes" raises the question of who should foster ends such as loyalty, integrity, mutual charity, and civic righteousness. These do not lie in the power of the state to bring about, though they are essential for decent human life.[54]

Religious teaching addresses this question. Because these ends are moral in their nature and relate to the moral capacity to distinguish between right and wrong, they are integral to the collective interest of society. Religion would accomplish more for the general well-being of society, cultivating mutual charity and forbearance, than politics would with its expedient attitude to moral rules as instruments of government. The end and purpose of human personhood are not limited by our capacities for pain and pleasure or by the goals of aversion of pain and pursuit of pleasure. For the clerics, structures of peaceful propagation and the influence on society of moral values help foster a culture of toleration in line with the Creator's will and purpose. Despite historical differences, this voluntarist view of religion should help foster a climate of mutual trust and comprehension with the modern West.

With respect to state and society, the Qur'an provides a model only for society. This led an Indian Muslim scholar to argue that Muslims are free to engage in state-building.[55] Assuming that society generates the state necessary for it, rather than that the state precedes its society, Muslims are free to adopt the political structure that best reflects their values and needs. Religion impinges on practical affairs by virtue of the influence it exerts in society, and it serves as a safeguard against arbitrary power to the extent that it is able to defend its independent moral authority. Pacifist teaching grasps this without assuming that religion has to be either politically useful or individually advantageous to be valid. The real force of the pacifist insight is that politics does not qualify or determine religion; rather, religion constrains politics and is required for it.

The Moral Deficit of Secular Government

Reflecting on the writers whose classic philosophy led to America's experiment in democratic freedom, Jefferson asserted that they fell short: they succeeded in reaching "tranquility of mind," but only by precepts

> related chiefly to ourselves . . . in developing our duties to others, they were short and defective. They embraced, indeed, the circles

> of kindred and friends, and inculcated patriotism, or the love of our country in the aggregate, as a primary obligation: toward our neighbors and countrymen they taught justice, but scarcely viewed them as within the circle of benevolence. Still less have they inculcated peace, charity and love to our fellow men, or embraced with benevolence the whole family of mankind.[56]

This expanded circle of benevolence, rather than narrow national jurisdiction or cultural entitlement, is the moral extent of our duty toward one another as human beings, something that secular thought did not address.

Islamic thought addresses this moral deficit by beginning with the Ruler of the universe, law as the expression of the Creator's will for all human society, and *maṣlahah* as positive enjoinment. The earthly ruler is the Creator's instrument of law and reason, which makes him the caliph (*khalífah*) and the state the caliphate (*khiláfah*), necessary for our common security but not sufficient for our ethical perfection. Revealed law directs worldly affairs toward God's justice and human responsibility for mutual justice. In this principle of reciprocal rights and responsibilities, we "give what is due *from* you and ask God for what is due *to* you," as Ibn Taymiyya put it in his *al-Siyásah al-shar'iyáh* ("Divine Government").[57] The content of divine law is available to human reason but only when guided by revealed law. Prophecy and wisdom provide the channel, not the substitute or replacement, of that law.[58] Political repression is the consequence of usurping God's law; overweening power encroaches on God's power, evoking the perpetual war Hobbes thought establishing the state would prevent.

Centuries earlier, Ibn Khaldun anticipated Hobbes by saying that human society has "need of a restraining force to keep men off each other in view of their animal propensities for aggressiveness and oppression of others." The remedy is a central political institution: the state.[59] Ibn Khaldun sought more than the Hobbesian notion of government, however; he saw a need for government under ethical constraint, necessary to prevent the idolatry of power. Its nineteenth-century proponents viewed secular dogma as a replacement for theology, which was regarded as indefinite, inadequate, and unreliable. In this view, secularism radiates the power of the "sacred in its influence on life," thanks to "the purity of material conditions," understood as conditions freed of religious influence, that can sustain the loftiest natures and elevate the lower parts of society, in the words of a leading authority.[60] But this secular formula as a reliable replacement for religion conflicts with all that pertains to the moral and spiritual in human nature. To force it is to trade in dogma. Political extremism merely repeats the problem of religious extremism at its end of the spectrum.

The principle of association as the ground of civil society not only lays the basis for rules and regulations, as Ibn Taymiyya argues, but also establishes norms of justice and mutual charity, as contended by the clerics. Echoing Ibn Taymiyya, Hobbes observed that compacts without the sword are but mere words. It may be added, however, that the sword may be necessary and adequate for administrative effectiveness and common security but not for virtue and civic philanthropy. Because of its origins in a monopoly of power backed by force, the Taymiyan power state (*qudrah*) as a state defined by power as necessary and sufficient without *maṣlahah*, not unlike the Hobbesian state, can be held to standards no higher than the simple calculation of its own brute power.[61] The state is a necessary firewall against anarchy—what Hobbes describes as perpetual war—making force and reprisal necessary for state authority. Without the state, societies of scale in terms of size and complexity are not viable, but it is equally true that without ethical values and the spirit of liberty, society is not worth abiding in. Al-Farábí (870–950), a scholar of Aristotle, used Islamic and Greek sources to frame a universal ethical view of society on the grounds that "there can be virtuous nations and cities of different religions, for all tend towards one same happiness and identical objects."[62]

Al-Farábí's view shifts the question from the specific social order to pure ideal forms. The idea of "one same happiness" conflicts with the reality of lived experience, where difference is not just an accident of space and time but an advantage one group might hold over another. The "same truth" can have varying interpretations by different groups.

Pacifist Islam: A Check on Political Power

Even with unrivaled authority as king of Mali, Mansa Músá did not attempt to immunize himself against the moral claims of religion. On the contrary, he sought learned religious counsel with the intention of applying that counsel to running the state. A ruler's behavior and conduct are not exempt from the jurisdiction of religion, he was told. That he sought this counsel indicates that Mansa Músá was willing to concede the truth of a higher authority. His plan to return to Mali to relinquish power to a successor before hastening back to Mecca to become "a dweller near the sanctuary" shows how he wished to yield the girdle of power for devotion to the rosary. Although Mansa Músá's example may be unusual, it is not out of keeping with the way the kings of Mali coveted spiritual *barakah* for which they looked to the clerical communities. It shows their acknowledgment that Islam has superior moral merit over power. It shows also how Islam as a religion may criticize rulers without the charge of sedition. In practice, however, a ruler without conscience would be hard to defy. But it is worth noting that Muslim rulers were not able to defy Islamic teaching without challenge from the scholars, however much the scholars might be bought.

The question of how the clerical scholars should relate to those in power presumes separate domains for religion and power. In 1400, as part of the sultan's delegation, Ibn Khaldun joined negotiations in Damascus with the Tartar conqueror, Tamerlane. He was offered a court position, which he declined. For his success in rescuing many of the city's important nobles before Tamerlane's sack of the city, Ibn Khaldun was appointed chief justice of Cairo. He died shortly thereafter in 1405 or 1406, at age seventy-four. Ibn Khaldun warned against mixing religion and worldly affairs lest we "patch our worldly affairs by tearing our religion to pieces. Thus, neither our religion lasts nor (the worldly affairs) we have been patching."[63]

A criticism often made with regard to rulers, and one that riles men prone to jihad, is that power tends to treat religion as a game. People in power acknowledge or ignore religion when it suits their purpose and otherwise toy with it for show—the criticism was made by Dan Fodio of Hausa Habe rulers. When not ornamental, religion is reduced to a plaything. Sunni 'Ali (r. 1464–1492), ruler of Songhay, adopted a Jekyll-and-Hyde attitude toward the hapless religious scholars of his state. He alternated between humiliating and torturing them to instill fear and plying them with gifts and favors to acknowledge their worth but also to subordinate them to his patronage.[64] It was the proverbial case of the stick for those who might harbor the thought of insubordination or treachery and the carrot for those who complied because they dreaded the threat of starvation. Sunni 'Alí declared, tongue in cheek, "Were it not for the scholars (*'ulamá*) life would not be pleasant or agreeable."[65] Sunni 'Alí's critics consider him a cruel tyrant who used religion in a cynical game of divide and rule. They believe that Sunni 'Alí's conduct warrants jihad as a remedy and as protection of the faith community. Yet many upright rulers have governed without Sunni 'Alí's cruel cynicism and have refused to wage jihad, or even to consider jihad as an option. For such rulers, commitment to Islam is not commitment to a winner-take-all strategy. Mansa Músá exemplifies this ethical understanding of religion and leadership.

That religion carried great weight with rulers is confirmed by the story of Askiya Muhammad, who became king of Songhay by wresting power from Sunni 'Alí. After overthrowing Sunni 'Alí in a military coup d'etat, Askiya Muhammad refrained from adopting jihad as state policy, preferring instead to observe the practice of religious pluralism and accommodation that had been the standard. Even in such an extreme time, religion exerted a moderating influence on affairs, with moderate clerical voices still audible in the upheaval.[66] During his pilgrimage in 1497, the askiya pled with the Sharif of

Mecca to appoint him *khalífah* (caliph) of Songhay, which would confer on the kingdom a much-coveted religious and diplomatic status. The Sharif said he would accede if the king would lay aside his crown for three days. The askiya agreed readily, and the investiture proceeded in the mosque before a large crowd. The askiya was adorned with the vestments of his new office as *khalífah*: a robe, cap, turban, and sword, and the title *amír al-mu'minín* (commander of the faithful).[67]

If the appointment went to Askiya Muhammad's head, it is not much evidenced in the policies he pursued on returning home. Only once, immediately after his return from Mecca in 1497–1498, did he wage jihad, against the neighboring Mossi and the Mesufa Berbers. He undertook no theocratic reform of government, imposed no Shari'ah law in the state, and required no religious test of his courtiers. On the contrary, he maintained and even enlarged the Songhay system of titles and offices inherited from Sunni 'Alí and dispensed justice according to traditional custom.[68]

A story that takes place after the askiya's return from Mecca describes an occasion in which he became frustrated by a *qádí*'s resistance to his orders. The *qádí* had sent royal message-bearers packing. The askiya traveled out to Timbuktu to confront the offending *qádí,* Mahmúd b. 'Umar, and demanded an explanation. The *qádí* reminded the askiya of his oath of obedience, when the king had declared, "I have come so that you may place yourself in safety between me and the fire of damnation. Help me and hold me by the hand lest I stumble into hell fire. I entrust myself in safe-keeping to you." Religion is to politics as the hedge is to the garden: religion forms a boundary around politics, sharing its earth without merging into it.

That this distinction occurred so early in Muslim practice shows the long history of the commitment of the clerics. Elias Saad's remarks on Timbuktu as a center of scholars may be applied to clerical centers like Touba: "The very existence of a large body of scholars . . . had its significance in the sphere of adaptation."[69] Gradualism helped to fold Islam into the habits and lifestyle of ordinary Muslims without respect to political or social status; it solidified the position of religious agents vis-à-vis rulers. The pattern reflects the civil nature of the crown–turban relationship with respect to the limits religion sets for political power and calls to mind St. Ambrose's telling defiance of Theodosius.[70]

When he accepted the offer of the position of chief justice of Cairo under the Mamluke sultan, Ibn Khaldun set out at once to reform the corrupt judicial system that clogged the courts. This earned him the enmity of officials who had the ear of the sultan, and they orchestrated his dismissal. The lesson was not lost on Ibn Khaldun, leading him to argue that the intellectual life in general was incompatible with politics, in this case because of the excessive tendency of intellectuals for abstraction and idealization that showed them to be isolated from ordinary life.[71]

This incompatibility is a running leitmotif in the sources. So is the principle that religion and politics are connected at the level of the common good and public interest, as Ibn Taymiyya maintains, without one being a replica of the other, as al-Ghazali insists.[72] As already noted, the religious canon does not concede absolute power to the ruler, though the code is not shut out from the affairs of society. Religion is beyond politics in the sense that its meaning and purpose derive from Scripture, which furnishes prescriptions and guidance for individuals and society. Political authority cannot rise above its assigned role of guardianship of the religious law, however interpreted, and may not repeal or replace it. The revealed law is supreme; the law of the sultan cannot overtake it. Instituting the worship (*iqámat al-salát*), observing Ramadan, purifying the household, honoring what is praiseworthy, abstaining from unlawful things, and accountability in the hereafter are the things that establish a pattern of social order. Ultimately they are matters of moral injunction, the sort left out of Hobbes's political repertoire. These things were part of clerical duties.

The Qur'an reminds the faithful that in the final reckoning "no soul for another shall give satisfaction, and no counterpoise shall be accepted from it, nor any intercession shall be profitable to it." (Qur'an ii:116, Arberry's translation.) Even with the safeguard of checks and balances, there is no political substitute for religion as moral frame of the social order. The Qur'anic materials we have considered stipulate moral accountability as ultimate personal responsibility without any hint of a corresponding political accountability. Human destiny is more than a matter of political calculation.

14

End of Jihad?

Tradition and Continuity

O, let me teach you how to knit again
This scattered corn into one mutual sheaf.

—Shakespeare

Taking Advantage of Colonial Rule

In the cases discussed in previous chapters, we have seen the complex responses of Muslim religious leaders to colonial penetration into their societies. Colonial rule introduced modern, global forces—political and economic—into the Muslim world. In the ensuing reconfiguration, religious leaders sought refuge in the privatization of religion, an analogue to the traditional *zawiya* system in which communities enjoy protection from being absorbed in the wider society. Meaning "assembly of group," the *zawiya* has served as an educational center, religious retreat, and residential enclave in towns. With a few significant exceptions, colonial bureaucracy left the domestic sphere of religious life alone, allowing religion to develop the character of a voluntary association. Under the sovereign nation-state and its international scope, lines of jurisdiction no longer coincided with the mandate of jihad as existed in the Sokoto caliphate and elsewhere, and militant Islam ceased to be a prerogative of government except as rebellion against legitimate authority. Colonial bureaucracy advanced the pacifist impulse by removing the theocratic option. Ironically, the secular nation-state helped to restore Islam's religious heritage of systematic jurisprudence and ethical thought.

From the beginning, the peaceful spread of Islam in West Africa has been more typical of the history of the religion than jihad. With conversion came the advantages of trade and cultural contact, and Islam gained momentum thereby. The jihad–pacifist polarity and secular–religious tension were mitigated by the spirit of social accommodation; religious specialists strengthened this accommodation with the supple use of Scripture and the canon, and of Shari'ah and *fiqh*. The legal rulings of al-Suyuti bolstered this accommodating understanding of religion, and Sufi influence provided additional spiritual support.

Colonial penetration had several other indirectly positive effects. It provided an impetus for the production of new scholarship and helped to suppress unrest and violence. In Morocco in 1910, the distinguished Maliki jurist al-Mahdi al-Wazzani undertook a comprehensive review of fatwas in eleven volumes "to reinforce the authority of Mālikī scholarship and to ensure the moral survival of the Muslim community" as it faced inevitable French colonial takeover. [1] The head of the Tijániyáh order, Abdullah Niasse of Kaolack, Senegal, commended the French for arriving just in time, because before "we lived in anarchy and were cutting each other's throats. We enslaved children and committed acts of brigandage on the roads."[2] There, too, colonial rule smothered outbreaks of violence and disorder and allowed the renewal of religion. In other parts of West Africa, Jakhanke communities saw much to be gained from cooperation with the French.[3]

The British made it a goal to play up the beneficial aspects of colonial rule to their Muslim subjects in Nigeria. In his autobiography, Alhaji Sir Ahmadu Bello, the Sardauna of Sokoto and a member of the Muslim establishment, described how in 1922 the colonial government created Katsina College, later called Barewa College. The college was created exclusively for the sons of the Muslim elite—for boys of "birth and standing," in official parlance—resulting in the exclusion of non-Muslims, including Christian children. Bello believed that this exclusion showed regrettable bias by the colonial administration. "There were no people from non-Muslim areas among us," Bello wrote, from his experience as a student of the college. "I see now that this was perhaps a fault."[4]

It cannot be denied, however, that the British were offering stability to religious institutions. Sir Hugh Clifford, governor-general at the time, saw the college as a means of launching Muslim values and institutions in a modern progressive nation. The college, he exhorted, should instill in the students the way good Muslims should live and carry out the observances of their religious duties. In a conversation at Cambridge University with the late E. P. T. Crampton, one of the last principals of the college before the British left Nigeria, Crampton confirmed the government's policy with regard to Muslims and agreed that it was done to promote Muslim interests. Mission schools tried to offer similar benefits to children of non-Muslim populations, becoming the last recourse for those children. Encountering the modern West promised lasting benefits for Muslim communities, though astute administrators calculated that success in raising loyal Muslim subjects would "give to England a wider and a more permanent influence upon the millions of the Soudan [sub-Saharan Africa] than can possibly be wielded by any other agency."[5]

Muslims availed themselves of opportunities afforded by colonial rule. However ramshackle and inconsistently run, the colonial bureaucratic superstructure was in many instances far more durable and effective than the sporadic structures erected by caliphal power. Rural migration into urban centers facilitated trade and the peaceful spread of Islam.[6] There is little in the peaceful aspects of colonial rule that conflicts with clerical views or with the spiritual message of Islam. The idea that Muslims must rule but never be ruled is baseless. Colonial rule offered enough advantages to persuade Muslims to adapt and cooperate. It paid huge dividends in the expansion of Muslim networks and educational organization.

Nationalist ideology in general held little appeal for Muslim clerics who feared a chauvinistic nationalism. Even during the colonial takeover, the religious culture remained vibrant enough to avert from Muslim societies comprehensive absorption by the West. It would be an irony to lose ground in the postcolonial sequel. Balancing the need to legitimize colonial rule with the need to respect religious sensibilities, officials adopted policies aiming to promote modern education without instigating defections from Islam. In a judicious mix of policies, colonial administrations established the rule of law and a justice system, and coupled that with incentives and rewards to expand Islam's influence in society. They enabled the Islamization of society rather than the Islamization of the state. That policy undercut armed jihad.

Anti-Western extremist elements had a hard time ignoring the cumulative achievement of modern Muslim society. The defenders of this achievement accepted the fact that the end of jihad had occurred, at least the end of jihad as the established right of an Islamic government. Accordingly, the "classical doctrine of jihad has been stripped of its militancy and is represented as an adequate legal system for maintaining peace in the domain of international relations."[7] Militant jihad may survive as a political weapon employed in response to particular grievances and frustrations, with academics portraying it as heroic resistance to the West,[8] but it is doubtful whether jihad can be restored to its position as an existential duty of the faith community backed by constituted authority. As a political weapon, jihad had to contend with more accepted ways of being Muslim in the modern world. Speaking in his capacity as an early nationalist leader who became a minister in the government of Modibo Keita of Mali (1961–1968), Mamadou Madeira Keita, a Muslim himself, made a pointed repudiation of jihad. "Naturally, a hundred years ago Islam was a pretext for a certain number of conquerors in Nigeria, or even in the Western Sudan, Senegal and Guinea, to carve themselves empires."[9] A Muslim scholar reflected on the trend toward the rejection of military jihad in favor of its primary sense as spiritual struggle and as an individual ethic. He concluded: "We do not doubt that the original sense will triumph in the end, so that jihad will become an instrument of justice and mercy, not of violence and war."[10]

Mervyn Hiskett considered the question of jihad with respect to Nigeria, arguing that Muslims first mobilized behind militancy in their resistance to colonial rule, and then when resistance proved costly and futile they turned to *taqiyya* (dissimulation) to keep a safe distance from an unbelieving colonial power.[11] *Taqiyya* is based on the Qur'anic injunction about the obligation of remaining "faithful" and true to Islam in situations of danger and hostility, with dispensation for withholding the truth and hiding one's true intentions to ride out the challenge (Qur'an 19:18; 49:13). This teaching was more systematically developed in Shi'ite Islam.

There is evidence for general Muslim use of *taqiyya* under colonial rule but not for the clerical attitude particularly. Under colonial rule, the clerics did not seek to wage a campaign to distinguish between believers and unbelievers and to force a choice but to distinguish between political power and religious authority. Attacking unbelievers was typically the preoccupation of jihad leaders and a point of major doctrinal difference with the clerics. The clerics did not abandon their principled opposition to the Islamization of political power.

Even if unwittingly, colonial rule helped not only to disarm the impulse of jihad but also to realign Muslim thought. As heirs to the colonial heritage, Senegal's President Leopold Senghor, a Catholic, and Prime Minister Mamadou Dia, a Muslim, came to similar conclusions about the human spirit as a common bond. The concept was originally articulated by the Jesuit paleontologist and philosopher Teilhard de Chardin. Drawing on Qur'anic scholarship, Mamadou Dia commended the cause of a common humanity as what he considered the necessary historical context for "the return to God." He viewed the *ummah* as a spiritual force rather than as a fossil, giving Muslims a volitional Islam committed to a common human destiny.[12] For his part, Senghor identified the theme of a common human destiny as the spirit of a politically independent Senegal:

> To build a new nation, to erect a new civilization which can lay claim to existence because it is humane, we shall try to employ not only enlightened reason but also dynamic imagination. Once we have put forth our full effort of heart and spirit and intellect, once we have achieved this inner revolution, the rest will be given to us in addition.[13]

The disparities of history involving masters and subjects, free people and slaves, as well as those of theology involving believers and nonbelievers, are here overcome in an intercultural common endeavor.[14] Among other places, Senegal is an outstanding vindication of that view.

The defeat of political Islam opened the way for the recovery of the clerical religious initiative. Indirectly, colonial rule ushered in a new era of separation of religion and power, including power related to economic enterprise, and fostered a climate for the peaceful propagation of religion as a part of civil society. Through its policy of indirect rule, the British administration in Nigeria advanced Islam—ironically, it did so by expanding Islam's sphere of influence in the middle belt in the course of trying to outflank and subdue it. This policy gave clerics the opportunity to propagate their religious mission in communities previously outside the sphere of Islamic authority. Local administration was left in the hands of Muslim religious officials who, trained and salaried, became a pillar of the native tribunals set up to run affairs. The British administration developed its policy of native authority guided by expediency and by the need to maintain public security as effectively as it was inexpensive to do so.

> They promised the emirs [of north Nigeria] that there would be no interference in religious matters and interpreted this to mean that Islam would be upheld as the religion of any state whose ruler called himself a Muslim and its people insulated against other religious influences. . . . This policy, besides assisting the spread of Islam, enabled Islamic law to gain greater influence.[15]

It spelled the demise of African customary law in the areas affected.

As Hiskett argues, despite the early resistance it faced, British rule in north Nigeria "was in many ways helpful to Islam" by protecting the religion "from a tide of social and political change that might, under other circumstances, have overwhelmed the now enfeebled Sokoto caliphate."[16] In a speech in the Legislative Council in March 1948, Abubakar Tafawa Balewa pleaded with the administration to change its policy of non-intervention in Muslim affairs and introduce modern education for girls, the opposition of the emirs and chiefs notwithstanding. "I would like to move that the British interfere in this way," he challenged.[17]

Jihad left society broken and exhausted. Colonial rule helped to reinvigorate Muslim ethics, the civil code, and spiritual life, creating conditions of revival. "The need to come to a new interpretation of the doctrine of jihad was felt after the defeat of the jihad movements," and Muslim leaders became increasingly aware that Western control posed little risk to Islam as a religious tradition.[18] Instead of fighting the new world order, the leaders argued, Muslims should embrace it. Some went even further, repudiating the antisecular campaign of the Islamists as a far greater threat to Islam than communism and secularism. According to Abdel Wahad al-Effendi of Sudan, the "Islamists can strike in its most vital places, where its enemies have never yet managed to inflict a wound."[19]

Al-Effendi's criticism is echoed in the views of the Egyptian legal scholar Khaled Abou El Fadl, who acknowledges the role of scholar-jurists as custodians and conveyors of Islam's heritage. According to El Fadl, in that role the jurists "used their moral weight to thwart tyrannous measures and at times led or legitimated rebellions against the ruling classes."[20]

Under modern conditions, however, both religious authority and political authority have been altered in a fundamental way. For one, modern conditions have turned the 'ulama "from 'vociferous spokesmen of the masses' into salaried state functionaries who play a primarily conservative, legitimist role for the ruling regimes in the Islamic world."[21] For another, the rise of what El Fadl calls "the modern praetorian state, with its hybrid practices of secularism, have opened the door for the state to become the maker and enforcer of the divine law."[22] The consequence, El Fadl argues, is the entrenchment of authoritarianism in various Islamic states, because the confiscation of the functions of the 'ulama removed safeguards against autocratic power. The issue is not about whether Muslims can embrace the modern secular nation state, for they have, but about whether secular political power is viable when it ignores the cumulative moral heritage of Islam or, conversely, when the moral heritage becomes mere fodder for crass political calculation. As it is, Islam's spiritual power continues to exert its influence on Muslim life and practice.

Al Effendi and El Fadl, joined by Bassam Tibi, the Syrian Muslim scholar based in Germany,[23] offer an honest recognition of the effects of the Western encounter. It shows how Western influences gave global scope to Islamic aspirations, providing the language and vehicle for their expression. Muslim scholars came to realize that the cultural range and diversity of the Muslim tradition would frame how Islam would enter and expand upon its modern errand. The tradition of pacifist autonomy set forth in this book belongs to that modern errand.

Local Muslim scholars in Nigeria have taken the argument in another direction. They note that colonial rule freed religion from the burden of power without weakening Islam's religious heritage, leaving scholars to shape society's formative character independently. Alhaji Junaidu, the Wazir of Sokoto and a descendant of Uthman Dan Fodio, reflected on the moral character of Muslim societies bearing the brunt of Western secular influence. At the Ahmadu Bello University convocation in Zaria, he called on the audience to integrate modern knowledge with the values of society, saying this integration would occur only by bringing modern values into alignment with religious teaching.

Drawing on the heritage of learning in Timbuktu, Wazirin Junaidu of the Sokoto Islamic establishment said that knowledge is more than technical competence or individual achievement and its acquisition more than for show. "All communities have an inner life, a spiritual dimension. . . . I am speaking here of the values which they have about their place in the world, about the correct relationship between men, about the proper ways to behave in conducting the affairs of men and about their own views of what constitutes their identity." However much society may be concerned with the pursuit of material benefit, all will be in vain if it is not also "concerned with self-discipline, piety and the love of learning, justice and truth." Madison's view that "before any man can be considered as a member of Civil Society, he must be considered as a subject of the Governor of the Universe," comes pretty close to Junaidu's conception of power.[24] This sentiment is echoed also in Tocqueville: "And what can be done with a people who are their own masters if they are not submissive to the Deity?"[25]

Wazirin Junaidu emphasized that true learning should have a community focus, such that those born and raised in the community recognize, affirm, and perpetuate the moral "codes of conduct on which the sacred community depends for its peace and harmony."[26] He cautioned that the political instrument, severed from conscience, undermines integrity and is a threat to the social order. This explains, he says, why modern political elites, who have suffered the loss of the moral sense, feel emboldened to violate the very laws they themselves make and break society's moral trust.[27] There is no indication in his call for retrieval of Islam's intellectual heritage that Wazirin Junaidu is proposing to introduce theocratic rule, or what Pakistani Muslim reformer Maulana Maududi called "theo-democracy"—democracy established under Islamic legal norms.[28] There was little prospect of the introduction of theocratic rule in Nigeria or anywhere else. Theocratic rule is not an option, not just because of pacifist clerical objections but because of opposition to violent jihad in the modern age. In an interview in early 1971 at his palace in Sokoto, the Wazirin expressed to me the view that society was unlikely to enjoy peace and justice without respecting its core values; no society could progress beyond its moral capacity or against it.

I emerged from the interview with the sense that, for Muslim leaders, political sovereignty under the rule of law is congruent with divine sovereignty based on revealed teaching. Laws exist to protect the safety and security we require as political entities, but without moral conscience, our political nature will cause us to manipulate and corrupt the laws we make. Even revealed law is not beyond abuse, though reducing it to the vagaries of politics makes abuse more certain. The power-state (*qudrah*), with force as its means and end, increases that situation. However much the heritage of hope and fidelity that religion instills had helped to mitigate the disappointment of colonial subjugation, secular forces bequeathed by imperial rule could still weaken that heritage. In several instances religious institutions have stepped in to offer food and shelter to the victims of war and political misrule. In an informal way, the *ummah* filled that role in many places, assuring the continuity of Islam's religious patrimony against political uncertainty and strife.[29] Given current upheavals, it may do so yet again.

The impact of modern ideas had not so much bypassed Islam as engaged it. Islam's political heritage had been probed by jurists and Sufi masters, as we have seen, and the fact that that political heritage had been too enfeebled to offer a credible response to modern challenges confirms its marginal role. But it would be an error to conclude that, because of its marginalized political heritage, Islam was sidelined and neutralized by modern developments. One scholar drew that conclusion, contending that "Islamic civilization is being gradually detached from its religious roots, and the gulf between the spiritual and secular spheres of life is widening." He writes, too, that Islam is unlikely "to exercise the profound political effect it has had in earlier periods" and so may be discounted for that reason.[30] The situation seems in fact to be the other way round. The *ummah* regrouped by engaging its religious heritage afresh. The outcome was an emerging unity of faith and practice across cultures and national jurisdictions. Jurists and religious authorities continued to maintain oversight over the religious canon, using it to limit and constrain rulers and to strip them of religious anointment when and where appropriate.

The swift reaction in Egypt to the Muslim Brotherhood's attempt to rule in the name of Islam while in power in a brief spell from 2012 to 2013 shows that Muslims are determined not to relinquish religious authority into the hands of political leaders, although much uncertainty continued to attend the bloody aftermath of the Brotherhood's ouster. Islam's religious initiative continues to be vital for individuals and societies alike, making possible the vocation of religious learning and pastoral mediation, more often without state involvement and sometimes against state interference. As pointed out by Sir Thomas Arnold, the spiritual energy of Islam is of far greater consequence than its political power.[31] The decline of religion that for so long was predicted seems to have bypassed Islam. In Muslim societies religious attendance has not declined.

Islamization of Society Versus Islamization of the State

The enduring strength of Islam in society contrasts starkly with futile efforts to make the nation-state effective. In the present-day context, religious thought continues to diverge on the relationship between Islamization and politics. One position promotes the Islamization of society wherein Islam is not a political product and is not put to antidemocratic ends. Involving shared social and cultural values and practices, as well as the observance of religious duties, such as prayer, pilgrimage, and devotion, the Islamization of society by officials of the *ummah* can proceed with little interference from the state. In that environment, Muslim projects of philanthropy, education, civic responsibility, and community development may be promoted alongside freedom for other communities. Civil and community engagement could give an otherwise restive youth a role and thus help check the drift toward disenchantment and extremism. This would also discourage political opportunism. Thus did Alhaji Aliyu, the Magaji Gari (a senior political councilor of the Sokoto Sultanate), dismiss the idea of political Islam as mere academic diversion, as "the view of radical academics" who ingratiated themselves with the government.[32] Aliyu argues that the Sharí'ah should not be turned into means of bullyragging and that Islam should contribute to promoting the common good and enjoin moral standards for conduct and behavior without state imposition. This is an implicit appeal to "commanding the good and prohibiting wrong." Muslims may, accordingly, embrace "soft" secularization by supporting the separation of church and state and taking their rightful place in national affairs.

The second position is the Islamization of the state via direct political action. Shaykh Gumi spoke for proponents of this position when he said that politics (*siyásah*) was more important than prayer (*salát*) or pilgrimage (*hajj*) for reasons of scale—this despite the fact that prayer, unlike politics, is one of the five pillars of faith.[33] A Muslim who shirks his prayer and devotion, according to Gumi, brings harm only to himself, whereas a politically delinquent Muslim implicates the larger Muslim community and its future. Deployed for tactical purposes to rally supporters, Gumi's bold statement was fodder for extremists prone to a literal understanding of religious texts. This appears to be the case with the Council of 'Ulamá in Nigeria's statement calling for the adoption of theocratic rule on the grounds that "for a government to be Islamic, Allah has to be the legislator through the Qur'an and the Sunna of the Prophet."[34] Chances of that outcome are slim. Reformist groups in north Nigeria are split not just on the idea of an Islamic government but on what form of Islam should pass muster. Confronted now by the ravages of Boko Haram, the internal debates have caused "fragmentation of sacred authority," in the words of Senegalese scholar Ousmane Kane, and show increasing remoteness of the project of an Islamic state.[35]

Opponents of Gumi pressed their case for the Islamization of society, arguing that it is the best route for Islam in a pluralist modern secular world. Suleman Kumo, a Muslim lawyer in private practice in Kano and a prominent Sharí'ah activist since 1978, was a member of a loose circle of critics of the politicization of Sharí'ah. Although known for his pro-Iranian leanings, Kumo objected to Sharí'ah law, arguing that incompetent and corrupt judges were pretending to mete out justice. Abuse, he said, was prevalent in these courts: "They are the worst courts. Ninety percent of the area judges, if you were to apply the Sharia rules that witnesses must be upstanding citizens, would not even be competent to testify."[36]

Called to serve on a state government–appointed committee called the Kano Forum, Kumo opened a dialogue with members of the militant *Ja'amutu Tajidmul* (Jamá'atu *Tajdid) Islami*, a breakaway group from the local Muslim Brothers. Kumo noted that the members were well-educated: engineers, medical students, and university-age men. These people wanted to be self-reliant and independent of the government but felt nevertheless that Islam should have a public role, though one well short of Shari'ah penal prescription.

Mohammed Tawfiq Landan, senior lecturer in law and head of the Department of Public Law at Ahmadu Bello University, Zaria, was another critic. In a prominent dissenting article, he attacked the method of Sharí'ah implementation as flawed and "violative of the rights of life and security" of the poor.[37] Echoing him was Mohammed Sani, a tailor and Muslim activist. In August of 2000, Sani preached at an open-air meeting to a crowd of fellow Muslims about the banners, bumper stickers, and posters featuring the photograph of the Islamist governor of Zamfara state, the first to introduce *hadd* (Shari'ah penal law). Sani pointed out that such partisan displays were a mockery of the claim that the debate was all about Shari'ah. "This is a political campaign, not sharia," he protested. Shari'ah, he challenged his audience, is from God, not from a governor. The implication was that political Islam is but wolf in sheep's clothing. Sani was thrown in jail for four months, his enemies charging him with disloyalty to the government—though, tellingly, not with disloyalty to religion. Abdul Kadir Jelani, a leading Muslim scholar and an advisor to the government, strained the issue when he warned, "Islam does not permit someone to criticize the government."[38]

The debate between the Islamization of the state and the Islamization of society shows the complex and vital role that still remained for Islam as a civil institution. Expanding the religion's influence in society can be distinguished from turning religion over to the state in the way Abdul Kadir Jelani proposed. In Nigeria, as elsewhere, Islam's political heritage may have retreated further than its ethical and religious teachings; educated clerics as members of the *'ulama* are best equipped in this situation to lead the religious community forward, not the political leaders.[39]

Beyond Jihad

The clerics of this study have faced controversies and challenges throughout history. In the radical view, jihad is presented as a panacea for Islam. Pacifist teaching did not offer a panacea for jihad and, in particular cases, did not even prevent dissension within clerical ranks. Religious teaching binds jihad with extensive moral stipulations. Pacifist practice posed real obstacles for jihad as an uncontested idea and for politics as required expression of the Muslim heritage. Throughout history, jihad did not spare Muslims; it is doubtful it would be any different now. Pacifist teaching does not forget that, and its influence should continue to diminish the appeal of a radical prescription of religion for society. The everyday nature of clerical work in counseling, teaching, mediation, study, worship, devotion, and pastoral engagement helped to fix the habits of Muslims, most of whom had never seen nor would ever see or be involved in jihad. Sufi movements have used spiritual devotion to direct their followers and sympathizers to practice the faith as a matter of personal discipline in "communities of grace," the title of Abun Nasr's study. The energy of Islam is more significant in those communities than in political or military endeavors.

Without jihad, the daily religious rhythm can quietly resume infusing society with the more benign influences of pastoral leadership and the circulation of materials for educational and spiritual training. Among the beneficial influences of Islam on society is the ban on the sale and consumption of alcohol, a measure that has averted from Muslim society the scourge of alcohol and its associated vices.[40] A distinct dry zone separates Muslim communities from non-Muslim regions of North and West Africa.

The disproportionate attention paid to jihad has obscured the significance of the peaceful pastoral theme in Muslim life and practice. The relative abundance of sources on jihad movements gives the impression that jihad was the decisive mode of the expansion of Islam and the continuing message of religious teaching, and bursts of violent radicalism reinforce that impression. After all, war makes for engaging history, and peace is bland by comparison. Yet, while the steel and fire of jihad make for good drama, by no means do they represent what Muslims value in religion. Islam's moral stock is not more evident in its most militant voices. To adapt Lord Acton, if the jihad view of Muslim history "has been an obstacle and a burden," the history of the alternative peaceful view "is the safest and the surest emancipation."

The end of jihad in terms of the state forcing religion on citizens was overtaken by the educational system of the clerics based on *tajdid* (making new) by a peaceful, gradual process, rather than by ultimatum and the injunction of jihad. Long before colonial rule, jihad had become a dubious project. We saw this in eighteenth-century Futa Jallon, where the secular Soriya split with the religious Alfaya to take turns governing. This was a harbinger of the end of jihad as a collective duty (*fard kifáya*). In due course Muslim rulers abandoned the idea of making war for religion, leaving jihad to fester with no canonical credibility or public legitimacy. Sentiments of militant jihad persisted while its stock in the *ummah* dwindled into residual fallout at the margin of society, there to become the ruthless cause of aggrieved individuals and groups. The phenomenon of radical Islam in the guise of Boko Haram in Nigeria and the Islamic State (of Iraq and the Levant) is regarded as a flagrant challenge to established governments in the Muslim world and beyond and in defiance of the constraints and restrictions of classical jihad. The aim of these radical groups to establish an Islamic caliphate has little foundation or justification in Shari'ah or *fiqh* and makes repudiation of them consistent with Islamic ethical obligation as well as being an imperative of faith.

Over the centuries pacifist clerics have been important bearers of Islam's spiritual heritage; they established for that purpose communities of practice and devotion, with the leaders providing pastoral guidance for generations of students and sympathizers. From time immemorial when caravan routes opened pathways for Islam, Muslim Africans took to themselves the Muslim name and kept it without jihad. Militants could not prevail against the steady, peaceful impulse that fed Islam's spiritual energy.

Without denying the role of warriors as carriers of religion in North and Northwest Africa, Futa Jallon, north Nigeria, and elsewhere, this book has proposed an alternative understanding of the historical and religious roots of society, finding those roots in peaceful teaching, religious observance, however perfunctory, and diversity of life and experience. Despite its checkered course, Islam's encounter with the modern West has simply accelerated the peaceful development that had been underway and on course from the beginnings of the Islamization of West Africa. Citing Ahmad Baba to that effect, Dan Fodio acknowledged the peaceful character of the early conversion of West Africa. The end of militant jihad as an unquestioned prerogative of Muslim society was brought about by activities and initiatives undertaken beyond "routes and kingdoms," leading to the widespread diversity and coexistence that have generally characterized the worldwide Muslim *ummah* today despite the heightened plight of minorities in the Arab world and elsewhere.

TIMELINE

550,000,000 BC—Formation of land mass of Africa

3,000–2,500 BC—Domestication of camels in Middle East and Northern Africa300 CE—Beginning of Ghana Empire

622—Founding of Islam

632—Death of the Prophet Muhammad

636—Muslim conquest of Syria; shortly after, 'Uqba ibn Náfi' founds Qayrawan in Tunisia

642—Muslim conquest of Egypt; Caliph 'Uthman orders the expansion of Islam to Ifriqiya (Africa)

651—*Baqt* treaty: Nubia agreed to supply slaves to Muslim rulers

656—Caliph 'Uthman is pursued to Medina and assassinated; beginning of the *fitnah* of the Sunni-Shi'ite division

666–667—'Uqba ibn Náfi' enters Fezzan region

698—Fall of Carthage

710—Muslims invade Spain

732—Arabs defeated by Frankish ruler Charles Martel

Late eighth century—Idris b. 'Abd Allah, claiming descent from the family of the prophet, flees political oppression in Baghdad, settles in the Maghrib, becomes chief of a Berber tribe, and founds the city of Fez

750–800—Founding of the Serakhulle state of Wagadu, merged into Ghana, first mentioned by al-Fazárí in 770

800s—Málikí law consolidates in Egypt

1045—Invasion of North Africa by the Banú Hilál and Banú Sulaym nomads

1050s—Arabs established themselves in colonies among the Berbers

1067—Abú 'Ubayd 'Abd Alláh b. 'Abd al-'Azíz al-Bakrí writes *Kitáb al-Masálik wa'l-Mamálik* (*The Book of Routes and Kingdoms*), a key source on the Almoravid movement and Ghana

1076—Purported conquest of Ghana by the Almoravids

1121–1122—Almohad revolt against the Almoravids
1174—Beginning of Saladin's reign
1193—Death of Saladin
1203—Soninke dynasty recaptures Ghana and restores the non-Muslim Soninke Empire
1224—Ghana transfers political center to Biru (Walata)
1235—Sumanguru, the conqueror of Ghana, is killed by Sunjata, the Malinke ruler; Sunjata converts to Islam. End of Ghana Empire; beginning of Mali Empire
1255—Mansa Wulé (Ulí), son of Sunjata, succeeds as king of Mali. He goes on pilgrimage to Mecca and dies in 1270
1317—Fall of Dongola
1324—Pilgrimage of Mansa Músá to Mecca via Cairo
1352—Ibn Battuta, the veteran Arab "the traveler of the age," visits West Africa
1455–1457—Diogo Gomes, first European to visit Sutukho clerical center
1482—The Portuguese build a massive fortress, São Jorge da Mina (Elmina), on the coast of what is now Ghan
1490s—'Abd al-Rahmán Jakhite travels to Kano, where he dies
1505—Fall of Alwa (on the lower escarpment of the Ethiopian plateau); death of Jalál al-Dín al-Suyútí of Egypt and of 'Abd al-Karím al-Maghílí of Tlemcen
1530s—Possible fragmentation of Diakhaba
1580s—Founding of the kingdom of Kabou
1600—The Fulbe assert control of a large area from the Sahel to Futa Jallon and the Upper Senegal
1590s—End of the Mali Empire
1600s—Founding of Bundu state
1730—Birth of Karamokhoba at Didecoto
1776—Birth of Karang Taslimanka; Karamokho Alfa goes insane and is replaced in the leadership of Futa Jallon by his nephew, Ibrahima Sori
1804—Karamokhoba founds Touba west of Labé
1817—Death of 'Uthman dan Fodio, founder of the Sokoto caliphate
1824—Death of Karamokhoba; Karang Taslimanka succeeds him as leader of Touba
1829—Death of Karang Taslimanka
1830—Birth of Karamokho Qutubo
1837—Death of Muhammad Bello, son of 'Uthman dan Fodio
1860—Birth of Karamokho Sankoung
1881—Muhammad Muṣṭafá ibn Muhammad Taslímí becomes leader of Touba; during his tenure, the French colonial administration enters the area
1885—Karamokho Qutubo succeeds as leader of Touba

1897—Alfa Yahya (and other African leaders) signs a treaty of capitulation dictated by the French, allowing the French to nominate successors to political office and guaranteeing them monopoly on commerce

1905—Death of Karamokho Qutubo. The French ban slavery

1906—Karamokho Sankoung succeeds Karamokho Qutubo as leader of Touba

1911—Karamokho Sankoung is exiled from Touba. The Conakry-Niger Railway begins running

1922—British colonial administration creates Katsina College (later called Barewa College) in Nigeria, exclusively for the sons of the Muslim elite

1928–1929—Death of Karamokho Sankoung

1956—Soriba Jabi, son of Karamokho Sankoung, leaves Touba to settle in Macca-Kolibantang

1958—Banfa Jabi, eldest son of Karamokho Sankoung, leaves Touba for Macca-Kolibantang

1974—Death of Banfa Jabi

1978—Death of Soriba Jabi, succeeded by his son Sekuba Majani Jabi

1980—Death of Mbalu Fode Jabi, son of Karamokho al-Maghili, also known as Karamokho Madi. Mbalu Fode served as Maliki mufti of Senegal. Succeeded by his eldest son, Sidiya Jabi

1987—Death of Sekuba Majani Jabi, succeeded by his son Soriba Jabi II

2004—Death of Soriba Jabi II; succeeded by his brother 'Abdullah Jabi

2007—Death of 'Abdullah Jabi; succeeded by Masire Sankung Jabi

GLOSSARY

adab	literature
'adát	customary practices deemed good and desirable
'adáwa	enmity of non-Muslims
adhán	call to prayer
ahl al-qafr	desert dwellers
al-amír al-mutawallí	vassal chief
al-harth	farming
al-mayl ilayhi	favor
al-muwahhid	Almohad; Muslim Unitarian
al-qirá'ah	Qur'an study
al-safar	travel
'álim mutafannin	erudite scholar
askiya	title for king
aslama	to surrender; to believe
'asr	afternoon prayer
assa	to found; to establish
award (*sing. wird*)	litanies
awliyá (**sing.** *walí*)	saints
babalawo	diviner
baqá	mystical subsistence; spiritual consummation
barakah	blessing; charisma
bay'ah	pledge of obedience
bayyá' al-maṭar	seller of rain
bid'a	innovation, deviation
bilád al-kufr	sphere of unbelief; pagan territory
borom bayré	popular personal appeal; personal charisma
burnús	highly decorative fitted gown
cherno (**pl.** *sernabe*)	scholar-cleric

dabara	cabbalistic technique
dá'í	missionary; propagator
dakákir	sacred images
dar al-khalt	sphere of mixing; syncretism
daraja-tio	possessor of charisma
dhimmí	non-Muslim protected people
dirham	unit of currency
faná	mystical annihilation of self
fanna	branch of study
fanna al-awfáq	higher studies
faqíh, fode	jurist
faqír	mendicant; dervish
faláh	flourishing
fard kifáya	collective duty
farida min Allah	duty imposed by God
fellahin	desert nomads
fergo	immigration
fina-ké	chartered royal bards
fiqh	jurisprudence
fitnah	civil strife, anarchy
fitnat ad-dunyá	worldly ordeal
fuqahá	jurists
garanké	tanners
hadd (**pl.** *hudúd*)	Shari'ah penal law
hajj	annual pilgrimage to Mecca
hijrah	emigration; withdrawal
hirábah	warfare that terrorizes society by targeting civilians
hisbah	commending good and forbidding harm; market supervision
'ibádah al-asnám	idol worshipers
'ibádát	duties owed only to God
'ijmá	collective consensus
ilhám	mystical illumination
'ilm	knowledge; science
imám ratti	religious superior; presiding imám
imámat al-ṣalát	leadership of prayer
imán	faith
intidhár	ultimatum in jihad
iqámat al-salát	instituting the worship
isnád	chain of transmission
istikhárah	consulting of the Qur'an for guidance

istisrár	concubinage
jamá'ah	community
jamu	salutation name
jangali	cattle tax
jihad fi sabil li-llah	struggle in the path of God
jong(o)	slave
karambaya	clerical residential quarter
karamokho	master of *qara'ah*; religious cleric
kautital mawubé	council of political elders of Timbo
khalífah	caliph, successor
khalwah	ritual seclusion
khiláfah	caliphate
khuṭbah	Friday sermon
kitáb	book
kufr	unbelief of non-Muslims
laqab	nickname, honorific
lithám	veil
lúghah	linguistics
madíh	eulogy
madrasah	Islamic school
mahr	gold
majlis (**pl.** *majális*)	clerical center
mansa	king
marabout	religious cleric
maşlahah mursala	concept of God's justice in harmony with human well-being
mawubé	Fulbe elders
mihna	Inquisition
mithqál	measure of gold
mori-ké	clerics
moro	local name for cleric
mudabbar	a qualified slave by circumstantial action
muhtasib	religious enforcement official; market inspector
mujahid	one engaged in jihad
mujáwir	keeper of the sanctuary in Mecca
mukátab	a qualified slave by contract
mukhálafah	difference between creation and the Creator's sovereign power
mulk	political office; kingship
mu'min	believer
murshid	religious guide; leader

murtadid	apostate; renegade
muruwwa	manliness; bravery
mushrif	overseer
muththalimún	the veiled ones
nahw	grammar
nawáfil	supererogatory devotions
niyah	religious intention; spiritual resolve
numu foro	goldsmiths
numu jong	blacksmiths
qabílah	family clan
qádí	judge who rules according to Islamic law
qara'ah	to read
Qaráfa	city of the dead; cemetery
qasm	branch or section of a community
qiyás	analogy; case law
qudrah	power-state
qutb	pole; spiritual pivot
rak'ah	standing position (in prayer)
rijál al-şálihína	upright leaders
ru'yá al-şálihah	*sound,* lucid dream
safar	travel
salat	prayer; worship
salát al-istikhárah	ritual prayer for guidance
salát al-istisqá	prayer for rain
sálik sabíl 'l-haqq	the traveler in search of truth
seringe	marabout; cleric
shahádah	Muslim creed
sharíf	descendant of the prophet; noble
siyásah	politics
sujúd	required prostration of Muslim worship
sunnah	way of life as prescribed by the Prophet
ta'bír	dream interpretation
tadhákara	rehearsal of learning
tafsir	exegesis of the Qur'an
tahajjud	nighttime prayer devotion
tahhadí	advance sign or challenge
tajdíd	renewal
takbír	declaration of Allah–u–akbar
takfir	anathema; anathematization
takshíf	caravan guide
taqiyya	dissimulation in pious cloak

taşawwuf	mysticism
taslím	concluding the prayer with peace greeting
tawallá	symbolic gift
tawhíd	theology of the one God
'ulamá	religious scholars
umaná	trustees of God
ummah	faith community
waláyah	institutional saintship
walí(o) (pl. awliyá)	saint; friend of God
wálio	disagreement
wiláyah	personal sainthood
wird	litany
wudú	ritual ablution
yadhbahuhá	sacrificial slaughter
zakat	obligatory alms
zalm	tyranny
zangos	stranger quarters
záwiyá	hostel
ziyárah	local pilgrimage
zuhhád	Muslim ascetics

NOTES

Introduction

1. E. A. Westermack, *Pagan Survivals in Mohammadan Civilization* (London, 1933; reprinted Amsterdam: Philo Press, 1973); A. J. Wensinck, *The Muslim Creed* (Cambridge, UK: Cambridge University Press, 1932).
2. Neil McHugh, *Holy Men of the Blue Nile* (Evanston, IL: Northwestern University Press, 1986), 126. See chapter 2 for more details.
3. E. W. Blyden, *Christianity, Islam and the Negro Race* (London, 1887; reprinted Edinburgh, UK: Edinburgh University Press, 1969), 10.
4. David Robinson suggests that Sufi orders and jihads played a major role in the introduction and expansion of Islam in Africa. David Robinson, *Muslim Societies in African History* (New York: Cambridge University Press, 2004), 28. It should be noted that after the conquest of North Africa the first jihad in West Africa discussed in this connection was that of Uthman dan Fodio in the nineteenth century, 139–151. We must assume that in the intervening centuries a good deal of accommodation and adaptation accounted for Islam's continued role in society.
5. Ibn Hawqal, *Şurat al-Ard*, "The Picture of the Earth," in *Corpus of Early Arabic Sources for West African History*, translated by J. F. P. Hopkins, edited by N. Levtzion and J. F. P. Hopkins (Cambridge, UK: Cambridge University Press, 1981), 47.
6. Ibid.
7. P. F. de Moraes Farias, "Silent Trade: Myth and Historical Evidence," *History in Africa* 1 (1974): 9–24, 14–15.
8. J. Spencer Trimingham, *A History of Islam in West Africa* (Oxford: Oxford University Press, 1962), 29; Nehemia Levtzion, *Ancient Ghana and Mali* (London: Metheun, 1973), 161.
9. Richard Jobson, *The Discovery of the River Gambra (1623)*, Series III, Vol. 2, Part I, edited by David P. Gamble and P. E. H. Hair (London: The Hakluyt Society, 1999), 142. This first critical edition supersedes earlier versions.
10. Levtzion, *Ancient Ghana*, 164.
11. Reuben Levy, *The Social Structure of Islam*, 2d ed. (Cambridge, UK: Cambridge University Press, 1965), 39, 192–193.
12. Arthur Darby Nock, *Conversion: The Old and the New in Religion from Alexander the Great to Augustione of Hippo* (Oxford: Oxford University Press, 1933; reprinted Baltimore: Johns Hopkins University Press, 1998). Blyden analyzes the roots of the distinctions Indo-European and classical traditions contributed to the idea of religion, with a consideration of the Islamic understanding. Edward W. Blyden, *Christianity, Islam and the Negro Race* (London: 1887, reprinted Edinburgh, UK: Edinburgh University Press, 1969), 241–259.
13. Paul Marty, cited in Christopher Harrison, *France and Islam in West Africa* (Cambridge, UK: Cambridge University Press, 1988), 108.

14. Cited in L. Sanneh, *Disciples of All Nations: Pillars of World Christianity* (New York: Oxford University Press, 2008), 45.
15. Michael Walzer, *The Revolution of the Saints: A Study in the Origins of Radical Politics* (Cambridge, MA: Harvard University Press, 1965), 134–135.
16. This influential thesis was first eloquently put forward by H. F. C. Smith, "A Neglected Theme of West African History: The Islamic Revolutions of the 19th Century," *Journal of the Historical Society of Nigeria* 2.2 (December 1961). This article was a seminal influence in shaping the field of scholarship on Islam in West Africa. John Ralph Willis, a pioneer scholar, dedicated to Smith (as H. F. C. S.) the edited volume of essays, *Studies in West African Islam*: Vol. 1, *The Cultivators of Islam* (London: Frank Cass, 1979).
17. Hugh Clapperton, the Scottish traveler, had an audience with Muhammad Bello, heir to the Sokoto Caliphate, in March 1824 and reported that, when shown a planisphere of the heavenly bodies, Bello knew all the signs of the Zodiac and some of the constellations and stars by their Arabic names. Clapperton said he was pestered constantly by local people, to be given "a charm in writing that entice people" to become customers. He noted widespread belief in dreams and in good and bad omens. E. W. Bovill, ed., *Mission to the Niger:* Vol. IV, *The Bornu Mission 1822–25,* Series II, Vol. 130 (London: Hakluyt Society 1966), 679. Also Hugh Clapperton, *Journal of a Second Expedition into the Interior of Africa from the Bight of Benin to Soccatoo* (London: John Murray, 1829), 224.
18. Ibn Khaldun's intellectual descendants, says Nicholson, "are the great mediaeval and modern historians of Europe—Machiavelli and Vico and Gibbon." Reynold A. Nicholson, *A Literary History of the Arabs* (Cambridge, UK: Cambridge University Press, 1962), 438–439.
19. Ibn Khaldun, *An Arab Philosophy of History, Selections from the Prologomena of Ibn Khaldun of Tunis (1332–1406)*, translated and edited by Charles Issawi (London: John Murray, 1950), 28.
20. 'Asharite scholars brought pressure to bear on the Sufis to force a clear distinction between God and what God created in order to avoid the pitfall of pantheistic deviation. The concept of *mukhálafah* was adopted for that purpose, though in Hanafi law it was used in exegetical interpretation. J. Spencer Trimingham, *The Sufi Orders in Islam* (Oxford: Clarendon Press, 1971), 231.

Chapter 1

1. Merrick Posnansky, "Anatomy of a Continent," in *The Africans: A Reader,* edited by Ali A. Mazrui and Toby Kleban Levine (New York: Praeger, 1986), 31–59.
2. T. N. Clifford and I. G. Gass, eds., *African Magmatism & Tectonics* (Edinburgh, UK: Oliver & Boyd, 1970), 14–15; John Reader, *Africa: A Biography of the Continent* (New York: Vintage Books of Random House, 1997), 10.
3. For a summary of the evidence see C. B. M. McBurney, *The Stone Age of Northern Africa* (Harmondsworth, UK: Penguin Books, 1960), 70–81.
4. McBurney, *Stone Age,* 67–68.
5. Ibid., 68.
6. Ibid., 69.
7. James Owen for *National Geographic News,* July 31, 2009. Sudan was recently subject to devastating floods following heavy rainfall in a region that experiences periods of intense drought alternating with periods of high levels of rainfall. In this particular incident, more than 300,000 people were affected and 74,000 homes damaged, according to United Nations reports. Isma'il Kushkush, "As Floods Ravage Sudan, Young Volunteers Revive a Tradition of Aid," *New York Times,* August 30, 2013, A7.
8. It was Jawhar al-Siqilli, the Sicilian, originally a Christian slave brought to Qayrawan, who established the Fatimid dynasty in Egypt in 969. Philip K. Hitti, *History of the Arabs* (London: Macmillan, 1968), 619.
9. Ibn Battuta, *Travels in Africa and Asia, 1325–1354,* translated and edited by H. A. R. Gibb (London: Routledge & Kegan Paul, 1929), 311–312.

10. W. Montgomery Watt, *Islamic Political Thought: The Basic Concepts* (Edinburgh, UK: Edinburgh University Press, 1968), 54–63; W. Montgomery Watt, *The Formative Period of Islamic Thought* (Oxford: Oneworld, 1998), 140.
11. Michael Brett and Elizabeth Fentress, *The Berbers* (Malden, MA: Blackwell, 1996), 87.
12. For a later history of the relations between Morocco and Andalusia see Andrew Hess, *The Forgotten Frontier: A History of the 16th Century Ibero-African Frontier* (Chicago: University of Chicago Press, 1978).
13. P. M. Holt, Ann K. S. Lambton, and Bernard Lewis, eds., *The Cambridge History of Islam*: Vol. 2A, *North Africa to the Sixteenth Century* (Cambridge, UK: Cambridge University Press, 1970), 216.
14. David J. Wasserstein, "How Islam Saved the Jews," Jordan Lectures, School of Oriental and African Studies, University of London, May 2012. See also Uri Rubin and Wasserstein, eds., *Dhimmis and Others: Jews and Christians and the World of Classical Islam* (Tel Aviv: Tel Aviv University, 1997). The emigration of Maimonides and his father, who was employed as court doctor to Saladin, reflects the renewal of intellectual life in areas under Muslim sway. Maimonides himself became head of the Cairene Jewish community and reports in his correspondence about the great respect Jews enjoyed in the Muslim Cairo of his time. G. E. von Grunebaum, *Classical Islam: A History, 600–1258*, translated by Katherine Watson (London: Allen & Unwin, 1970), 178.
15. J. J. Saunders, *A History of Medieval Islam* (London: Routledge & Kegan Paul, 1965), 189.
16. P. Joseph Stamer, *Islam in Sub-Saharan Africa* (Estella, Spain: Editorial Verbo Divino, 1995), 11.
17. *The Cambridge History of Islam*: Vol. 2A, 224.
18. Abdullahi Ahmed An-Na'im, *Islam and the Secular State: Negotiating the Future of Shari'a* (Cambridge, MA: Harvard University Press, 2008), 284–285.
19. An-Na'im, *Islam and the Secular State*, 285.
20. Michael Brett, "Islam and Trade in the *Bilád al-Súdán*, Tenth-Eleventh Century A.D.," *Journal of African History* 24.4 (1983): 432. See also W. Madelung, "A Treatise of the Sharif al-Murtada on the Legality of Working for the Government," *Bulletin of the School of Oriental and African Studies* 43 (1980): 18–31.
21. E. M. Sartain, *Jalál al-dín al-Suyútí*: Vol. 1, *Biography and Background* (Cambridge, UK: Cambridge University Press, 1975), 87–91, 103–106. The second volume of this book consists of the text, *Al-Tahadduth bi ni'mat alláh*.
22. H. A. R. Gibb, *Studies in the Civilization of Islam: Collected Essays*, edited by Stanford J. Shaw and William R. Polk (London: Routledge & Kegan Paul, 1962), 149.
23. David de Santillana, "Law and Society," in *The Legacy of Islam*, edited by Sir Thomas Arnold and Alfred Guillaume (Oxford: Oxford University Press, 1931), 304.
24. R. Stephen Humphreys, *Islamic History: A Framework for Inquiry*, 2d ed. (Princeton, NJ: Princeton University Press, 1991), 210.
25. Ignaz Goldziher, *Introduction to Islamic Theology and Law*, translated by Andras Hamori and Ruth Hamori (Princeton, NJ: Princeton University Press, 1981), 52. The book was first published in German as *Vorlesungen über den Islam* (Heidelberg, 1910).
26. An-Na'im, the Sudanese legal scholar, has argued that Shari'ah and *fiqh* are both human constructions. An-Na'im, *Islam and the Secular State*, 35–36. The view has echoes elsewhere, such as Muhammad Khalid Masud, *Muslim Jurists' Quest for the Normative Basis of Shari'a* (Leiden: Institute for the Study of Islam in the Modern World, 2001), 14; Reuben Levy, *The Social Structure of Islam*, 2d ed. (Cambridge, UK: Cambridge University Press, 1965), 248–249.
27. Goldziher, *Introduction to Islamic Theology and Law*, 55. Qur'an 2:185; 22:78.
28. Duncan B. Macdonald, *The Development of Muslim Theology, Jurisprudence and Constitutional Theory* (New York: Scribner's, 1903; reprinted Beirut: Khayats, 1965), 238.
29. Cited in Ahmad Bábá, *Mi'ráj al-Su'úd, Ahmad Bábá's Replies on Slavery*, annotated and translated by John O. Hunwick and Fatima Harrak (Rabat: Institute of African Studies, University Mohammed V Souissi, 2000), 15n.
30. Fernand Braudel, *Mediterranean and the Mediterranean World in the Age of Philip II*, translated by Sian Reynolds (New York: Harper & Row, 1972).

31. Ibn Khaldun, *Kitáb al-'ibar, Corpus of Early Islamic Sources* (Cambridge, UK: Cambridge University Press, 1981), 333.
32. Writing in 951, Ibn Hawqal visited Sijilmása, whose commercial strength he described as considerable, saying the city conducted a vigorous caravan trade with *bilád al-Súdán*. He described the people of Sijilmása as distinguished by their dignity, refinement of character, and cosmopolitan outlook. "They are known for their ready charity and show a manly concern for one another. Though there are among them some old feuds and quarrels they put them aside in time of need and cast them away . . . I saw at Awdaghast a warrant in which was the statement of a debt owed to one of them [the people of Sijilmása] by one of the merchants of Awdaghast, in the sum of 42,000 dinars. I have never seen or heard anything comparable to this story in the East. When I told it to the people in 'Iráq, Fárs, and Khúrasán it was considered remarkable." Ibn Hawqal, *Kitáb Súrat al-Ard*, "Book of the Picture of the World," in *Corpus of Early Arabic Sources for West African History* (Cambridge, UK: Cambridge University Press, 1981), 47. Sijilmása's prosperity was threatened under the Almohads but appears to have emerged without lasting damage.
33. Abí Zar', *Corpus of Early Arabic Sources*, 239. On Ibn Yásín see H. T. Norris, "New Evidence on the Life of 'Abdulláh b. Yásín and the Origins of the Almoravid Movement," *Journal of African History* 12.2 (1971): 255–268.
34. Brett and Fentress, *The Berbers*, 100.
35. H. T. Norris, *Súfí Mystics of the Niger Desert: Sídí Mahmúd and the Hermits of Aïr* (Oxford: Clarendon Press, 1990), 92–95.
36. Ibn Mazruq, *Musnad*, edited and translated by E. Lévi-Provençal, *Hespéris*, v (1925); J. Spencer Trimingham, *History of Islam in West Africa* (Oxford: Oxford University Press, 1962), 23n.
37. Nehemia Levtzion, "'Abd Allah b. Yasin and the Almoravids," *Studies in West African Islamic History:* Vol. 1, *The Cultivators of Islam*, edited by John Ralph Willis (London: Frank Cass, 1979), 79–80. See also P. F. de Moraes Farias, "The Almoravids: Some Questions Concerning the Character of the Movement During Its Periods of Closest Contact With the Western Sudan," *Bulletin de l'Institut Fondemantale de l'Afrique Noir*, Série B, 29.3–4 (1967): 794–878.
38. In his detailed review of the *Corpus*, Humphrey Fisher of the School of Oriental and African Studies, University of London, took issue with the claim that an Almoravid-led jihad resulted in the conquest of Ghana. No such conquest took place, Fisher challenges. After we have examined all the evidence, "what other judgement is possible, than that there was no Almoravid conquest and enforced conversion of Ghana. This watershed in west African history simply did not exist." Humphrey J. Fisher, "Early Arabic Sources and the Almoravid Conquest of Ghana," *Journal of African History* 23 (1982): 549–560, quote on 558. He returned to the issue in several other articles, with D. Conrad, "The Conquest That Never Was: Ghana and the Almoravids," *History in Africa* 9 (1982): 21–59, and Humphrey J. Fisher and David C. Conrad, "The Conquest that Never Was: Ghana and the Almoravids," part II, *History in Africa* 10 (1983): 53–78; "What's in a Name? The Almoravids of the Eleventh Century in the Western Sudan," *Journal of Religion in Africa* 22.4 (1992): 290–317.
39. Ibn Abí Zar', *Kitáb al-anís al-mutrib bi-rawd al-qirtás fí akhbár mulúk al-maghrib wa-tárikh madínat Fás* ("The Entertaining Companion in the Garden of Paper on the History of the Kings of the Maghrib and the City of Fez"), translated by J. F. P. Hopkins, edited by N. Levtzion and J. F. P. Hopkins, in *Corpus of Early Arabic Sources for West African History*, 240.
40. Abí Zar', *Kitáb al-anís al-mutrib*, 240.
41. Brett, "Islam and Trade."
42. T. E. Lawrence, *Seven Pillars of Wisdom: A Triumph* (London: Penguin Books, 1962), 36.
43. Charles Doughty, *Passages from Arabia Deserta*, selected by Edward Garnett (London: Penguin Books, 1956), 52.
44. Ibn Battuta, *Rihlah*, in *Corpus of Early Arabic Sources*, 283.
45. Brett, "Islam and Trade," 439.
46. Ibn Tumart, "The Muslim Creed." Rachid Bourouiba, *Ibn Tumart* (Alger, Algeria: SNED, 1974); Constance B. Hilliard, ed., *Intellectual Traditions of Pre-Colonial Africa*, (Boston: McGraw-Hill, 1998), 199.

47. Roger Le Tourneau, *The Almohad Movement in North Africa in the Twelfth and Thirteenth Centuries*, Princeton Studies on the Near East (Princeton, NJ: Princeton University Press, 1969).
48. Jean-Louis Triaud, *Islam et Sociétés Soudanaises au Moyen-Age: Etude historique, Recherches Voltaiques* 16 (Paris: Centre National de la Recherche Scientifque, 1973), 51.
49. von Grunebaum, *Classical Islam*, 182.
50. von Grunebaum, *Classical Islam*, 181–182.
51. The view is attributed to the disciples of John Wycliffe (d. 1384) who declared: "It will never go well in England till all the things be in common and no one can have more than another." Edward P. Cheyney, *The Dawn of a New Era, 1250–1453* (New York: Harper Torchbooks, 1962), 334.
52. Cited in von Grunebaum, *Classical Islam*, 111–113.
53. Ibn Khaldun, *Histoire des Berbères et des Dynasties Musulmanes de l'Afrique Septentrionale:* Vol. 1, new ed., translated and edited by Le Baron de Slane (Paris: Librairie Orientaliste, 1982), 33.
54. Ibn Khaldun, *An Arab Philosophy of History: Selections from the Prologomena of Ibn Khaldun of Tunis (1332–1406)*, edited and translated by Charles Issawi (London: John Murray, 1950), 57–58.
55. Khaldun, *Histoire des Berbères et des Dynasties Musulmanes de l'Afrique Septentrionale*, 4 vols, translated by Le Baron de Slane (Paris: Librairie Orientaliste, 1982), Vol. 1, 28.
56. Holt et al., *The Cambridge History of Islam:* Vol. 2A, 225.
57. For a general account of what was considered "the clash of civilizations" of its time see Stephen O'Shea, *Sea of Faith: Islam and Christianity in the Medieval Mediterranean World* (New York: Walker, 2006). Also Nigel Cliff, *The Last Crusade: The Epic Voyages of Vasco da Gama* (New York: Harper Perennial, 2012).
58. Gomes Eanes de Azurara (Zurara), *The Chronicle of the Discovery and Conquest of Guinea*, 2 vols. (London: Hakluyt Society, 1896, 1899; Vol. 2 reprinted New York: Burt Franklin, 1963), 192.

Chapter 2

1. Ibn Khaldun, *An Arab Philosophy of History: Selections from the Prologomena of Ibn Khaldun of Tunis (1332–1406)*, edited and translated by Charles Issawi (London: John Murray, 1950), 31.
2. F. H. El-Masri, editor and translator of Dan Fodio's *Bayán Wujúb al-Hijra*, says he has no knowledge in Islam of the rule that says that when the ruler is non-Muslim and the population is Muslim his or her land should be considered a land of unbelief and warranting waging jihad against the ruler and the land. *Bayán Wujúb al-Hijra* edited and translated by F. H. El-Masri (Khartoum: Khartoum University Press, 1979), 50n. One hadith that comes close in fact is making a different point: "*Kama takunu kadhalika yu'ammaru alaykum*" (*Mishkat al-Masabih*), meaning "As you are, so shall be your rulers."
3. Nehemia Levtzion examines the question of matrilineality with respect to Ghana in his article, "Was Royal Succession in Ancient Ghana Matrilineal?" *The International Journal of African Historical Studies* 1 (1972): 91–93.
4. According to Mercier, 'Ubayd Allah b. al-Habib, governor of Ifriqiya, dispatched an expedition between 734 and 740 commanded by his son, Ismá'íl, and the *amír* al-Habíb b. Abú 'Ubaydah from Tanjír bearing south into *bilád al-súdán*. They returned with a large booty, including a rich cull of slaves. Ernest Mercier, *Histoire de l'Afrique Septentrionale:* Vol. 1 (Paris: Ernest Leroux, 1888), 206.
5. Ibn Battuta says the caravan guide, *takshif*, is a familiar role in the trans-Saharan trade He is hired by caravan merchants because "he is known for his honesty and he acts as [the merchant's] partner" in the business (*fa-yushárikuh fí dhálik*). *Rihlah*, in *Corpus of Early Arabic Sources for West African History* (Cambridge, UK: Cambridge University Press, 1981), 283–284.
6. Nehemia Levtzion, *Ancient Ghana and Mali* (London: Methuen, 1973), 145–146.
7. Al-'Umarí quotes Mansa Músá as saying that his predecessor actually commissioned a naval flotilla first of two hundred ships and then, this time with the king himself in charge,

of two thousand to set sail across the Atlantic in order to discover its furthest limits. The king and his flotilla never returned, and nothing further was heard of them. Mansa Músá assumed office in those mysterious circumstances. Historians have in more recent times tried to crack the mystery but without success. Yet it is not necessary to solve the conundrum to acknowledge that the rulers of Mali harbored maritime ambitions, proof that their power brought them at least within political range of the Atlantic coast. *Corpus of Early Arabic Sources*, 268–269.

8. In Futa Toro in Senegal, where matrilineal structures were once dominant, the Muslim Tokolor teach their children that at the Day of Resurrection a mother will not recognize her own son, nor a father his; only the maternal uncle will find his nephew, his sister's son. H. Gaden, *Proverbes et maxims: Peuls et Toucouleurs* (Paris: University of Paris, 1931), 19.
9. For a summary discussion see A. S. Tritton, "Islam and the Protected Religions," *Journal of the Royal Asiatic Society*, part III, (July 1928): 485–508.
10. Michael Brett, "Islam and Trade in the *Bilád al-Súdán*, Tenth-Eleventh Century A.D.," *Journal of African History* 24.4 (1983): 436.
11. *Corpus of Early Arabic Sources*, 170. See later for more references on Yáqút.
12. Ibn Battuta, *Travels in Asia and Africa, 1325–1354*, translated and edited by H. A. R. Gibb (London: Routledge & Kegan Paul, 1929; reprinted 1983), 329, 380–381. In his own travels in Africa, Mungo Park, the eighteenth-century Scottish geographer, wrote about time he spent in Sansanding, a town of eight to ten thousand inhabitants at that time. Mungo Park, *Travels in the Interior Districts of Africa* (Durham, NC: Duke University Press, 2000), 201–203, 214.
13. Mervyn Hiskett, *The Course of Islam in Africa* (Edinburgh, UK: Edinburgh University Press, 1994), 93–94.
14. Pekka Masonen and Humphrey J. Fisher, "Not Quite Venus From the Waves: The Almoravid Conquest of Ghana in the Modern Historiography of West Africa," *History in Africa* 23 (1996): 197–231.
15. Mervyn Hiskett, *The Development of Islam in West Africa* (New York: Longman, 1984), 23.
16. Ibid.
17. In this curious volte-face, Hiskett reiterates in his conclusions (p. 302) that the Almoravids conquered Ghana and imposed Islam on the people.
18. Ibn Khaldun, *An Arab Philosophy of History: Selections from the Prologomena of Ibn Khaldun of Tunis (1332–1406)*, edited and translated by Charles Issawi (London: John Murray, 1950), 31.
19. Alexis de Tocqueville, *Democracy in America* (London: Everyman's Library, 1994), 299.
20. Al-Maqrízí writes: "The king of Ghana was the greatest of kings but then the Veiled Men overcame them and their authority dwindled away. The people of Súsú (spelled with a sád) [then] conquered them. After this the people of Málí became powerful and ruled over them." *Corpus of Early Arabic Sources*, 355.
21. Levtzion, *Ancient Ghana and Mali*, 59. Of the many versions of Sunjata Keita, see Djibril Tamsir Niane, *Sundiata: An Epic of Old Mali*, rev. ed., Longman African Writers Series (New York: Longman, 2006); Banna Kanute and Bamba Suso, *Sunjata: Gambian Versions of the Mande Epic*, translated and annotated by Gordon Innes with Bakari Sidibe (New York: Penguin, 1999); and John William Johnson, trans. and ed., *The Epic of Son-Jara: A West African Tradition*, text by Fa-Digi Sisòkò (Bloomington: Indiana University Press, 1992).
22. J. Spencer Trimingham, *A History of Islam in West Africa* (Oxford: Oxford University Press, 1962), 234.
23. Humphrey J. Fisher, "Early Arabic sources and the Almoravid Conquest of Ghana: review article," *The Journal of African History* 23. 4 (1982): 559–560. Nehemia Levtzion responded to the Almoravid conquest debate in a draft article he sent to this writer entitled, "Berber Nomads and the Sudanese States: The Historiography of the Desert-Sahel Interface." The article was presented at the International Conference on Manding Studies, Bamako, Mali, March 15–19, 1993. Levtzion concluded that conquest is not be necessary to explain the constant turnover in relations between the Berbers and populations in sub-Saharan Africa, which indicates retreat from the claim.

24. Elias S. Saad, *Social History of Timbuktu: The Role of Muslim Scholars and Notables, 1400–1900* (Cambridge, UK: Cambridge University Press, 1983), 35. See also Dierk Lange, "Les Rois de Gao-Sané et les Almoravides," *Journal of African History* 32.2 (1991): 251–275. David Robinson has a brief notice on the issue without elaboration. David Robinson, *Holy War of Umar Tal: The Western Sudan in the Mid-Nineteenth Century* (Oxford: Clarendon Press, 1985), 369.
25. 'Uthman ibn Fudi, *Bayán Wujúb al-Hijra 'ala al-'Ibád*, edited and translated by F. H. El-Masri (Khartoum: Khartoum University Press, 1979), 51.
26. Ibid.
27. Griots are members of the *nyamakala* caste, what social scientists call ascriptive occupational groups.
28. Niane, *Sundiata*, 17. Klein summarizes the functions of the griot as one who "as a musician gave pleasure. As a praise-sayer, he was feared and catered to. As a genealogist, he was a source of legitimacy. As a historian, he was society's collective memory." Martin A. Klein, *Islam and Imperialism in Senegal: Sine-Saloum, 1847–1914* (Edinburgh, UK: Edinburgh University Press, 1968), 10.
29. Trimingham, *A History of Islam*, 3. See also Levtzion, *Ancient Ghana and Mali*, 191, 209.
30. In one Muslim region the ruler traveled flanked on one side by a cleric, called *mori-ké*, and on the other by a *fina-ké*. The *fina* by that stage were members of an endogamous clan of *jeli* or griots who acted as masters of ceremony at the various *rites de passage*. Trimingham, *A History of Islam*, 80n.
31. Gordon Innes, trans. and ed., *Kelefa Saane* (London: University of London, School of Oriental and African Studies, 1978), 7–11. This book is the published outcome of the oral traditions brought together and translated by Bakary Sidibe. Despite his being acknowledged as the one who introduced the editor to the two bards of the accounts, Sidibe was in fact the translator and supplier of much of the information in the notes. I was familiar with Sidibe's work at School of Oriental and African Studies as well as in the field. Further information on Kabou is provided in Sekéné Modi Cissoko, "Prophéties de roi Mandingue: Mansa dâli," *Notes Africaines* 120 (1968): 123–124; and "L'empire de Kabou XVIe–XIXe," paper presented at the Manding Conference, School of Oriental and African Studies London, 1972. Considerable discography exists on Kabou, including Sori Kandia, Jeli Foday Suso, Jeli Nyama Suso, and Jeli Bai Konte,
32. This writer attended a public musical performance at the Atlantic Hotel, Banjul, put on by the visiting Cathedral Choir of Dakar that featured a griot Kora player. Uneasy about being on public display with a Catholic choral group, the Kora player preceded his appearance on the platform with a self-conscious justification to the effect that as a professional musician he was not in it to propagate anyone's religion but to ply his craft for a fee. The Catholic choir offered an appealing stage for his art, causing him to reflect on how the mosque would not give him such space. His feigned protest at the appearance of his being coopted was an attempt to preempt Muslim criticism. From the long enthusiastic applause of the audience at the conclusion, however, the kora player was left in no doubt that the choral setting was a natural milieu for his craft and that his Muslim reputation was not a deal-breaker.

Chapter 3

1. Nehemia Levtzion, *Ancient Ghana and Mali* (London: Methuen, 1973), 8.
2. J. D. Y. Peel, *Christianity, Islam and Orisa Religion: Three Traditions in Comparison and Interaction* (Berkeley: University of California Press, 2015), 4–5.
3. Abd al-Rahmán al-Sa'dí, *Ta'ríkh al-Súdán*, edited with text and translation by O. Houdas (Paris: Librairie d'Amerique et d'Orient, Adrien Maisonneuve, 1964), Ar. 12–13.
4. The title is given to a holy man of Nubia where tombs "are visible and visited (*záhir yuzár*) and abundant rain is obtained by them." Neil McHugh, *Holy Men of the Blue Nile: Religious Leadership and the Genesis of an Arab Islamic Society in the Nilotic Sudan, 1500–1850*, PhD dissertation, Northwestern University, 1986, 120.
5. Philip Curtin, a historian of Africa, encourages this imputation when he writes of the clerics who in their traditions speak often of a holy figure duly declining to accept to

become a chief or ruler because he sees that as in conflict with his religious role; still, says Curtin, "the commercial value of this attitude is obvious." It is not clear how or why. Philip D. Curtin, "Pre-Colonial Trading Networks and Traders: The Diakhanké," in *The Development of Trades and Markets in Pre-Colonial West Africa*, edited by Claude Meillasoux (London: Oxford University Press, 1971), 229–230. Also Philip Curtin, *Economic Change in Precolonial Africa: Senegambia in the Era of the Slave Trade* (Madison: University of Wisconsin Press, 1975), 80.

6. Levtzion, *Ancient Ghana and Mali*, 151.
7. Ibn Fadl Alláh al-'Umarí, *Masálik al-absár*, in *Corpus of Early Arabic Sources of West African History* (Cambridge, UK: Cambridge University Press, 1981), 262. The information is based on the authority of what Mansa Músá reported in Cairo.
8. For discussion of the gold trade in this region see Phillip D. Curtin, "The Lure of Bambouk Gold," *Journal of African History* 4 (1973): 623–631.
9. Shiháb al-Dín Ahmad Ibn Fadl Alláh al-'Umarí, *Al-Ta'ríf bi al-mustalah al-sharíf* ("Instruction on the Noble Convention") (Cairo, 1894); *Corpus of Early Arabic Sources*, 276. See also Jean-Louis Triaud, *Islam et Sociétés Soudanaises au Moyen-Age* (Paris: Centre National de la Recherche Scientifique, 1973), 88.
10. *Corpus of Early Arabic Sources*, 169–170.
11. P. F. de Moraes Farias, "Silent Trade: Myth and Historical Evidence," *History in Africa* 1 (1974): 11–12.
12. Cited in C. R. Boxer, *Four Centuries of Portuguese Expansion, 1415–1825: A Succinct Survey* (Johannesburg: Witwatersrand University Press, 1965), 26–27.
13. This story is reproduced in Ibn Battuta, perhaps copied from al-'Umarí. *Corpus of Early Arabic Sources*, 294.

Chapter 4

1. Ibn Fadl Alláh al-'Umarí, *Masálik al-Absár fí Mamálik al-Amsár*, "Pathways of Vision in the Realms of the Metropolises," in *Corpus of Early Arabic Sources for West African History* (Cambridge, UK: Cambridge University Press, 1981), 267.
2. Mahmúd al-Ka'tí, *Ta'ríkh al-Fattásh*, translated by O. Houdas and M. Delafosse (Paris: Librairie d'Amerique et d'Orient, Adrien-Maisonneuve, 1964), 34, tr. 59.
3. Al-Maqrízí, *Al-tibr al-masbúk*, in *Corpus of Early Arabic Sources*, 351.
4. The idea is encapsulated in a *hadíth* considered sound, *sahíh*, as follows: *innnama al-amal bi al-níyáh* (the worth of a work of faith is according to the intention behind it).
5. Saláh al-Dín Munajjid, *Mamlakah Máliyah 'ind al-jugrifiyín al-muslimín*: Vol. I (Beirut: Dár al-Kitáb al-Jadídah, 1963), 58.
6. Family law reforms in Syria and Tunisia, for example, stipulated that the Qur'anic injunction exhorting the husband to provide materially for his wives and to be transparently equitable and impartial toward them (Qur'an 4:128–129) should be construed as an insurmountable legal obstacle to polygamy because complete impartiality is humanly impossible. In this understanding, the intent of the Scriptural injunction is deemed to be tantamount to an outright ban on polygamy. It is an interpretation induced by changed circumstances. N. J. Coulson, *A History of Islamic Law* (Edinburgh, UK: Edinburgh University Press, 1964), 208–211. Also Sir Norman Anderson, "Modernization: Islamic Law," in *Northern Africa: Islam and Modernization*, edited by Michael Brett (London: Routledge, 1973), 73–83.
7. Ibn Abí Zayd al-Qayrawání, *La Risálah: Epítre sur les elements du dogme et de la loi de l'Islám selon le rite mâlikite*, edited and translated by L. Bercher, Quatrième ed. (Alger, Algeria: Ēditions Jules Carbonel, 1952), 178. For an English translation see Ibn Abí Zayd, *The Risála: Treatise on Málikí Law*, edited and translated by Joseph Kenny (Minna, Nigeria: Islamic Education Trust, 1992), 119–120, and Neil B. E. Baillie, *A Digest of Muhammadan Law* (Lahore, Pakistan: Premier Book House, 1974), 367. A second volume (1975) by the same title is devoted to Shí'ite law as a variation of the Sunní tradition. Al-Sharíshí (d. 1222) says in his commentary (*sharh*) on al-Harírí's *Maqámát*, "Assemblies," that Maghribi merchants travel to Ghana as guests of the ruler, and while there they purchased slaves to keep as concubines. *Corpus of Early Arabic Sources*, 153.

8. In his work *Al-Tibr al-masbúk fí man hajja min al-mulúk* ("Moulded Gold, on Those Kings Who Made the Pilgrimage"), al-Maghrízí (d. 1441), who studied under Ibn Khaldun in Cairo, says the king brought with him the mythic number of "14,000 slave girls for his personal service." It beggars the imagination. *Corpus of Early Arabic Sources*, 351.
9. A story carried by al-Maghrízí reports that in a similar situation a king of Takrúr in Cairo on his way to the pilgrimage in 1351 asked to be excused from meeting the sultan so as to be spared observance of the custom of prostration. I am inclined to put such qualms to religious scruples rather than to kingly pride. The rulers of Ghana exempted Muslims from similar court etiquette for religious reasons rather than from any concern with questions of personal pride.
10. Al-Maqrízí, who reports the story, does so with additional details without seemingly raising an eyebrow. He writes: "It is said that [Mansa Músá] brought with him 14,000 slave girls for his personal service. The members of his entourage proceeded to buy Turkish and Ethiopian slave girls, singing girls, and garments." *Corpus of Early Arabic Sources*, 351.
11. In April 2012 Tuareg radical secessionists laid siege to Timbuktu, drove out government troops and targeted the mosque, which they damaged. It was feared that the city's famous library was ransacked, with serious loss to the holdings there. It emerged later, however, that the books and papers escaped destruction, thanks to Abdel Kader Haidara, owner of the city's private collection of manuscripts, who had hidden the manuscripts and dispersed them in over one thousand boxes. Colin Schultz, "Timbuktu's Priceless Manuscripts are Safe After All," *Smithsonian.com*, February 4, 2013.
12. Cited in J. O. Hunwick, "An Andalusian in Mali: A Contribution to the Biography of Abú Isháq al-Sáhilí, c. 1290–1346," *Paideuma* 36 (1990): 59–66, quote on 60.
13. Ibn Khaldun, *Kitáb al-'ibar wa diwá al-mubtada' wa al-khabar fí ayyám al- 'arab wa al-'ajam wa al-barbar, Corpus of Early Arabic Sources*, 335.
14. Ibid., 341.
15. Ibid., 335.
16. Ibn Battuta, *Journey*, in *Corpus of Early Arabic Sources*, 324–325.
17. Ibid., 295–296.
18. Reporting on this legal tradition, al-Maghrízí says that Mansa Músá "bought several books on Malikite jurisprudence."
19. In a letter seeking a *fatwa* ruling (*istiftá'*) addressed to al-Suyútí in Cairo, a scholar from West Africa describes how the popularity of works on Málikí law is so great that the Qur'an and Sunnah are neglected. John Hunwick, trans. and ed., "*As'ila wárida min al-Takrúr fí Shawwál 898* ("Notes on a Late Fifteenth Century Document Concerning al-Takrúr"), in *African Perspectives*, edited by Christopher Allen and R. W. Johnson (Cambridge, UK: Cambridge University Press, 1970), 17–18.
20. Al-Maqrízí, *Al-tibr al-Masbúk* in *Corpus of Early Arabic Sources*, 351.
21. David de Santillana, "Law and Society," in *The Legacy of Islam*, edited by Sir Thomas Arnold and Alfred Guillaume (London: Oxford University Press, 1931), 304. Fazlur Rahman pointed out a similar fact about Islam's cultural openness, saying, "Of the three Western religions Islam is the least race- and color-conscious, embracing as it does Arabs, Turks, Persians, Indians, Malaysians, Indonesians, blacks, and Berbers who constitute a single Muslim community with its center of gravity at Mecca." Fazlur Rahman, *Health and Medicine in the Islamic Tradition: Change and Identity* (New York: Crossroad, 1989), 17. It should, however, be noted that Christianity is no less diverse in its embrace of race and color, whatever its shortcomings on either front.
22. In his observations on religion and political freedom in America, Alexis de Tocqueville reflects on this issue. "Despotism," he contends, "may govern without faith, but liberty cannot . . . . How is it possible that society should escape destruction if the moral tie is not strengthened in proportion as the political tie is relaxed? And what can be done with a people who are their own masters if they are not submissive to the Deity?" Alexis de Tocqueville, *Democracy in America* (London: Everyman's Library, 1994), 307.
23. The founders of the other legal schools fared little better at the hands of rulers: Abú Hanífa (d. 770–771) was tortured and poisoned to death on the orders of the caliph; Sháfi'í (d. 819–820) was dumped in a dungeon in Baghdad for his refusal to bow to the powers that

be. But for the intervention of Shaybání, his student and faithful acolyte, he would have suffered worse fate. The school of Imám Hanbal (d. 855), the most conservative of the schools, was the last to be recognized. His persecution at the hands of the rulers became a badge of defiance and honor for his followers who adhered to a rigorist understanding of Qur'an and *sunnah*. For this reason, Sharí'ah can be said to have been written in the blood, sweat, and tears of its founders. Even if the world has forgotten their moral sacrifice, their achievement has continued to influence the lives of the world's Muslims.

24. Alexander David Russell and 'Abdullah al-Ma'mún Suhrawardy, ed. and trans., *First Steps in Muslim Jurisprudence, Consisting of Excerpts from Bákúrat al-Sa'd of Ibn Abí Zayd* (1906; reprinted London: Luzac, 1963), xix–xx.

Chapter 5

1. Ibn Battuta, *Travels in Africa and Asia, 1325–1354*, translated and edited by H. A. R. Gibb (London: Routledge & Kegan Paul, 1929), 327. This description is very reminiscent of the *kankurang* masquerade tradition of the Mandinka of Senegambia that combines use of code language, dance, and music, perhaps a loose cultural survival long detached from its source in imperial ritual.
2. Ibid., 329.
3. Ibid., 330.
4. Nehemia Levtzion, "Rural and Urban Islam in West Africa: An Introductory Essay," in *Rural and Urban Islam*, edited by Nehemia Levtzion and Humphrey J. Fisher (Boulder, CO: Lynne Rienner, 1987), 3.
5. Nehemia Levtzion and Randall Pouwels, eds., *The History of Islam in Africa* (Athens: Ohio University Press, 2000), 11.
6. J. D. Y. Peel, *Christianity, Islam, and Orisa-Religion: Three Traditions in Comparison and Interaction* (Oakland: University of California Press, 2016. DOI: http://dx.doi.org/10.1525/luminos.8): 137–140.
7. J. H. Saint-Père, *Les Serakollé de Guidimakha* (Paris: Larose, 1925), 26.
8. Anne Raffenel, *Voyage dans l'Afrique occidentale: comprenant l'exploration du Sénégal . . . exécuté, en 1843 et 1844, par une commission composée de MM. Huard-Bessinières, Jamin, Raffenel, Peyre-Ferry et Pottin-Patterson* (Paris: A. Bertrand, 1846), 281.
9. N. Levtzion, *Muslims and Chiefs in West Africa: A Study of Islam in the Middle Volta Basin in the Pre-Colonial Period* (Oxford: Clarendon Press, 1968), 111–113.
10. M. E. Mage, *Voyage dans le Soudan occidental* (Sénégambie-Niger) *1863–1866* (Paris: Librairie de L. Hachette et cie, 1868), 672.
11. The differences in spelling are more a matter of orthography than that of substance, and field work has confirmed this.
12. In the language, "Suware" is a compound word from *sú* (horse) and *waré* (piebald). Ivor Wilks notes this compound use of the word but mistranslates *waré* as "red." Ivor Wilks, "Transmission of Islamic Learning in the Western Sudan," in *Literacy in Traditional Societies*, edited by Jack Goody (Cambridge, UK: Cambridge University Press, 1968), 178.
13. Wilks, "Transmission of Islamic Learning," 176–181.
14. E. M. Sartain, *Jalal al-Din al-Suyuti*: Vol. 1, *Biography and Background* (Cambridge, UK: Cambridge University Press, 1975), 50–51.
15. The *Mukhtasar* went on to acquire high prestige among the Muslim Hausa. "Hausa clerics so prize the *Mukhtasar* of Khalil that if one mentions *al-Kitab* [the book] they think the reference is to Khalil's treatise and not the Qur'an." J. Spencer Trimingham, *Islam in West Africa* (Oxford: Clarendon Press, 1959), 82.
16. Delafosse criticized colonial expansion in Africa, saying the motive was the desire to subjugate Africans not, as was claimed, the happiness of the people. "That is only an excuse that we can give ourselves after the event, it was never our design." Colonial expansion was motivated by the desire to dispossess "the peoples of their independence for the profit of our country." Maurice Delafosse, "Sur l'orientation nouvelle de la politique indigene," 146, cited in Christopher Harrison, *France and Islam in West Africa* (Cambridge, UK: Cambridge University Press, 1988), 145.

17. Maurice Delafosse, *Traditions Historiques et Légendaires de l'Afrique Occidental,* Paris: Comité de l'Afrique francaise, 1913), 7. See also A. Bathily, "A Discussion of the Traditions of Wagadu, With Some Reference to Ancient Ghana, Including a Review of Oral Accounts, Arabic Sources and Archeological Evidence," *Bulletin de l'Institut Française de l'Afrique Noire* 37 (1975): 1–94.
18. J. Spencer Trimingham, *A History of Islam in West Africa* (Oxford: Oxford University Press, 1962), 31. Trimingham was one of the earliest scholars of the subject, though his meticulous knowledge of sources was somewhat undermined by his premature opinions. He had switched his scholarly interest to other fields by the time I met him at the American University of Beirut, Lebanon.
19. Abd al-Rahmán al-Sa'dí, *Ta'ríkh al-Súdán,* edited with text and translation by O. Houdas (Paris: Librairie d'Amerique et d'Orient, Adrien Maisonneuve, 1964), Arabic text, 71. Hunwick adopts the Soninke interpretation of the name. J. O. Hunwick, *Timbuktu and the Songhay Empire: Al-Sa'dí's Ta'ríkh al-Súdán Down to 1613* (Leiden: Brill, 1999), 102. See also J. O. Hunwick, trans. and ed., *Sharí'a in Songhay: The Replies of al-Maghílí to the Questions of Askia al-Hájj Muhammad* (Oxford: Oxford University Press, 1985), 110, 110n. The explanation in the Arabic text that the name "Askiya" is derived from a phrase in the local language, *a si kiyá,* translated as "he shall not be it," is odd, especially when that is given as the reason for the title of the king. It would make more sense if the phrase was intended to say, *lá yakúnu [illá] iyáhu* (he shall not be anything but that). If Askiya Muhammad was related to the Silla patronymic, as Hunwick argues, it would buttress his Serakhulle pedigree, though that is not critical to the argument at hand.
20. Hunwick, *Timbuktu and Songhay,* 104–105.
21. D. Lange and S. Berthoud, "L'Intérieur de l'Afrique occidantle d'après Giovanni Lorenzo (XVIe siècle)," *Cahiers d'histoire mondiale* 14 (1972): 298–351.
22. G. R. Crone, ed. and trans., *The Voyages of Cadamosto and Other Documents on Western Africa in the Second Half of the Fifteenth Century* (London: Hakluyt Society, 1937), 135, 139, 140. The editor says "Caragoles" are Soninké.
23. Gaspard Mollien, *Travels in Africa to the Sources of the Senegal and Gambia in 1818* (London: C. Knight, 2nd ed., 1824), 50, 130, 213, 288, 308.
24. Muhammad Bello [d. 1837], *Infáq al-Maysúr,* edited by C. E. J. Whitting (London: Luzac., 1957), 208; also E. J. Arnett, *The Rise of the Sokoto Fulani* (Lagos, Nigeria, 1922), 137–138. In their translation of the *Ta'ríkh al-Fattásh,* Houdas and Delafosse repeat the Almoravid conquest claim in which the Soninke of Ghana were defeated and Islamized. Mahmúd Ka'tí bin al-Hájj al-Mutawwakil Ka'tí, *Ta'ríkh al-Fattásh,* translated and edited by O. Houdas and M. Delafosse (Paris: Librairie d'Amerique et d'Orient, Adrien-Maisonneuve, Paris, 1964), 78n.
25. Trimingham claims that the name is a Wolof designation as Sere-kule, or Sarakole, meaning "red men," though the people so designated call themselves Soninke. Trimingham, *Islam in West Africa,* 13n. John Ralph Willis repeats this claim. John Ralph Willis, ed., *Studies in West African Islam*: Vol. I, *The Cultivators of Islam* (London: Frank Cass, 1979), 35. But Willis acknowledges that the name "Soninke" was used of a pagan warrior group as testified by A. Raffenel, *Voyage dans l'Afrique occidentale française, 1843–1844* (Paris: A. Bertrand, 1846), 491. Delafosse says the Fulbe used the term "Soninke" in the same way for the warrior class. Maurice Delafosse, *Haut Sénégal-Niger*: Vol. 1 (Paris: Larose, 1912), 123, 281. See also J. H. Saint-Père, *Les Serakholle du Guidimaka* (Paris: Larose, 1925), 26. D'Arcy, the British governor of the Gambia, introduced the concept of the Marabout–Soninke split when he wrote in 1862 that the Mandinka are divided into the two parties: the Marabouts were distinguished by adherence to Islam and abstension from alcohol, while the Soninke were noteworthy for being "lawless and dissipated, plundering when they can." In D'Arcy's view, becoming a Soninke was not a matter of ethnic identity but of religious identity. Martin A. Klein, *Islam and Imperialism in Senegal: Sine-Saloum, 1847–1914* (Edinburgh, UK: Edinburgh University Press, 1968), 69–70. All this evidence proves we need not place any confidence in a Wolof or Senegambian invention of the name. It may suggest only that the Serakhulle lived, and still live, in greater Senegambia.

26. Mungo Park, *Travels in the Interior Districts of Africa*, edited by Kate Ferguson Marsters (Durham, NC: Duke University Press, 2000), 89–90. This edition does not include the journal of the 1805 expedition.
27. Charlotte Quinn, *Mandingo Kingdoms of the Senegambia* (London: Longman, 1972).
28. Charles Monteil, "La Légend de Ouagadou et l'Origine des Soninké," in *Mélanges Ethnologiques* (Dakar: IFAN, 1953), 372.
29. The master of the Qur'an school in the Jakhanke quarter in in the town of Brikama, Gambia, explained that elementary Qur'anic exegesis, consisting of short, simple explanations of Qur'anic verses, was conducted in the Serakhulle language for the children of the clerics. Our meeting happened to be interrupted by a woman visitor who came to report the impending departure for the hajj of a family relative. The cleric offered prayers for safe travel and for a successful hajj. The conversation was in Serakhulle.
30. Growing up in the Gambia I heard the Serakhulle language spoken around me. I thereby acquired a smattering of the language.
31. Philip D. Curtin, "Precolonial Trading Networks and Traders: The Diakhanké," in *The Development of Trades and Markets in Pre-Colonial West Africa*, edited by Claude Meillasoux (London: Oxford University Press, 1971), 229–230. Also Philip D. Curtin, *Economic Change in Precolonial Africa: Senegambia in the Era of the Slave Trade* (Madison: University of Wisconsin Press, 1975), 80.
32. Elias N. Saad, *Social History of Timbuktu: The Role of Muslim Scholars and Notables, 1400–1900* (Cambridge, UK: Cambridge University Press, 1983), 31.
33. Monteil, "La Legende," 372.
34. Delafosse, *Traditions Historiques*, 7; Monteil, "La Legende," 372.
35. Trimingham, *Islam in West Africa*, 75.
36. I. M. Lewis, the British sociologist, observes that the Muslim religious calendar "gives uniformity to the regulation of life . . . Similar regularities bridging the great ethnic and cultural diversities of this vast region are evident in the traditional pattern of Islamic instruction." I. M. Lewis, "Africa South of the Sahara," in *The Legacy of Islam*, 2d ed., edited by Joseph Schacht and C. E. Bosworth, (Oxford: Clarendon Press, 1974), 107.
37. Edward W. Blyden, *Christianity, Islam and the Negro Race* (London, 1887; reprinted Edinburgh, UK: Edinburgh University Press, 1969), 176.
38. Emily Osborn reports on local traditions in Kankan on the expansion of al-Hajj Salim's community there. Emily Lynn Osborn, *Our New Husbands Are Here: Households, Gender, and Politics in a West African State from the Slave Trade to Colonial Rule* (Athens: Ohio University Press, 2011), 24–34, 50–62.
39. Pierre Smith, "Les Diakhanké: Histoire d'une dispersion," *Bulletins et mémoires de la Société d'anthropologie de Paris* Série 8, 11 (1965): 231–262.
40. Wilks, "Transmission of Islamic Learning," 179.
41. A local saying cited in Wilks, "Transmission of Islamic Learning," 170.
42. Gordon Innes, trans. and ed., *Kelefa Saane: His Career Recounted by Two Mandinka Bards* (London: School of Oriental and African Studies, University of London, 1978), 57.
43. Peterson describes one such cleric, Mamadou Gassemba (Gassama?) from Futa Jallon who traveled with a bottle of ink, a small animal skin sack containing a miscellany of loose papers in Arabic writing, gazelle horns decorated with leather, a shell with horsehair, and six cowries. He made his living making amulets and providing divination services for clients. Plying the open road was his way of life. Brian J. Peterson, *Islamization From Below: The Making of Muslim Communities in Rural French Sudan, 1880–1960* (New Haven, CT: Yale University Press, 2011), 108.
44. Wilks, "Transmission of Islamic Learning," 171.
45. Ibn Khaldun, *An Arab Philosophy of History: Selections from the Prologomena of Ibn Khaldun of Tunis (1332–1406)*, edited and translated by Charles Issawi (London: John Murray, 1950), 133. One criticism of this theory is that it has no explanatory or predictive value, that it is simply stating the obvious, namely, that solidarity is the property of any group that happens to possess it. Al-Azmeh, who mounts this criticism, accuses Ibn Khaldun of nominalism, which is the school of thought, Al-Azmeh says, that was dominant among orthodox Muslim thinkers of the time. Aziz Al-Azmeh, *Ibn Khaldun: An Essay*

in Reinterpretation (London: Frank Cass, 1982). It is not clear what import this criticism has for historical study.

46. Wilks, "Transmission of Islamic Learning," 179.
47. Charles Monteil, *Les empires du Mali: Etude d'histoire et de sociologie soudanaises* (Paris: Larose, 1929; reprinted in *Bulletin du Comité d'Ētudes Historiques et Scientifiques de l'Afrique Occidentale Française* [Paris: Larose, 1968], 44–45).
48. Charles Monteil, "Etat actuel de nos connaissances sur l'Afrique occidentale française: Le coton chez les noirs," in *Bulletin du Comité d'Ētudes Historiques et Scientifiques de l'Afrique Occidentale Française,* 9.4 (1926). Reprinted as a book under the same title, Paris: E. Larosse, 1927.
49. Ka'tí, *Ta'ríkh al-Fattásh,* Ar. 179, tr. 314. *Ta'ríkh al-Fattásh* was begun by Mahmúd al-Ka'tí (b. 1468) in 1519 and completed by his grandson, Ibn Mukhtár, in about 1664. On the authorship see N. Levtzion, "A 17th Century Chronicle by Ibn al-Mukhtár: A Critical Study of the *Ta'ríkh al-Fattásh,*" *Bulletin of the School of Oriental & African Studies* 34 (1971), 571–593.
50. In the Sufi tradition one of the qualities of the *walí* (saint) is the gift *of mujáb al-du'a* (efficacious prayer). See Ignaz Goldziher, *Muslim Studies*: Vol. 2, translated and edited by C. R. Barber and S. M. Stern (London: Allen & Unwin), 269.
51. Ka'tí, *Ta'ríkh al-Fattásh,* Ar. text 180, tr. 315.
52. Ahmad Bábá, *Mi'ráj al-Su'úd: Ahmad Bábá's Replies on Slavery,* edited and translated by John Hunwick and Fatima Harrak (Rabat: Institute of African Studies, University Mohammed V Souissi, 2000), 52.
53. Ibid., 50–51.
54. Richard Jobson, *The Discovery of the River Gambra (1623), Part II: Other Early Sources on River Gambia [1455–1684].* Edited by David P. Gamble and P. E. H. Hair (London: Hakluyt Society, 1999), 260–261.
55. Ibid., 265–266.
56. Ibid., 266.
57. Ibid., 277.
58. Ibid., 277.
59. Ibid., 122.
60. Jobson was unaware of the fact that the Qur'an contains accounts of Adam and Eve, material that was available in Medina at the time of Muhammad, thanks to thriving Jewish communities in the town. W. Montgomery Watt, *Muhammad at Medina* (Oxford: Clarendon Press, 1962).
61. Jobson, *Discovery,* 122–123.
62. Ibid., 124.
63. Ibid., 125.
64. Ibid., 128.
65. Ibid., 126.
66. Ibid., 126–127, 127n.
67. Ibid., 129.
68. Ibid., 130.
69. Ibid., 130.
70. Ibid., 131.
71. Commenting on the work of Jules Brévié, Delafosse assures his audience that in the modification to native policy he was recommending, he did not wish to give the impression that the colonial crusade against Islam should be abandoned. Harrison, *France and Islam,* 146.
72. Mungo Park, *Travels in Africa* (London: Everyman, 1969), 273. This edition includes the journal of the 1805 expedition.
73. Ibid., 274.
74. Blyden, *Christianity, Islam and the Negro Race,* 185.
75. Park, *Travels in Africa,* 1969, 273.
76. Jobson, *Discovery,* 148.
77. Philip D. Curtin, "*Jihad* in West Africa: Early Phases and Inter-relations in Mauritania and Senegal," *The Journal of African History* 12.1 (1971): 11–24.

78. For a strong apologetic of the clerical heritage of al-Hajj Salim Suware by the leading scholar of the Jabi-Gassama tradition, see the work of 'Abd al-Qádir Gassama Ṭúbawí, better known as Al-Hajj Soriba, *Kitáb al-Bushrá: Sharh al-Mirqát al-Kubrá* (Tunis: Matba'ah al-Manár, n.d.).
79. Jamil M. Abun-Nasr, *Muslim Communities of Grace: The Sufi Brotherhoods in the Islamic Religious Life* (New York: Columbia University Press, 2007), 7–25.
80. Trimingham, *Islam in West Africa*, 92.

Chapter 6

1. M. A. al-Hájj, "A 17th Century Chronicle on the Origins and Missionary Activities of the Wangarawa," *Kano Studies* 1.4 (1968): 7–16.
2. Humphrey J. Fisher, "The Mecca Pilgrimage in Black African History: Counting the Demographic Coast," *Africa Events* (July/August 1986): 45–48.
3. Traditions about the introduction of this Málikí legal text to West Africa vary enormously, including the claim that the first scholar in Timbuktu who introduced the teaching of the work in the city was al-Hajj Ahmad b 'Umar Aqít, traveled to Kano where he lived and taught. 'Abd al-Rahmán al-Sa'dí, *Ta'ríkh al-Súdán*, edited with text and translation by O. Houdas (Paris: Librairie d'Amerique et d'Orient, Adrien Maisonneuve, 1964), 37; Elias N. Saad, *Social History of Timbuktu: The Role of Muslim Scholars and Notables, 1400–1900* (Cambridge, UK: Cambridge University Press, 1983), 58.
4. *AW*, 12.
5. H. R. Palmer, "The Kano Chronicle," *Journal of the Royal Anthropological Institute* 38 (1908): 70. See also Elias N. Saad, "Islamization in Kano: Sequence and Chronology," *Kano Studies*, New Series 1.4 (1979): 52–66; John O. Hunwick, "A Historical Whodunit: The So-Called 'Kano Chronicle' and Its Place in the Historiography of Kano," *History in Africa* 21 (1994): 127–146; John O. Hunwick, "Songhay, Borno and Hausaland in the Sixteenth Century," in *History of West Africa*: Vol. 1, 2d ed., edited by J. F. A. Ajayi and Michael Crowder (London: Longman, 1976), 264–301.
6. Al-Zarnújí, *Instruction to the Student: The Method of Learning*, in *Classical Foundations of Islamic Educational Thought*, edited by Bradley J. Cook and Fathi H. Malkawi (Provo, UT: Brigham Young University Press, 2010), 135.
7. Cook and Malkawi, *Classical Foundations*, 96.
8. *AW*, 14, Ar. text 20.
9. The Tijániyah first came to Nigeria at the hands of al-Hájj 'Umar Tall (1794–1864) when he visited Sokoto on his way to Mecca. A convert to the Tijániyah from that visit was Modibbo Muhammad Rájí (d. 1862), chief minister of the Sokoto caliphate. Yet, not to antagonize the mainly Qádiriyáh establishment, Rájí kept his conversion secret. Eventually, in 1855, he migrated with his family to Adamawa where he nurtured a nucleus Tijániyah community. After the fall of the Segu state in 1890, numerous elements of the Tijániyah order emigrated to north Nigeria to establish strongholds in Kano and Zaria.
10. See, for example, A. Bonnel de Mézières, "Les Diakhanké de Banisiraïla et du Bondou," *Notes Africaines* 41 (1949): 21–25.
11. Mungo Park, *Travels in the Interior Districts of Africa* (Durham, NC: Duke University Press, 2000), 296.
12. Al-Sa'dí, *Ta'ríkh al-Fattásh*, tr. 119.
13. Gaspard Mollien, *Travels in Africa to the Sources of the Senegal and Gambia in 1818*, 2d ed. (London: Sir R. Phillips, 1820), 79.
14. André Rançon, *Le Bondou* (Bordeaux: G. Gounouilhou, 1894), 6.
15. William Gray and Staff Surgeon Dochard, *Travels in Western Africa, 1818–1821* (London: Murray, 1825), 179–180.
16. Park, *Travels in Africa*, 104.
17. Ibid., 106.
18. Baron Charles Athanase Walckenaer, *Histoire générale des voyages*: Vol. 7 (Paris: Chez Lefèvre, 1826–1831), 161ff.
19. Pierre Smith, "Les Diakhanké: histoire d'une dispersion." *Bulletins et mémoires de la Société d'anthropologie de Paris*, Série 8, 11 (1965): 244, 253, 255.

20. Park, *Travels in Africa*, 305. Unless where the edition is stated as different.
21. Ibid., 266.
22. Ibid., 309–311.
23. Ibid., 373.
24. J. Spencer Trimingham. *A History of Islam in West Africa* (Oxford: Oxford University Press, 1962), 236.
25. G. R. Crone, ed., *The Voyages of Cadamosto and other Documents on Western Africa in the Second Half of the Fifteenth Century* (London: Hakluyt Society, 1937), 143–144. Cadamosto was in West Africa in 1455–1456. Nehemia Levtzion, *Ancient Ghana and Mali* (London: Methuen, 1973), 98–99.
26. Al-Sa'dí, *Ta'ríkh al-Súdán*, 15–16.
27. Park, *Travels in Africa*, 105.
28. Ahmad Baba, *Mi'ráj al-Şu'úd ilá nayl hukm Majlab al-súd* (*The Ladder of Ascent towards Grasping the Law Concerning Transported Blacks*), edited and translated by John Hunwick and Fatima Harrak (Rabat: Institute of African Studies, University Mohammed V Souissi, 2000).
29. In a popular musical piece consisting of at least forty rhymed stanzas, Jeli Foday Suso performs a parody of the theme of pious marabouts trading on their reputation by cutting the image of pomp and sanctity. The type, he says, is too familiar to be missed.
30. The emir of Hausa, Alfa 'Umar b. Muhammad al-Hausi, defended solidarity with fellow Muslims by citing Ahmad b. Hanbal to the effect that "the brotherhood of imán precedes that of blood." Cited in John Ralph Willis, *In the Path of Allah: The Passion of al-Hajj 'Umar: An Essay into the Nature of Charisma in Islam* (London: Frank Cass, 1989), 73.
31. Richard Jobson, *The Discovery of the River Gambra (1623)*, edited by David P. Gamble and P. E. H. Hair (London: Hakluyt Society, 1999), Part I, 132–133.
32. Watt, *The Formative Period of Islamic Thought* (Oxford: Oneworld, 1998), 30. Also Baber Johansen, *Contingency in a Sacred Law: Legal and Ethical Norms in the Muslim Fiqh* (Leiden: Brill, 1999), 21.
33. *As'ila wárida min al-Takrúr fí Shawwál 898* (*Questions Arriving From al-Takrúr in the Month of Shawwál 898/July-August 1493*), edited and translated by John Hunwick as "Notes on a Late Fifteenth-Century Document Concerning 'al-Takrúr'," in *African Perspectives: Papers in the History, Politics and Economies of Africa Presented to Thomas Hodgkin*, edited by Christopher Allen and R. W. Johnson (Cambridge, UK: Cambridge University Press, 1970), 7–33.
34. One assessment speaks of the fact that the Jakhanke ties to Malik Sy contributed to the weakening of the jihad impulse of Malik Sy's movement to push him toward moderation. The rulers of Bundu heeded the pacifist counsels of the Jakhanke to pursue a policy of moderation at the inception of the Bundu state. Michael A. Gomez, *Pragmatism in the Age of Jihad: The Precolonial State of Bundu* (Cambridge, UK: Cambridge University Press, 1992), 50.
35. The chronicle is titled *Ta'ríkh al-Madaniyyu* and accessioned at the Institute of African Studies, University of Ghana, Legon as IASAR/451. The *mufti* who is the author of the chronicle describes his own clerical lineage as that of the Jabi family, with Touba his birthplace. The details of the chronicle are virtually identical to other clerical chronicles referenced in this book.
36. H. T. Norris, *Súfí Mystics of the Niger Desert* (Oxford: Clarendon Press, 1990), 107.
37. Cited in Faríd al-Dín 'Aṭṭár, *Tadhkírat al-Awliyá* (*Memorial of Saints*), edited and translated by Reynold A. Nicholson (Leiden: Brill 1905–1907), Vol. II, 8; Reuben Levy, *The Social Structure of Islam*, 2d ed. (Cambridge, UK: Cambridge University Press, 1965), 212.
38. Shiháb al-Dín 'Umar b. Muhammad Suhrawardí [d. 1234], *'Awárif al-Ma'árif*, translated by Lieut. Col. H. Wilberforce Clarke as *A Dervish Textbook* (London: Octagon Press, 1980), 26. A Sháfi'ite scholar and head of a *ribát* in Baghdad, Suhrawardí, like many of his fellow-Şúfís, placed no confidence in the caliphate for the religious leadership of the *ummah* even though the caliph al-Násir recruited him to promote stronger bonds with religious leaders. In the final analysis, Suhrawardí believed that submission to spiritual authority is the only way to observe submission to the authority of God and to that of

the Prophet. Jamil M. Abun-Nasr, *Muslim Communities of Grace: The Sufi Brotherhoods in Islamic Religious Life* (New York: Columbia University Press, 2007), 63–64.

39. Park's book had enormous literary influence on such writers as Conrad, Hemingway, George Eliot, Thoreau, and Wordsworth.
40. Park, *Travels in Africa*, 9. This edition comprises only Park's first expedition of 1795–1797.
41. *Parliamentary Debates*, February 23, 1807, "Slave Trade Abolition Bill," 987.

Chapter 7

1. Thierno Diallo, *Alfa Yaya: roi du Labé (Fouta Djallon)* (Dakar: Editions ABC, 1976), 11–14.
2. Djibril Tamsir Niane, "Récherches sur l'empire du Mali au Moyen Age," *Récherches Africaines Études guinéenes*, nouvelle série 1 (1960): 17–36, 23; Walter Rodney, *History of the Upper Guinea Coast: 1545–1800* (Oxford: Oxford University Press, 1970), 223–226, 229.
3. Sometimes also "zongo," these quarters are familiar in many parts of West Africa. See R. C. Abraham, *Dictionary of the Hausa Language* (London: University of London Press, 1962); also Nehemia Levtzion, *Muslims and Chiefs in West Africa* (Oxford: Oxford University Press, 1968), 23, 105–106.
4. C. A. L. Reichardt, *Grammar of the Fulde Language* (London: Church Missionary Society, 1876), 319; Omar Jamburiah, "The Story of the Jihad of the Foulahs," *Sierra Leone Studies* 3 (1919): 30–34.
5. Claude Halle, "Notes sur Koly Tenguella, Olivier de Sanderval et les ruines de Gueme-Sangan," *Récherches Africaines* 1 (1960): 37. The dates indicate that the event took place during the reign of the first askiya, Muhammad b. Abi Bakr, who ruled 1493–1529.
6. J. Spencer Trimingham, *History of Islam in West Africa* (Oxford: Oxford University Press, 1962), 150–151.
7. G. R. Crone, ed. and trans. *The Voyages of Cadamosto and Other Documents on Western Africa in the Second Half of the Fifteenth Century* (London: Hakluyt Society, 1937), 144.
8. H. A. S. Johnston, *The Fulani Empire of Sokoto* (London: Oxford University Press, 1967), 21–26.
9. John Ralph Willis, "The Torodbe Clerisy: A Social View," *Journal of African History* 19.2 (1978): 195–212.
10. L. Tauxier, *Moeurs et histoire des Peulhs* (Paris: Payot, 1937), 219.
11. André Arcin, *Histoire de la Guinée Française* (Paris: A. Challamel, 1911), 82.
12. Ibid., 80. Alfred le Chatelier, *L'Islam dans l'Afrique Occidentale* (Paris: G. Steinhell, 1899), 161–162.
13. Jean Bayol, *Voyage en Sénégambie: Haut-Niger, Bambouck, Fouta Djallon et Grand-Bélédougou, 1880–1885* (Paris: Baudoin, 1888), 106–110; Yves Person, "The Atlantic Coast and the Southern Savannahs," in *History of West Africa*: Vol. 2, edited by J. F. Ade Ajayi and Michael Crowder (London: Longman, 1974), 286.
14. Bayol, *Voyage*, 101.
15. Paul Marty, *L'Islam en Guinée* (Paris: E. Leroux, 1921), 4–5.
16. According to some sources, Ibrahima Sori died in 1793.
17. Walter Rodney, "Jihad and Social Revolution in Fouta Djalon in the Eighteenth Century," *Journal of the Historical Society of Nigeria* 4.2 (1968), 277.
18. Arcin, *Histoire*, 88.
19. Bayol, *Voyage*, 103; Arcin, *Histoire*, 87.
20. Arcin, *Histoire*, 89.
21. Ibid., 95. J. Suret-Canale and Boubacar Barry, "The Western Atlantic Coast to 1800," in *History of West Africa*: Vol. 1, edited by J. F. Ade Ajayi and Michael Crowder (Longman: Longman, 1976), 495.
22. Ibid., 493, 495.
23. J. M. Gray, *A History of the Gambia* (Cambridge, UK: Cambridge University Press, 1940; reprinted London: Frank Cass, 1966), 458–459.
24. Gaspard Mollien, *Travels in Africa to the Sources of the Senegal and Gambia in 1818*, (London: C. Knight, 2nd ed., 1824), 130.
25. Arcin, *Histoire*, 80–81.

26. The statement is by Marie-François Joseph Clozel of Côte d'Ivoire, cited in Christopher Harrison, *France and Islam in West Africa* (Cambridge, UK: Cambridge University Press, 1988), 99.
27. Ibid., 124–125.
28. Louis Joseph Barot, *Guide pratique de l'Européen dans l'Afrique Occidentale a l'usage des militaires, fonctionnaires, commerçants, colons, & tourists* (Paris: Flammarion, 1902), 316–317; Harrison, *France and Islam*, 32.
29. Jules Brévié, *L'Islamisme contre'naturisme' au Soudan français: Essai de psychologie politique coloniale* (Paris, 1923), 184, cited in Harrison, *France and Islam*, 147. Brévié was director of the Department of Political and Administrative Affairs, Dakar, before becoming governor-general of French West Africa. He was a follower of the ideas of Levy Bruhl.
30. Harrison, *France and Islam*, 122.
31. Ibid., 124.
32. Ibid., 100.
33. Richard Critchfield, *Shahhat: An Egyptian* (Syracuse, NY: Syracuse University Press, 1978), 219.
34. I. M. Lewis, ed., *Islam in Tropical Africa*, 2d ed. (Bloomington: Indiana University Press, 1980), 91.
35. For a discussion of the issue, see Rodney, "Jihad and Social Revolution." Also Mervyn Hiskett, *The Sword of Truth: The Life and Times of the Shehu Ususman Dan Fodio* (New York: Oxford University Press, 1973), 105–107.
36. Cheikh Hamidou Kane, *Ambiguous Adventure* (London: Heinemann, 1972), 79–80.

Chapter 8

1. Yves Person, "The Atlantic Coast and the Southern Savannahs," in *History of West Africa*: Vol. 2, edited by J. F. Ade and Michael Crowder (London: Longman, 1974), 285.
2. H. Gaden, *Proverbes et Maximes Peuls et Toucouleurs* (Paris: Institut d'ethnologie, Université de Paris, 1931), 68.
3. Amadou Hampaté Bâ, *A Spirit of Tolerance: The Inspiring Life of Tierno Bokar* (Bloomington, IN: World Wisdom, 2008), 29.
4. 'Abd al-Qạdir Gassama Ṭúbawí (Al-Hajj Soriba), *Kitáb al-Bushrá: Sharh al-Mirqát al-Kubrá* (Tunis: Matba'ah al-Manár, n.d.), 192. The author of this work, who was born in Touba in Guinea and moved to Senegal, died in 1974. He was a direct descendant of Karamokhoba and, as an informant of this study, was very encouraging of it.
5. Ibn Jama'ah, "A Memorandum for Listeners and Lecturers: Rules of Conduct for the Learned and the Learning," in *Classical Foundations of Islamic Educational Thought*, edited by Bradley J. Cook and Fathi H. Malkawi (Provo, UT: Brigham Young University Press, 2010), 191.
6. Abí al-Fadl 'Iyád bin Músá was a twelfth-century Málikí jurist, and one-time *qádí* of Córdoba and Ceuta.
7. This was a standard text for the scholars of Timbuktu. The *qádí* Mahmúd (d. 1548) was among the scholars who studied the work. J. O. Hunwick, ed. and trans. *Timbuktu and the Songhay Empire: Al-Sa'dí's Ta'ríkh al-Súdán Down to 1613*, translation of 'Abd al-Rahmán Sa'dí's *Ta'rikh al-Súdán* (Leiden: Brill, 1999), 54.
8. Jama'ah, "A Memorandum."
9. See also Elias N. Saad, *Social History of Timbuktu: The Role of Muslim Scholars and Notables, 1400–1900* (Cambridge, UK: Cambridge University Press, 1983), 58–93.
10. This may be the same individual who was also the teacher of al-Hajj 'Umar al-Fútí. John Ralph Willis, *In the Path of Allah: The Passion of al-Hajj 'Umar: An Essay into the Nature of Charisma in Islam* (London: Frank Cass, 1989), 82.
11. J. Spencer Trimingham, *Islam in West Africa* (Oxford: Clarendon Press, 1959), 122.
12. 'Abd al-Ghaní al-Nábulsí, *Ta'tír al-Anám fí Ta'bír al-Manám*, 2 vols. (Cairo: Dār Iḥyā' al-Kutub al-'Arabīyah, 1972). I purchased a copy of the work at the Sandaga market in Dakar, proof that there is a market in West Africa for such highly technical work.

13. Ibn Khaldun, *Al-Muqaddimah: An Introduction to History*, edited and translated by Franz Rosenthal (Princeton, NJ: Princeton University Press, 1967), Vol. 1, 207–213; Vol. 3, 70–75; on dream-interpretation specifically see Vol. 3, 103–110.
14. For a discussion of the subject in the Muslim heartlands see Albert Hourani, *A History of the Arab Peoples* (Cambridge, MA: Harvard University Press, 1991), 204–205.
15. Gregory of Nyssa (d. 394) drew from religious persecution a consoling thought about dreams. He wrote that sleep brings about a state in which reason is not extinguished but smolders like a fire, in which dreams break forth in insights and new hope.
16. Jack Goody, "Restricted Literacy in Northern Ghana," in *Literacy in Traditional Societies* (Cambridge, UK: Cambridge University Press, 1968), 226. Humphrey J. Fisher, "The Ivory Horn: Oneirology, Chiefly Muslim, in Black Africa," unpublished paper, SOAS, London. See also Ousmane Kane, "Reconciling Islam and Pre-Islamic Beliefs: A Reflection on a Talismanic Textile of the Art Institute of Chicago," *Islam et Sociétés au Sud du Sahara* 2 (2009): 137–161.
17. Joseph Greenberg, *The Influence of Islam on a Sudanese Religion* (New York: J. J. Augustin, 1966), 12–13, 27, 41; Mu'izz Goriawala, "Maguzawa: The Influence of the Hausa Muslims on the Beliefs and Practices of the Maguzawa, the Traditional Religionists of Kano and Katsina," *Orita: Ibadan Journal of Religious Studies* 4.2 (1970): 115–123. The name "Maguzawa" is said to be derived from *majus*, the *magian* of the Qur'an (22:17).
18. L. Sanneh, *The Jakhanke Muslim Clerics: A Study of Islam in Senegambia* (Lanham, MD: University Press of America, 1989), 99.
19. J. Suret-Canale, "Touba in Guinea: Holy Place of Islam," in *African Perspectives*, edited by Christopher Allen and R. W. Johnson (Cambridge, UK: Cambridge University Press, 1970), 57.
20. Al-Hajj Soriba, *Kitáb al-Bushrá*, 193.
21. Emily Lynn Osborn, *Our New Husbands Are Here: Households, Gender, and Politics in a West African State from the Slave Trade to Colonial Rule* (Athens: Ohio University Press, 2011), 50–56.
22. *TKB*.
23. Willis, *In the Path of Allah*, 198–199. To show that he was no pacifist, al-Bakka'í was instrumental in bringing about the death of al-Hajj 'Umar when he set fire to the stockade in which al-Hajj 'Umar had taken refuge. Willis's book is a sophisticated intellectual account of jihad.
24. Al-Kuntí's own spiritual pedigree is traced to the sixteenth-century scholar Muhammad Baghayagho al-Fulání. Saad, *Social History of Timbuktu*, 249.
25. John Hanson and David Robinson, eds. and trans., *After Jihad: The Reign of Ahmad al-Kabir in the Western Sudan* (East Lansing: Michigan State University Press, 1991), 84. Al-Bakka'í was pilloried for his flip-flop on jihad. *After Jihad*, 86. See also 'Abd el-Qadir Zabadia, "The Career of Ahmad al-Bekkay in the Oral Evidences and Recorded Documents," *Revue d'Histoire Maghrébine* 3 (1975): 75–83.
26. John Ralph Willis, *The Jihád of al-Hajj 'Umar al-Fútí: Its Doctrinal Basis etc.*, PhD dissertation, University of London, 1970, 62–63. See also Willis, *In the Path of Allah*, 95.
27. Al-Ghazali, *Ayyuha al-walad*, in *Classical Foundations*, 99.
28. Cited by Ibn Jama'ah, "A Memorandum for Listeners and Lecturers: Rules of Conduct for the Learned and the Learning," in *Classical Foundations*, 190.
29. Khaldun, *Al-Muqaddimah*, Vol. 1, 449–450. Translation slightly altered.
30. A similar organization of Timbuktu into "kundas," with a proliferation of Manding and Jakhanke-sounding names, suggests explicit Suwarian influence. Saad, *Social History of Timbuktu*, 113, 116, 118, 128–129.
31. For a discussion of castes in Muslim West Africa see Trimingham, *Islam in West Africa*, 136–138.
32. Information from al-Hajj Mbalu Fode Jabi-Gassama, Marssassoum, Casamance, January 18, 1973. The informant, a descendant of Karamokhoba, was Málikí *mufti* of Senegal; in line with his clerical pacifist scruples he kept a studied distance from Dakar as the center of national politics.
33. Ahmad Bábá, *Mi'ráj al-Su'úd, Ahmad Bábá's Replies on Slavery*, edited and translated by John Hunwick and Fatima Harrak (Rabat: Institute of African Studies, University Mohammed V Souissi, 2000), 52.

34. Mahmúd al-Ka'ti, *Ta'ríkh al -Fattásh*, translated by O. Houdas and M. Delafosse (Paris: Librairie d'Amerique et d'Orient, Adrien-Maisonneuve, 1964), text 60–61, tr. 116–117; text 179, tr. 314.
35. Khaldun, *Al Muqaddimah*, Vol. 1, 188–194.
36. Romans 8:8.
37. David de Santillana, "Law and Society," in *The Legacy of Islam*, edited by Sir Thomas Arnold and Alfred Guillaume (London: Oxford University Press, 1931), 288–289.
38. Neil McHugh, *Holy Men of the Blue Nile: The Making of an Arab-Islamic Community in the Nilotic Sudan, 1500–1850* (Evanston, IL: Northwestern University Press, 1986), 119.
39. Vincent Monteil, *L'Islam noir* (Paris: Seuil, 1964), 137.
40. While it is not a prominent part of West African Islam, the cult of saints occurs widely in North Africa and elsewhere, where devotees undertake visitations to the tombs of saints for prayer and devotion. Saint veneration in the relevant instances is based on the idea of the personal *barakah* of a charismatic religious personage. Trimingham, *Islam in West Africa*, 88–91.
41. Al-Hajj Soriba, *Kitáb al-Bushrá*, 195.
42. The story seems to follow a recognized pattern, for a similar account is given of al-Kuntí himself, who once interrupted leading public prayers because, as he explained later, he had learned of the birth of an exceptional child, 'Umar b. Fútí. Willis, *In the Path of Allah*, 78.
43. Al-Hajj Soriba, *Kitáb al-Bushrá*, 195. The Sakho lineage was the founder of the state of Tamba, which lay to the east of Futa Jallon. David Robinson, *The Holy War of 'Umar Tal: The Western Sudan in the Mid-Nineteenth Century* (Oxford: Clarendon Press, 1985), 126.
44. C. K. Meek, *Tribal Studies in Northern Nigeria* (London: K. Paul, Trench, Trubner & Co., 1931), Vol. 1, 269.
45. Hunwick, ed. and trans. *Timbuktu and the Songhay Empire*, 135.
46. Al-Ka'ti, *Ta'ríkh al-Fattásh*, text 60–61, tr. 116–117.
47. Ibid., text 61, tr. 117.
48. Abd al-Rahmán Al-Sa'dí, *Ta'ríkh al-Súdán*, translated and edited by O. Houdas (Paris: Librairie d'Amerique et d'Orient, Adrien-Maisonneuve, 1964), 176. See also Hunwick, ed. and trans., *Timbuktu and the Songhay Empire*, 164.
49. In one account, the donation was received by the *qádí* without prejudice. Subsequently the *askia* sent some building materials, four thousand pieces altogether, which were used to complete construction work on the mosque. Hunwick, ed. and trans., *Timbuktu and the Songhay Empire*, 154.
50. Ahmad Baba, *Jalb al-Ni'mah*, quoted in Saad, *Social History of Timbuktu*, 152. In exile in Morocco, Ahmad Baba was granted an interview with the sultan Ahmad al-Mansur (r. 1578–1603), the son of an African concubine. Ahmad Baba refused to talk to the sultan when he found him concealed behind a curtain, saying that by speaking without being seen the sultan was imitating God. The curtain was removed. Humphrey J. Fisher, "The Western and Central Sudan and East Africa," in *The Cambridge History of Islam*: Vol. 2A (Cambridge, UK: Cambridge University Press, 1970), 360.
51. J. Spencer Trimingham, *The Sufi Orders in Islam* (Oxford: Clarendon Press, 1971), 48, 225. The distinction is widely recognized. An eighteenth-century Muslim Chinese Sufi leader, Ma Laichi, established succession to barakah as saintship to ensure that "the family's accumulated wealth would not dissipate nor its religious power wane." Melanie Jones-Leaning and Douglas Pratt, "Islam in China: From Silk Road to Separatism," *The Muslim World* 102 (April 2012), 323.
52. The context suggests 'Abd al-Qádir al-Jílání, also known as al-Jílí in some sources.
53. Al-Hajj Soriba, *Kitáb al-Bushrá*, 196.
54. Trimingham, *Sufi Orders*, 45.
55. Ibn Khaldun was critical of al-'Arabí's ideas. Khaldun, *Al-Muqaddimah*, Vol. 1, 398n; Vol. 3, 172.
56. 'Abdullah ibn Muhammad ('Abdullah dan Fodio) affirms the teaching of *lá yuhtadá bi qiyás*, which means "that all that God gives and withholds, no reason can be known for it, for the wisdom of the Eternal is above being related to cause." 'Abdullah ibn Muhammad, *Tazyín al-Waraqát* ("Ornament of Letters"), edited and translated by M. Hiskett (Ibadan,

Nigeria: Ibadan University Press, 1963), tr. 127, Arabic text 78. For a discussion of the place of speculative theology in Islam see Khaldun, *Al-Muqaddimah*, Vol. 3, 34–55.

57. The words are those of al-Junayd. Annemarie Schimmel, *Mystical Dimensions of Islam* (Chapel Hill: University of North Carolina Press, 1975), 58.
58. Trimingham, *Sufi Orders*, 224–225.
59. Muhammad Bello, *Uṣúl al-Siyásah*, edited and translated by B. G. Martin, "A Muslim Political Tract from Northern Nigeria," in *Aspects of West African Islam*, edited by Daniel F. McCall and Norman R. Bennett, Boston University Papers on Africa, Vol. V (Boson: African Studies Center, Boston University, 1971), 63–86, quote on 82.
60. Al-Ghazálí on *Hisba*. 'Abd al-Rahmán b. Nasr al-Shayzarí, *Niháyat al-Rutba al-Hisba*, edited and translated by R. P. Buckley (Oxford: Oxford University Press, 1999), 151. See also Michael Cook, *Commanding Right and Forbidding Wrong in Islamic Thought* (Cambridge, UK: Cambridge University Press, 2000), 428–459.
61. Al-Shayzarí, *Niháyat al-Rutba al-Hisba*, 151–152.
62. Reuben Levy, *The Social Structure of Islam*, 2d ed. (Cambridge, UK: Cambridge University Press, 1965), 334.
63. Cited in Levy, *Social Structure of Islam*, 334n.
64. Cook, *Commanding Right*, 99.
65. Ibid., 448.
66. For a critical assessment of Ibn Khaldun, see Aziz al-Azmeh, *Ibn Khaldun: An Essay in Interpretation* (London: Frank Cass, 1982) and Michael Brett, "Morocco and the Ottomans: The Sixteenth Century in North Africa" [Review essay], *Journal of African History* 25 (1984): 331–341.
67. C. H. Becker, *Christianity and Islam* (New York: Harper, 1909), 9.
68. J. Spencer Trimingham, *The Christian Approach to Islam in the Sudan* (London: Oxford University Press, 1948), 29–30.
69. J. P. Hubbard, "Government and Islamic Education in Northern Nigeria (1900–40)," in *Conflict and Harmony in Education in Tropical Africa*, edited by Godfrey N. Brown and Mervyn Hiskett (London: Allen & Unwin, 1975), 154–155.
70. J. Spencer Trimingham, "The Phases of Islamic Expansion and Islamic Culture Zones in Africa," in *Islam in Tropical Africa*, edited by I. M. Lewis, (Bloomington: Indiana University Press, 1980), 102.
71. Haroun al-Rashid Adamu, *The North and Nigerian Unity: Some Reflections on the Political, Social and Educational Problems of Northern Nigeria* (Lagos: Daily Times, 1973): 57.
72. *TKB*, fo. 8.
73. *TKB*, fo.6
74. *TKB*, fo. 8.
75. Ibn Jubayr, *Rihlah*, translated by R. J. C. Broadhurst, in *Anthology of Islamic Literature: From the Rise of Islam to Modern Times*, edited by James Kritzeck (New York: New American Library, 1964), 218.
76. Marty, *L'Islam en Guinée*, 109.
77. This work has maintained its appeal for the clerics as is evident by the fact that a handwritten copy of it was given to this writer by al-Hajj Banfa, a senior member of the Jabi-Gassama community.
78. Marty, *L'Islam en Guinée*, annexe xx.
79. *TSK*, fo. 8.
80. Paul Marty, *L'Islam en Guinée: Fouta Diallon* (Paris: E. Leroux, 1921), 110.
81. *TKB*, fo. 9. I interviewed a son of Karamokho Qutubo, al-Hajj Mbalu Fode Jabi-Gassama, who by that time had moved to Casamance. He was Málikí *muftí* of Senegal.
82. Marty, *L'Islam en Guinée*, 109–110.
83. Ibid., 110.
84. Ibid.
85. Suret-Canale, "Touba in Guinea, 63.
86. For the text of the treaty, including the Arabic version, see Marty, *L'Islam en Guinée*, 535–538.
87. Suret-Canale, "Touba in Guinea," 63.

88. Ibid.
89. Ibid.
90. Hollis R. Lynch, *Edward Wilmot Blyden: Pan-Negro Patriot, 1832–1912* (New York: Oxford University Press, 1970).
91. Church Missionary Society Archives: CA 1/047, E. W. Blyden to Venn, January 19, 1872.
92. M. D. Gouldsbury, *Expedition to the Upper Gambia, August 1881*, Enclosure 1 in no. 17 (London: Public Records Office, June, 22, 1881).
93. Marty, *L'Islam en Guinée*, 127.

Chapter 9

1. Hosea 10:10.
2. The name is borrowed from 'Abd al-Karím al-Maghílí (d. 1505–1506), a North African scholar and a counselor to Askiya Muhammad Turé of Songhay. Respected for his learning, al-Maghílí found little appeal in Songhay for his radical jihad ideas. That was different for the Fulani *mujáhids* led by 'Uthmán dan Fodio (Ibn Fúdí) (d. 1817), and his son, Muhammad Bello (d. 1837), who both cited him in support of the jihad program they launched in Hausaland from 1804. In their turn the British colonial administration in north Nigeria adopted one of al-Maghílí's works as representing one of the best models of administration for the newly conquered Muslim territories. The work in question was *Táj al-Dín fí má Yajíbu 'alá al-Mulúk wa al-Saláṭín, The Crown of Religion Concerning the Obligations of Princes: An Essay on Moslem Kingship by Sheikh Mohammed al-Maghílí of Tlemcen*, translated by T. H. Baldwin (Beirut: Imprimerie Catholique, 1932). As lieutenant-governor of north Nigeria (1925–1930), H. R. Palmer obtained a copy of al-Maghílí's *The Crown of Religion*, which he included in the collection of the Shahuci Judicial School, established in 1928, and in that of the School of Arabic Studies in Kano, established in 1947. It established al-Maghílí in the canon of West African Muslim scholarship. See Mervyn Hiskett, "An Islamic Tradition of Reform in the Western Sudan from the Sixteenth to the Eighteenth Century," *Bulletin of the School of Oriental and African Studies* 25.3 (1962): 577–596, and O. S. A. Ismail and A. Y. Aliyu, "Bello and the Tradition of Manuals of Islamic Government and Advice to Rulers," in *Nigerian Administration Research Project, Second Interim Report* (Zaria: Ahmadu Bello University, 1975).
3. Paul Marty, *L'Islam en Guinée: Fouta Diallon* (Paris: E. Leroux, 1921), 111.
4. Marty expressed this sentiment eloquently to his superiors. Christopher Harrison, *France and Islam in West Africa* (Cambridge, UK: Cambridge University Press, 1988), 134.
5. Jamil M. Abun-Nasr, *Muslim Communities of Grace: The Sufi Brotherhoods in the Islamic Religious Life* (New York: Columbia University Press, 2007), 170–171. See also Charles C. Stewart and E. K. Stewart, *Islam and Social Order in Mauritania* (Oxford: Oxford University Press, 1973), 109, 115–122, 128; also Aziz A. Batran, "The Kunta, Sidi Mukhar al-Kunti, and the Office of Shaykh al-Ṭaríqa al-Q̧ádiriyya," in *Studies in West African Islamic History*: Vol. 1, *The Cultivators of Islam*, edited John Ralph Willis (London: Frank Cass, 1979), 113–146. The Kunta followed a harsh custom in which a father of many sons would designate as his heir one with a religious aptitude and put the others to death. Kunta chains of spiritual eminence (*qutbaniyah*) were for that reason a string of isolated names (*afrad*). Aziz A. Batran, "The Kunta, Sidi Mukhar al-Kunti, and the Office of Shaykh al-Ṭaríqa al-Q̧ádiriyya," in *Studies in West African Islamic History,* 115.
6. Marty, *L'Islam en Guinée*, 112–113.
7. Ibid., 113.
8. Ibid.
9. J. Suret-Canale, "Touba in Guinea: Holy Place of Islam," in *African Perspectives*, edited by Christopher Allen and R. W. Johnson (Cambridge, UK: Cambridge University Press, 1970).
10. Marty, *L'Islam en Guinée*, 124.
11. Suret-Canale, "Touba in Guinea," 64.
12. Nehemia Levtzion, "Merchants Vs. Scholars and Clerics in West Africa: Differential and Complementary Roles," in *Rural and Urban Islam in West Africa*, edited by Nehemia Levtzion and Humphrey J. Fisher (Boulder, CO: Lynne Rienner, 1987), 37.

13. Suret-Canale reports that these women were daughters of Ba Gassama, but the age chronology makes that unlikely. Besides, Sankoung's own sons confirmed that the women were Ba Gassama's sisters. Suret-Canale, "Touba in Guinea," 68.
14. Ibid., 68–69.
15. Ibid., 69.
16. Ibid., 70. Al-Hajj Soriba, Sankoung's son, says vaguely each side sustained wounds.
17. Suret-Canale, "Touba in Guinea," 70.
18. Field notes, al-Hajj Soriba Jabi, at Macca-Kolibantang, Senegal Orientale, September 12, 1972.
19. Letter of March 22, 1909, *Archives Nationale de Guinée* 1.E 17, cited in Suret-Canale, "Touba in Guinea," 70.
20. Marty, *L'Islam en Guinée*, 116. The kettle-drum is sounded normally only for the Friday prayer, for funerals, and in emergencies. A night-time occurrence would be extremely rare.
21. Suret-Canale, "Touba in Guinea," 72.
22. Marty, *L'Islam en Guinée*, 117.
23. P. M. Holt, *The Mahdist State in the Sudan: 1881–1898* (Oxford: Clarendon Press, 1958).
24. Camille Guy, "Proposition d'internement d'indigènes de la Guinée pour faits d'insurection contre l'autorité de la France," Report by the Governor of the Colonies and Lt.-Governor of Guinea, Archives Fédérales de Dakar 84, Session de 1911.
25. Cited in Harrison, *France and Islam*, 83.
26. Suret-Canale, "Touba in Guinea," 160–164.
27. Marty, *L'Islam en Guinée*, 118.
28. Harrison, *France and Islam*, 84.
29. Governor-General de Coppet in Harrison, *France and Islam*, 177. For a discussion of the origin of the practice of "eleven beads" and "twelve beads" as a Tijaniyya rite, see Amadou Hampaté Bâ, *A Spirit of Tolerance: The Inspiring Life of Tierno Bokar* (Bloomington, IN: World Wisdom, 2008), 44–57.
30. Louis Brenner, *West African Sufi: The Religious Heritage and Spiritual Search of Cerno Bokar Saalif Taal* (Berkeley: University of California Press, 1984), 56.
31. The trial was covered in the local newspaper, *L'A.O.F. Echo de la côte occidentale d'Afrique*, from September 20, 1911. See L. Sanneh, *The Crown and the Turban: Muslims and West African Pluralism* (Boulder, CO: Westview Press, 1997), chapter 4: "Tcherno Aliou, the *Walí* of Goumba: Islam, Colonialism, and the Rural Factor in Futa Jallon, 1867–1912," 73–99.
32. Harrison, *France and Islam*, 86–89.
33. Marty, *L'Islam en Guinée*, 116.
34. Ibid., 118.
35. Ibid., 114.
36. Suret-Canale, "Touba in Guinea," 74; Harrison, *France and Islam*, 91.
37. Marty, *L'Islam en Guinée*, 115. Sankoung testified in his "Sur la Puissance de Chrétiens (1912) that he "placed his total confidence in God against all the evils of the century." Archives of IFAN, Fonds Vieillard, Dakar.
38. Marty, *L'Islam en Guinée*, 118.
39. Suret-Canale, "Touba in Guinea," 72.
40. Marty, *L'Islam en Guinée*, 117.
41. Suret-Canale, "Touba in Guinea," 65.
42. Al-Hajj Soriba Jabi, Macca-Kolibantang, December 9, 1972; al-Hajj Mbalu Fode Jabi, Marssassoum, January 18, 1973.
43. Marty, *L'Islam en Guinée*, 119. The Qur'an allows the marrying of slave women, provided someone else has owned them. Slave women can also be freed by a legal contract, *kitabah*; such a slave is called a *mukátabah*. In the case of an implied contract, such as a slave woman having a child by the master, she is an *umm al-walad*, sometimes also a *mudabbarah*—the implied contract entitling her to manumission is called the *tadbír*. Qur'an iv: 24; xxiv: 32–33. Joseph Schacht, *The Origins of Muhammadan Jurisprudence* (Oxford: Clarendon Press, 1950), 277, 325–327. 'Abd al-Rahman III, the first caliph of Córdoba, fathered an heir by his slave, Marjan, thus making her entitled to manumission as *umm walad*. Maribel Fierro, *'Abd al-Rahman III: The First Cordoban Caliph* (Oxford: Oneworld Publications, 2005), 81.

44. John Hunwick and Eve Troutt Powell, eds., *The African Diaspora in the Mediterranean Lands of Islam* (Princeton, NJ: Markus Wiener, 2002), 14–16, 224.
45. W. G. Palgrave, *A Year's Journey Through Central and Eastern Arabia*, 5th ed. (London: Macmillan, 1869), 270–271; see also Reuben Levy, *The Social Structure of Islam*, 2d ed. (Cambridge, UK: Cambridge University Press, 1965), 73–83.
46. J. S. Hogendorn and Paul E. Lovejoy, "The Reform of Slavery in Early Colonial Northern Nigeria," in *The End of Slavery in Africa*, edited by Suzanne Miers and Richard Roberts (Madison: University of Wisconsin Press, 1988), 391–414. The British finally abolished slavery in Nigeria in 1936, the same year the French abolished slavery in Mauritania. In the Gambia, colonial authorities conceded the fact that "domestic slavery had been for so long a time one of the foundations of native society that its immediate abolition was neither desirable nor even practicable." J. M. Gray, *A History of the Gambia* (Cambridge, UK: Cambridge University Press; reprinted London: Frank Cass, 1966), 475. Fear of emancipation made Muslim leaders averse to allowing "their herdsmen and their women-folk to take refuge on British soil." Gray, *History of Gambia*, 475.
47. Gray, *History of the Gambia*, 475.
48. Martin A. Klein, *Slavery and Colonial Rule in French West Africa* (Cambridge, UK: Cambridge University Press, 1998).
49. The story of Muhammad Kaba Saghanughu illustrates how the fortunes of religion and slavery are intertwined. He was captured and shipped off the West African coast, finally ending up as a slave in Jamaica where in about 1820 he wrote a religious tract in Arabic, evidence that he carried his faith with him. Yacine Daddi Addoun and Paul Lovejoy, "The Arabic Manuscript of Muhammad Kaba Saghanughu of Jamaica, c. 1820," in *Creole Concerns: Essays in Honour of Kamau Brathwaite*, edited by Annie Paul (Kingston: University of the West Indies Press, 2007), 313–340. One study describes a major slave exodus in modern-day Mali in the late nineteenth century. The town in question had recently been established, and the slaves, who were some two-thirds of the population, had not been long enough in slavery to forget their non-slave past. Their harsh treatment fomented their resolve to stage a mass exodus, threatening the entire local slave system. Richard Roberts and Martin A. Klein, "The Banamba Slave Exodus of 1905 and the Decline of Slavery in the Western Sudan," *Journal of African History* 21 (1980): 375–394. See also Richard Roberts, "The End of Slavery in the French Soudan, 1905–1914," in *End of Slavery in Africa*, 282–307.
50. Humphrey J. Fisher, "Liminality, *Hijra* and the City," in *Rural and Urban Islam*, 170–171.
51. A study of the introduction of Islam among the Yoruba of Nigeria calls attention to the work of returning slaves who as Muslims facilitated the establishment of Islam in their communities. T. G. O. Gbadamosi, *The Growth of Islam among the Yoruba, 1841–1908* (London: Longman Group, 1978), 84, 90–91. The book was actually published in March 1979. See also Brian J. Peterson, *Islamization from Below: The Making of Muslim Communities in Rural French Sudan, 1880–1960* (New Haven, CT: Yale University Press, 2011), 90–100, 237.
52. For a summary of the law on manumission in Islam see F. A. Klein, *The Religion of Islam* (London: Curzon Press, 1906; reprinted 1979), 196n–199n. The statement by Klein that slavery is a divine institution in Islam and so cannot be declared illegal has to be modified by the fact that slavery is qualified in several ways, including providing means for its abolition.
53. Alexander David Russell and Abdullah al-Ma'mún Suhrawardy, eds. and trans., *First Steps in Muslim Jurisprudence* (London: Luzac, 1963), xiv.
54. Bradley J. Cook and Fathi H. Malkawi, eds., *Classical Foundations of Islamic Educational Thought*, Islamic Translation Series (Provo, UT: Brigham Young University Press, 2010), 44–45.
55. Marty, *L'Islam en Guinée*, 119.
56. J. D. Hargreaves, *A Life of Sir Samuel Lewis* (London: Oxford University Press, 1958), p. ix.
57. African slave markets existed in the Islamic world where specialized trading guilds controlled the traffic. See Terence Walz, "Notes on the Organisation of the African Trade in Cairo, 1800–1850," *extrait des Annales Islamologiques* (Cairo, XI, 1972): 263–286.
58. Harrison, *France and Islam*, 89.

59. Cited in Harrison, *France and Islam*, 77.
60. The words are those of Mariani, the Inspector of Muslim Education, in Harrison, *France and Islam*, 79.
61. Harrison, *France and Islam*, 85.
62. The Interministerial Commission on Muslim Affairs, created in Paris, was tasked with responsibility for surveillance of Muslim activity in French West Africa. Harrison, *France and Islam*, 95.
63. For a detailed examination of this subject, see Winston McGowan, "Fula Resistance to French Expansion into Futa Jallon, 1889–1896," *Journal of African History* 22.2 (1981): 245–261.
64. Cited in Harrison, *France and Islam*, 75.
65. Harrison, *France and Islam*, 59.
66. Cited in Peterson, *Islamization From Below*, 88.
67. In January 1910, Paul Brocard, the French administrator of Sine-Saloum in Senegal, wrote in a memo to the lieutenant-governor a temperamental reference to the Syrian and Lebanese traders, saying they "have nothing that generally induces native respect for the white race." Fear of commercial competition was behind this jaundiced view. Martin A. Klein, *Islam and Imperialism in Senegal: Sine-Saloum, 1847–1914* (Edinburgh, UK: Edinburgh University Press, 1968), 187–189. In due course the French government assumed control of Syria under a United Nations mandate following the Armistice of 1918. To protect the Maronites from absorption in the Muslim population, France backed in the 1940s the creation of Lebanon as a separate political entity, becoming thereby the guarantor of Maronite identity.
68. Cited in Harrison, *France and Islam*, 53–54.
69. Mariot in Harrison, *France and Islam*, 58–59.
70. Governor-General E. Roume in Harrison, *France and Islam*, 43.
71. Harrison, *France and Islam*, 176.
72. Shakespeare, *Henry V*, Act IV, Scene 1.
73. W. H. Withrow, ed., *Methodist Magazine and Review* 56 (July–December 1902), 117.
74. Suret-Canale, "Touba in Guinea," 77.
75. Ibid., 76.
76. On the career of Blaise Diagne, see G. W. Johnson, *The Emergence of Black Politics in Senegal: The Struggle for Power in the Four Communes, 1900–1920* (Stanford, CA: Stanford University Press, 1971).
77. Suret-Canale, "Touba in Guinea," 77.
78. Marty, *L'Islam en Guinée*, 124–125.
79. Suret-Canale, "Touba in Guinea," 78.
80. Marty, *L'Islam en Guinée*, 128.
81. In 1977 the president issued a statement emphasizing the government's position on Islam. The ruling party, he declared, "is uncompromising in its insistence on serving the people." The party "will pursue its objective with revolutionary conviction." The Jakhanke must understand that the Revolution is not anti-Muslim because Islam supports the aims of the Revolution. "L'Islam au Service du Peuple," *Revue RDA* (October 1977). See Moustapha Diallo, *L'Islam et son influence sur la Société Djakanka de Touba (Gawal)*, Memoire de Diplome de Fin d'Etudes Superieures, Institut Polytechnique Gamal Abdel Nasser, Conakry, July 1980, 91.
82. The CD is titled *Wambara* (Stern's Africa), 1999. Listed on the National Geographic World Music site. Toumani Diabate of Mali in his CD *Djelika* dedicated a song to "Sankoun Djabi," in all likelihood the Sankoung Jabi of Macca-Kolibantang. All this shows the influence of the clerics in the popular imagination. *Djelika*, Hannibal Records, HNCD 1380, 1995.

Chapter 10

1. As pointed out with reference to Ibn Khaldun's theory of the culture of personal charisma versus institution-building, the phenomenon is not peculiar to sub-Saharan Africa. Reynold A. Nicholson, *A Literary History of the Arabs* (Cambridge, UK: Cambridge University Press, 1962), 440.
2. Paul Marty, *L'Islam en Guinée: Fouta Diallon* (Paris: E. Leroux, 1921), 133–134.

3. Ibid.
4. Ibid., 136.
5. Ibid., 137–137.
6. Ibid., 140–142.
7. Ibid., 111.
8. Paul Marty, "L'Islam en Mauritanie et au Sénégal," *Revue du Monde Musulman* 31 (1915–1916): 448–452.
9. J. Spencer Trimingham, *Islam in West Africa* (Oxford: Clarendon Press, 1959), 38.
10. Shaykh Abu Bakr Saidy Jallow, *Bughyat al-Sá'il wa Ghunyat al-'Aqil* ("The Desire of the Inquirer and the Wealth of the Wise") (Islamabad, Pakistan: Da'wah Academy, International Islamic University), 1992. The words cited are from the Foreword by Imam Abdoulie Jobe, Chief Imam of Banjul.
11. Marty, "L'Islam en Mauritanie," 456.
12. Ibid., 457.
13. Ibid.

Chapter 11

1. For a discussion of Islam and state in West Africa see J. Spencer Trimingham, *Islam in West Africa* (Oxford: Clarendon Press, 1959), 138–143.
2. J. M. Gray, *A History of the Gambia* (Cambridge, UK: Cambridge University Press, 1940; reprinted London: Frank Cass, 1966), 388, 388n.
3. 'Abd al-Qádir was taken prisoner to France where Louis Napoleon, who became Napoleon III, freed him on a state pension. He eventually moved to Damascus where, in 1860, following attacks instigated by local Ottoman authorities, he played a critical role in saving the lives of an estimated twelve thousand Christians, including the French consul and his staff. He died in Damascus in 1883, and in 1966, on the fourth anniversary of the country's independence after the bitter Algerian war, his remains were transferred to his home country; a national shrine was built in Constantine with a mosque bearing his name.
4. The reference is to Adullam mentioned in 1 Samuel 22:1–2 where the distressed, the discontented, and economic insolvents joined cause with David when he fled from Saul. "Adullamite" was the term originally applied to members of a dissident political group of Liberal British Members of Parliament who seceded from the governing party, causing defeat of its reform program.
5. The idea comes from John S. Galbraith, *Reluctant Empire: British Policy on the South African Frontier, 1834–1854* (Berkeley: University of California Press, 1963).
6. Gray, *History of the Gambia*, 338–339.
7. Examples of the colonial role in siding with Muslims in relations with non-Muslim Africans are given in Niels Kastfelt, *Religion and Politics in Nigeria: A Study in Middle Belt Christianity* (London: British Academic Press, 1994), 41–42, and in Andrew F. Barnes, "Evangelization Where It Is Not Wanted: Colonial Administrations and Missionaries in Northern Nigeria During the First Third of the Twentieth Century," *Journal of Religion in Africa* 25.4 (1995): 412–441. Similar colonial intervention is reported of German Togoland, where administrators sided with a local Muslim scholar who faced hostility from the chiefs. In 1902 the scholar in question struck a partnership with officials who maneuvered to install him as chief imam of Kete-Krachi and encouraged him to write down the customs and traditions of the resident Hausa community. L. Sanneh, *Translating the Message: The Missionary Impact on Culture* (Maryknoll, NY: Orbis Books, 2009), 158–159.
8. Gray, *History of the Gambia*, 389.
9. John D. Hargreaves, *A Life of Sir Samuel Lewis* (London: Oxford University Press, 1958).
10. David Robinson, *The Holy War of 'Umar Tal: The Western Sudan in the Mid-Nineteenth Century* (Oxford: Clarendon Press, 1985), 116–117.
11. See L. Sanneh, *Abolitionists Abroad: American Blacks and the Making of Modern West Africa* (Cambridge, MA: Harvard University Press, 2001), 122–123.

12. For an account of African religious life in Freetown see Michael Banton, *West African City: A Study of Tribal Life in Freetown* (London: Oxford University Press, 1957, reprinted 1969, 121–141.
13. Hargreaves, *Life of Sir Samuel Lewis*, 19.
14. The assimilationist policy was against giving any room to indigenous institutions, and it banned mother-tongue education. The appointment in 1940 of Félix Eboué as governor-general of French Equatorial Africa led to questions about the wisdom of the policy. One of the most famous colonial administrators, Eboué came from French Guiana. He championed decentralization of power to the colonies and support for African political institutions as symbols of African initiative. In a statement in November 1941, Eboué noted that a native policy must replace the policy of assimilation, and with it the notion that traditional political institutions are inert, immobile, fit only to be uprooted. "It is clear that custom changes and will change, and that we are not here to sterilize it by fixing it." Eboué died in 1944. Excerpt in Robert O. Collins, ed., *Western African History: Text and Readings* (New York: Marcus Wiener, 1990), 115–116.
15. Martin A. Klein, *Islam and Imperialism in Senegal: Sine-Saloum, 1847–1914* (Edinburgh, UK: Edinburgh University Press, 1968), 73; and Martin A. Klein, "The Moslem Revolution in 19th Century Senegambia," in *Boston Papers in African Studies*, edited by J. Butler (Boston: Boston University Publications, 1966).
16. Gray, *History of the Gambia*, 424; Charlotte Quinn, Mandingo Kingdoms of the Senegambia, 1972; Charlotte Quinn, "Maba Diakhou Ba: Scholar-Warrior of the Senegambia," *Ta'ríkh* 2.3 (1968): 1–12.
17. Gray, *History of the Gambia*, 428.
18. Frances Anne Leary, "The Role of the Mandinka in the Islamization of the Casamance," in *Papers on the Manding*, edited by C. T. Hodge (Bloomington: Indiana University Publications, 1971), 240. Leary documents examples of Jakhanke opposition to Fode Kaba but does not relate it to the pacifist theme of Jakhanke history.
19. Leary, "Islamization of the Casamance," 241.
20. On Musa Molo see Paul Marty, "L'Islam en Mauritanie et au Sénégal," *Revue du Monde Musulman* 31 (1915–1916): 448-452; Charlotte Quinn, "A Nineteenth Century Fulbé State," *Journal of African History* 12 (1971).
21. Gray, *History of the Gambia*, 452–453.
22. Cited in Gray, *History of the Gambia*, 452.
23. This prayer ritual was standard procedure for jihad leaders, all of whom employed it. "Before making a decision they went into retreat to receive guidance." J. Spencer Trimingham, *The Influence of Islam Upon Africa* (London: Longman, Green and Co, 1968), 84.
24. Henri Frey, *Campagnes dans le Haut-Sénégal et dans le Haut-Niger, 1885–1886* (Paris: Pion, 1888), 252, 253–254.
25. Alfred le Chatelier, *L'Islam dans l'Afrique occidentale* (Paris: G. Steinhell, 1899), 216.
26. Charles Monteil, *Les Khassonké* (Paris: E. Leroux, 1915), 374; Abdoulaye Bathily, "Mamadou-Lamine Daramé et la résistance anti-impérialiste dans le Haut-Sénégal (1885–87)," *Notes Africaines* 125 (1970): 22.
27. The military incidents are reported in detail in the French colonial archives in Paris, ANSOM, Sénégal, IV, 44d, *Affaire Zimmermann et les Serakolé*, Rapport ait à l'enquete ordonnée le 22 julliet, 1875.
28. Cited in Daniel Nyambarza, "Le marabout El-Hadj Mamadou-Lamine d'après les archives françaises," *Cahiers d'Ētudes Africaines* 11.1 (1969): 130.
29. Mervyn Hiskett, *The Course of Islam in Africa* (Edinburgh, UK: Edinburgh University Press, 1994), 113.
30. Le Chatelier, *L'Islam dans l'Afrique occidentale*, 218–219.
31. Frey, *Campagnes dans le Haut-Sénégal*, 210; A. Sabatié, *Le Sénégal* (St. Louis, Senegal: Imprimerie du Gouvernement, 1925), 214–215; Pierre Smith, "Les Diakhanké: Histoire d'une dispersion," *Bulletins et mémoires de la Société d'anthropologie de Paris*, Série 8, 11 (1965): 248.
32. Marty, "L'Islam en Mauritanie," 310–313.
33. Ibid., 317–318.

34. John D. Hargreaves, "The Tokolor Empire of Ségou and Its Relations With the French," in *Boston Papers in African Studies,* edited by J. Butler (Boston: Boston University Publications, 1966), 139.
35. Marty, "L'Islam en Mauritanie," 311.
36. Archives national section outré mer (ANSOM), Paris, *Mission 18, d'après Mission Galliéni 1886–87,* "Mission de Capitaine Martin en Bambouk."
37. "Les Diakhanké ne sont pas guerriers." ANSOM, "Mission de Capitaine Martin en Bambouk."
38. Smith, "Les Diakhanké," 256.
39. Ibid., 248–249.
40. L. Sanneh, *The Jakhanke Muslim Clerics: A Study of Islam in Senegambia* (Lanham, MD: University Press of America, 1989), 83–86.
41. There is a brief reference to al-Hajj Kemoring Jakhite discussing the possible origins of the ancient stone circles of the area, with comments on sources of Jakhanke scholarship. Florence Mahoney, "The Stone Circles of Senegambia," *Ta'ríkh* 2.2 (1968): 1–11.
42. Humphrey J. Fisher, "The Early Life and Pilgrimage of al-Hájj Muhammad al-Amín the Soninké (d. 1887)," *Journal of African History* 12.3 (1970): 51–69.
43. Gray, *History of the Gambia,* 448.
44. Gray, *History of the Gambia,* 449.
45. Muhammad Rabadan, *Mahometism Fully Explained (Written in Spanish and Arabic in the Year 1603 for the Instruction of the Moriscoes in Spain)*: Vol. 2., translated and edited by J. Morgan (London: E. Curll, W. Mears, and T. Payne, 1723–1725), 297f, 345f.
46. Richard W. Bulliet, "The Individual in Islamic Society," in *Religious Diversity and Human Rights,* edited by Irene Brown, J. Paul Martin, and Wayne L. Proudfoot (New York: Columbia University Press, 1996), 183.

Chapter 12

1. M. Hiskett, *The Sword of Truth: The Life and Times of the Shehu Usuman dan Fodio* (New York: Oxford University Press, 1973), 97. See also 'Abdullah b. Fudi, *Tazyín al-Waraqát* (Ibadan, Nigeria: Ibadan University Press, 1963), 121.
2. H. A. S. Johnson, *The Fulani Empire of Sokoto* (London: Oxford University Press, 1967), 178.
3. Hiskett, *Sword of Truth,* 107.
4. Ibid., 112. In his *Bayán Wujúb al-Hijra,* Dan Fodio devotes a chapter on the illegality of offering gifts to governors. 'Uthman Ibn Fudi, *Bayán Wujúb al-Hijra 'ala-l i'ibád,* edited and translated by F. H. El-Masri (Khartoum: Khartoum University Press 1979), 74–75.
5. Murray Last, *The Sokoto Caliphate* (London: Longmans, Green and Co.) 1967, 59.
6. Ibid., 208.
7. Hiskett, *Sword of Truth,* 110.
8. Dan Fodio writes: "The government of a country is the government of its King without question. If the King is a Muslim, his land is Muslim; if he is an Unbeliever, his land is a land of Unbelievers." Dan Fodio acknowledges the existence of scattered Muslim communities in Borno but says here as elsewhere that the exception proves the rule. He cites an authority to the effect that the sporadic presence of Muslims makes no difference to the common religious picture of Borno. "You should prefer the usual to the unusual; for the usual and the common is what we want to elucidate." Dan Fodio, *Tanbíh al-Ikhwán* ("The Admonition to the Brethren"), 1811. Excerpt in *Nigerian Perspectives: An Historical Anthology,* edited by Thomas Hodgkin (London: Oxford University Press, 1960), 192. The rule is repeated elsewhere: "the law of the country is the law of the ruler." Fudi, *Bayán,* 50, 50n, 55. But this claim, according to El-Masri, has no basis in Islam.
9. John Hunwick, "Sub-Saharan Africa and the Wider World of Islam: Historical and Contemporary Perspectives," *Journal of Religion in Africa* 26.3 (August 1996): 233.
10. According to the authorities, the believer who commits a mortal sin is still a believer; he may be regarded as impious or as a hypocrite but not, as the Khárijites would have it, an infidel. F. A. Klein, *The Religion of Islam* (London: Curzon Press, 1906; reprinted 1979), 44, 44n.

11. Jalal al-Din al-Suyuti, *As'ila wárida min al-Takrúr fi Shawwál 898*, edited and translated by J. O. Hunwick, in *African Perspectives: Papers in the History, Politics, and Economies of Africa Presented to Thomas Hodgkin*, edited by Christopher Allen and R. W. Johnson (Cambridge, UK: Cambridge University Press, 1970), 23, 27.
12. Cited in Reuben Levy, *The Social Structure of Islam*, 2d ed. (Cambridge, UK: Cambridge University Press, 1965), 213.
13. Subhí Mahmassaní, *Turáth al-khulafá' al-ráshidún fí al-fiqh wa al-qadá'* (Beirut: Dár al-'ilm li al-Maláyín, 1984), 229, cited in Abdullah Saeed, *Interpreting the Qur'an: Towards a Contemporary Approach* (Abingdon, UK: Routledge, 2006), 136.
14. "The al-Kánamí-Bello Correspondence," in *Nigerian Perspectives*, 201.
15. *Nigerian Perspectives*, 200.
16. Louis Brenner, "Muhammad al-Amin al-Kanimi and Religion and Politics in Bornu," in *Studies in West African Islam*: Vol. 1, *The Cultivators of Islam*, edited by John Ralph Willis (London: Frank Cass, 1979), 168.
17. Eusebius, *The History of the Church*, translated and edited by G. A. Williamson (Harmondsworth, UK: Penguin Books, 1965), 192.
18. Sir Thomas Arnold, *The Preaching of Islam: A History of the Propagation of the Muslim Faith* (New York: Scribner's, 1913), 414.
19. *Kitáb al-Imára* ("The Book of Government"), *Sáhíh* of Muslim.
20. *Nigerian Perspectives*, 201.
21. See Levy, *Social Structure of Islam*, 222.
22. Statement of Al-Azhar and intellectuals [on a] Bill of Rights, March 2012. Grand Sheik Ahmed al-Tayeb of al-Azhar University urged Muslim Brotherhood members to renounce violence and said his institution would resist political efforts to influence religious scholars, according to a translation by Egyptian newspaper *Al-Masry Al-Youm*. Oren Dorell, "Political Islam on the Defensive Across the Middle East," *USA Today*, August 21, 2013.
23. Ignaz Goldziher, *Introduction to Islamic Theology and Law*, translated by Andras Hamori and Ruth Hamori (Princeton, NJ: Princeton University Press, 1981), 55. Qur'an 2:185; 22:78.
24. Qur'an 18:103–104.
25. *Nigerian Perspectives*, 200.
26. John Ralph Willis, "Jihad fi sabil li-l'llah: Its Doctrinal Basis in Islam and Some Aspects of Its Evolution in Nineteenth-Century West Africa," *Journal of African History* 8.3 (1967): 395–415. On jihad in classical sources, see Majid Khaduri, *War and Peace in the Law of Islam* (Baltimore, MD: Johns Hopkins University Press, 1955).
27. The Qur'an supports pluralism and communities of difference: "O mankind, We have created you male and female, and appointed you races and tribes, that you may know one another" (Qur'an 49:13.).
28. H. A. R. Gibb, *Studies in the Civilization of Islam: Collected Essays*, edited by Stanford J. Shaw and William R. Polk (London: Routledge & Kegan Paul, 1962), 149.
29. This rule is one of the five principles of the Mu'tazilites, the Rationalists of Islam, who explained it as the use of the tongue, hand, and sword in maintaining justice and punishing wrong. Qur'an 3:100; Michael Cook, *Commanding Right and Forbidding Wrong in Islamic Thought* (Cambridge, UK: Cambridge University Press, 2000).
30. Stefan Reichmuth, "Islamic Education and Scholarship in Sub-Saharan Africa," in *The History of Islam in Africa*, edited by Nehemia Levtzion and Randall Pouwels (Athens: Ohio University Press, 2000), 420.
31. Al-Bakri, *Kitab al-Masalik* in *Corpus of Early Arabic for West African History*, translated by J. F. P. Hopkins, edited by N. Levtzion and J. F. P. Hopkins (Cambridge, UK: Cambridge University Press, 1981), 87.
32. N. Levtzion, "Islam in West African Politics: Accommodation and Tension Between the 'Ulamá' and the Political Authorities," *Cahiers d'études africaines* 71 (1978): 333–345.
33. Ibn Battuta, *Rihlah*, in *Corpus of Early Arabic Sources*, 289–290.
34. Ahmad Bábá, *Mi'ráj al-Su'úd Ahmad Bábá's Replies on Slavery*, edited and translated by John Hunwick and Fatima Harrak (Rabat: Institute of African Studies, University Mohammed V Souissi, 2000).

35. Ahmad Shafiq Bek, *Al-Riq fí'l-Islám*, excerpt in *The African Diaspora in the Mediterranean Lands of Islam*, edited by John Hunwick and Eve Troutt Powell (Princeton, NJ: Markus Wiener, 2002), 14.
36. Allan G. B. Fisher and Humphrey J. Fisher, *Slavery and Muslim Society in Africa: The Institution in Saharan and Sudanic Africa and the Trans-Saharan Trade* (New York: Anchor Books, 1972).
37. Ahmad b. Khalid al-Nasiri, a nineteenth-century Moroccan scholar, lamented "the indiscriminate enslavement of the people of the Sudan, and the importation of droves of them every year to be sold in the markets in town and country where men trade in them as one would trade in beasts. . . . People have become so inured to that, generation after generation, that many common folk believe that the reason for being enslaved according to the Holy Law is merely that a man should be black in color and come from those regions." *African Diaspora*, xx. Blyden appeals to religious sentiment when he quotes a Muslim African slavemaster. The slavemaster said that it is the case that the slave may be "nearer to God than his master, as was the case with the Children of Israel who, in their time, on account of the revelation granted to them, were superior to all other people; yet God gave them in service to Pharaoh, with all his arrogance and Heathenism." The master should, therefore, "seek from [the slave] with kindness what God has decreed to you of profit from him." Edward W. Blyden, *Christianity, Islam and the Negro Race* (London: 1887; reprinted Edinburgh, UK: Edinburgh University Press, 1969), 319–320. The issue of slaves and ex-slaves continued to rankle in Muslim society. Mauritania abolished slavery in 1981, but the practice continued unabated. A law making enslavement punishable with up to ten years in prison, introduced in 2007, has never been implemented. Anti-Slavery International, a human rights organization, reports on its website that some 600,000 people are estimated to be enslaved in Mauritania. *Mail & Guardian*, August 22, 2011. See also Mariella Villasante de Beauvais, ed., *Groupes serviles au Sahara: Approche comparative à partir du cas de arabophones de Mauritanie* (Paris: Centre National de Recherches Scientifique, 2000), and El-Arby Ould Saleck, *Les Haratins: Le paysage politique mauritanien* (Paris: L'Harmattan, 2003).
38. On this subject see Robert C. Davis, *Christian Slaves, Muslim Masters: White Slavery in the Mediterranean, The Barbary Coast, and Italy, 1500–1800* (London: Palgrave Macmillan, 2003), and Giles Milton, *White Gold: The Extraordinary Story of Thomas Pellow and Islam's One Million White Slaves* (New York: Farrar, Straus and Giroux, 2004). Eve Troutt Powell discusses the question of race and slavery in the Middle East in "The Silence of the Slaves," in *African Diaspora*, xxv–xxxvii.
39. Tertullian, *Apologia*, chap. 39.
40. Frederick D. Maurice, *The Religions of the World and Their Relations to Christianity* (London: Macmillan, 1886), 28.
41. Muhammad ibn Ali ibn Tabataba, *Al-Fakhri: On the Systems of Government and the Moslem Dynasties* [composed in 1301–1302], translated by C. E. J. Whitting (London: Luzac & Company, 1947), 14. The work is divided into two sections, the first concerned with statecraft and government and the second with dynasties and their succession.
42. Muhammad Qasim Zaman, *Modern Islamic Thought in a Radical Age: Religious Authority and Internal Criticism* (New York: Cambridge University Press, 2012), 52. Watt noted that the religious scholars of the caliphate were interested only in the advancement of their careers, and the resulting "perversion of scholarship and pursuit of wealth and celebrity [were] soul-destroying." W. Montgomery Watt, *Islamic Political Thought: The Basic Concepts* (Edinburgh, UK: Edinburgh University Press, 1968), 76.
43. Francis Robinson, "The British Empire and the Muslim World," in *The Oxford History of the British Empire: The Twentieth Century*, edited by Judith M. Brown and William Roger Louis (New York: Oxford University Press, 1999), 406.
44. Al-Ghazali, *Ayyuha al-walad*, in *Classical Foundations of Islamic Educational Thought*, edited by Bradley J. Cook and Fathi H. Malkawi (Provo, UT: Brigham Young University Press, 2010), 105.
45. Jamil M. Abun Nasr, *Muslim Communities of Grace: The Sufi Brotherhoods in the Islamic Religious Life*. New York: Columbia University Press, 2007), 56.

46. Cook, *Commanding Right*, 53.
47. Abun-Nasr, *Muslim Communities of Grace*, 35.
48. Afaf Lutfi al-Sayyid Marsot, "The Ulama of Cairo in the Eighteenth and Nineteenth Centuries," in *Scholars, Saints, and Sufis: Muslim Religious Institutions in the Middle East Since 1500*, edited by Nikki Keddie (Berkeley: University of California Press, 1972), 149.
49. L. Carl Brown, *Religion and State: The Muslim Approach to Politics* (New York: Columbia University Press, 2000), 3.
50. For an interesting discussion on the continuing vitality of legal reasoning in Islam, see Wael B. Hallaq, "Was the Gate of *Ijtihád* Closed?" *International Journal of Middle East Studies* 16 (1984): 3–41. It should be recognized that defending the right of *ijtihád* is quite different from having the capability to implement changes in the structure of law. Baber Johansen, *Contingency in a Sacred Law: Legal and Ethical Norms in the Muslim Fiqh* (Leiden: Brill, 1999), 447.
51. Ghislaine Lydon, *On Trans-Saharan Trails: Islamic Law, Trade Networks, and Cross-Cultural Exchange in Nineteenth Western Africa* (Cambridge, UK: Cambridge University Press, 2009).
52. Patricia Crone notes that, in contrast to the Western tradition, antinomian Sufis embarked on escape from religious authority rather than from the world. They wished to remove shackles, but only of the religious kind. While religious law was dispensable for salvation, "one could not live without law or government in the here and now." Patricia Crone, *God's Rule: Government and Islam, Six Centuries of Medieval Islamic Political Thought* (New York: Columbia University Press, 2004), 324.
53. Cook, *Commanding Right*, 459–460.
54. 'Abdullah dan Fodio, *Tazyín al-Waraqát*, 100, Arabic text 43.
55. Cook, *Commanding Right*, 8–9.
56. Ibid., 106, 106n.
57. Cook, *Commanding Right*, 112–113, 192. A modern Muslim scholar, S. Pervez Manzoor, argues that the nature of Shari'ah defies the temporal character of positive law. See discussion of his views in David L. Johnston, *Earth, Empire and Sacred Text: Muslims and Christians as Trustees of Creation* (London: Equinox, 2010), 389.
58. L. Sanneh, *The Jakhanke Muslim Clerics: A Study of Islam in Senegambia* (Lanham, MD: University Press of America, 1989), 17.
59. Maurice Delafosse, *Traditions Historiques et Légendaires de l'Afrique Occidental* (Paris: Comité de l'Afrique française, 1913).
60. Humphrey J. Fisher, "The Juggernaut's Apologia: Conversion to Islam in Black Africa," *Africa* 55.2 (1985): 157.
61. Bernard Lewis, *The Emergence of Modern Turkey*, 2d ed. (London: Oxford University Press, 1968), 405.
62. Zuesse makes a distinction between religions of structure and religions of salvation, arguing that religions of structure try to remove their members from relying on inner experience to focusing on symbols in this word, using constant repetition and dramatization achieve that end. Religions of salvation, on the other hand, "inculcate a type of concentration which systematically removes attention from sensory experience, and focuses it on internal processes of subjective thought and awareness." E. M. Zuesse, *Ritual Cosmos: The Sanctification of Life in an African Religion* (Athens: Ohio University Press, 1979), 8. The typology needs amending, certainly with respect to Islam, which has both a structural appeal and a salvific dimension.
63. Donal B. Cruise O'Brien, *The Mourides of Senegal: The Political and Economic Organization of an Islamic Brotherhood* (Oxford: Clarendon Press, 1971), 147–158.
64. A study of the life of a modern Sufi in North Africa may be taken as representative of the genre. Martin Lings, *A Moslem Saint of the Twentieth Century: Shaikh Ahmad al-'Alawí, His Spiritual Heritage and Legacy*, 3d ed. (Cambridge, UK: Islamic Texts Society, 1993). Dahiru Maigari, an anti-Sufi scholar of north Nigeria, published a work in 1981 attacking Sufi promises of rewards and denouncing Sufism as foreign to Islam. He said Sufism originated in Neoplatonism and in the teachings of the Upanishads. That line of attack draws its fire from theistic opposition to monism and seeks to define Sufism as alien

and illegitimate for Muslims. Muhammad Sani ‘Umar, “Sufism and Its Opponents in Nigeria: The Doctrinal and Intellectual Aspects,” *Islamic Mysticism Contested: Thirteen Centuries of Controversies and Polemics*, edited by in Frederick de Jong and Bernd Radtke (Leiden: Brill, 1999). Also Martin Klein, *Islam and Imperialism in Senegal: Sine-Saloum, 1847–1914* (Edinburgh, UK: Edinburgh University Press, 1968), 64.

65. Ivor Wilks, “Transmission of Islamic Learning in the Western Sudan,” in *Literacy in Traditional Societies*, edited by Jack Goody (Cambridge, UK: Cambridge University Press, 1968), 170.
66. Christopher Harrison, *France and Islam in West Africa* (Cambridge, UK: Cambridge University Press, 1988), 108.
67. Born Joseph-Desiré Mobutu, President Mobutu of Zaire (r. 1965–1997) changed his name to Mobutu Sese Seko Kuku Ngbendu Wa Za Banga when he launched a program of *l'authenticité* requiring the adoption of African names in place of Christian names.
68. Imam Malik, *Al-Muwatta* (Cambridge, UK: Cambridge University Press, 1982).
69. Trimingham, *Islam in West Africa* (Oxford: Clarendon Press, 1959), 82.
70. Blyden, *Christianity, Islam and the Negro Race*, 176.
71. Amadou Hampaté Bâ, *A Spirit of Tolerance: The Inspiring Life of Tierno Bokar* (Bloomington, IN: World Wisdom, 2008), 167–168.
72. Marion M. Preminger, *The Sands of Tamanrasset: The Story of Charles de Foucauld* (New York: Hawthorn, 1961), 55. Also Charles de Foucauld, *Meditations of a Hermit: The Spiritual Writings of Charles de Foucauld*, translated by C. Balfour (London: Burns & Oates, 1981). On the prayer life as a daily exercise in Islam, see Constance Padwick, *Muslim Devotions* (London: SPCK, 1961), and Marion Holmes Katz, *Prayer in Islamic Thought and Practice* (Cambridge, UK: Cambridge University Press, 2013).
73. Jefferson wrote: “Difference of opinion is advantageous in religion.” Thomas Jefferson, *Notes on the State of Virginia* (Paris, 1782).

Chapter 13

1. Under Jules Ferry (d. 1893), a statesman in the Third Republic and an aggressive promoter of French colonial expansion, France adopted an anticlerical policy that included a ban on teaching religion in public schools, coupled with the issue of decrees between1880 and 1881 that dissolved the Jesuits and other Catholic religious bodies and forbade their members to direct or teach in any educational establishment. As governor-general of French Equatorial Africa to which position he was appointed in 1940, Félix Eboué (d. 1944), born in French Guiana, reversed some of these policies. He referred to the principles of the French Revolution and the Napoleonic Code as prevailing norms of governance, saying, however, France should not impose them on the colonies. To enforce them, he argued, would require “the settling in the colony of a foreign race that would take the place of the indigenous tribes,” which was not in France's interest. Eboué, however, was writing in wartime conditions and died before the conclusion of the war. At the Brazzaville Conference of 1944, opened by General Charles de Gaule, Eboué's reform ideas were adopted, but the conference specifically rejected independence or self-government for the colonies. Nevertheless, rapid developments of postwar reconstruction and realignment brought about independence for the colonies in quick succession. Excerpt in Robert O. Collins, ed., *Western African History: Text and Readings* (New York: Marcus Wiener, 1990), 113–116. Jean-Louis Triaud, “Islam in Africa Under French Colonial Rule,” in *The History of Islam in Africa*, edited by Nehemia Levtzion and Randall L. Pouwels (Athens: Ohio University Press, 2000), 170. Triaud divides the French colonial attitude toward Islam into several phases, pointing out that administrators had changing perceptions of the religion. The French did not have “a Muslim policy,” strictly speaking. Their responses varied according to circumstance.
2. Bryan-Paul Frost and Jeffrey Sikkenga, eds., *History of American Political Thought* (Lanham, MD: Lexington Books, 2003), 142.
3. J. Spencer Trimingham, *Islam in West Africa* (Oxford: Clarendon Press, 1959), 206.
4. Brian J. Peterson, *Islamization From Below: The Making of Muslim Communities in Rural French Sudan, 1880–1960* (New Haven, CT: Yale University Press, 2011), 193.

5. Cited in E. I. J. Rosenthal, *Islam and the Modern National State* (Cambridge, UK: Cambridge University Press, 1965), 212.
6. Thomas Hodgkin, ed., *Nigerian Perspectives: An Historical Anthology* (London: Oxford University Press, 1960), 201.
7. The claim made in Michael Cook's book, *Commanding Right and Forbidding Wrong in Islamic Thought* (Cambridge, UK: Cambridge University Press, 2000), is that the ethical obligation to command right and forbid wrong is answered in a rigorous fashion in few cultures. The Islamic tradition, it is claimed, presents the most striking exception. The book set out to demonstrate that in just over seven hundred pages.
8. In one of his works, al-Ghazali defines *maṣlahah* "as the preservation of the *maqsúd* (objective) of the law (*Shar'*) which consists of five things: preservation of religion, of life, of reason, of descendants and of property. What assures the preservation of these five principles is *maṣlahah* and whatever fails to preserve them is *mafsada* (evil) and its removal is *maṣlahah*." *Muṣṭafá min 'ilm al-uṣúl*, 2 vols. (Baghdad: Muthanná), Vol. 1, 286–287, cited in David Johnston, "A Turn in the Epistemology and Hermeneutics of Twentieth Century Uṣúl al-Fiqh," *Islamic Law and Society* 11.2 (2004): 246. See also Muhammad Khalid Masud, *Muslim Jurists' Quest for the Normative Basis of Sharí'a*, (Leiden: International Institute for the Study of Islam in the Modern World, 2001).The idea of *maṣlahah* was prominent in discussions in early Islam in terms of the teaching that God's justice obliges Him to do what is best (*aslah*) for His creatures, a reasoning calculated to resolve the conflict between free will and predestination. Baber Johansen, *Contingency in a Sacred Law: Legal and Ethical Norms in the Muslim Fiqh* (Leiden: Brill, 1999), 18.
9. Reuben Levy, *The Social Structure of Islam*, 2d ed. (Cambridge, UK: Cambridge University Press, 1965), 168.
10. Muhammad Khalid Masud, *Muslim Jurists' Quest*, 208–209.
11. Patricia Crone, *God's Rule Government and Islam, Six Centuries of Medieval Islamic Political Thought* (New York: Columbia University Press, 2004), 394.
12. Ibid., 393.
13. Ibid., 394. Ibn Taymiyya's position on government has been described as that of a utilitarian moralist. He does not believe that power is inherently corrupt and so is unconvinced about the need or value of conscientious objection. Cook, *Commanding Right*, 156–157.
14. Crone, *God's Rule*.
15. Levy, *Social Structure of Islam*, 224–225.
16. Ibn Khaldun, *Al-Muqaddimah: An Introduction to History*, 3 vols., edited and translated by Franz Rosenthal (Princeton, NJ: Princeton University Press, 1967), Vol. 1, 450.
17. Cited in Nizam al-Mulk, *Siyásat-náma*, or *Siyar al-Mulúk*, translated by Hubert Drake, *The Book of Government or Rules for Kings* (London: Routledge & Kegan Paul, 1960), 63.
18. *Kawkab Waqqad* is the title of a Sufi manual written by Shaykh Mukhtár al-Kuntí. It was copied and distributed in printed version by al-Hajj Banfa. It is a work of Sufi initiation and devotion.
19. Karl Kautsky, *Communism in Central Europe in the Time of the Reformation* (London: Unwin, 1897), 187.
20. Lewis W. Spitz, *The Protestant Reformation, 1517–1559* (New York: Harper Torchbooks, 1987), 170.
21. Kautsky, *Communism in Central Europe*, 187.
22. Spitz, *The Protestant Reformation*, 169–174.
23. Christopher Hill, *The English Bible and the Seventeenth-Century Revolution* (London: Penguin Books, 1994), 35, 310–311.
24. John Woolman, *The Journal of John Woolman* (Chicago: Henry Regnery Company, 1950). The *Journal* is an autobiographical work covering the period 1720 to 1770. Similar to his heartfelt letter to a couple who were mourning the loss of their child, the *Journal* is a sensitive, gentle exploration of the interior life of Woolman and a moving presentation of the Quaker religious conscience on slavery. But it leaves unattended any necessary organizing social principle to oppose slavery. Personal individual urgency on the issue seems to find no parallel in a corresponding public social urgency. Woolman's papers were consulted at The Quaker Collection, Haverford College Library.

25. Albert C. Applegarth, *Quakers in Pennsylvania* (Baltimore, MD: Johns Hopkins University Press, 1892), cited in A. James Reichley, *Religion in American Public Life* (Washington, DC: Brookings Institution, 1985), 81.
26. Reichley, *Religion in American Public Life*, 81.
27. In his conflict with John Winthrop of Massachusetts, Williams returned to England to secure a charter for his new settlement at Providence, speaking of the need to erect a "hedge or wall of Separation between the Garden of the Church and the Wilderness of the world." More than 150 fifty years later, Jefferson used the phrase in his assurance to the Danbury Baptists in 1801 about maintaining "a wall of separation between Church and state."
28. Thomas G. Sanders, *Protestant Concepts of Church and State: Historical Backgrounds and Approaches for the Future* (New York: Doubleday, 1964), 132.
29. Hill contends that toleration was often materially motivated. Trading considerations, as Defoe notes in *Robinson Crusoe*, "necessitated tolerance not only of Catholics but also of Muslims and adherents of even more alien faiths." Christopher Hill, *The English Bible and the Seventeenth-Century Revolution* (London: Penguin Books, 1994), 412; Lord Acton, *Essays in The Study and Writing of History*: Vol. 2, edited by J. Rufus Fears (Indianapolis, IN: Liberty Classics, 1986), 516.
30. Lord Brooke Fulke Greville (d. 1628) declared in his poem, *Mustapha*,

    Yet when each of us in his own heart looks
    He finds the God there far unlike his books.

    For a study of Islamic literary influences in medieval English literature, see Dorothee Melitzki, *The Matter of Araby in Medieval England* (New Haven, CT: Yale University Press, 2005).
31. September 4, 1864, *Collected Works of Abraham Lincoln*, vol. 7.
32. Christopher Hill, *Change and Continuity in 17th Century England*, rev. ed. (New Haven, CT: Yale University Press, 1991), 114. The Yorkshire shepherd, William Dewsbury, declared in 1656 that conviction of the heart replaced Scripture as the tribunal of authority. It is only a small step from there to the sovereignty of human reason. Hill, *The English Bible*, 235–236. It is as such that Gerrard Winstanley preferred the word Reason to God. Hill, *The English Bible*, 309–310, 349–350, 417.
33. John Winthrop, "A Model Christian Charity (1630)," in *The Puritans in America: A Narrative Anthology*, edited by Alan Heimert and Andrew Delbanco (Cambridge, MA: Harvard University Press, 1985), 89; also Perry Miller and Thomas H. Johnson, eds., *The Puritans: A Sourcebook of their Writings*: Vol. I, rev. ed., (New York: Harper Torchbooks, 1963), 197. This anthology preserves the seventeenth-century language of the original texts.
34. Lord Acton, "The Political Causes of the American Revolution," in *Essays in the History of Liberty, Selected Writings:* Vol. 1, edited by J. Rufus Fears (Indianapolis, IN: Liberty Classics, 1986), 259–261. For an appraisal of Acton, see Irene Colton Brown, "The Historian as Philosopher," *History Today* 31 (October 1981): 49–53.
35. Hobbes asked rhetorically, "Had it not been much better that those seditious preachers, which were not perhaps 1,000, had been all killed before they had preached? It had been, I confess, a great massacre, but the killing of 100,000 [in the civil wars] is a greater." Cited in Paul S. Seaver, *The Puritan Lectureships: The Politics of Religious Dissent, 1560–1662* (Stanford, CA: Stanford University Press, 1970), 70.
36. William Barclay, *Thou Shalt Not Kill: War and the Church in the Past* (Nyack, NY: Fellowship of Reconciliation, 1966), 24.
37. Dennis Donoghue, "A Voluble Presence in the World," review of *Bertrand Russell: A Life* by Caroline Moorehead, *New York Times Book Review*, October 31, 1993. See also Bertrand Russell, *Autobiography* (London: Unwin, 1978), 666–670, 696, 707–724.
38. The words are those of the Puritan divine, Thomas Adams, cited in R. H. Tawney, *Religion and the Rise of Capitalism* (London: Penguin Books, 1926; reprinted 1962), 241.
39. Alexander David Russell and Abdullah al-Ma'mún Suhrawardy, eds. and trans., *First Steps in Muslim Jurisprudence* (London: Luzac, 1963), xiii.
40. Reynold A. Nicholson, *A Literary History of the Arabs* (Cambridge, UK: Cambridge University Press, 1962), 93–94.

41. Levy, *Social Structure of Islam*, 194. See also Qur'an 3:128.
42. Cited in Harrison, *France and Islam in West Africa* (Cambridge, UK: Cambridge University Press, 1988), 38.
43. For a discussion of *imán* see W. Montgomery Watt, *The Formative Period of Islamic Thought* (Oxford: Oneworld, 1998), 126–136.
44. Antinomian tendencies made their appearance in early Islam but were promptly nipped in the bud by the scholars. Ignaz Goldziher, *Introduction to Islamic Theology and Law*, translated by Andras Hamori and Ruth Hamori (Princeton, NJ: Princeton University Press, 1981), 59. In his *Al-Farq Bayna 'l-Firaq*, "On Divisions Among the Sects," Abú Mansúr 'Abd al-Qádir ibn Ṭáhir al-Baghdádí (d. 1037) describes groups in Islam that took an extreme position of faith as moral immunity because the saved can do no wrong. Such groups, however, soon jettisoned themselves from the religious mainstream. Translated as *Moslem Schisms and Sects: History of the Various Philosophic Systems Developed in Islam*, edited and translated by Kate Chambers Seelye (New York: Columbia University Press, 1920). The teaching is upheld according to the fifteenth-century commentary on *al-Mawáqif fi 'ilm al-kalám* of 'Abdu al-Dïn 'Abd al-Rahmán (d. 1355), 634, where it is reiterated that no Muslim can be declared an unbeliever or an infidel even if he or she opposes the truth. Al-Suyuti similarly condemns antinomianism (*ibahah*) as uncanonical. E. M. Sartain, ed., *Jalal al-Din al-Suyuti*: Vol. 1, *Biography and Background* (Cambridge, UK: Cambridge University Press, 1975), 36.
45. Jamil M. Abun Nasr, "Islam and Socialism in Africa," in *Christian and Islamic Contributions Towards Establishing Independent States in Africa South of the Sahara*, edited by Ernst J. Tetsch (Stuttgart: Institute for Foreign Cultural Relations, 1979), 121, 123. The law on property and inheritance was a major issue in the West African reform tradition. Mervyn Hiskett, "An Islamic Tradition of Reform in the Western Sudan from the Sixteenth to the Eighteenth Century," *Bulletin of the School of Oriental and African Studies* 25.3 (1962): 588.
46. See chapter 8 for more details on al-Maghílí.
47. Humphrey J. Fisher, "Slavery and Seclusion in Northern Nigeria: A Further Note," *Journal of African History* 32 (1991): 123–135, quote on 133.
48. It is relevant to the argument to point out that when he examined the importance of toleration Locke was constrained to contemplate its root in religion despite his own experience of religious upheavals around him. Removing religion, he argued, drains toleration of its value completely. If you deny the truth of God, Locke contends, "promises, covenants, and oaths, which are the bonds of society, can have no hold" on us. "The taking away of God, though not even in thought, dissolves all. Besides also, those that by their atheism undermine and destroy a religion, can have no pretense of religion whereupon to challenge the privilege of a toleration." John Locke, *A Letter Concerning Toleration, 1689* (Buffalo, NY: Prometheus Books, 1990), 64.
49. Kenneth Cragg argues that *faláh* cannot be compelled, for it is based on "moral persuasion." Kenneth Cragg, *Call of the Minaret*, 2d ed. (Maryknoll, NY: Orbis Books, 1985), 145.
50. Crone, *God's Rule*, 395. See also Ira M. Lapidus, "The Separation of State and Religion in the Development of Early Islamic Society," *International Journal of Middle East Studies* 6.4 (October 1975): 363–385.
51. Nicholson, *Literary History of the Arabs*, 438–439.
52. Abú Hátim al-Rází, *The Proofs of Prophecy*, translated and edited by Tarif Khalidi (Provo, UT: Brigham Young University Press, 2011), 178.
53. Bernard Lewis, *The Political Language of Islam* (Chicago: University of Chicago Press, 1988), 31.
54. Charles Taylor, "Modes of Secularism," in *Secularism and Its Critics*, edited by R. Bhargava (New Delhi: Oxford University Press, 1998), 35.
55. Asghar Ali Engineer, *The Islamic State* (New Delhi: Vikas Publishing House, 1994).
56. April 1803, *The Letters of Thomas Jefferson, 1743–1826*.
57. Cited in Albert Hourani, *Arabic Thought in the Liberal Age, 1798–1939* (London: Oxford University Press, 1970), 19.
58. Griffel writes that although he adopted the philosophical method, al-Ghazali supports the view that revelation gives fuller knowledge than reason. Frank Griffel, *Al-Ghazali's Philosophical Theology* (New York: Oxford University Press, 2009), 116.

59. Ibn Khaldun, *An Arab Philosophy of History: Selections from the Prologomena of Ibn Khaldun of Tunis (1332–1406)*, edited and translated by Charles Issawi (London: John Murray, 1950), 100.
60. George J. Holyoake, *The Principles of Secularis* (London: Austin & Co., 1870), 11. The cause is taken up in Olivier Roy, *Holy Ignorance: When Religion and Culture Part Ways* (New York: Columbia University Press, 2010).
61. Cook, *Commanding Right*, 155, 157.
62. Hourani, *Arabic Thought*, 18.
63. A verse attributed to Abú al-'Atáhiyah and cited by Ibn Khaldún, *Al-Muqaddimah:* Vol 1, 427.
64. 'Abd al-Rahmán al-Sa'dí, *Ta'ríkh al-Fattásh*, edited with text and translation by O. Houdas (Paris: Librairie d'Amerique et d'Orient, Adrien Maisonneuve, 1964), Ar. text, 44, tr. 82–83.
65. J. O. Hunwick, ed. and trans. *Timbuktu and the Songhay Empire: Al-Sa'dí's Ta'ríkh al-Súdán Down to 1613*, translation of 'Abd al-Rahmán Sa'dí's *Ta'rikh al-Súdán* (Leiden: Brill, 1999), 95.
66. It is pertinent to the issue to note that one scholar whom Sunni 'Alí treated well refrained from speaking ill of him after his death, preferring instead neither to praise nor to blame him. The scholar's "clear impartiality raised him high in the estimation of the jurist Abú al-Barakát Mahmúd," *Timbuktu and the Songhay Empire*, 94.
67. '*Timbuktu and the Songhay Empire*, 105. Hunwick has pointed out that it was the 'Abbasid caliph of Cairo who appointed Askiya Muhammad as his deputy for the "lands of Takrúr." It was in Cairo that Askiya Muhammad met al-Suyútí, the Egyptian jurist, whose counsel he sought.
68. John Hunwick, "Religion and State in the Songhay Empire, 1464–1491," in *Islam in Tropical Africa*, edited by I. M. Lewis (Bloomington: Indiana University Press, 1980), 138. See also Charlotte Blum and Humphrey J. Fisher, "Love for Three Oranges, or, The *Askiya's* Dilemma: The *Askiya*, al-Maghili and Timbuktu, c. 1500," *Journal of African History* 34.1 (1993): 65–91.
69. Elias N. Saad, *Social History of Timbuktu: The Role of Muslim Scholars and Notables, 1400–1900* (Cambridge, UK: Cambridge University Press, 1983), 232.
70. David Potter, *Prophets and Emperors: Human and Divine Authority from Augustus to Theodosius* (Cambridge, MA: Harvard University Press, 1994).
71. Ibn Khaldun, *Al-Muqaddimah:* Vol. 1, 382f.
72. Al-Ghazali, "Ayyuha al-walad," in *Classical Foundations of Islamic Educational Thought*, edited by Bradley J. Cook and Fathi H. Malkawi (Provo, UT: Brigham Young University Press, 2010), 105.

Chapter 14

1. When in 1910 Morocco was facing the prospect of French military occupation, a leading jurist, al-Mahdī al-Wazzānī (1849–1923), undertook a massive eleven-volume compilation of Maliki fatwas, called *al-Mi'yār al-jadīd* ("The New Standard") as a bulwark against colonial usurpation of Morocco's Islamic heritage. As a comprehensive legal digest the *Mi'yār* provides ethical rules and guidelines for Muslim society undergoing rapid social change. Etty Terem, "Redefining Islamic Tradition: Legal Interpretation as a Medium for Innovation in the Making of Modern Morocco," *Islamic Law and Society* 20.4 (2013): 425–475.
2. Cited in Christopher Harrison, *France and Islam in West Africa, 1860–1960* (Cambridge, UK: Cambridge University Press, 1988), 119.
3. Brian J. Peterson, *Islamization From Below: The Making of Muslim Communities in Rural French Sudan, 1880–1960* (New Haven, CT: Yale University Press, 2011), 76.
4. Alhaji Sir Ahmadu Bello, *My Life* (Cambridge, UK: Cambridge University Press, 1962), 31.
5. Michael Banton, *West African City: A Study of Tribal Life in Freetown* (London: Oxford University Press, 1957, reprinted 1969), 119.
6. For a study of this theme see Peterson, *Islamization From Below*. Peterson's point seems valid that one of the transformations taking place in Islam under colonial rule in the area of his study was that it went quietist and jihad-averse, though that did not mean the end of

anti-Muslim sentiment among disparate populations. It should be stressed also that rural Islam never lost its hold in Muslim Africa. For a summary of the historical evidence, see Nehemia Levtzion, "Rural and Urban Islam in West Africa: An Introductory Essay," in *Rural and Urban Islam in West Africa*, edited by Nehemia Levtzion and Humphrey J. Fisher (Boulder, CO: Lynne Rienner, 1987), 1–20.

7. Rudolph Peters, *Islam and Colonialism: The Doctrine of Jihad in Modern History* (The Hague: Mouton, 1979), 150. Also see my review under the same title: L. Sanneh, *Journal of Religion in Africa* 12.1 (1981): 77.
8. Thomas Hodgkin, *African Political Parties* (London: Penguin Books, 1961), 165.
9. Madeira Keita, "The Single Party in Africa," *Présence Africaine* 30 (1960): 35.
10. Muhammad Saïd al-Ashmawy, *Islam and the Political Order* (Washington, DC: Council for Research in Values and Philosophy, 1994), 76. The work was originally published in Arabic as *Al-Islám al-siyásí* (Cairo: Dár Síná, 1987).
11. Mervyn Hiskett, *The Course of Islam in Africa* (Edinburgh, UK: Edinburgh University Press, 1994), 115.
12. This echoes what Teilhad de Chardin said concerning the stages of spirituality: "We are not human beings having a spiritual experience. We are spiritual beings having a human experience."
13. Léopold Sédar Senghor, "West Africa in Evolution," in *Africa: A Foreign Affairs Reader*, edited by Philip W. Quigg (New York: Praeger, 1964), 289–290.
14. For a study of the thought of Mamadou Dia and Leopold Sedar Senghor, see Kenneth Cragg, *The Pen and the Faith: Eight Modern Muslim Writers and the Qur'an* (London: Allen & Unwin, 1985), 32–52.
15. J. Spencer Trimingham, *Islam in West Africa* (Oxford: Clarendon Press, 1959), 204–205.
16. Hiskett, *The Course of Islam*, 116.
17. Cited in Haroun al-Rashid Adamu, *The North and Nigerian Unity: Some Reflections on the Political, Social and Educational Problems of Northern Nigeria* (Lagos: Daily Times, 1973), 33. Adamu was the Political editor of the *Daily Times* newspaper.
18. Peters, *Islam and Colonialism*, 160.
19. Gilles Kepel, *Jihad: The Trail of Political Islam* (Cambridge, MA: Belknap Press of Harvard University Press, 2002), 362.
20. Khaled Abou El Fadl, "Islam and the Challenge of Democracy," *The Boston Review of Books* (April/May 2003), 6–12, quote on 8.
21. El Fadl, "Islam and the Challenge of Democracy," 8.
22. Ibid., 8.
23. Bassam Tibi, *Islam and the Cultural Accommodation of Social Change* (Boulder, CO: Westview Press, 1990).
24. Robert Rutland, ed., *The Papers of James Madison* (Chicago: University of Chicago Press, 1973), Vol. VIII, June 20, 1785, 299.
25. Alexis de Tocqueville, *Democracy in America* (London: Everyman's Library, 1994), 307.
26. Alhaji Junaidu, "The Relevance of the University to our Society," Speech of Acceptance, Abdullahi Bayero University, Zaria, Nigeria, 1972. Published in *Nigerian Journal of Islam*, 2.2 (June 1972–June, 1974): 55–58.
27. Ibid., 57.
28. James Piscatori, *Islam, Islamists, and the Electoral Principle in the Middle East* (Leiden: International Institute for the Study of Islam in the Modern World, 2000), 20–21.
29. Imam Muhammad Ashafa and Pastor James Wuye launched in 1995 a reconciliation campaign in Nigeria following violent civil upheavals in their communities. They were armed militia leaders at strife with each other before they decided to seek forgiveness and reconciliation. They assumed international recognition and were invited to visit the Middle East and elsewhere spreading their message of forgiveness and reconciliation. A DVD was produced and distributed under the auspices of the United States Institute of Peace under the title of *The Imam and the Pastor*, available on YouTube.
30. I. M. Lewis, ed., *Islam in Tropical Africa* (Bloomington: Indiana University Press, 1980), 91.
31. Sir Thomas Arnold, *The Preaching of Islam: A History of the Propagation of the Muslim Faith*, 2nd rev. ed. (New York: Scribner's Sons, 1913), 426. Translated into Arabic as *Da'wah ila*

al-Islām: baḥth fī tārīkh nashr al-'aqīdah al-Islāmīyah/ta'līf Tūmās W. Arnold; tarjamahu ilá al-'Arabīyah wa-'allaqa 'alayhi Ḥasan Ibrāhīm Ḥasan, 'Abd al-Majīd 'Ābidīn, Ismā'īl al-Nah (Al-Qāhirah: Maktabat al-Nahḍah al-Miṣrīyah, 1970).

32. Interview, *This Week*, April 6, 1987. This condemnation of those 'ulamá who are under the thumb of temporal rulers is a well-rehearsed one in the literature. Al-Ghazali and al-Suyúti have both mounted attacks on religious scholars who ingratiate themselves with rulers, a reflection of how widespread the practice was but also how irregular it felt.
33. Report in *Quality* (Lagos, October 1987) and cited in Simeon Ilesanmi, *Religious Pluralism and the Nigerian State* (Athens, OH: Center for International Studies, 1997), 186. The statement echoes a hadith that says that "One day of fighting is of greater value with God than fasting a whole month" (*ribát yawm fí sabíl li-lláh khayrun min siyám shahri*).
34. Umar M. Birai, "Islamic Tajdid and the Political Process in Nigeria," in *Fundamentalism and the State: Remaking Polities, Economies, and Militance*, edited by Martin E. Marty and R. Scott Appleby (Chicago: Chicago University Press, 1993), 190. See also Abdul-Fattah Olayiwola, *Islam in Nigeria: One Crescent, Many Voices* (Lagos, Nigeria: Sakirabe Publishers, 2007): 38, 95.
35. Ousmane Kane has examined the reformist groups in north Nigeria and their ideological roots. The agenda of these groups shows they are trying to deal with a fast-changing modern situation. Ousmane Kane, *Muslim Modernity in Postcolonial Nigeria: A Study of the Society for the Removal of Innovation and Reinstatement of Tradition* (Leiden: Brill, 2003), 69–103; also Ousmane Kane, "Izala: The Rise of Muslim Reformism in Northern Nigeria," in *Accounting for "Fundamentalisms": The Dynamic Character of Movements*, edited by Martin Marty and R. Scott-Appleby (Chicago: University of Chicago Press, 1994), 490–512.
36. Karl Maier, *This House Has Fallen: Nigeria in Crisis* (London: Penguin Books, 2000), 178.
37. *The Guardian*, January 8, 2002.
38. *Christian Science Monitor*, February 22, 2001.
39. Johannes Harnischfeger, *Democratization and Islamic Law: The Sharia Conflict in Nigeria* (Frankfurt: Campus Verlag, 2008), 197–220, gives a summary of differences on the Shari'ah issue among Muslims.
40. Alcohol addiction had become a serious social problem in the Delta region of Nigeria by the first decade of the twentieth century. A Nigerian Christian charismatic leader, Garrick Sokare Braide (d. 1918), along with other Christian leaders, led a campaign against alcohol, and annual consumption, estimated at nearly 3 million gallons of gin and rum, fell sharply as a result. Braide was arraigned and charged with economic sabotage. The dramatic fall in excise revenue from the alcohol tax created a huge shortfall in government revenues. Godwin Tasie, *Christian Missionary Enterprise in the Niger Delta, 1864–1918* (Leiden: Brill, 1978), 188.

BIBLIOGRAPHY

Abraham, R. C. *Dictionary of the Hausa Language*. 2d ed. London: University of London Press, 1962.

Abuja, J. Bala. "Koranic and Modern Law Teaching in Hausaland." *Nigeria* 37 (1951), 25–28.

Acton, Lord. "The Study of History," in *Essays in the Study of and Writing of History*. Edited by J. Rufus Fears. Indianapolis: Liberty Classics, 1986.

Acton, Lord. "The Political Causes of the American Revolution." In *Essays in the History of Liberty, Selected Writings*: Vol. I. Edited by J. Rufus Fears. Indianapolis: Liberty Classics, 1986.

Adamu, Haroun al-Rashid. *The North and Nigerian Unity: Some Reflections on the Political, Social and Educational Problems of Northern Nigeria*. Lagos: Daily Times, 1973.

Addoun, Yacine Daddi, and Paul Lovejoy. "The Arabic Manuscript of Muhammad Kaba Saghanughu of Jamaica, c. 1820." In *Creole Concerns: Essays in Honour of Kamau Brathwaite*. Edited by Annie Paul. Kingston: University of the West Indies Press, 2007.

Adeleye, Rowland Aderemi. *Power and Diplomacy in Northern Nigeria, 1804–1906*. London: Longman, 1971.

Ahmad, Imad A. "Islam and Freedom." *Religion and Liberty* 3.5.

Alao, Nurudeen. "Education in Islam: The Challenge of Numbers, Breadth and Quality." In *Islam in Africa: Proceedings of the Islam in Africa Conference*. Edited by Nura Alkali, Adamu Adamu, Awwal Yadudu, Rashid Motem, and Haruna Salihi. Ibadan, Nigeria: Spectrum Books, 1993.

Alharazim, M. Saif'ud Deen. "The Origin and Progress of Islam in Sierra Leone." *Sierra Leone Studies*, Old Series, 21 (1939).

Aminu, Jibril. "Towards a Strategy for Education and Development in Africa." In *Islam in Africa: Proceedings of the Islam in Africa Conference*. Edited by Nura Alkali, Adamu Adamu, Awwal Yadudu, Rashid Motem, and Haruna Salihi. Ibadan, Nigeria: Spectrum Books, 1993.

Anderson, Benjamin, and Edward W. Blyden. *Narrative of a Journey to Musardu, the Capital of the Western Mandingoes, With Appendix to Benjamin Anderson's Journey to Musadu: An Exact Facsimile of a Letter from the King of Musadu to the President of Liberia, Written by a Young Mandingo, at Musadu, in Arabic, in the Latter Part of 1868*. New York: Lithographing, Engraving & Printing Co., 1870; reprinted with introduction by Humphrey J. Fisher, London: Frank Cass, 1971.

Anderson, J. N. D. *Islamic Law in Africa*. London: H. M. Stationery Office, 1954; reprinted London: Frank Cass, 1970.

———. "Modernization: Islamic Law." In *Northern Africa: Islam and Modernization*. Edited by Michael Brett. London: Routledge, 1973.

Applegarth, Albert C. *Quakers in Pennsylvania.* Baltimore, MD: Johns Hopkins University Press, 1892.

Archives Féderales de Dakar. 7 G 99, Dossier no. 1. "Affaire Tierno Aliou ou le Oualy de Goumba." 1910–1912.

———. Dossier no. 170. "Administrative Report of Kindia." April 19, 1911.

Arcin, André. *Histoire de la Guinée Française.* Paris: A. Challamel, 1911.

Arnaud, Robert. "L'Islam et la politique musulmane française en Afrique occidentale française suivi de la singulière légende des Soninkés." *Bulletin du Comité d'Afrique Française, Renseignements Coloniaux* (1911).

Arnett, E. J. *The Rise of Sokoto Fulani.* Lagos, 1922.

Arnold, Sir Thomas. *The Preaching of Islam: A History of the Propagation of the Muslim Faith.* New York: Scribner's, 1913.

Asad, M. *Principles of State and Government in Islam.* Gibraltar: Dar al-Andalus, 1980.

'Aṭṭár, Faríd al-Dín. *Tadhkírat al-Awliyá (Memorial of Saints)*: Vol. II. Edited and translated by Reynold A. Nicholson. Leiden: Brill, 1905–1907, 8.

Azmeh, Aziz al-. *Ibn Khaldun: An Essay in Interpretation.* London: Frank Cass, 1982.

Azurara, Gomes Eanes de. *The Chronicle of the Discovery and Conquest of Guinea.* 2 vols. London: Hakluyt Society, 1896, 1899; reprinted New York: Burt Franklin, 1963.

Bâ, Amadou Hampaté. *A Spirit of Tolerance: The Inspiring Life of Tierno Bokar.* Bloomington, IN: World Wisdom, 2008.

Bâ, Amadou Hampaté, and J. Daget. *L'Empire Peuhl du Macina.* Paris: Mouton, 1962.

Bábá, Ahmad. *Mi'ráj al-Su'úd, Ahmad Bábá's Replies on Slavery.* Edited and translated by John O. Hunwick and Fatima Harrak. Rabat: Institute of African Studies, University Mohammed V Souissi, 2000.

Baghdádí, Abú Mansúr 'Abd al-Qádir ibn Ṭáhir al-. *Moslem Schisms and Sects: History of the Various Philosophic Systems Developed in Islam.* Edited and translated by Kate Chambers Seelye. New York: Columbia University Press, 1920.

Baillie, Neil B. E. *A Digest of Muhammadan Law.* Lahore, Pakistan: Premier Book House, 1974.

Bakri, al-. "Kitab al-Masalik." In *Corpus of Early Arabic Sources for West African History.* Translated by J. F. P. Hopkins. Edited by N. Levtzion and J. F. P. Hopkins. Cambridge, UK: Cambridge University Press, 1981.

Balogun, Isma'íl A. B., trans. and ed. *The Life and Works of 'Uthmán dan Fodio.* Lagos: Islamic Publications Bureau, 1975.

Banton, Michael, *West African City: A Study of Tribal Life in Freetown.* London: Oxford University Press, 1957; reprinted 1969.

Barakatullah, Mohammad, *The Khilafat.* London: Luzac, 1924.

Barclay, William. *Thou Shalt Not Kill: War and the Church in the Past.* Nyak, NY: Fellowship of Reconciliation, 1966.

Barot, Louis Joseph. *Guide pratique de l'Européen dans l'Afrique Occidentale a l'usage des militaries, fonctionnaires, commerçants, colons, & tourists.* Paris: Flammarion, 1902.

Barry, Boubacar. *Senegambia and the Atlantic Slave Trade.* Cambridge, UK: Cambridge University Press, 1998.

———. "Senegambia From the Sixteenth to the Eighteenth Century: Evolution of the Wolof, Serer, and Tukulor." In *UNESCO General History of Africa:* Vol. 5. Berkeley: University of California Press, 1992.

Bathily, Abdoulaye. "A Discussion of the Traditions of Wagadu, With Some Reference to Ancient Ghana, Including a Review of Oral Accounts, Arabic Sources and Archeological Evidence." *Bulletin de l'Institut Française de l'Afrique Noire* 37 (1975): 1–94.

———. "Mamadou-Lamine Daramé et la résistance anti-impérialiste dans le Haut-Sénégal (1885–87)." *Notes Africaines* 125 (1970): 20–32.

Batran, Aziz A. "The Kunta, Sidi Mukhar al-Kunti, and the Office of Shaykh al-Ṭaríqa al-Qádiriyya." In *Studies in West African Islamic History:* Vol. I, *The Cultivators of Islam.* Edited by John Ralph Willis. London: Frank Cass, 1979.

Battuta, Ibn. *Journey*. In *Corpus of Early Arabic Sources for West African History*. Translated by J. F. P. Hopkins. Edited by N. Levtzion and J. F. P. Hopkins. Cambridge, UK: Cambridge University Press, 1981.

———. *Travels in Africa and Asia, 1325–1354*. Translated and edited by H. A. R. Gibb. London: Routledge & Kegan Paul, 1929.

Bayol, Jean. *Voyage en Sénégambie: Haut-Niger, Bambouck, Fouta Djallon et Grand-Bélédougou, 1880–1885*. Paris: Baudoin, 1888.

Becker, C. H. *Christianity and Islam*. New York: Harper, 1909.

Beeston, A. F. L. *Samples of Arabic Prose in Its Historical Development*. Oxford: Oxford University Press, 1977.

Bek, Ahmad Shafiq. "Al-Riq fi'l-Islám" [Excerpt]. In *The African Diaspora in the Mediterranean Lands of Islam*. Edited by John Hunwick and Eve Troutt Powell. Princeton, NY: Markus Wiener, 2002.

Bello, Alhaji Sir Ahmadu. *My Life*. Cambridge, UK: Cambridge University Press, 1962.

Bello, Muhammad. *Infáq al-Maysúr*. Edited by C. E. J. Whitting. London: Luzac & Co., 1957.

———. *Uṣúl al-Siyásah*. Edited and translated by B. G. Martin. In *Aspects of West African Islam*. Edited by Daniel F. McCall and Norman R. Bennett. Boston: African Studies Center, Boston University, 1971.

Benjamin, Thomas. *The Atlantic World: Europeans, Africans, Indians and Their Shared History, 1400–1900*. New York: Cambridge University Press, 2009.

Berque, Jacques. *Les Nawāzil el muzāra'a du Mi'yār Al Wazzānī: Étude et traduction*. Rabat: Felix Moncho, 1940.

———. "Ville et univesité: apercu sur l'histoire de l'ecole de Fès." *Revue Historique de Droit Française et Étranger* 27 (1949).

Bickford-Smith, Vivian. "Meanings of Freedom: Social Position and Identity Among Ex-Salves and Their Descendants in Cape Town, 1875–1910." In *Breaking the Chains*. Edited by Nigel Worden and Clifton Crais. Johannesburg: Witwatersrand University Press, 1994.

Birai, Umar M. "Islamic Tajdid and the Political Process in Nigeria." In *Fundamentalism and the State: Remaking Politics, Economies, and Militance*. Edited by Martin E. Marty and R. Scott Appleby. Chicago: Chicago University Press, 1993.

Birks, J. S. *Across the Savannas to Mecca: The Overland Pilgrimage Routes from West Africa*. London: Christopher Hurst, 1978.

Bivar, A. D. H. "The *Wathíqat Ahl al-Súdán*: A Manifesto of the Fulani Jihád." *The Journal of African History* 2 (1961): 235–243.

Bivar, A. D. H., and Mervyn Hiskett. "The Arabic Literature of Nigeria to 1804: A Provisional Account." *Bulletin of the School of Oriental and African Studies* 25 (1962).

Blake, J. W. *Europeans in West Africa, 1450–1560*. London: Hakluyt Society, 1942.

Blasdell, R. A. "The Use of the Drum for Mosque Services." *The Muslim World* 30 (1940): 41–45.

Blasdoe, C. H., and K. M. Robey. "Arabic Literacy and Secrecy Among the Mende of Sierra Leone." *Man* 21 (1986): 202–226.

Blum, Charlotte, and Humphrey J. Fisher. "Love for Three Oranges, or, The *Askiya's* Dilemma: The *Askiya*, al-Maghili and Timbuktu, c. 1500." *The Journal of African History* 34.1 (1993): 65–91.

Blyden, Edward W. *Christianity, Islam and the Negro Race*. London: 1887; reprinted Edinburgh, UK: Edinburgh University Press, 1969.

———. "The Koran in Africa." *Journal of the African Society* 4 (January 1905).

Bocardé, B. "Notes sur la Guinée portugaise ou Sénégambie méridionale." *Bulletin de la Société de Géographie*, Séries 3, 12 (1849): 265–350.

Boulégue, Jean. "Contribution à la chronologie du royaume du Saloum." *Bulletin de l'Institut Fondamental d'Afrique Noire*, Séries B, 28 (1966): 657–662.

———. *La Sénégambie du milieu du XVe siècle et début du XVIIe siècle*. Unpublished thesis. University of Paris, 1969.

Bovill, E. W. *The Golden Trade of the Moors: West African Kingdoms in the Fourteenth Century*. London: Oxford University Press, 1958.

———, ed. *Mission to the Niger:* Vol. IV, *The Bornu Missio, 1822–25*. London: Hakluyt Society, 1966.

Boxer, C. R. *Four Centuries of Portuguese Exploration, 1415–1825: A Succinct Survey*. Johannesburg: Witwatersrand University Press, 1965.

Braudel, Fernand. *Mediterranean and the Mediterranean World in the Age of Philip II*. Translated by Sian Reynolds. New York: Harper & Row, 1972.

Bravmann, René A. "A Fragment of Paradise." *The Muslim World* 78 (1988): 29–37.

———. *Islam and Tribal Art in West Africa*. Cambridge, UK: Cambridge University Press, 1974.

Brenner, Louis. "Muhammad al-Amin al-Kanimi and Religion and Politics in Bornu." In *Studies in West African Islam:* Vol. 1, *The Cultivators of Islam*. Edited by John Ralph Willis. London: Frank Cass, 1979.

Brenner, Louis, and M. Last. "Role of Language in West African Islam." *Africa* 55.4 (1985): 432–446.

Brett, Michael. "Islam and Trade in the *Bilád al-Súdán*, Tenth–Eleventh Century A.D." *The Journal of African History* 24.4 (1983), 431–440.

———. "Morocco and the Ottomans: The Sixteenth Century in North Africa." *The Journal of African History* 25 (1984): 331–341.

Brett, Michael, and Elizabeth Fentress. *The Berbers*. Malden, MA: Blackwell, 1996.

Brévié, Jules. *L'Islamisme contre "naturisme" au Soudan français: Essai de psychologie politique coloniale*. Paris: Ernest Leroux, 1923.

Brown, Godfrey N., and Mervyn Hiskett, eds. *Conflict and Harmony in Education in Tropical Africa*. London: Allen & Unwin, 1976.

Brown, Irene Colton. "The Historian as Philosopher." *History Today* 31 (1981): 49–53.

Bulliet, Richard W. "The Individual in Islamic Society." In *Religious Diversity and Human Rights*. Edited by Irene Brown, J. Paul Martin, and Wayne L. Proudfoot. New York: Columbia University Press, 1996.

Burney, C. B. M. *The Stone Age of Northern Africa*. Harmondsworth, UK: Penguin Books, 1960.

Bury, J. B. *The Ancient Greek Historians*. Harvard Lane Lectures. London: Macmillan, 1908; reprinted New York: Dover, 1958.

Callaghy, Thomas. *The State–Society Struggle: Zaire in Comparative Perspective*. New York: Columbia University Press, 1984.

Chatelier, Alfred le. *L'Islam dans l'Afrique Occidentale*. Paris: G. Steinhell, 1899.

Christellow, Allan. *Muslim Law Courts and the French Colonial State in Algeria*. Princeton, NJ: Princeton University Press, 1985.

Clapperton, Hugh. *Journal of a Second Expedition into the Interior of Africa From the Bight of Benin to Soccatoo*. London: John Murray, 1829.

Clifford, T. N., and I. G. Gass, eds. *African Magmatism and Tectonics*. Edinburgh, UK: Oliver & Boyd, 1970.

Colley, Linda. *Captives: Britain, Empire, and the World, 1600–1850*. New York: Anchor Books, 2002.

Cook, Bradley J., and Fathi H. Malkawi, eds. *Classical Foundations of Islamic Educational Thought*. Provo, UT: Brigham Young University Press, 2010.

Cook, Michael. *Commanding Right and Forbidding Wrong in Islamic Thought*. Cambridge, UK: Cambridge University Press, 2000.

Cooper, Frederick. "The Problem of Slavery in African Studies." *The Journal of African History* 20.1 (1979): 103–125.

Coulson, N. J. *A History of Islamic Law*. Edinburgh, UK: Edinburgh University Press, 1964.

Cragg, Kenneth. *Call of the Minaret*. Maryknoll, NY: Orbis Books, 1985.

———. *Counsels in Contemporary Islam*. Edinburgh, UK: Edinburgh University Press, 1965.

Critchfield, Richard. *Shahhat: An Egyptian*. Syracuse, NY: Syracuse University Press, 1978.

Crone, G. R., ed. and trans. *The Voyages of Cadamosto and Other Documents on Western Africa in the Second Half of the Fifteenth Century*. London: Hakluyt Society, 1937.

Crone, Patricia. *God's Rule: Government and Islam, Six Centuries of Medieval Islamic Political Thought.* New York: Columbia University Press, 2004.

Curtin, Philip D. *Economic Change in Pre-Colonial Africa: Senegambia in the Era of the Slave Trade.* Madison: University of Wisconsin Press, 1975.

———. "*Jihad* in West Africa: Early Phases and Inter-Relations in Mauritania and Senegal." *The Journal of African History* 12.1 (1971).

———. "Pre-Colonial Trading Networks and Traders: The Diakhanké." In *The Development of Trades and Markets in Pre-Colonial West Africa.* Edited by Claude Meillasoux. London: Oxford University Press, 1971.

———. "The Lure of Bambouk Gold." *The Journal of African History* 4 (1973): 623–631.

Davidson, Basil. *The Black Man's Burden: Africa and the Curse of the Nation-State.* London: James Currey, 1992.

Davis, Robert C. *Christian Slaves, Muslim Masters: White Slavery in the Mediterranean, The Barbary Coast, and Italy, 1500–1800.* London: Palgrave-Macmillan, 2003.

Deeb, M.-J. "Islam and Arab Nationalism in Al-Qaddhafi's Ideology." *Journal of South Asian and Middle Eastern Studies* 2.2 (1978): 12–26.

Delafosse, Maurice. *Traditions Historiques et Légendaires de l'Afrique Occidental.* Paris: Comité de l'Afrique française, 1913.

Diallo, Moustapha. *L'islam et son influence sur la Société Djakanka de Touba (Gawal): Mémoire de Diplôme de Fin d'Etudes Superieures.* Conakry, Guinea: Institut Polytechnique, 1980.

Diallo, Thierno. *Alfa Yaya: roi du Labé (Fouta Djallon).* Dakar: Editions ABC, 1976.

Dilley, Roy M. "Spirits, Islam and Ideology: A Study of a Tukulor Weavers' Song (Dillire)." *Journal of Religion in Africa* 17.3 (1987): 245–279.

Doi, A. R. I. "Islamic Education in Nigeria (11th Century to the 20th Century)." *Islamic Culture* 46 (1972), 1–16.

Donald, Leland. "Arabic Literacy Among the Yalunka of Sierra Leone." *Africa* 44 (1974): 71–81.

Donoghue, Dennis. "A Voluble Presence in the World. Review of *Bertrand Russell: A Life*, by Caroline Moorehead." *New York Times Book Review*, October 31, 1993.

Doughty, Charles. *Passages From Arabia Deserta.* London: Penguin Books, 1956.

Duffy, James. *A Question of Slavery: Labour Policies in Portuguese Africa and the British Protest, 1850–1920.* Cambridge, MA: Harvard University Press, 1967.

Earthy, E. D. "The Impact of Mohammedanism on Paganism in the Liberian Hinterland." *Numen* 2 (1955): 206–216.

Engineer, Asghar Ali. *The Islamic State.* New Delhi: Vikas Publishing, 1994.

Euba, Titilola. "Muhammad Shitta Bey and the Lagos Muslim Community (1850–1895)." *Nigerian Journal of Islam* 2.1 (July 1971–January 1972), 7–18.

Eusebius. *The History of the Church.* Translated and edited by G. A. Williamson. Harmondsworth, UK: Penguin Books, 1965.

Fadera, al-Hájj Muhammad Fádilu. *Kitáb Tahdhíru Ummati 'l-Muhammadiyát min Ittibái 'l-firqati Ahmadiyát (A Warning to the Muslim Community on the Dangers of Following the Ahmadiyah Sect).* Dakar, n.d.

Faksh, M. "Concepts of Rule and Legitimation in Islam." *Journal of South Asian and Middle Eastern Studies* 13.3 (1990): 21–36.

Farias, P. F. de Moraes. "Great States revisited: review article, " *The Journal of African History* 15. 3 (1974), 479–488.

———. "Silent Trade: Myth and Historical Evidence." *History in Africa* 1 (1974): 9–24.

———. "The Almoravids: Some Questions Concerning the Character of the Movement During its Periods of Closest Contact With the Western Sudan." *Bulletin de l'Institut Fondemantale de l'Afrique Noir*, Série B, 29.3–4 (1967): 794–878.

Fierro, Maribel. *'Abd al-Rahman III: The First Cordoban Caliph.* Oxford: Oneworld, 2005.

Fisher, Humphrey J. "A Muslim Wilberforce? The Sokoto *Jihád* as Anti-Slavery Crusade: An Enquiry into Historical Causes." In *De la traite à l'esclavage: Actes du colloque international sur la traite des Noirs, Nantes, 1985.* 2 vols. Edited by Serge Daget. Nantes: Centre de recherche sur l'histoire du monde atlantique, 1988.

Fisher, Humphrey J. "Early Arabic sources and the Almoravid Conquest of Ghana: review article." *The Journal of African History* 23 (1982): 549–560.

———. "Hassebu: Islamic Healing in Black Africa." In *Northern Africa: Islam and Modernization*. Edited by Michael Brett. London: Frank Cass, 1973.

———. "Islamic Education and Religious Reform in West Africa." In *Education in Africa*. Edited by Richard Jolly. Nairobi, Kenya: East African Publishing House, 1969.

———. "Liminality, *Hijra*, and the City." In *Rural and Urban Islam in West Africa*. Edited by Nehemia Levtzion and Humphrey J. Fisher. Boulder, CO: Lynne Rienner, 1987.

———. "Prayer and Military Activity in the History of Muslim Africa South of the Sahara." *The Journal of African History* 12 (1971): 391–406.

———. "Slavery and Seclusion in Northern Nigeria: A Further Note." *The Journal of African History* 32 (1991): 123–135.

———. "The Early Life and Pilgrimage of al-Hájj Muhammad al-Amín the Soninké (d. 1887)." *The Journal of African History* 12 (1970): 51–69.

Fisher, Allan G. B., and Humphrey J. Fisher. *Slavery and Muslim Society in Africa: The Institution in Saharan and Sudanic Africa and the Trans-Saharan Trade*. New York: Anchor Books, 1972.

Foucauld, Charles de. *Meditations of a Hermit: The Spiritual Writings of Charles de Foucauld*. Translated by C. Balfour. London: Burns & Oates, 1981.

Frey, Henri. *Campagnes dans le Haut-Sénégal et dans le Haut-Niger, 1885–1886*. Paris: Pion, 1888.

Fudi, 'Abdullah b. *Idá' al-Nusúkh*. In Mervyn Hiskett, "Materials Relating to the State of Learning Among the Fulani Before Their Jihád." *Bulletin of the School of Oriental and African Studies* 19 (1957), 104–149.

———. *Tayzin al-Waraqát*. Ibadan, Nigeria: Ibadan University Press, 1963.

Fudi, 'Uthman Ibn. *Bayán Wujúb al-Hijra 'ala 'I-'Ibád*. Edited and translated by F. H. El-Masri. Khartoum: Khartoum University Press, 1979.

———. *Ihya al-Sunna wa Ikhmad al-Bid'a*. In Ismail A. B. Balogun. *A Critical Edition of the Ihya al-Sunna wa Ikhmad al-Bid'a of 'Uthman b. Fudi, Popularly Known as Usuman Dan Fodio*. PhD dissertation, University of London, 1967.

———. *Kitáb al-Farq bayna Wiláyát Ahl al-Islám wa bayna Wiláyát Ahl al-Kufr*. In Mervyn Hiskett. "*Kitáb ak-Farq*: A Work on the Habe Kingdoms Attributed to 'Uthmán dan Fodio." *Bulletin of the School of Oriental and African Studies* 23 (1960), 550–578.

———. *Núr al-Albáb*. In Ismaël Hamet. "*Nour-el-Elbabe* (Lumière des Coeurs) de Cheïkh Otmane ben Mohammed ben Otmane dit Ibn-Foudiou." *Revue Africaine: Bulletin des Travaux de la Société Historique Algérienne* 41 (1897) and 42 (1898), 58–70.

Gaden, H. *Proverbes et maxims Peuls et Toucouleurs*. Paris: Institut d'ethnologie, Université de Paris, 1931.

Gassama, 'Abd al-Qádir Túbawí. *Kitáb al-Bushrá: Sharh al-Mirqát al-Kubrá*. Tunis: Matba'ah al-Manár, n.d.

Gbadamosi, T. G. O. *The Growth of Islam Among the Yoruba, 1841–1908*. London: Longman Group, 1978.

———. "The Imamate Question Among Yoruba Muslims." *Journal of the Historical Society of Nigeria* 6 (1972): 229–237.

Ghazali, Abdul Karim. "A Muslim Propaganda Play: De Man Way De Play Gyambul Wit God." *The Sierra Leone Bulletin of Religion* 3.2 (December 1961).

Ghazali, Abdul Karim, and L. Proudfoot. "A Muslim Propaganda Play and a Commentary." *The Sierra Leone Bulletin of Religion* 3.2 (December 1961), 72–79.

Ghazali, al-. "Ayyuha al-walad." In *Classical Foundations of Islamic Educational Thought*. Edited by Bradley J. Cook and Fathi H. Malkawi. Provo, UT: Brigham Young University Press, 2010, 88–107.

Gibb, H. A. R. *Studies in the Civilization of Islam: Collected Essays*. Edited by Stanford J. Shaw and William R. Polk. London: Routledge & Kegan Paul, 1962.

Gibbon, Edward. *The Decline and Fall of the Roman Empire*. 3 vols. New York: Modern Library, 1932.

Golberry, Sylvain. *Fragments d'un Voyage en Afrigue 1785–87*. 2 vols. Paris: Treuttel et Würtz, 1802.

Goldziher, Ignaz. *Introduction to Islamic Theology and Law*. Translated by Andras Hamori and Ruth Hamori. Princeton, NJ: Princeton University Press, 1981.

———. *Muslim Studies*, 1889/90, Translated and edited by C. R. Barber & S. M. Stern, London: George Allen & Unwin, 2 vols., 1967–1971.

Gomez, Michael A. *Pragmatism in the Age of Jihad: The Precolonial State of Bundu*. Cambridge, UK: Cambridge University Press, 1992.

Goody, Jack. "Restricted Literacy in Northern Ghana." In *Literacy in Traditional Societies*. Cambridge, UK: Cambridge University Press, 1968.

———. "The Impact of Islamic Writing on the Oral Cultures of West Africa." *Cahiers d'études africaines* 11.3 (1971): 455–466.

Goriawala, Mu'izz. "Maguzawa: The Influence of the Hausa Muslims on the Beliefs and Practices of the Maguzawa, the Traditional Religionists of Kano and Katsina." *Orita: Ibadan Journal of Religious Studies* 4.2 (1970): 115–123.

Gouldsbury, M. D. *Expedition to the Upper Gambia, August 1881*. London: Public Records Office, 1881.

Gray, J. M. *A History of the Gambia*. Cambridge, UK: Cambridge University Press, 1940; reprinted London: Frank Cass, 1966.

Gray, William, and Staff Surgeon Dochard. *Travels in Western Africa, 1818–1821*. London: John Murray, 1825.

Green, J. "Islam, Religio-Politics and Social Change." *Comparative Studies in Society and History* 27 (1985). 312–322.

Greenberg, Joseph. *The Influence of Islam on a Sudanese Religion*. New York: J. J. Augustin, 1966.

Griffel, Frank. *Al-Ghazali's Philosophical Theology*. New York: Oxford University Press, 2009.

Grunebaum, Gustav E. von. "Pluralism in the Islamic World." *Islamic Studies* 1.2 (June 1962): 37–59.

Guy, Camille. *Proposition d'internement d'indigènes de la Guineèe pour faits d'insurection contre l'autorité de la France*. Dakar: Archives Fédérales de Dakar, 1911.

Hájj, M. A. al-. "A 17th Century Chronicle on the Origins and Missionary Activities of the Wangarawa." *Kano Studies* 1.4 (1968): 7–16.

Hair, P. E. H. "A Jesuit Document on African Enslavement." *Slavery & Abolition* 19 (1998): 118–127.

Hallam, W. K. R. *The Life and Times of Rabih Fadl Allah*. Elm Court, UK: Arthur H. Stockwell, 1977.

Hallaq, Wael B. *A History of Islamic Legal Theories: An Introduction to Sunni Usul al-Fiqh*. Cambridge, UK: Cambridge University Press, 1999.

———. "Was the Gate of *Ijtihád* Closed?" *International Journal of Middle East Studies* 16 (1984): 3–41.

Halle, Claude. "Notes sur Koly Tenguella, Olivier de Sanderval et les ruines de Gueme-Sangan." *Récherches Africaines* 1 (1960), 37–41.

Hanson, John, and David Robinson, eds. and trans. *After Jihad: The Reign of Ahmad al-Kabir in the Western Sudan*. East Lansing: Michigan State University Press, 1991.

Harnischfeger, Johannes. *Democratization and Islamic Law: The Sharia Conflict in Nigeria*. Frankfurt: Campus Verlag, 2008.

Harrison, Christopher. *France and Islam in West Africa*. Cambridge, UK: Cambridge University Press, 1988.

Haynes, Jeff. *Religion in Third World Politics*. Boulder, CO: Lynne Rienner, 1994.

Hawqal, Ibn. *Kitáb Súrat al-Ard, "Book of the Picture of the World."* In *Corpus of Early Arabic Sources for West African History*. Translated by J. F P. Hopkins. Edited by N. Levtzion and J. F. P. Hopkins. Cambridge, UK: Cambridge University Press, 1981.

Hess, Andrew. *The Forgotten Frontier: A History of the 16th Century Ibero-African Frontier*. Chicago: University of Chicago Press, 1978.

Hill, Christopher. *Change and Continuity in 17th Century England*. New Haven, CT: Yale University Press, 1991.

Hill, Christopher. *The English Bible and the Seventeenth-Century Revolution.* London: Penguin Books, 1993.

Hilliard, Constance. "Zuhúr al-Basátin and Ta'ríkh al-Turubbe: Some Legal and Ethical Aspects of Slavery in the Sudan as Seen in the Works of Shaykh Musa Kamara." In *Slaves and Slavery in Muslim Africa.* 2 vols. Edited by John Ralph Willis. London: Frank Cass, 1985.

———, ed. *Intellectual Traditions of Pre-Colonial Africa.* Boston: McGraw-Hill, 1998.

Hiskett, Mervyn. "An Islamic Tradition of Reform in the Western Sudan from the Sixteenth to the Eighteenth Century." *Bulletin of the School of Oriental and African Studies* 25 (1962): 577–596.

———. *The Course of Islam in Africa.* Edinburgh, UK: Edinburgh University Press, 1994.

———. *The Development of Islam in West Africa.* London: Longman, 1984.

———. "The Maitatsine Riots in Kano, 1980: An Assessment." *Journal of Religion in Africa* 17.3 (1987): 209–223.

———. "The Nineteenth Century Jihads in West Africa." In *The Cambridge History of Africa: Vol. 5, From c. 1790 to c. 1870.* Cambridge, UK: Cambridge University Press, 1976.

———. *The Sword of Truth: The Life and Times of the Shehu Ususman Dan Fodio.* New York: Oxford University Press, 1973.

Hitti, Philip K. *History of the Arabs.* London: Macmillan, 1968.

Hocking, William Ernest. *The Coming World Civilization.* New York: Harper, 1956.

Hodgkin, Thomas. "Islam and National Movements in West Africa." *The Journal of African History* 3.2 (1962): 323–327.

———. "Islam, History and Politics." *The Journal of Modern African Studies* 1.1 (1963): 91–97.

———. "The Fact of Islamic History (II): Islam in West Africa." *Africa South* 2.3 (1958): 88–99.

———, ed. *Nigerian Perspectives: An Historical Anthology.* London: Oxford University Press, 1960.

Hogendorn, J. S. "The Economics of Slave Use on Two 'Plantations' in the Zaria Emirate of the Sokoto Caliphate." *The International Journal of African Historical Studies* 10.3 (1977): 369–383.

Hogendorn, J. S., and Paul E. Lovejoy. "The Reform Slavery in Early Colonial Northern Nigeria." In *The End of Slavery in Africa.* Edited by Suzanne Miers and Richard Roberts. Madison: University of Wisconsin Press, 1988.

Holt, P. M., Ann K. Lambton, and Bernard Lewis, eds. *The Cambridge History of Islam:* Vol. 2A. Cambridge, UK: Cambridge University Press, 1970.

Holyoake, George J. *The Principles of Secularism.* London: Austin & Co., 1870.

Hopewell, James F. *Muslim Penetration into French Guinea, Sierra Leone and Liberia Before 1850.* Unpublished PhD dissertation, Columbia University, New York, 1958.

Hourani, Albert. *A History of the Arab Peoples.* Cambridge, MA: Harvard University Press, 1991.

———. *Arabic Thought in the Liberal Age, 1798–1939.* London: Oxford University Press, 1970.

Humblot, P. "Du nom proper et des appellations chez les Malinké des vallées du Niandan et du Milo." *Bulletin du Comité d'Etudes Historiques et Scientifiques de l'Afrique Occidental Française* 1 (1918), 523–539.

Humphrey J. Fisher and Conrad, D. "The Conquest That Never Was: Ghana and the Almoravids." Part II. *History of Africa* 10 (1983): 53–78.

———. "What's in a Name? The Almoravids of the Eleventh Century in the Western Sudan." *Journal of Religion in Africa* 22.4 (1992): 290–317.

Humphreys, R. Stephen. *Islamic History: A Framework for Inquiry.* 2d ed. Princeton, NJ: Princeton University Press, 1991.

Hunwick, J. O. "A Historical Whodunit: The So-Called 'Kano Chronicle' and Its Pace in the Historiography of Kano." *History in Africa* 21 (1994).

———. "An Andalusian in Mali: A Contribution to the Biography of Abú Isháq al-Sáhilí, c. 1290–1346." *Paideuma* 36 (1990): 59–66.

———. "Religion and State in the Songhay Empire, 1464–1491." In *Islam in Tropical Africa*. Edited by I. M. Lewis. Bloomington: Indiana University Press, 1980.
———. "Songhay, Borno, and Hausaland in the Sixteenth Century." In *History of West Africa*. Edited by J. F. A. Ajayi and Michael Crowder. London: Longman, 1976.
———. "Sub-Saharan Africa and the Wider World of Islam: Historical and Contemporary Perspectives." *Journal of Religion in Africa* 26 (1996): 230–257.
———. "The Influence of Arabic in West Africa." *Transactions of the Historical Society of Ghana* 7 (1964): 24–41.
———, ed. *Religion and National Integration in Africa: Islam, Christianity, and Politics in the Sudan and Nigeria*. Evanston, IL: Northwestern University Press, 1992.
———, ed. and trans. *Shari'a in Songhay: The Replies of al-Maghílí to the Questions of Askia al-Hájj Muhammad*. Oxford: Oxford University Press, 1985.
———, ed. and trans. *Timbuktu and the Songhay Empire: Al-Sa'dí's Ta'ríkh al-Súdán Down to 1613*. Translation of 'Abd al-Rahmán Sa'dí's *Ta'ríkh al-Súdán*. Leiden: Brill, 1999.
Hunter, Thomas. *The Development of an African Tradition of Learning Among the Jakhanke of West Africa*. Unpublished PhD dissertation, University of Chicago, 1976.
Ilesanmi, Simeon. *Religious Pluralism and the Nigerian State*. Athens, OH: Center for International Studies, 1997.
Ingham, K. *Politics in Modern Africa: The Uneven Tribal Dimension*. London: Routledge, 1990.
Ismail, O. S. A., and A. Y. Aliyu. "Bello and the Tradition of Manuals of Islamic Government and Advice to Rulers." In *Nigerian Administration Research Project, Second Interim Report*. Zaria: Ahmadu Bello University, 1975.
Jama'ah, Ibn. "A Memorandum for Listeners and Lecturers: Rules of Conduct for the Learned and the Learning." In *Classical Foundations of Islamic Educational Thought*. Edited by Bradley J. Cook and Fathi H. Malkawi. Provo, UT: Brigham Young University Press, 2010.
Jamburiah, Omar. "The Story of the Jihad of the Foulahs." *Sierra Leone Studies* 3 (1919), 30–34.
Jansen, G. H. *Militant Islam*. London: Pan Books, 1979.
Jimeh, S. A. "A Critical Appraisal of Islamic Education With Particular Reference to Critical Happenings on the Nigerian Scene." *Nigerian Journal of Islam* 2.1 (July 1971–January 1972), 31–50.
Jobson, Richard. *The Discovery of the River Gambra (1623). Part I: Jobson's Texts and Part II: Other Early Sources on River Gambia [1455–1684]*. Edited by David P. Gamble and P. E. H. Hair. London: Hakluyt Society, 1999.
Johansen, Baber. *Contingency in a Sacred Law: Legal and Ethical Norms in the Muslim Fiqh*. Leiden: Brill, 1999.
Johnson, G. W. *The Emergence of Black Politics in Senegal: The Struggle for Power in the Four Communes, 1900–1920*. Stanford, CA: Stanford University Press, 1971.
Johnson, H. A. S. *The Fulani Empire of Sokoto*. London: Oxford University Press, 1967.
Johnson, John William, ed. and trans. *The Epic of Son-Jara: A West African Tradition*. Bloomington: Indiana University Press, 1992.
Johnston, David. "A Turn in the Epistemology and Hermeneutics of Twentieth Century Uṣúl al- Fiqh." *Islamic Law and Society* 11 (2004): 233–282.
———. *Earth, Empire and Sacred Text: Muslims and Christians as Trustees of Creation*. London: Equinox, 2010.
Johnston, H. A. S. *The Fulani Empire of Sokoto*. London: Oxford University Press, 1967.
Jones-Leaning, Melanie, and Douglas Pratt. "Islam in China: From Silk Road to Separatism." *The Muslim World* 102 (2012): 308–334.
Jubayr, Ibn. *Rihlah*. Translated by R. J. C. Broadhurst. In *Anthology of Islamic Literature: From the Rise of Islam to Modern Times*. Edited by James Kritzeck. New York: New American Library, 1964.
Junaidu, Alhaji. "The Relevance of the University to Our Society" [Speech of acceptance, Abdullahi Bayero University, 1972]. *Nigerian Journal of Islam* 2 (1972–1974).
Kane, Cheikh Hamidou. *Ambiguous Adventure*. London: Heinemann, 1972.

Kane, Ousmane. "Izala: The Rise of Muslim Reformism in Northern Nigeria." In *Accounting for "Fundamentalisms": The Dynamic Character of Movements.* Edited by Martin Marty and R. Scott-Appleby. Chicago: University of Chicago Press, 1994.

———. *Muslim Modernity in Postcolonial Nigeria: A Study of the Society for the Removal of Innovation and Reinstatement of Tradition.* Leiden: Brill, 2003.

———. "Reconciling Islam and Pre-Islamic Beliefs: A Reflection on a Talismanic Textile of the Art Institute of Chicago." *Islam et Sociétés au Sud du Sahara* 2 (2009), 137–161.

Ka'tí, Mahmúd al-. *Ta'rikh al-Fattásh.* Translated by O. Houdas and M. Delafosse. Paris: Librairie d'Amerique et d'Orient, Adrien-Maisonneuve, 1964.

Kautsky, Karl. *Communism in Central Europe in the Time of the Reformation.* London: Unwin, 1897.

Keddie, Nikki R. *An Islamic Response to Imperialism: Political and Religious Writings of Sayyid Jamal Al-Din "al-Afghani."* Berkeley: University of California Press, 1983.

———. *Scholars, Saints, and Sufis: Muslim Religious Institutions in the Middle East Since 1500.* Berkeley: University of California Press, 1972.

Kepel, Gilles. *Jihad: The Trail of Political Islam.* Cambridge, MA: Belknap Press of Harvard University Press, 2002.

Khadduri, Majid. *War and Peace in the Law of Islam.* Baltimore, MD: Johns Hopkins University Press, 1955.

Khaldun, Ibn. *Al-Muqaddimah: An Introduction to History.* 3 vols. Edited and translated by Franz Rosenthal. Princeton, NJ: Princeton University Press, 1967.

———. *An Arab Philosophy of History: Selections from the Prologomena of Ibn Khaldun of Tunis (1332–1406).* Edited and translated by Charles Issawi. London: John Murray, 1950.

———. *Histoire des Berbères et des Dynasties Musulmanes de l'Afrique Septentrionale.* 4 vols. Translated by Le Baron de Slane. Paris: Librairie Orientaliste, 1982.

———. *"Kitáb al- 'ibar wa diwá al-mubtada' wa 'l-khabar fi ayyám al- 'arab wa 'l- 'ajam wa 'l-barbar."* In *Corpus of Early Arabic Sources for West African History.* Translated by J. F. P. Hopkins. Edited by N. Levtzion and J. F. P. Hopkins. Cambridge, UK: Cambridge University Press, 1981.

Klein, F. A. *The Religion of Islam.* London: Curzon Press, 1906.

Klein, Martin A. *Islam and Imperialism in Senegal: Sine-Saloum, 1847–1914.* Edinburgh, UK: Edinburgh University Press, 1968.

———. "The Moslem Revolution in 19th Century Senegambia." In *Boston Papers in African Studies.* Edited by J. Butler. Boston: Boston University Publications, 1966.

Kunti, Shaykh Mukhtar al-. *Kawkab al-Waqqád.* Privately printed by al-Hajj Banfa Jabi, Macca-Kolibantang, Senegal.

Kushkush, Isma'il. "As Floods Ravage Sudan, Young Volunteers Revive a Tradition of Aid." *New York Times,* August 30, 2013.

Labouret, H. "Les Manding et leur language." *Bulletin du Comité d'Etudes Historiques et Scientifiques de l'Afrique Occidental Française* 17 (1934), 1–270.

Landau, R. "The Karaoune at Fez." *The Muslim World* 48 (1958).

Lange, D. "Les Rois de Gao-Sané et les Almoravides." *The Journal of African History* 32.2 (1991): 251–275.

Lange, D., and S. Berthoud. "L'Intérieur de l'Afrique occidantle d'après Giovanni Lorenzo (XVIe siècle)." *Cahiers d'histoire mondiale* 14 (1972): 299–351.

Lapidus, Ira M. "The Seperation of State and Religion in the Development of Early Islamic Society." *International Journal of Middle East Studies* 6 (1975): 363–385.

Last, Murray. "A Note on Attitudes to the Supernatural in the Sokoto Jihad." *Journal of the Historical Society of Nigeria* 4 (1967): 3–13.

———. "Aspects of Administration and Dissent in Hausaland: 1800–1968." *Africa* 40.4 (October 1970): 345–357.

———. *The Sokoto Caliphate.* London: Longmans, Green, and Co., 1967.

Launay, Robert. *Beyond the Stream: Islam and Society in a West African Town.* Berkeley: University of California Press, 1992.

Lawrence, T. E. *Seven Pillars of Wisdom: A Triumph*. London: Penguin Books, 1962.
Lemaire, J. J. *Voyage to the Canaries, Cape Verde and the Coast of Africa* (1682). Translated by E. Goldsmid. Privately printed, Edinburgh, UK, 1887.
Lemu, B. A. "Islamisation of Education: A Primary Level Experiment in Nigeria." *Muslim Educational Quarterly* 2 (1988): 70–80.
Le Tourneau, Roger. "North Africa to the Sixteenth Century." In *The Cambridge History of Islam:* Vol. 2A. Edited by P. M. Holt, Ann K. S. Lambton, and Bernard Lewis. Cambridge, UK: Cambridge University Press, 1970.
Leary, Frances Anne. "The Role of the Mandinka in the Islamization of the Casamance." In *Papers on the Manding*. Edited by C. T. Hodge. Bloomington: Indiana University Publications, 1971.
Levtzion, Nehemia. "A 17th Century Chronicle by Ibn al-Mukhtár: A Critical Study of the *Ta'rikh al-Fattásh*." *Bulletin of the School of Oriental and African Studies* 34 (1971): 571–593.
———. "Abd Allah b. Yasin and the Almoravids." In *Studies in West African Islamic History:* Vol. I, *The Cultivators of Islam*. Edited by John Ralph Willis. London: Frank Cass, 1979.
———. *Ancient Ghana and Mali*. London: Methuen, 1973.
———. "Ancient Ghana: A Reassessment of Some Arabic Sources," *Rev. franc. d'Histoire d'Outre-Mer* LXVI (1979): 139–147.
———. "Islam in West African Politics: Accommodation and Tension Between 'Ulamá' and the Political Authorities." *Cahiers d'études africaines* 71 (1978): 333–345.
———. *Muslims and Chiefs in West Africa: A Study of Islam in the Middle Volta Basin in the Pre-Colonial Period*. Oxford: Clarendon Press, 1968.
———. "Rural and Urban Islam in West Africa: An Introductory Essay." In *Rural and Urban Islam in West Africa*. Edited by Nehemia Levtzion and Humphrey J. Fisher. Boulder, CO: Lynne Rienner, 1987.
———. "Was Royal Succession in Ancient Ghana Matrilineal?" *The International Journal of African Historical Studies* 1 (1972): 91–93.
Levtzion, Nehemia, and Randall Pouwels, eds. *The History of Islam in Africa*. Athens: Ohio University Press, 2000.
Levy, Reuben. *The Social Structure of Islam*. 2d ed. Cambridge, UK: Cambridge University Press, 1965.
Lewicki, T. "Les origins de l'Islam dans les tribus berbères du Sahara occidentale: Musa ibn Nusayr et 'Ubayd Allah ibn al-Habhah." *Studia Islamica* 32 (1970), 203–214.
———. "Un état soudainais médiéval inconnu: Le royaume de Zafun(u)." *Cahiers d'ētudes africaines* 11 (1971): 501–525.
Lewis, Bernard. *The Political Language of Islam*. Chicago: Chicago University Press, 1998.
Lewis, I. M. "Africa South of the Sahara." In *The Legacy of Islam*. Edited by Joseph Schacht and C. E. Bosworth. Oxford: Clarendon Press, 1974.
———, ed. *Islam in Tropical Africa*. Bloomington: Indiana University Press, 1980.
Lings, Martin. *A Moslem Saint of the Twentieth Century: Shaikh Ahmad al-'Alawí, His Spiritual Heritage and Legacy*. Cambridge, UK: Islamic Texts Society, 1993.
Locke, John. *A Letter Concerning Toleration, 1689*. Buffalo, NY: Prometheus Books, 1990.
Lovejoy, Paul E. "Concubinage and the Status of Women Slaves in Early Colonial Northern Nigeria." *The Journal of African History* 29.2 (1988): 245–266.
Lugard, Lord Frederick. "'Slavery in All Its Forms." *Africa* 6.1 (1933): 1–14.
Lydon, Ghislaine. *On Trans-Saharan Trails: Islamic Law, Trade Networks, and Cross-Cultural Exchange in Nineteenth Western Africa*. Cambridge, UK: Cambridge University Press, 2009.
Lynch, Hollis R. *Edward Wilmot Blyden: Pan-Negro Patriot, 1832–1912*. New York: Oxford University Press, 1970.
Macdonald, Duncan B. *The Development of Muslim Theology, Jurisprudence and Constitutional Theory*. Beirut: Khayats, 1965.
Madelung, W. "A Treatise of the Sharif al-Murtada on the Legality of Working for the Government." *Bulletin of the School of Oriental and African Studies* 43 (1980): 18–31.

Mage, M. E. *Voyage dans le Soudan occidental (Sénégambie-Niger) 1863–1866*. Paris: Librairie de L. Hachette et ciel, 868.

Maghili, Mohammed al. *Táj al-Dín fí má Yajíbu álá al-Mulúk wa al-Saláṭín (The Crown of Religion Concerning the Obligations of Princes: An Essay on Moslem Kingship)*. Translated by T. H. Baldwin. Beirut: Imprimerie Catholique, 1932.

Mahoney, Florence. "The Stone Circles of Senegambia." *Ta'rikh* 2 (1968): 1–11.

Maier, Karl. *This House Has Fallen: Nigeria in Crisis*. London: Penguin Books, 2000.

Mallat, Chibli. *Introduction to Middle Eastern Law*. Oxford: Oxford University Press, 2007.

Manga, Al-Amin Abu. "Resistance to the Western System of Education by the Early Migrant Community of Maiurno (Sudan)." In *Islam in Africa: Proceedings of the Islam in Africa Conference*. Edited by Nura Alkali, Adamu Adamu, Awwal Yadudu, Rashid Motem, and Haruna Salihi. Ibadan, Nigeria: Spectrum Books, 1993.

Manning, Patrick. *Slavery and African Life: Occidental, Oriental, and the African Slave Trades*. Cambridge, UK: Cambridge University Press, 1990.

Maranz, David E. *Peace Is Everything: The Worldview of Muslims and Traditionalists in the Senegambia*. Dallas: International Museum of Cultures, 1993.

Martin, B. G. *Muslim Brotherhoods in 19th Century Africa*. Cambridge, UK: Cambridge University Press, 1976.

Marty, Paul. *Etudes sur l'Islam et les tribus du Soudan:* Vol. II. Paris: E. Leroux, 1920.

———. *L'Islam en Guinée: Fouta Diallon*. Paris: E. Leroux, 1921.

———. "L'Islam en Mauritanie et au Sénégal." *Revue du Monde Musulman* 31 (1915–1916): 448–452.

Masonen, Pekka, and Humphrey J. Fisher, "Not Quite Venus From the Waves: The Almoravid Conquest of Ghana in the Modern Historiography of West Africa." *History in Africa* 23 (1996): 197–232.

Masri, F. H. el-. "The Life of Shehu Usuman dan Fodio Before the Jihad." *Journal of the Historical Society of Nigeria* 2.4 (1963): 435–448.

Masud, Muhammad Khalid. *Muslim Jurists' Quest for the Normative Basis of Shari'a*. Leiden: Institute for the Study of Islam in the Modern World, 2001.

Mauny, Raymond. *Tableau géographique de l'ouest africain*. Dakar: Institut Française de l'Afrique Noire, 1961.

Maurice, Frederick D. *The Religions of the World and Their Relations to Christianity*. London: Macmillan, 1886.

Mazrui, Ali A. "African Islam and Comprehensive Religion: Between Revivalism and Expansion." In *Islam in Africa: Proceedings of the Islam in Africa Conference*. Edited by Nura Alkali, Adamu Adamu, Awwal Yadudu, Rashid Motem, and Haruna Salihi. Ibadan, Nigeria: Spectrum Books, 1993.

Mazrui, Ali A., and Toby Kleban Levine, eds. *The Africans: A Reader*. New York: Praeger, 1986.

Mazruq, Ibn. *Musnad*. Edited and translated by E. Lévi-Provençal, *Hespéris* 5 (1925.)

McGowan, Winston. "Fula Resistance to French Expansion into Futa Jallon, 1889–1896." *The Journal of African History* 22 (1981): 245–261.

McHugh, Neil. *Holy Men of the Blue Nile: The Making of an Arab-Islamic Community in the Nilotic Sudan, 1500–1850*. Evanston, IL: Northwestern University Press, 1986.

Meek, C. K. *Tribal Studies in Northern Nigeria*. London: K. Paul, Trench, Trubner & Co., 1931.

Melitzki, Dorothee. *The Matter of Araby in Medieval England*. New Haven, CT: Yale University Press, 2005.

Mercier, Ernest. *Histoire de l'Afrique Septentrionale*. Paris: E. Leroux, 1888.

Merkl, Peter H., and Ninian Smart, eds. *Religion and Politics in the Modern World*. New York: New York University Press, 1985.

Mézières, A Bonnel de. "Les Diakhanké de Banisraïla et du Bondou." *Notes Africaines* 41 (January, 1949).

Miller, Perry, and Thomas H. Johnson, eds. *The Puritans: A Sourcebook of Their Writings:* Vol. I. New York: Harper Torchbooks, 1963.

Miskin, Tijani, El-. "Da'wa and the Challenge of Secularism: A Conceptual Agenda for Islamic Ideologues." In *Islam in Africa: Proceedings of the Islam in Africa Conference*. Edited by Nura Alkali, Adamu Adamu, Awwal Yadudu, Rashid Motem, and Haruna Salihi. Ibadan, Nigeria: Spectrum Books, 1993.

Mitchell, Peter K. "A Note on the Distribution in Sierra Leone of Literacy in Arabic, Mende and Temne." *African Language Review* 7 (1968): 90–100.

Milton, Giles. *White Gold: The Extraordinary Story of Thomas Pellow and Islam's One Million White Slaves*. New York: Farrar, Straus and Giroux, 2004.

Mollien, Gaspard. *Travels in Africa to the Sources of the Senegal and Gambia in 1818*. 2d ed. London: Sir R. Phillips, 1820.

Monteil, Charles. "Etat actuel de nos connaissances sur l'Afrique occidentale française: Le coton chez les noirs." *Bulletin du Comité d'Ētudes Historiques et Scientifiques de l'Afrique Occidentale Française* 9.4 (1927).

———. *Les empires du Mali: Etude d'histoire et de sociologie soudanaises*. Paris: Librairie Larose, 1929; reprinted Paris: G.-P Maisonneuve et Larose, 1968.

———. "La Légend de Ouagadou et l'Origine des Soninké." In *Mélanges Ethnologiques*. Dakar: IFAN, 1953, 134–149.

———. "Le site de Goundiourou." *Bulletin du Comité d'Etudes Historiques et Scientifiques de l'Afrique Occidental Française* 11.4 (1928), 647–653.

Monteil, Vincent. "Marabouts." In *Islam in Africa*. Edited by J. Kritzeck and W. H. Lewis. New York: Van-Nostrand, 1969.

Morton-Williams, Peter. "The Fulani Penetration into Nupe and Yoruba in the Nineteenth Century." In *History and Social Anthropology*. Edited by I. M. Lewis. London: Tavistock, 1968.

Munajjid, Saláh al-Dín. *Mamlakah Máliyah 'ind al-jugrifiyín al-muslimín:* Vol. 1. Beirut: Dár al-Kitáb al-Jadídah, 1963.

Nabulsi, 'Abd al-Ghani al- [1641–1731]. *Ta'tir al-Anam fi Ta'bir al-Manam*. 2 vols. Cairo: Dār Iḥyā' al-Kutub al-'Arabīyah, 1972.

Na'īm, 'Abd Allāh Aḥmad, *Islam and the Secular State: Negotiating the Future of Shari'a*. Cambridge, MA: Harvard University Press, 2008.

Nasr, Jamil M. Abun-. "Islam and Socialism in Africa." In *Christian and Islamic Contributions Towards Establishing Independent States in Africa South of the Sahara*. Edited by Ernst J. Tetsch. Stuttgart: Institute for Foreign Cultural Relations, 1979.

———. *Muslim Communities of Grace: The Sufi Brotherhoods in the Islamic Religious Life*. New York: Columbia University Press, 2007.

Niane, Djibril Tamsir. *Récherches sur l'empire du Mali au Moyen Age*. Récherches Africaines *Études guinéenes*, nouvelle série 1 (1960): 17–36, 23.

Nicholson, Reynold A. *A Literary History of the Arabs*. Cambridge, UK: Cambridge University Press, 1962.

Nielsen, Rich. "Jihadi Radicalization of Muslim Clerics." Cambridge, MA: Department of Government, Harvard University, 2012.

Nizám al-Mulk. *The Book of Government for Kings (Siyását náma)*. London: Routledge & Kegan Paul, 1960.

Nock, Arthur Darby. *Conversion: The Old and the New in Religion from Alexander the Great to Augustine of Hippo*. Oxford: Oxford University Press, 1933; reprinted Baltimore, MD: Johns Hopkins University Press, 1998.

Noirot, E. *A Travers le Fouta Djallon at le Bambouc*. Paris, 1889.

Norris, H. T. "New Evidence on the Life of 'Abdullah b. Yásín and the Origins of the Almoravid Movement." *The Journal of African History* 12 (1971): 255–268.

———. *The Arab Conquest of the Western Sudan*. Oxford: Oxford University Press, 1986.

———. *The Tuaregs: Their Islamic Legacy and Its Diffusion in the Sahel*. Warminster, UK: Aris & Phillips, 1975.

Nyambarza, Daniel. "Le marabout El-Hadj Mamadou-Lamine d'après les archives françaises." *Cahiers d'études africaines* 11 (1969): 124–145.

O'Brien, Donal B. Cruise. *The Mourides of Senegal: The Political and Economic Organization of an Islamic Brotherhood.* Oxford: Clarendon Press, 1971.

Okunola, Muri. "The Relevance of Shar'ia [sic.] to Nigeria." In *Islam in Africa: Proceedings of the Islam in Africa Conference.* Edited by Nura Alkali, Adamu Adamu, Awwal Yadudu, Rashid Motem, and Haruna Salihi. Ibadan, Nigeria: Spectrum Books, 1993.

Olayiwola, Abdul-Fattah, *Islam in Nigeria: One Crescent, Many Voices,* Lagos, Nigeria: Sakirabe Publishers, 2007.

Oloruntimehin, B. O. "Senegambia Mahmadou Lamine." In *West African Resistance: The Military Response to Colonial Occupation.* Edited by Michael Crowder. New York: Africana Publishing, 1971.

Osborn, Emily Lynn. *Our New Husbands Are Here: Households, Gender, and Politics in a West African State from the Slave Trade to Colonial Rule.* Athens: Ohio University Press, 2011.

Oseni, Z. I. "Islamic Scholars as Spiritual Healers in a Nigerian Community." *Islamic Culture* 62.4 (1988), 75–88.

O'Shea, Stephen. *Sea of Faith: Islam and Christianity in the Medieval Mediterranean World.* New York: Walker, 2006.

Oyelade, Emmanuel O. "Sir Ahmadu Bello, the Sardauna of Sokoto: The Twentieth Century Mujaddid (Reformer) of West Africa." *Islamic Quarterly* 27.4 (1983): 223–231.

———. "Trends in Hausa/Fulani Islam Since Independence: Aspects of Islamic Modernism in Nigeria." *Orita: Ibadan Journal of Religious Studies* 14.1 (1982): 3–15.

Paden, John N. *Religion and Political Culture in Kano.* Berkeley: University of California Press, 1973.

Padwick, Constance. *Muslim Devotions: A Study of Prayer-Manuals in Common Use.* London: SPCK, 1961.

Palmer, H. R. "The Kano Chronicle." *Journal of the Royal Anthropological Institute* 38 (1908): 58–98.

Park, Mungo. *Travels in Africa.* London: Everyman, 1969.

———. *Travels in the Interior Districts of Africa.* Durham, NC: Duke University Press, 2000.

Peel, J. D. Y. *Christianity, Islam, and Orisa-Religion: Three Traditions in Comparison and Interaction.* Oakland: University of California Press, 2016.

———. *Religious Encounter and the Making of the Yoruba.* Bloomington: Indiana University Press, 2000.

Person, Yves. "The Atlantic Coast and the Southern Savannahs." In *History of West Africa:* Vol. 2. Edited by J. F. Ade Ajayi and Michael Crowder. London: Longman, 1974.

Peters, Rudolph. *Islam and Colonialism: The Doctrine of Jihad in Modern History.* The Hague: Mouton, 1979.

Peterson, Brian J. *Islamization From Below: The Making of Muslim Communities in Rural French Sudan, 1880–1960.* New Haven, CT: Yale University Press, 2011.

Piscatori, James. *Islam, Islamists, and the Electoral Principle in the Middle East.* Leiden: International Institute for the Study of Islam in the Modern World, 2000.

Pollet, Eric, and Grace Winter. *La société soninké (Dyahunu, Mali).* Brussels: Université Bruxelles, 1971.

Porter, G. "A Note on Slavery, Seclusion and Agrarian Change in Northern Nigeria." *The Journal of African History* 30.4 (1989): 487–491.

Posnansky, Merrick. "Anatomy of a Continent." In *The Africans: A Reader.* Edited by Ali A. Mazrui and Toby Kleban Levine. New York: Praeger, 1986.

Potter, David. *Prophets and Emperors: Human and Divine Authority from Augustus to Theodosius.* Cambridge, MA: Harvard University Press, 1994.

Powell, Eve Troutt. "The Silence of Slaves." In *The African Diaspora in the Mediterranean Lands of Islam.* Edited by John Hunwick and Eve Troutt Powell. Princeton, NJ: Markus Wiener, 2002.

Preminger, Marion M. *The Sands of Tamanrasset: The Story of Charles de Foucauld.* New York: Hawthorn, 1961.

Proudfoot, Leslie. "Mosque-Building and Tribal Separatism in Freetown." *Africa* 29.4 (1959): 405–416.

———. "Muslims Among Akus in Freetown." *Africa* 24.3 (1954).

———. "Towards Muslim Solidarity in Freetown." *Africa* 31 (1961): 147–157.

Proudfoot, Leslie, and H. S. Wilson. "Muslim Attitudes to Education in Sierra Leone." *The Muslim World* 50.2 (January 1960): 86–98.

Qayrawání, Ibn Abí Zayd al-. *La Risálah: Epítre sur les elements du dogme et de la loi de l'Islam selon le rite mâlikite*. Edited and translated by L. Bercher. Alger: Ēditions Jules Carbonel, 1952.

Quellien, Alain. *La politique musulmane dans l'Afrique occidentale française*. Paris: Ēmile Larose, 1910.

Quinn, Charlotte. "A Nineteenth Century Fulbe State." *The Journal of African History* 12 (1971), 427–440.

———. *Mandingo Kingdoms of the Senegambia*. London: Longman, 1972.

Rabadan, Muhammad. *Mahometism Fully Explained (Written in Spanish and Arabic in the Year 1603 for the Instruction of the Moriscoes in Spain)*. 2 vols. Translated and edited by J. Morgan. London: E. Curll, W. Mears, and T. Payne, 1723–1725.

Raffenel, Anne. *Voyage dans l'Afrique occidentale: comprenant l'exploration du Sénégal... exécuté, en 1843 et 1844, par une commission compose de MM. Huard-Bessinières, Jamin, Raffenel, Peyre-Ferry et Pottin-Patterson*. Paris: A. Bertrand, 1846.

Rahman, Fazlur. *Health and Medicine in the Islamic Tradition: Change and Identity*. New York: Crossroad, 1989.

Rází, Abú Hátim al-. *The Proofs of Prophecy*. Edited and translated by Tarif Khalidi. Provo, UT: Brigham Young University Press, 2011.

Reader, John. *Africa: A Biography of the Continent*. New York: Vintage Books, 1997.

Reeck, Darrell L. "Islam in a West African Chiefdom: An Interpretation." *The Muslim World* 62.3 (1972): 183–194.

Reeve, Henry Fenwick. *The Gambia, Its History: Ancient, Mediaeval and Modern*. London: John Murray, 1912.

Reichardt, C. A. L. *Grammar of the Fulde Language, With an Appendix of Some Original Traditions*. London: Church Missionary Society, 1876.

Rippen, A., and J. Knappert, eds. *Textual Sources on Islam*. Manchester, UK: Manchester University Press, 1986.

Roberts, Richard. "The End of Slavery in the French Soudan, 1905–1914." In *The End of Slavery in Africa*. Edited by Suzanne Miers and Richard Roberts. Madison: University of Wisconsin Press, 1988.

Roberts, Richard, and Martin A. Klein. "The Banamba Slave Exodus of 1905 and the Decline of Slavery in the Western Sudan." *The Journal of African History* 21 (1980): 375–394.

Robertson, Claire C., and Martin Klein, eds. *Women and Slavery in Africa*. Madison: University of Wisconsin Press, 1983.

Robinson, Charles Henry. *Dictionary of the Hausa Language*. Cambridge, UK: Cambridge University Press, 1900.

Robinson, David. *Muslim Societies in African History*. New York: Cambridge University Press, 2004.

———. *The Holy War of 'Umar Tal: The Western Sudan in the Mid-Nineteenth Century*. Oxford: Clarendon Press, 1985.

Robinson, Francis. "The British Empire and the Muslim World." In *The Oxford History of the British Empire: The Twentieth Century*. Edited by Judith M. Brown and William Roger Louis. Oxford: Oxford University Press, 1999.

Rodney, Walter. *History of the Upper Guinea Coast: 1545–1800*. Oxford: Oxford University Press, 1968.

———. "Jihad and Social Revolution in Fouta Djalon in the Eighteenth Century." *Journal of the Historical Society of Nigeria* 4 (1968): 269–284.

Rosenthal, E. I. J., *Islam and the Modern National State*. Cambridge, UK: Cambridge University Press, 1965.

———. *Political Thought in Medieval Islam*. Cambridge, UK: Cambridge University Press, 1958.

Roy, Olivier. *Holy Ignorance: When Religion and Culture Part Ways*. New York: Columbia University Press, 2010.

Rubin, Uri, and David J. Wasserstein, eds. *Dhimmis and Others: Jews and Christians and the World of Classical Islam*. Tel Aviv: Tel Aviv University, 1997.

Ruete, Emily. *Memoirs of an Arabian Princess from Zanzibar*. New York: Markus Wiener, 1989.

Russell, Alexander David, and 'Abdullah al-Ma'mún Suhrawardy, eds. and trans. *First Steps in Muslim Jurisprudence*. London: Luzac, 1963.

Russell, Bertrand. *Autobiography*. London: Unwin, 1978.

Rutland, Robert, ed. *The Papers of James Madison*. Chicago: University of Chicago Press, 1973.

Ryan, Patrick J. "Environmental Factors in Religious Change: Perspectives from the Sahel and Savannah of West Africa." Unpublished paper, Fordham University, 2013.

———. *Imale: Yoruba Participation in the Muslim Tradition*. Ann Arbor, MI: Scholars Press, 1978.

Saad, Elias N. "Islamization in Kano: Sequence and Chronology." *Kano Studies*, New Series, 1.4 (1979): 52–66.

———. *Social History of Timbuktu: The Role of Muslim Scholars and Notables, 1400–1900*. Cambridge, UK: Cambridge University Press, 1983.

Sabatié, A. *Le Sénégal: Sa conquête et son organization*. St. Louis, Senegal: Imprimerie du Gouvernement, 1925.

Sa'dí, 'Abd al-Rahmán al-. *Ta'rikh al-Súdán*. Edited with text and translation by O. Houdas. Paris: Librairie d'Amerique et d'Orient, Adrien Maisonneuve, 1964.

Saint-Père, J. H. *Les Serakollé de Guidimakha*. Paris: Larose, 1925.

Saleck, El-Arby Ould. *Les Haratins: Le paysage politique mauritanien*. Paris: L'Harmattan, 2003.

Sanneh, L. *Abolitionists Abroad: American Blacks and the Making of Modern West Africa*. Cambridge, MA: Harvard University Press, 2001.

———. "Field-Work Among the Jakhanke of Senegambia." *Présence Africaine* 93 (1975): 92–112.

———. "Modern Education Among Freetown Muslims and the Christian Stimulus." In *Christianity in Independent Africa*. Edited by Edward Fashole-Luke, Richard Gray, Adrian Hastings, and Godwin Tasie. Bloomington: Indiana University Press, 1978.

———. "Saints and Virtue in African Islam: An Historical Approach." In *Saints and Virtues*. Edited by John Stratton Hawley. Berkeley: University of California Press, 1987.

———. "Tcherno Aliou: The Wali of Goumba: Islam, Colonialism, and the Rural Factor in Futa Jallon, 1867–1912." In *Rural and Urban Islam in West Africa*. Edited by Nehemia Levtzion and Humphrey J. Fisher. Boulder, CO: Lynne Rienner, 1987.

———. *The Crown and the Turban: Muslims and West African Pluralism*. Boulder, CO: Westview Press, 1997.

———. "The Domestication of Islam and Christianity in Africa." *Journal of Religion in Africa* 11.1 (1980): 1–12.

———. "The Jakhanke Clerical Tradition in Futa Jallon." *Journal of Religion in Africa* 12.1–2 (1981): 105–126.

———. *The Jakhanke Muslim Clerics: A Study of Islam in Senegambia*. Lanham, MD: University Press of America, 1989.

———. "The Origins of Clericalism in West African Islam." *The Journal of African History* 17.1 (1976): 49–72.

Santerre, Renaud. *Pédagogie musulmane d'Afrique noire: L'école coranique peul du Camroun*. Montreal: Les presses de l'Université de Montreal, 1973.

Santillana, David de. "Law and Society." In *The Legacy of Islam*. Edited by Sir Thomas Arnold and Alfred Guillaume. London: Oxford University Press, 1931.

Sartain, E. M. *Jalál al-dín al-Suyútí, Vol. I: Biography and Background*. Cambridge, UK: Cambridge University Press, 1975.

Saul, Mahir. "The Quranic School Farm and Child Labour in Upper Volta." *Africa* 54.2 (1984): 71–87.

Saunders, J. J. *A History of Medieval Islam*. London: Routledge & Kegan Paul, 1965.

Schacht, Joseph. "Islamic Law in Contemporary States." *American Journal of Comparative Law* 8 (1959): 133–147.

———. *The Origins of Muhammadan Jurisprudence*. Oxford: Clarendon Press, 1950.

Schultz, Colin. "Timbuktu's Priceless Manuscripts are Safe After All," *Smithsonian.com*, February 4, 2013.

Searing, James F. *West African Slavery and Atlantic Commerce: The Senegal River valley, 1700–1860*. Cambridge, UK: Cambridge University Press, 1993.

Seaver, Paul S. *The Puritan Lectureships: The Politics of Religious Dissent, 1560–1662*. Stanford, CA: Stanford University Press, 1970.

Sesay, S. I. "Koranic Schools in the Provinces." *Sierra Leone Journal of Education* 1.1 (April 1966): 24–26.

Shayzarí, 'Abd al-Rahmán b. Nasr al-. *Niháyat al-Rutba al-Hisba*. Translated and edited by R. P. Buckley. Oxford: Oxford University Press, 1999.

Sitwell, Cecil. *South Bank Report*. Public Record Office, Ref. 76/19, 1893.

Sivan, Emmanuel. *Radical Islam: Medieval Theology and Modern Politics*. New Haven, CT: Yale University Press, 1985.

Smart, Joko H. M. "Place of Islamic Law Within the Framework of the Sierra Leone Legal System." *African Law Studies* 18 (1980): 87–102.

Smith, H. F. C. "A Neglected Theme of West African History: The Islamic Revolutions of the 19th Century." *Journal of the Historical Society of Nigeria* 2.2 (December 1961): 169–185.

Smith, Pierre. "Les Diakhanké: Histoire d'une dispersion." *Bulletins et mémoires de la Société d'anthropologie de Paris*, Série 8, 11 (1965): 231–262.

Snelgrave, William. *A New Account of Some Parts of Guinea and the Slave Trade*. London: Bible and Crown, 1734.

Soh, Siré-Abbas. *Chroniques du Foûta Sénégalais*. Edited by Maurice Delafosse and H. Gaden. Paris: E. Leroux, 1913.

Soleillet, Paul. *Voyage à Ségou: 1878–1879*. Edited by Gabriel Gravier. Paris: Challamel aïné, 1887.

Stamer, P. Joseph. *Islam in Sub-Saharan Africa*. Estella, Spain: Editorial Verbo Divino, 1995.

Stenning, Derrick. J. *Savannah Nomads: A Study of the Wodaabe Pastoral Fulani of Western Bornu*. London: Oxford University Press, 1959.

Stewart, Charles C., and E. K. Stewart. *Islam and Social Order in Mauritania*. Oxford: Oxford University Press, 1973.

Stibb, Captain Bartholomew. "Voyage Up the Gambia in the Year 1723." In *Travels into the Inland Parts of Africa*. Edited by Francis Moore. London: E. Cave, 1738.

Suhrawardi. *Al-'Awárif al-Ma' árif* (*Bounties of Divine Knowledge*). Translated by Lieut. Col. H. Wilberforce Clarke as *A Dervish Textbook*. London: Octagon Press, 1980.

Suret-Canale, J. "Touba in Guinea: Holy Place of Islam." In *African Perspectives*. Edited by Christopher Allen and R. W. Johnson. Cambridge, UK: Cambridge University Press, 1970.

Suret-Canale, J., and Boubacar Barry. "The Western Atlantic Coast to 1800." In *History of West Africa*: Vol. 1. Edited by J. F. Ade Ajayi and Michael Crowder. London: Longman, 1976.

Suyuti, Jalal al-Din al-."*As'ila wárida min al-Takrúr fi Shawwál 898*." Edited and translated by J. O. Hunwick. In *African Perspectives: Papers in the History, Politics, and Economies of Africa Presented to Thomas Hodgkin*. Edited by Christopher Allen and R. W. Johnson. Cambridge, UK: Cambridge University Press, 1970.

Tabataba, Muhammad ibn 'Ali ibn. *Al-Fakhri: On the Systems of Government and the Moslem Dynasties*. Translated by C. E. J. Whitting. London: Luzac & Company, 1947.

Tambo, David. "The Sokoto Caliphate Slave Trade in the Nineteenth Century." *The International Journal of African Historical Studies* 9.2 (1976): 187–217.

Tangban, O. E. "The Hajj and the Nigerian Economy: 1960–1981." *Journal of Religion in Africa* 21.3 (August 1991): 241–255.

Tauxier, L. *Le Noir de Bondoukou*. Paris: Leroux, 1921.

———. *Moeurs et histoire des Peulhs*. Paris: Payot, 1937.

Tawney, R. H. *Religion and the Rise of Capitalism*. London: Penguin Books, 1926.

Taylor, Charles. "Modes of Secularism." In *Secularism and Its Critics*. Edited by R. Bhargava. New Delhi: Oxford University Press, 1998.

Terem, Etty. "Redefining Islamic Tradition: Legal Interpretation as a Medium for Innovation in the Making of Modern Morocco." *Islamic Law and Society* 20.4 (2013): 425–475.

Terrier, Auguste et Charles Mourey. *L'expansion française et le formation territorial (L'ouvre de la Troisième République en Afrique Occidentale)*. Paris: E Larot, 1910.

The Ramadan Vision. Freetown, July 1947.

Tibi, Bassam. *Islam and the Cultural Accommodation of Social Change*. Boulder, CO: Westview Press, 1990.

Tocqueville, Alexis de. *Democracy in America*. London: Everyman's Library, 1994.

Tourneau, Roger Le. *The Almohad Movement in North Africa in the Twelfth and Thirteenth Centuries*. Princeton Studies on the Near East. Princeton, NJ: Princeton University Press, 1969.

Triaud, Jean-Louis. *Islam et Sociétés Soudanaises au Moyen-Age: Etude historique*. Recherches Voltaiques 16. Paris: Centre National de la Recherche Scientifique, 1973.

Trimingham, J. Spencer. *A History of Islam in West Africa*. Oxford: Oxford University Press, 1962.

———. *Islam in West Africa*. Oxford: Clarendon Press, 1959.

———. *The Influence of Islam Upon Africa*. London: Longman, Green, and Co., 1968.

———. *The Sufi Orders in Islam*. Oxford: Clarendon Press, 1971.

Tritton, A. S., "Islam and the Protected Religions," *Journal of the Royal Asiatic Society*, part III (July, 1928): 485–508.

'Umar, Muhammed Sani. "Sufism and Its Opponents in Nigeria: The Doctrinal and Intellectual Aspects." In *Islamic Mysticism Contested: Thirteen Centuries of Controversies and Polemics*. Edited by Frederick de Jong and Bernd Radtke. Leiden: Brill, 1999.

'Umarí, Ibn Fadl Alláh al-. "*Masálik al-Absár fí Mamálik al-Amsár*" (Pathways of Vision in the Realms of the Metropolises). In *Corpus of Early Arabic Sources for West African History*. Translated by J. F P. Hopkins. Edited by N. Levtzion and J. F. P. Hopkins. Cambridge, UK: Cambridge University Press, 1981.

Vatikiotis, P. *Islam and the State*. London: Routledge, 1991.

Verdat, M. "Le Ouali de Goumba." *Études Guinéennes* 3 (1949): 3–81.

Villasante-de Beauvais, Mariella, ed. *Groupes serviles au Sahara: Approche comparative à partir du cas de arabophones de Mauritanie*. Paris: Centre National de Recherches Scientifique, 2000.

Vuillet, Jean. "Recherches au sujet de religions professées en Sénegambie, anciennement ou á l'epoque actuelle." *Comptes Rendus Mensuels des Séances de l'Academie des Sciences Coloniales* 12.8, 1952, 413–426.

Walckenaer, Baron Charles Athanase. *Histoire générale des voyages*. 11 vols. Paris: Didot, 1826–1831.

Waldman, M. R. "The Fulani Jihad: A Reassessment." *The Journal of African History* 6.3 (1965): 20–32.

Walz, Terence, "Notes on the Organisation of the African Trade in Cairo, 1800–1850." *extrait des Annales Islamologiques*, Cairo, XI, 1972.

Walzer, Michael. *The Revolution of Saints: A Study in the Origins of Radical Politics*. Cambridge, MA: Harvard University Press, 1965.

Waqidi, Muhammad ibn 'Umar al- [752–829]. *Muhammad in Medina*. Translated and abbreviated. Berlin: G. Reimer, 1882.

Warburg, Gabriel R. *Ideological and Practical Considerations Regarding Slavery in the Mahdist State and the Anglo-Egyptian Sudan: 1881–1918*. Edited by Paul Lovejoy. Beverly Hills, CA: SAGE, 1981.

Ware, Rudolph T.III. *The Walking Qur'an: Islamic Education, Embodied Knowledge, and History in West Africa*. Chapel Hill: University of North Carolina Press, 2014.

Washington, Captain. "Some Accounts of Mohammedu-Sisei, a Mandigo of Nyani-Maru on the Gambia." *Journal of the Royal Geographical Society* 8 (1838): 449–454.

Wasserstein, David J. "How Islam Saved the Jews." Jordan Lectures, School of Oriental and African Studies, University of London, May 2012.

Wasserstein, David J., and Uri Rubin, eds. *Dhimmis and Others: Jews and Christians and the World of Classical Islam*. Tel Aviv: Tel Aviv University, 1997.

Watt, W. Montgomery. *Islamic Fundamentalism and Modernity*. London: Routledge, 1990.

———. *Islamic Political Thought: The Basic Concepts*. Edinburgh, UK: Edinburgh University Press, 1968.

———. *Muhammad at Medina*. Oxford: Clarendon Press, 1962.

———. *The Formative Period of Islamic Thought*. Oxford: Oneworld, 1998.

Weber, Max. *The Sociology of Religion*. Translated by Ephraim Fischoff. Boston: Beacon Press, 1963.

Wensinck, A. J. *The Muslim Creed: Its Genesis and Historical Development*. Cambridge, UK: Cambridge University Press, 1932.

Westerlund, David, ed., *Questioning the Secular State: The Worldwide Resurgence of Religion in Politics*. London: Christopher Hurst, 1995.

Westermack, E. A. *Pagan Survivals in Mohammadan Civilization*. London, 1933; reprinted Amsterdam: Philo Press, 1973.

Wilks, Ivor. "Transmission of Islamic Learning in the Western Sudan." In *Literacy in Traditional Societies*. Edited by Jack Goody. Cambridge, UK: Cambridge University Press, 1968.

Willis, John Ralph. *In the Path of Allah: The Passion of al-Hajj 'Umar: An Essay into the Nature of Charisma in Islam*. London: Frank Cass, 1989.

———. "Jihad fi sabil li-l'llah: Its Doctrinal Basis in Islam and Some Aspects of its Evolution in Nineteenth-Century West Africa." *The Journal of African History* 8 (1967): 395–415.

———. "The Jihád of al-Hajj 'Umar al-Fútí: Its Doctrinal Basis, etc." PhD dissertation, University of London, 1970.

———, ed. *Studies in West African Islam:* Vol. I, *The Cultivators of Islam*. London: Frank Cass, 1979.

Winthrop, John. "A Model Christian Charity (1630)." In *The Puritans in America: A Narrative Anthology*. Edited by Alan Heimert and Andrew Delbanco. Cambridge, MA: Harvard University Press, 1985.

Wolf, Eric. "The Social Organization of Mecca and the Origins of Islam." *Southwestern Journal of Anthropology* 7 (1951), 329–356.

Wood, W. Raymond. "An Archeological Appraisal of Early European Settlements in the Senegambia." *The Journal of African History* 8.1 (1967): 39–64.

Yahya, Dahiru. "Colonialism in Africa and the Impact of European Concepts and Values: Nationalism and Muslims in Nigeria." In *Islam in Africa: Proceedings of the Islam in Africa Conference*. Edited by Nura Alkali, Adamu Adamu, Awwal Yadudu, Rashid Motem, and Haruna Salihi. Ibadan, Nigeria: Spectrum Books, 1993.

Yamusa, S. *The Political Ideas of the Jihad Leaders: Being a Translation, Edition and Analysis of* Usúl al-Siyása *by Muhammad Bello and Diya al-Hukkum by Abdullahi b. Fodio*. Master's thesis, Abdullahi Bayero College, Kano, 1975.

Yusuf, Bilikisu. "Da'wa and Contemporary Challenges Facing Muslim Women in Secular States—Yamusa, S., A Nigerian Case Study." In *Islam in Africa: Proceedings of the Islam in Africa Conference*. Edited by Nura Alkali, Adamu Adamu, Awwal Yadudu, Rashid Motem, and Haruna Salihi. Ibadan, Nigeria: Spectrum Books, 1993.

Zabadia, ʻAbd el-Qadir. "The Career of Ahmad al-Bekkay in the Oral Evidences and Recorded Documents." *Revue d'Histoire Maghrébine* 3 (1975): 75–83.

Zaman, Muhammed Qasim. *Modern Islamic Thought in a Radical Age: Religious Authority and Internal Criticism*. New York: Cambridge University Press, 2012.

Zar', Ibn Abí. "*Kitáb al-anis al-mutrib bi-rawd al-qirtás fi akhbár mulúk al-maghrib wa-tárikh madinat Fás*" (The Entertaining Companion in the Garden of Paper on the History of Kings of the Maghrib and the City of Fez). In *Corpus of Early Arabic Sources for West African History*. Translated by J. F P. Hopkins. Edited by N. Levtzion and J. F. P. Hopkins. Cambridge, UK: Cambridge University Press, 1981.

Zarnújí, al-. "Instruction to the Student: The Method of Learning." In *Classical Foundations of Islamic Educational Thought*. Edited by Bradley J. Cook and Fathi H. Malkawi. Provo, UT: Brigham Young University Press, 2010.

Zayd, Ibn Abí. *The Risála: Treatise on Máliki Law*. Translated and edited by Joseph Kenny. Minna, Nigeria: Islamic Education Trust, 1992.

INDEX